WE HEREBY REFUSE

JAPANESE AMERICAN RESISTANCE TO WARTIME INCARCERATION

PRODUCED BY

WING LUKE
MUSEUM

IN PARTNERSHIP WITH

CHIN MUSIC
PRESS

SEATTLE • WASHINGTON

WE HEREBY REFUSE

JAPANESE AMERICAN RESISTANCE TO WARTIME INCARCERATION

SCRIPT BY

FRANK ABE

STORY BY

FRANK ABE & TAMIKO NIMURA

JIM AKUTSU & MITSUYE ENDO ARTWORK BY

ROSS ISHIKAWA

HIROSHI KASHIWAGI ARTWORK BY

MATT SASAKI

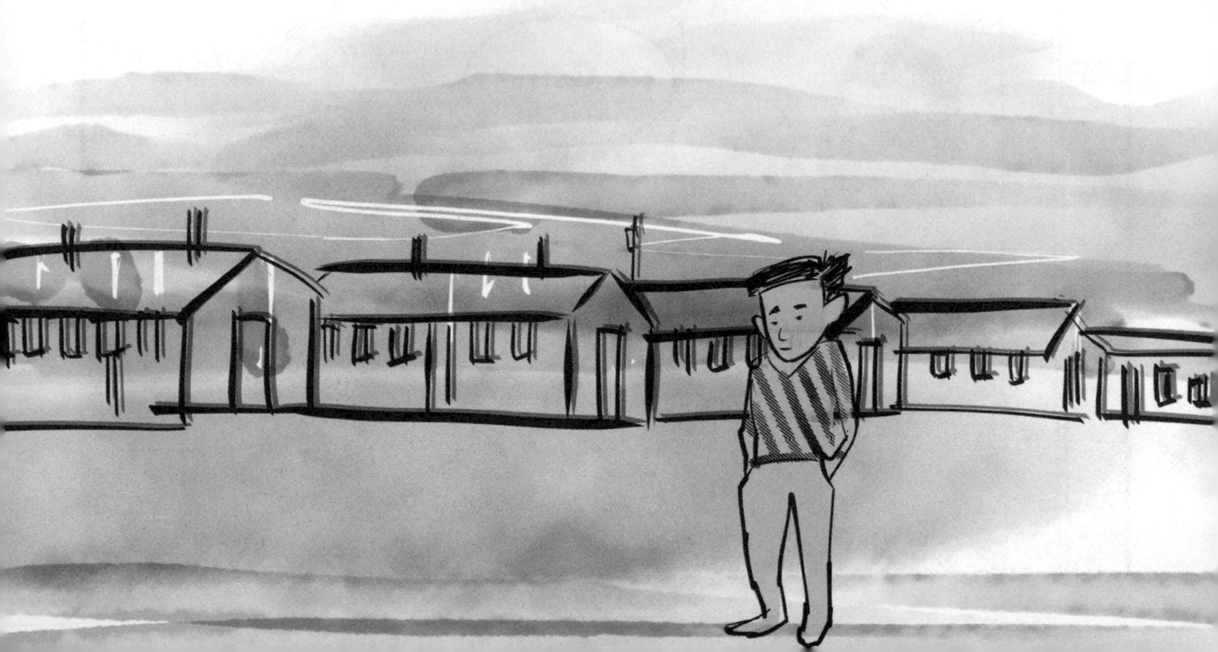

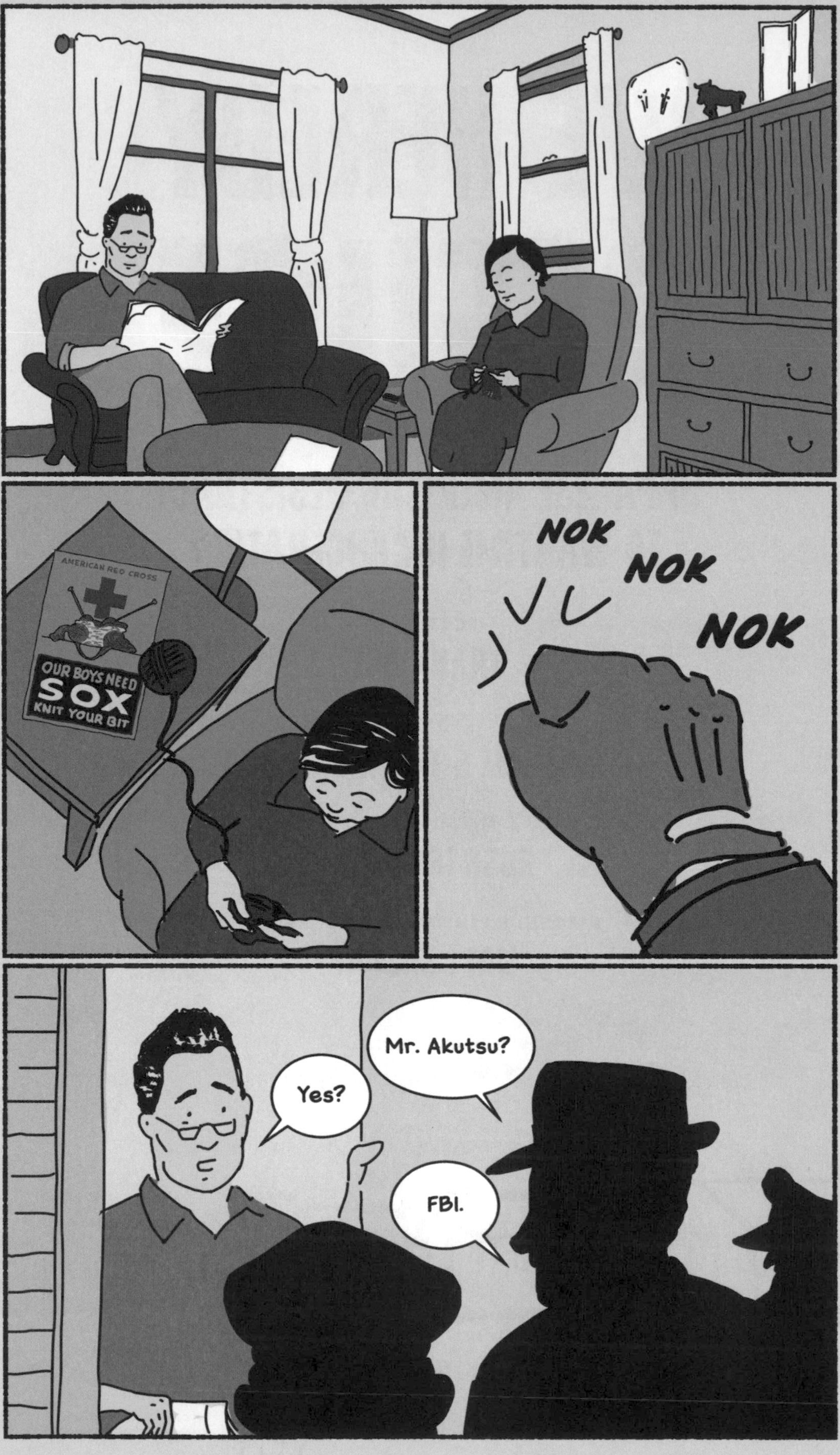
AMERICAN RED CROSS
OUR BOYS NEED
SOX
KNIT YOUR BIT
NOK
NOK
NOK
Mr. Akutsu?
Yes?
FBI.

HAJIME JIM AKUTSU

SEATTLE, WASHINGTON × AGE 22

KIYONOSUKE

NAO

GENE

LIVES WITH PARENTS AND BROTHER IN A HOME THEY OWN ON SEATTLE'S FIRST HILL.

FAMILY OPERATES A SHOE REPAIR SHOP AT 6TH AND KING IN CHINATOWN.

STUDYING CIVIL ENGINEERING IN COLLEGE.

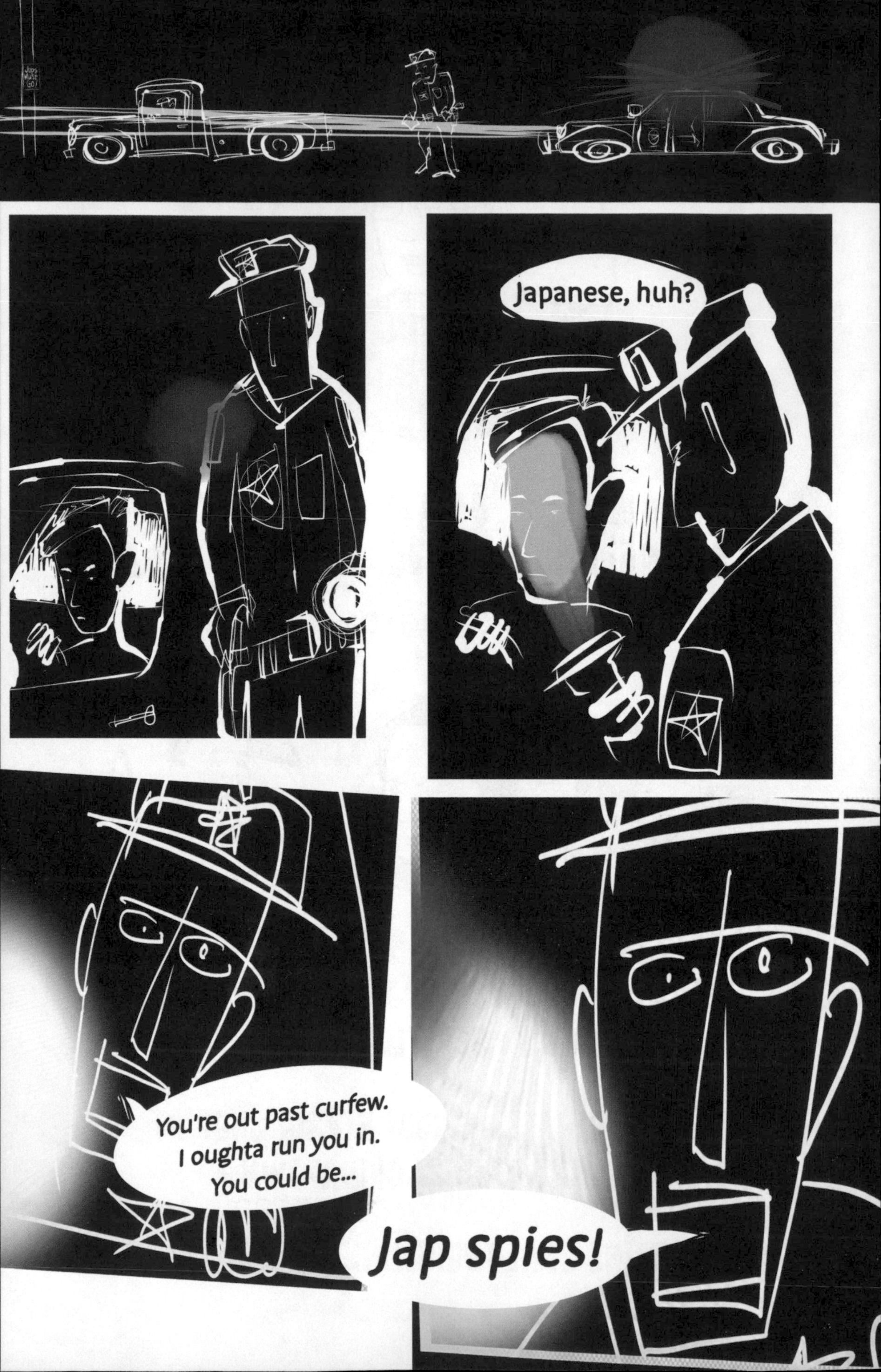
JAPS MUST GO!
Japanese, huh?
You're out past curfew. I oughta run you in. You could be...
Jap spies!

HIROSHI KASHIWAGI

PENRYN, CALIFORNIA × AGE 19

LIVES WITH MOTHER, BROTHER, AND SISTER
ON A FARM OUTSIDE SACRAMENTO.

FATHER IN A TUBERCULOSIS SANATORIUM.

RECENT HIGH SCHOOL GRADUATE,
WAITING TO ENROLL IN COLLEGE.

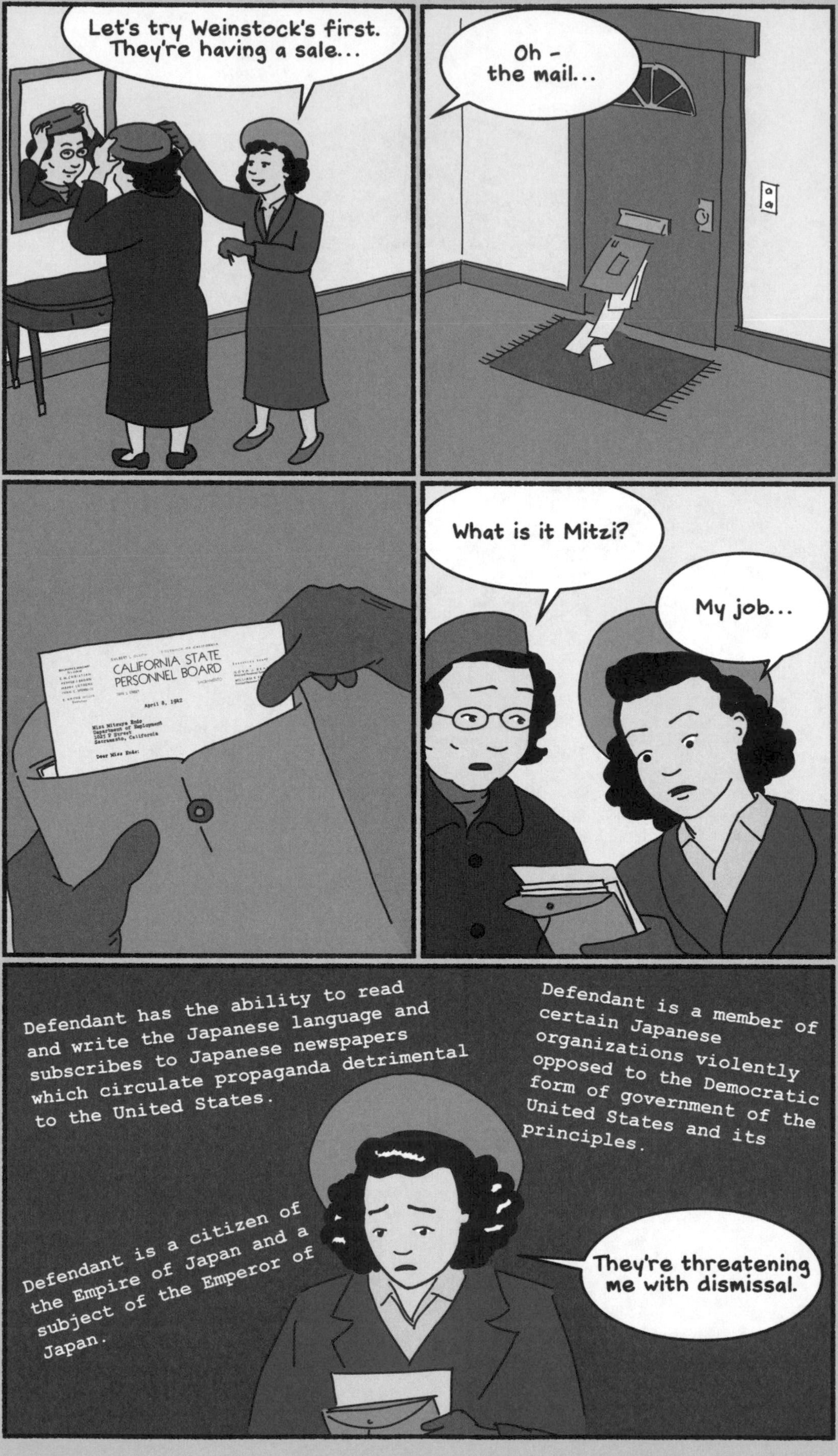
Let's try Weinstock's first. They're having a sale...
Oh - the mail...
CALIFORNIA STATE PERSONNEL BOARD
April 8, 1942
Miss Mitsuye Endo
Department of Employment
1025 P Street
Sacramento, California
Dear Miss Endo:
What is it Mitzi?
My job...
Defendant has the ability to read and write the Japanese language and subscribes to Japanese newspapers which circulate propaganda detrimental to the United States.
Defendant is a member of certain Japanese organizations violently opposed to the Democratic form of government of the United States and its principles.
Defendant is a citizen of the Empire of Japan and a subject of the Emperor of Japan.
They're threatening me with dismissal.

MITSUYE ENDO

SACRAMENTO, CALIFORNIA × AGE 21

LIVES WITH PARENTS AND TWO
SISTERS IN AN APARTMENT IN
SACRAMENTO'S JAPANTOWN.

BROTHER IN U.S. ARMY.

WORKS FOR A CALIFORNIA STATE
AGENCY AS A TYPIST.

COURT
DIVISION
MAY AND NOVEMBER
APRIL AND OCTOBER
N DIVISION
FEBRUARY AND JULY

DEPARTMENT OF JUSTICE

UNITED STATES ATTORNEY
WESTERN DISTRICT OF WASHINGTON

Seattle, Washington
May 18, 1942

Mr. Edward J. Ennis
Director, Alien Enemy Control Unit
Department of Justice
Washington, D. C.

Re: KIYONOSUKE AKUTSU

Sir:

We are forwarding herewith the findings and recommendation of Alien Enemy Hearing Board number One for this district, in which it is recommended that the above named alien enemy be interned, in which recommendation this office concurs.

Respectfully,

J. Charles Dennis

J. CHARLES DENNIS
United States Attorney

HS:ih
encs

JUN 4 '42 AM

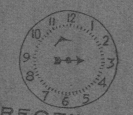

146-13-2-82-48
DEPARTMENT OF JUSTICE
JUN 3 1942 P.M.
DIVISION OF RECORDS
ALIEN ENEMY UNIT

RECEIVED
ALIEN ENEMY CONTROL UNIT

Docketed MCK 6-4-42

— PART ONE —

RUMORS AND LIES

FEBRUARY 1942

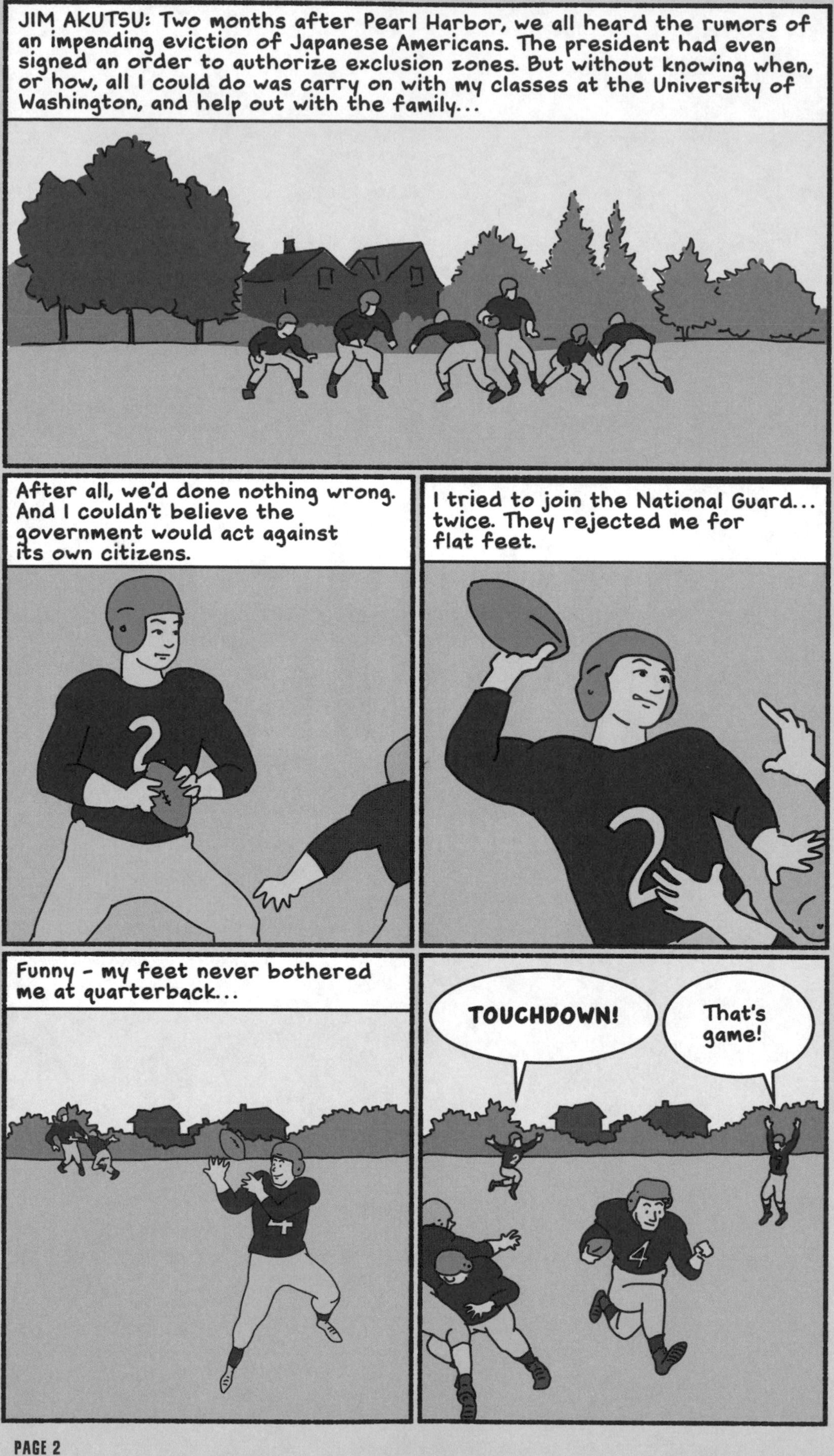
JIM AKUTSU: Two months after Pearl Harbor, we all heard the rumors of an impending eviction of Japanese Americans. The president had even signed an order to authorize exclusion zones. But without knowing when, or how, all I could do was carry on with my classes at the University of Washington, and help out with the family...
After all, we'd done nothing wrong. And I couldn't believe the government would act against its own citizens.
I tried to join the National Guard... twice. They rejected me for flat feet.
Funny - my feet never bothered me at quarterback...
TOUCHDOWN!
That's game!

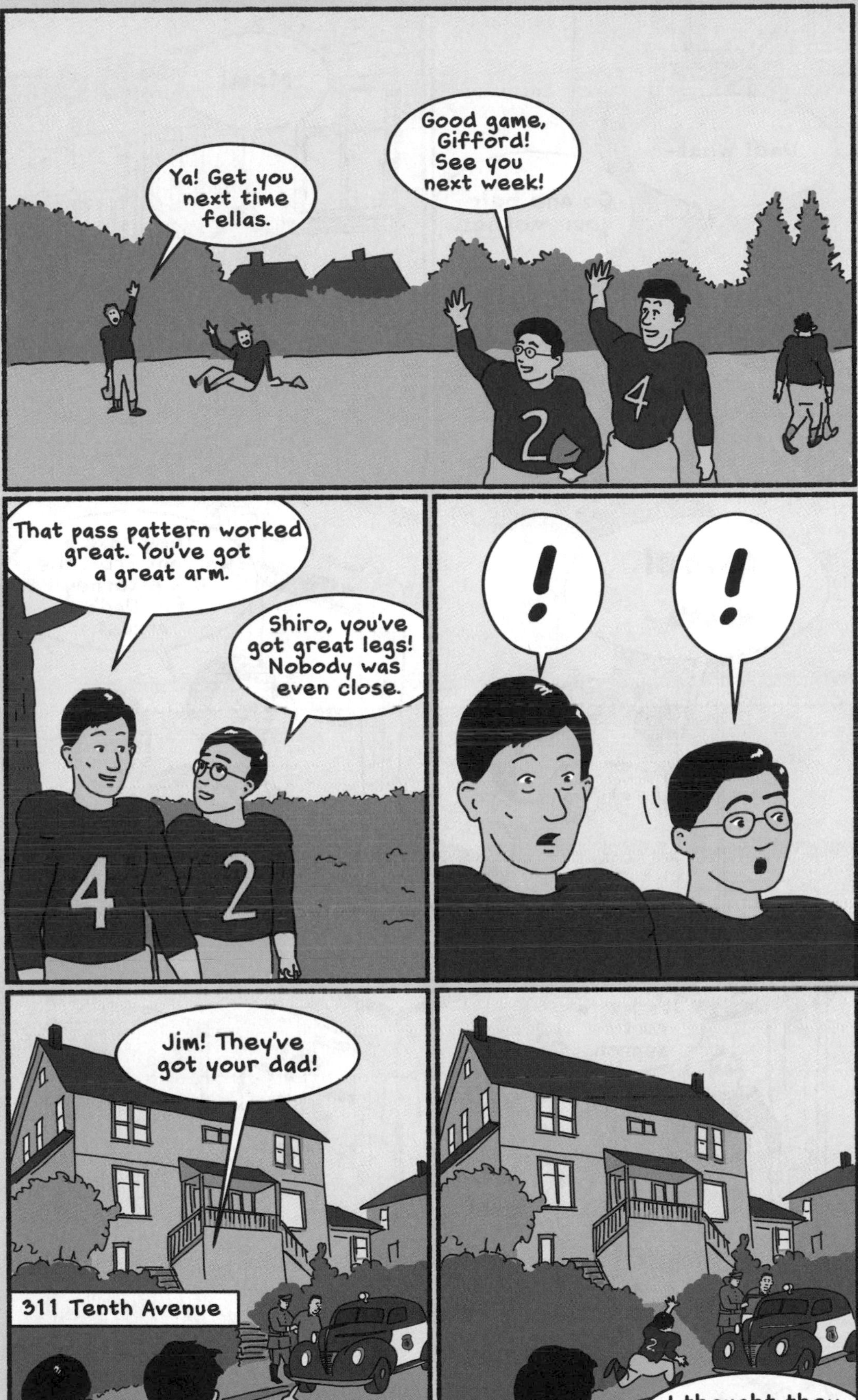
Ya! Get you next time fellas.
Good game, Gifford! See you next week!
That pass pattern worked great. You've got a great arm.
Shiro, you've got great legs! Nobody was even close.
!
!
Jim! They've got your dad!
311 Tenth Avenue
I thought they were done making arrests.

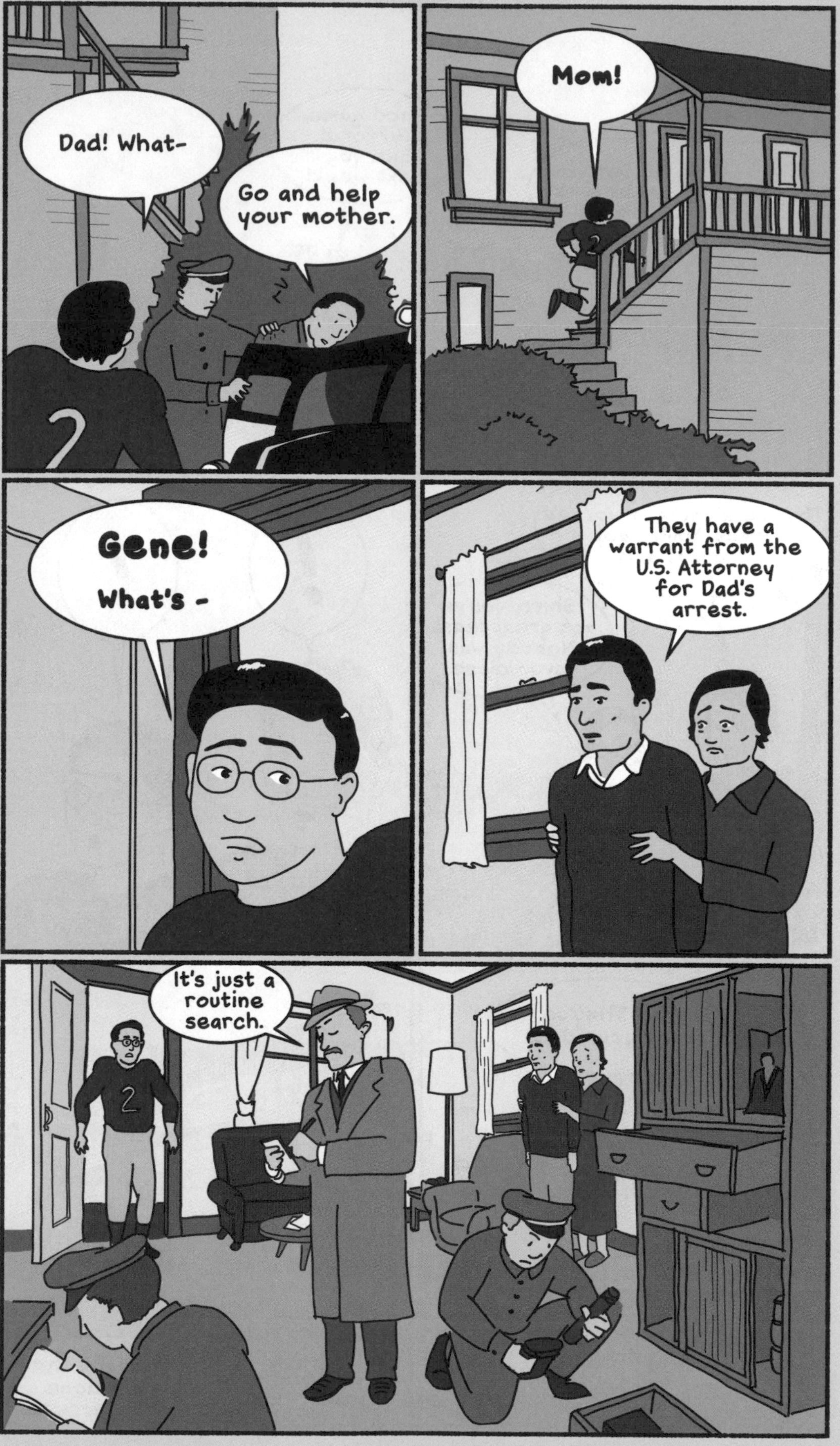
Dad! What-
Go and help your mother.
Mom!
Gene!
What's -
They have a warrant from the U.S. Attorney for Dad's arrest.
It's just a routine search.

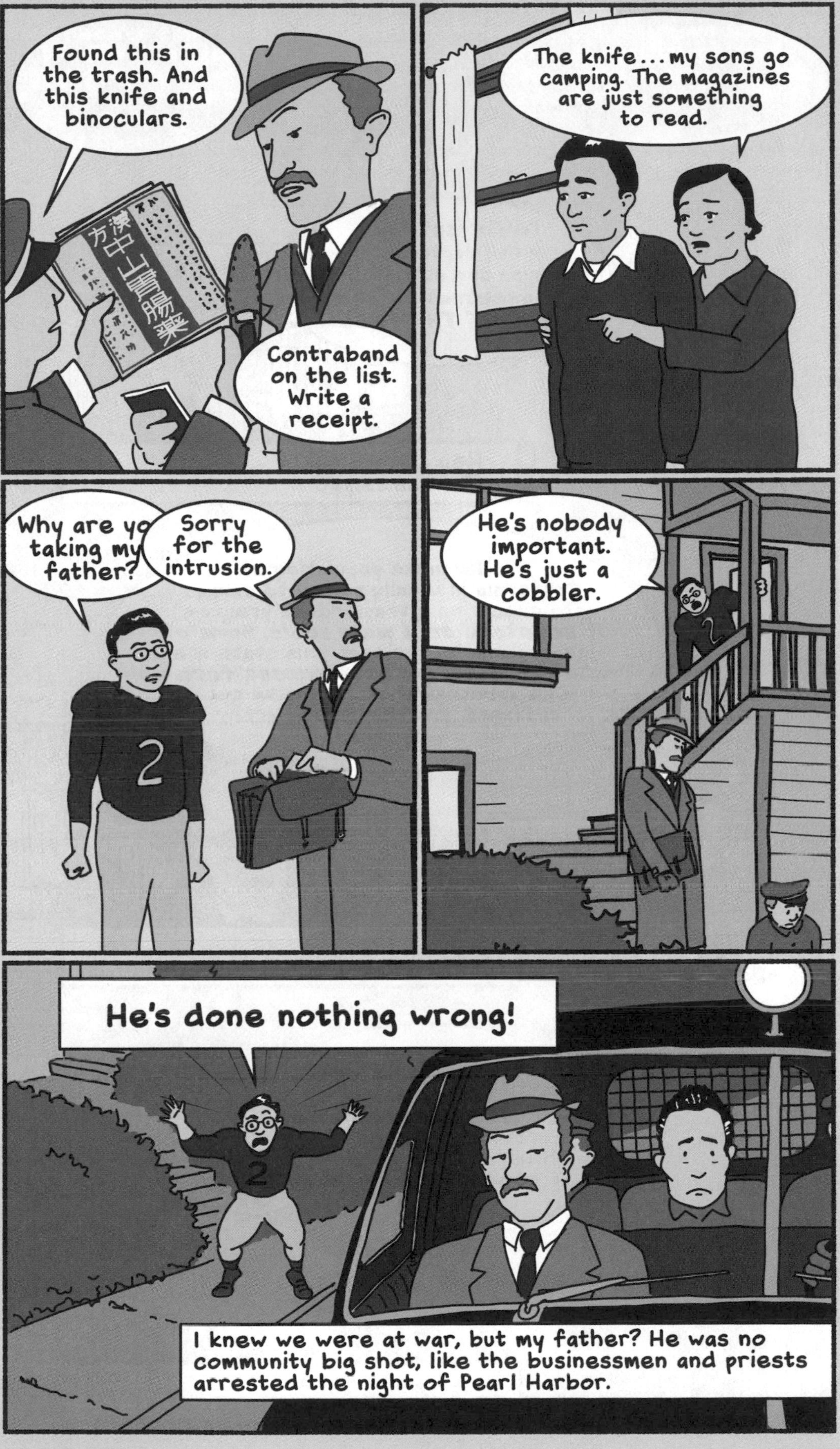

Found this in the trash. And this knife and binoculars.
Contraband on the list. Write a receipt.
The knife... my sons go camping. The magazines are just something to read.
Why are yo taking my father?
Sorry for the intrusion.
He's nobody important. He's just a cobbler.
He's done nothing wrong!
I knew we were at war, but my father? He was no community big shot, like the businessmen and priests arrested the night of Pearl Harbor.

We were simply visible targets for retaliation. Here I was a *Nisei*, born in Seattle, a citizen by birthright under the Constitution - while my parents, *Issei* who emigrated from Japan, were denied by law to become naturalized U.S. citizens because of their race. This was their home too.

The nation was scared, sure, but I didn't see how that excused the venom and wild conspiracy theories from political leaders.

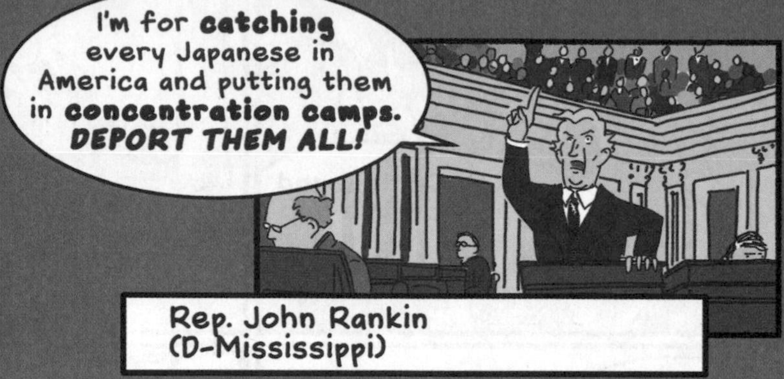
I'm for catching every Japanese in America and putting them in concentration camps. DEPORT THEM ALL!
Rep. John Rankin (D-Mississippi)

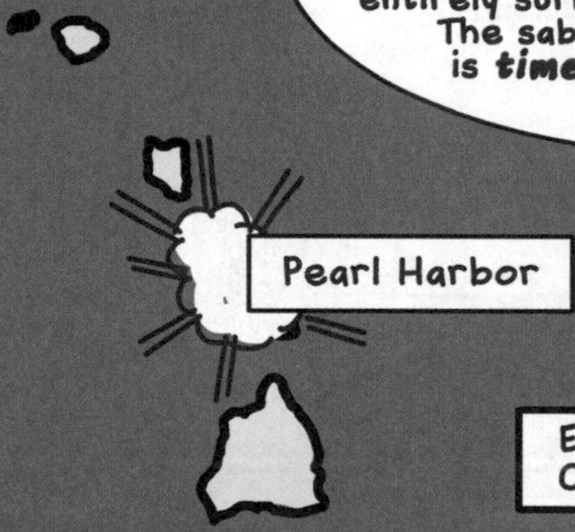
Pearl Harbor

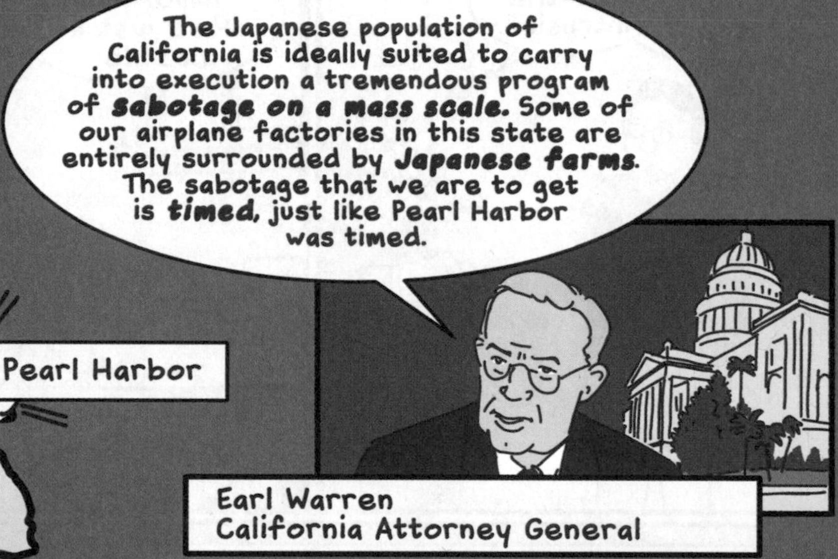
The Japanese population of California is ideally suited to carry into execution a tremendous program of sabotage on a mass scale. Some of our airplane factories in this state are entirely surrounded by Japanese farms. The sabotage that we are to get is timed, just like Pearl Harbor was timed.
Earl Warren California Attorney General

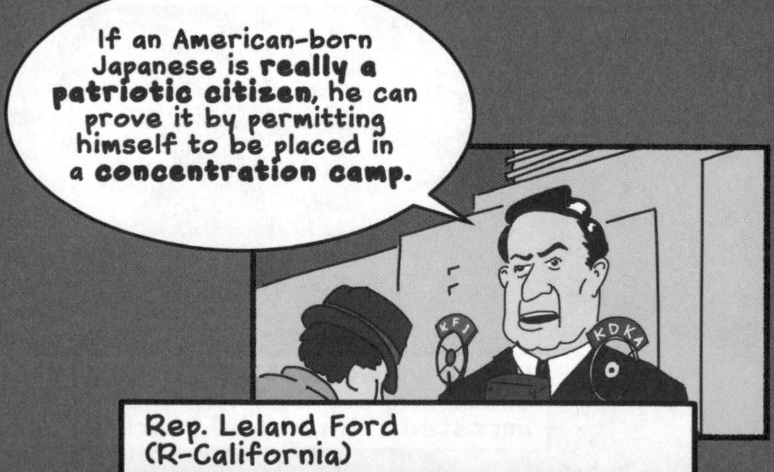
If an American-born Japanese is really a patriotic citizen, he can prove it by permitting himself to be placed in a concentration camp.
KFI
KDKA
Rep. Leland Ford (R-California)

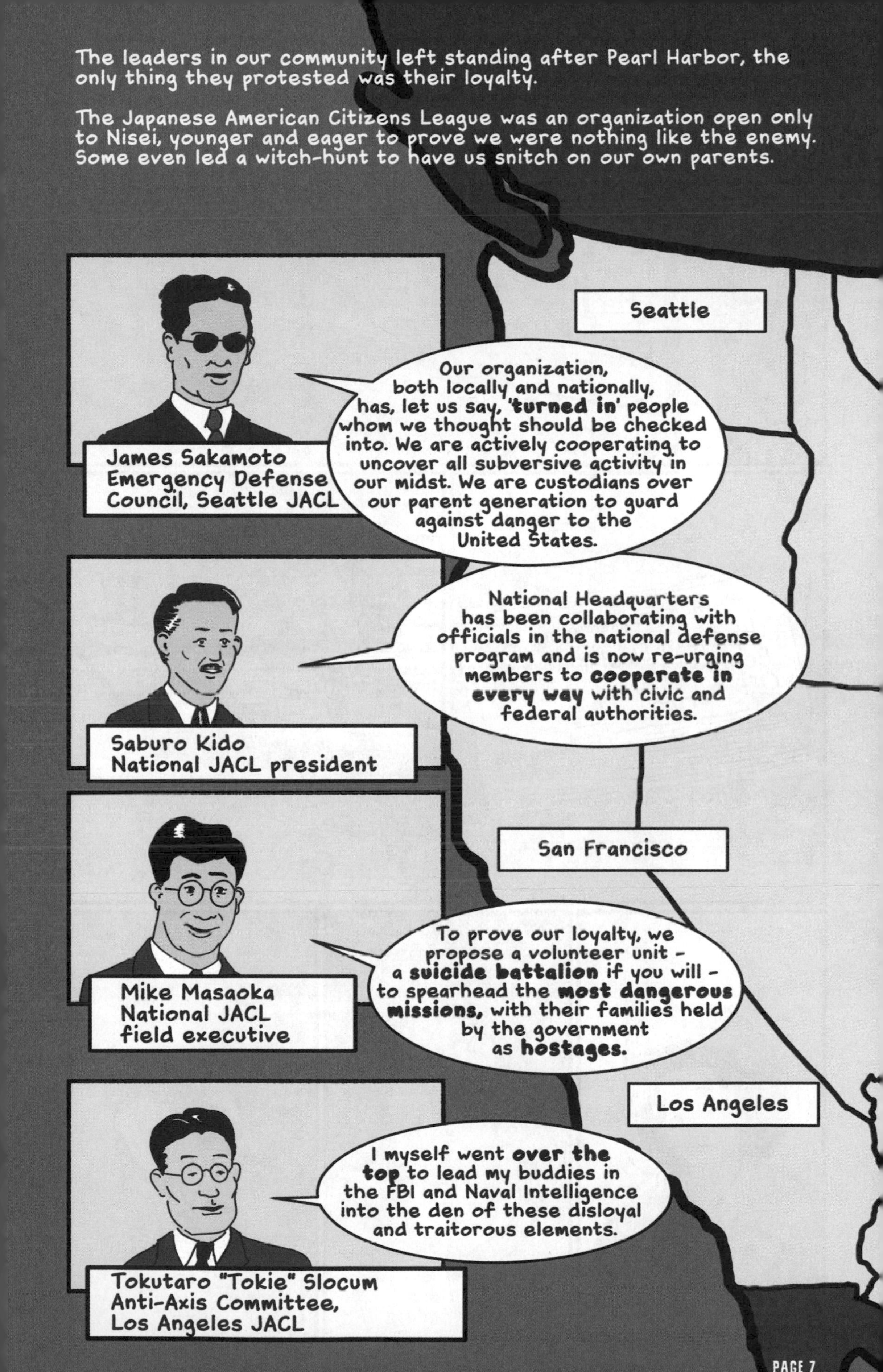
The leaders in our community left standing after Pearl Harbor, the only thing they protested was their loyalty.
The Japanese American Citizens League was an organization open only to Nisei, younger and eager to prove we were nothing like the enemy. Some even led a witch-hunt to have us snitch on our own parents.
Seattle
Our organization, both locally and nationally, has, let us say, '**turned in**' people whom we thought should be checked into. We are actively cooperating to uncover all subversive activity in our midst. We are custodians over our parent generation to guard against danger to the United States.
James Sakamoto Emergency Defense Council, Seattle JACL
National Headquarters has been collaborating with officials in the national defense program and is now re-urging members to **cooperate in every way** with civic and federal authorities.
Saburo Kido National JACL president
San Francisco
To prove our loyalty, we propose a volunteer unit - a **suicide battalion** if you will - to spearhead the **most dangerous missions,** with their families held by the government as **hostages.**
Mike Masaoka National JACL field executive
Los Angeles
I myself went **over the top** to lead my buddies in the FBI and Naval Intelligence into the den of these disloyal and traitorous elements.
Tokutaro "Tokie" Slocum Anti-Axis Committee, Los Angeles JACL

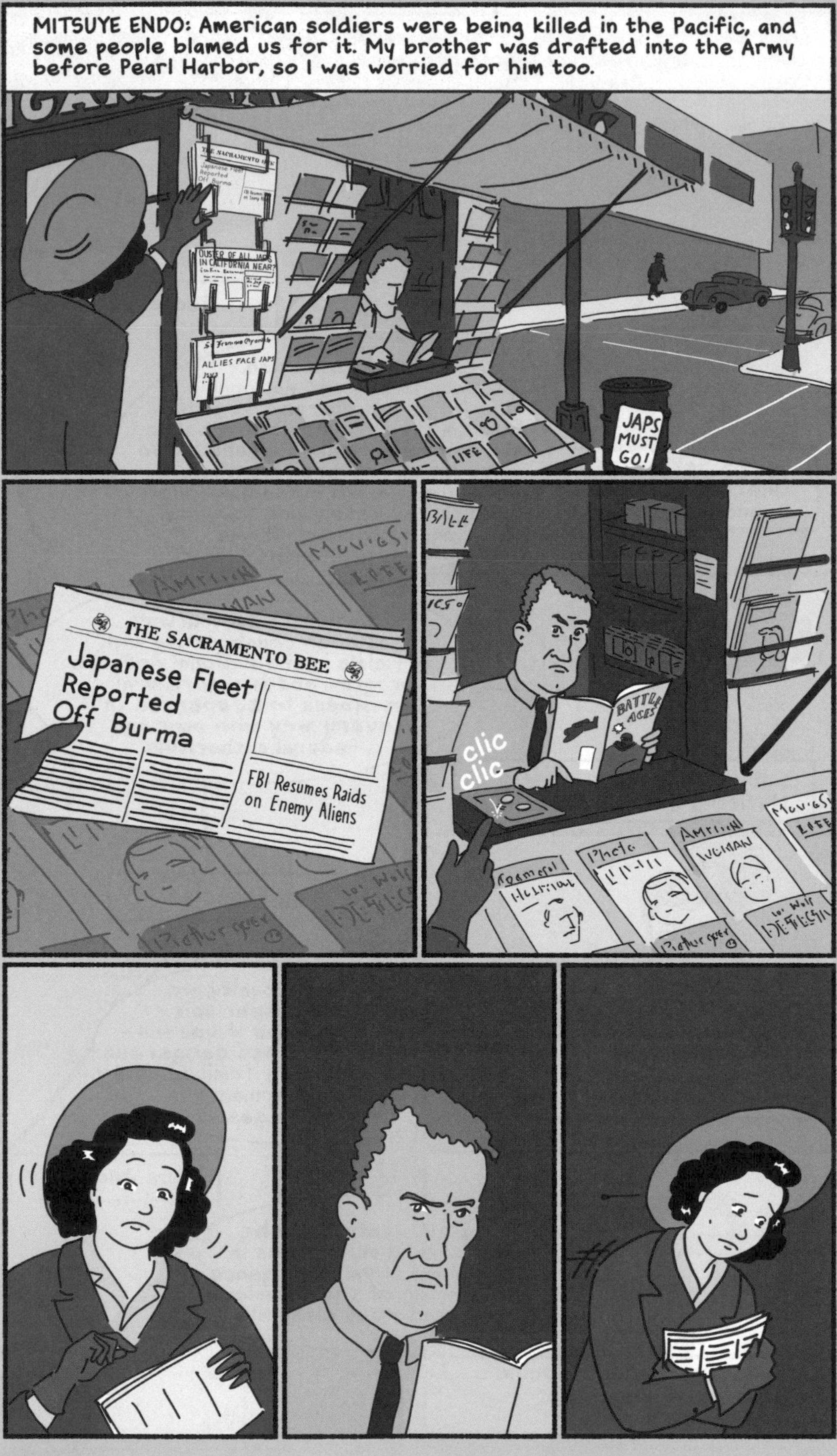
MITSUYE ENDO: American soldiers were being killed in the Pacific, and some people blamed us for it. My brother was drafted into the Army before Pearl Harbor, so I was worried for him too.
OUSTER OF ALL JAPS IN CALIFORNIA NEAR?
ALLIES FACE JAPS
JAPS MUST GO!
LIFE
THE SACRAMENTO BEE
Japanese Fleet Reported Off Burma
FBI Resumes Raids on Enemy Aliens
BATTLE ACES
clic
clic

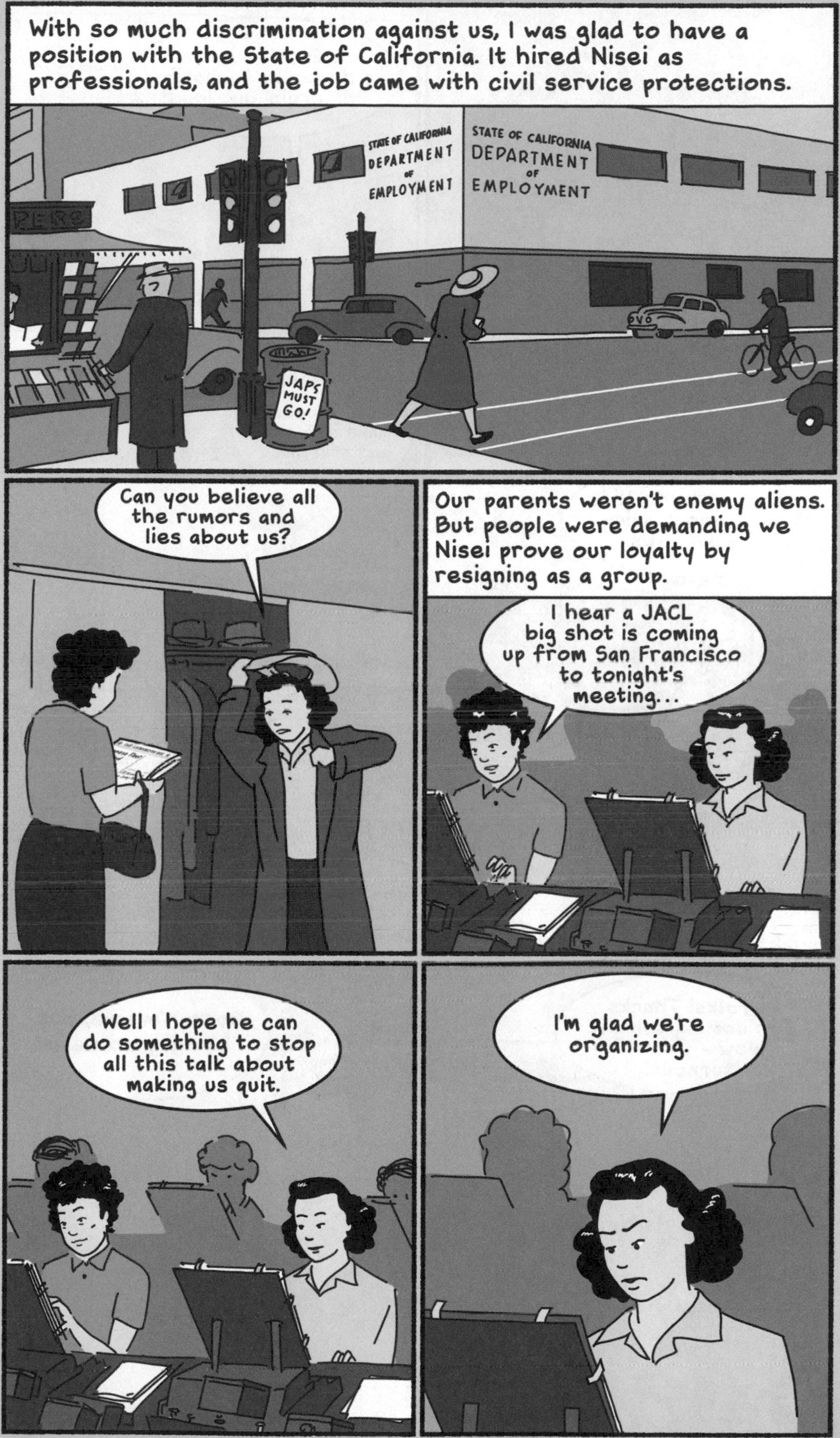
With so much discrimination against us, I was glad to have a position with the State of California. It hired Nisei as professionals, and the job came with civil service protections.
STATE OF CALIFORNIA DEPARTMENT OF EMPLOYMENT
STATE OF CALIFORNIA DEPARTMENT OF EMPLOYMENT
JAPS MUST GO!
Can you believe all the rumors and lies about us?
Our parents weren't enemy aliens. But people were demanding we Nisei prove our loyalty by resigning as a group.
I hear a JACL big shot is coming up from San Francisco to tonight's meeting...
Well I hope he can do something to stop all this talk about making us quit.
I'm glad we're organizing.

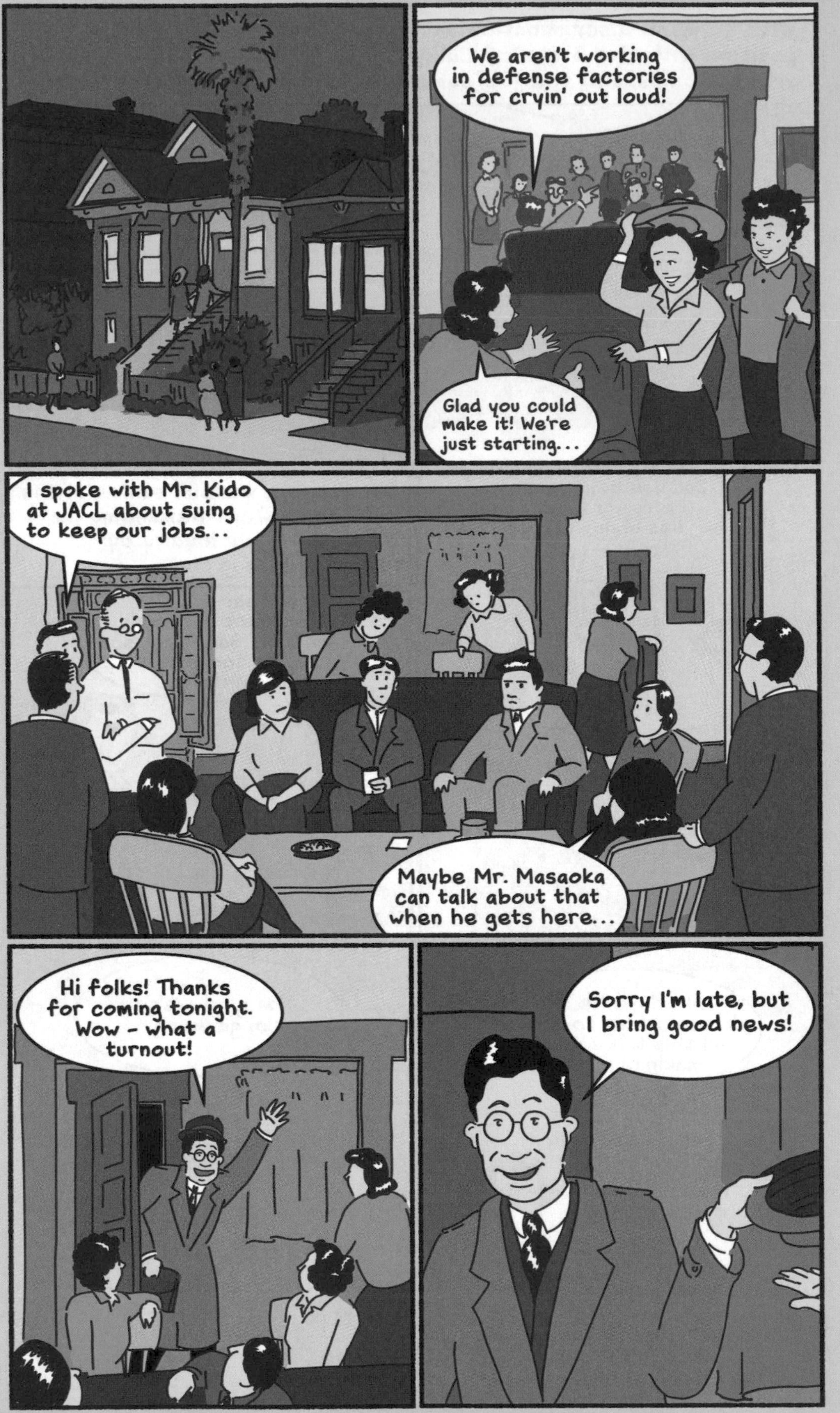
We aren't working in defense factories for cryin' out loud!
Glad you could make it! We're just starting...
I spoke with Mr. Kido at JACL about suing to keep our jobs...
Maybe Mr. Masaoka can talk about that when he gets here...
Hi folks! Thanks for coming tonight. Wow - what a turnout!
Sorry I'm late, but I bring good news!

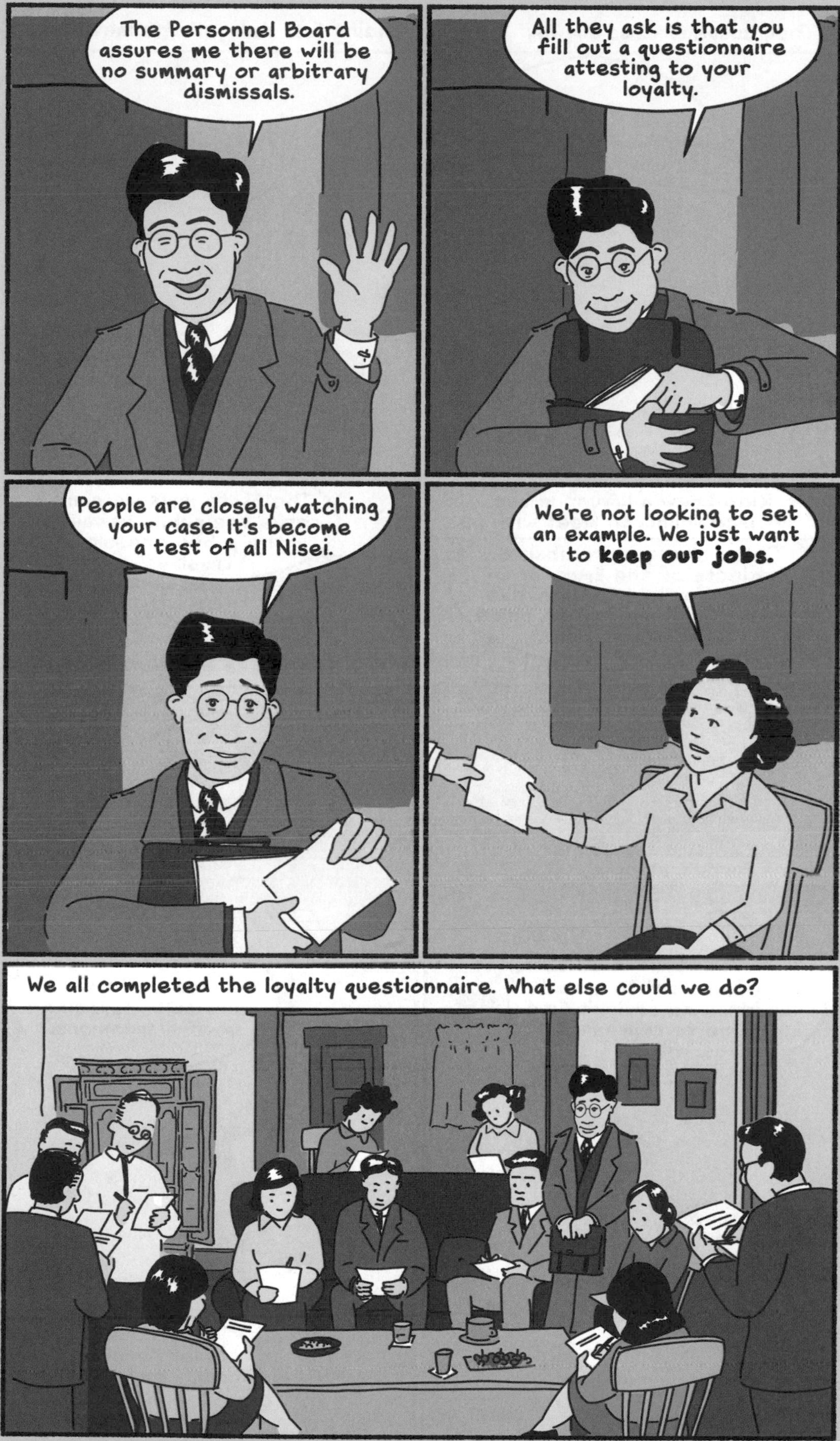
The Personnel Board assures me there will be no summary or arbitrary dismissals.
All they ask is that you fill out a questionnaire attesting to your loyalty.
People are closely watching your case. It's become a test of all Nisei.
We're not looking to set an example. We just want to **keep our jobs.**
We all completed the loyalty questionnaire. What else could we do?

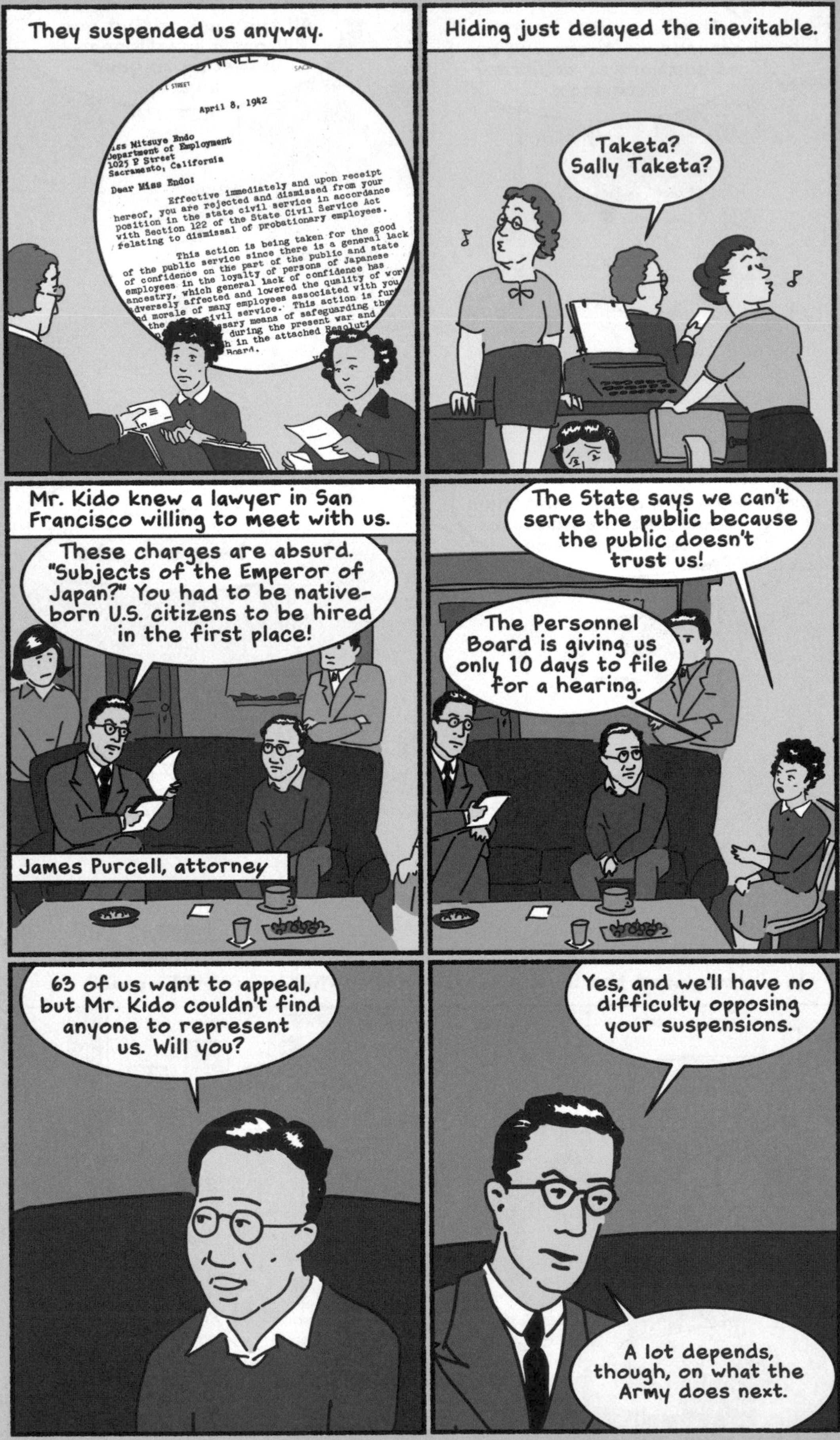
They suspended us anyway.
April 8, 1942
iss Mitsuye Endo
Department of Employment
1025 P Street
Sacramento, California
Dear Miss Endo:
Effective immediately and upon receipt hereof, you are rejected and dismissed from your position in the state civil service in accordance with Section 122 of the State Civil Service Act relating to dismissal of probationary employees.
This action is being taken for the good of the public service since there is a general lack of confidence on the part of the public and state employees in the loyalty of persons of Japanese ancestry, which general lack of confidence has adversely affected and lowered the quality of wor and morale of many employees associated with you the civil service. This action is fur sary means of safeguarding the during the present war and h in the attached Resoluti Board.
Hiding just delayed the inevitable.
Taketa? Sally Taketa?
Mr. Kido knew a lawyer in San Francisco willing to meet with us.
These charges are absurd. "Subjects of the Emperor of Japan?" You had to be native-born U.S. citizens to be hired in the first place!
James Purcell, attorney
The State says we can't serve the public because the public doesn't trust us!
The Personnel Board is giving us only 10 days to file for a hearing.
63 of us want to appeal, but Mr. Kido couldn't find anyone to represent us. Will you?
Yes, and we'll have no difficulty opposing your suspensions.
A lot depends, though, on what the Army does next.

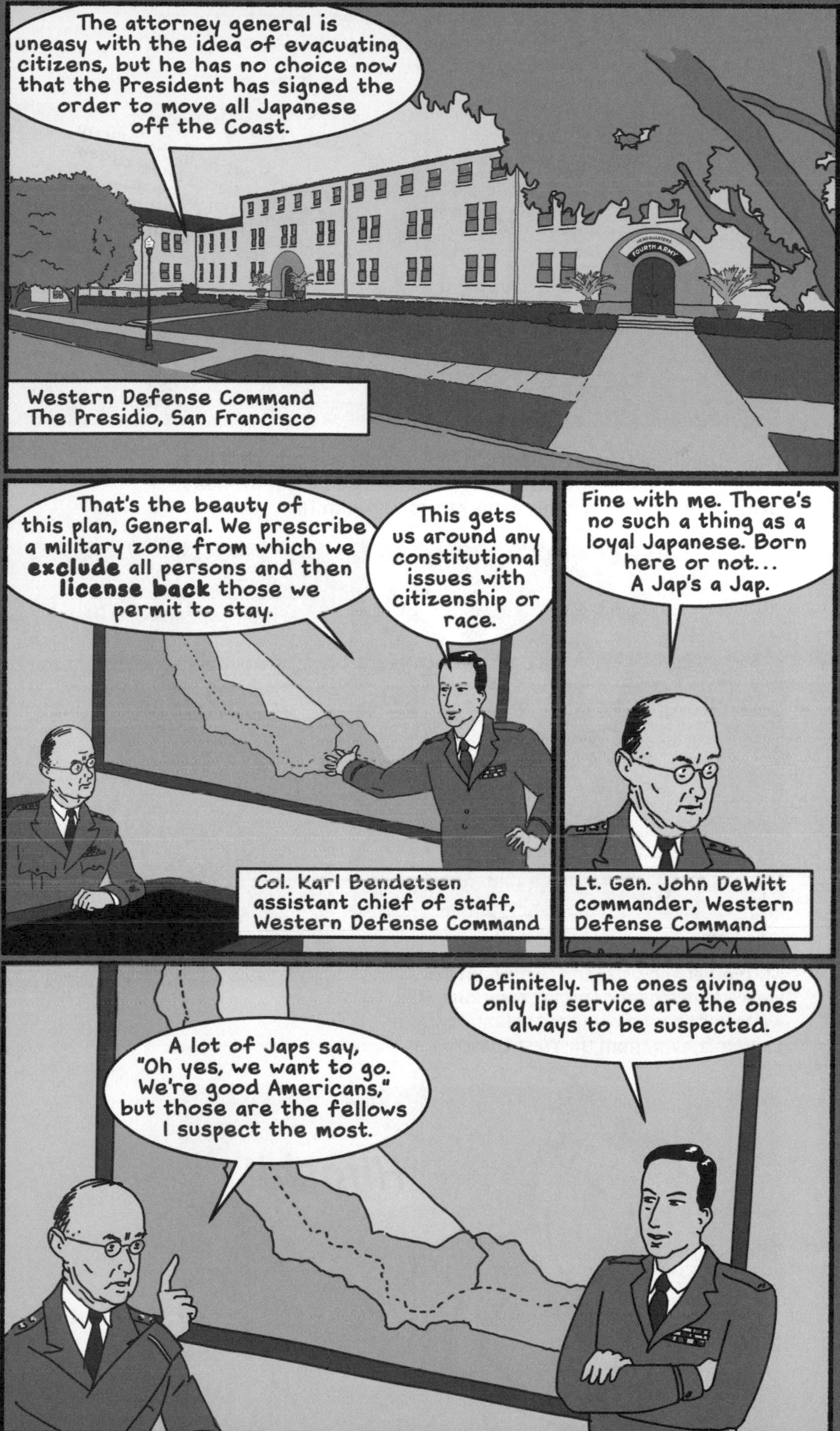

The attorney general is uneasy with the idea of evacuating citizens, but he has no choice now that the President has signed the order to move all Japanese off the Coast.
HEADQUARTERS FOURTH ARMY
Western Defense Command The Presidio, San Francisco
That's the beauty of this plan, General. We prescribe a military zone from which we **exclude** all persons and then **license back** those we permit to stay.
This gets us around any constitutional issues with citizenship or race.
Col. Karl Bendetsen assistant chief of staff, Western Defense Command
Fine with me. There's no such a thing as a loyal Japanese. Born here or not... A Jap's a Jap.
Lt. Gen. John DeWitt commander, Western Defense Command
A lot of Japs say, "Oh yes, we want to go. We're good Americans," but those are the fellows I suspect the most.
Definitely. The ones giving you only lip service are the ones always to be suspected.

HIROSHI KASHIWAGI: I was two years out of high school, helping my family sharecrop on a fruit ranch, and waiting for my younger brother to graduate so I could go to college – no different from any other idealistic American youth, ready and willing to serve my country if called upon.

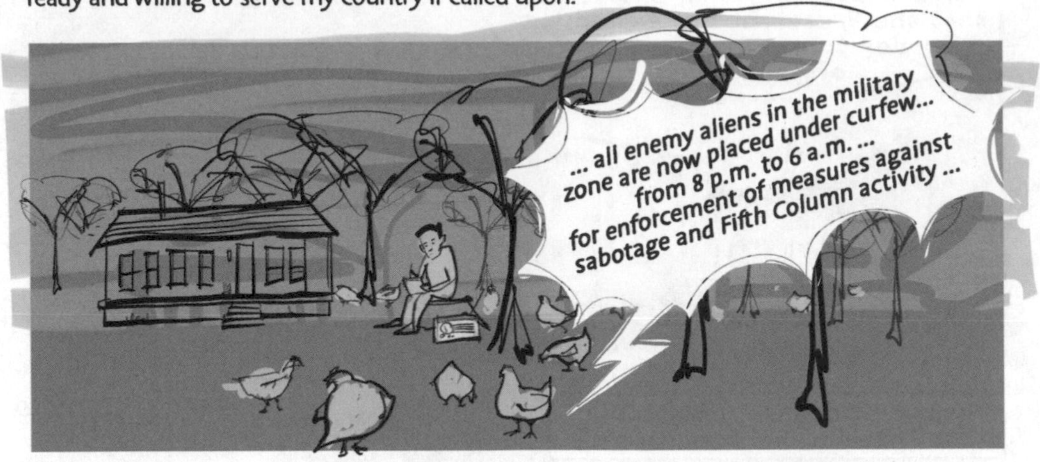
... all enemy aliens in the military zone are now placed under curfew... from 8 p.m. to 6 a.m. ... for enforcement of measures against sabotage and Fifth Column activity ...

I raised our hens from day-old chicks – beautiful New Hampshire Reds. I kept a notebook and listened to my little Zenith radio. But the news made me worry for my father in the sanatorium with TB.

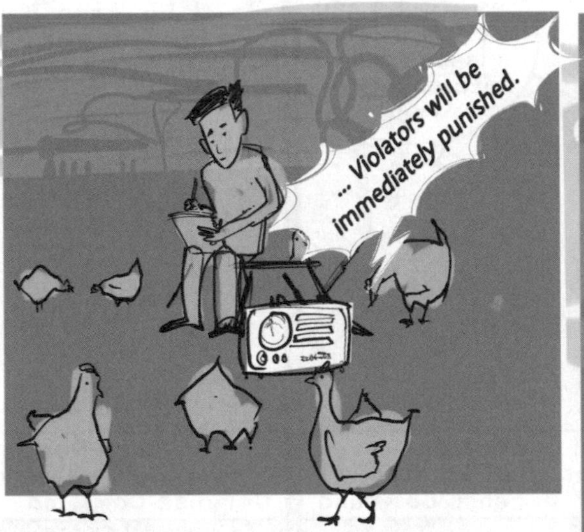
... Violators will be immediately punished.

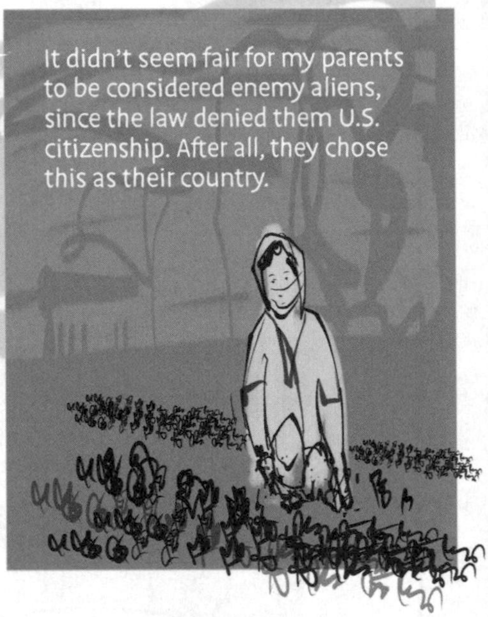
It didn't seem fair for my parents to be considered enemy aliens, since the law denied them U.S. citizenship. After all, they chose this as their country.

My brother and sister and I were born here, so we were citizens and I wasn't panicking. Still, we talked about moving out voluntarily from California, away from the West Coast.

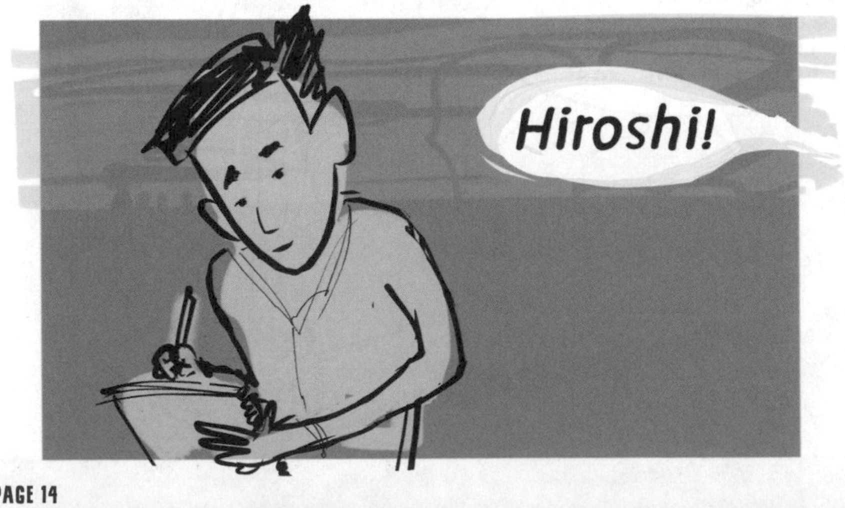
Hiroshi!

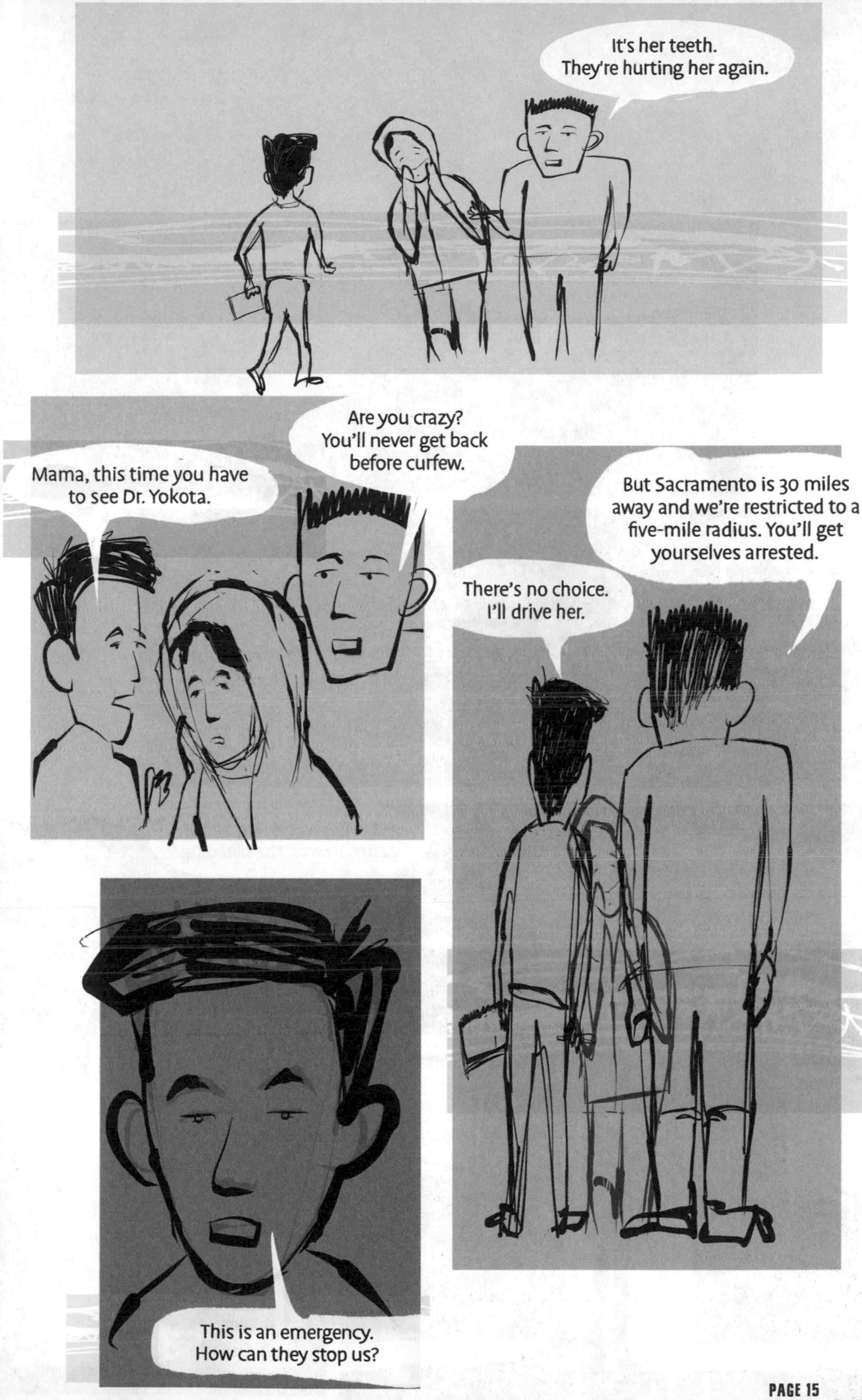
It's her teeth. They're hurting her again.
Mama, this time you have to see Dr. Yokota.
Are you crazy? You'll never get back before curfew.
There's no choice. I'll drive her.
But Sacramento is 30 miles away and we're restricted to a five-mile radius. You'll get yourselves arrested.
This is an emergency. How can they stop us?

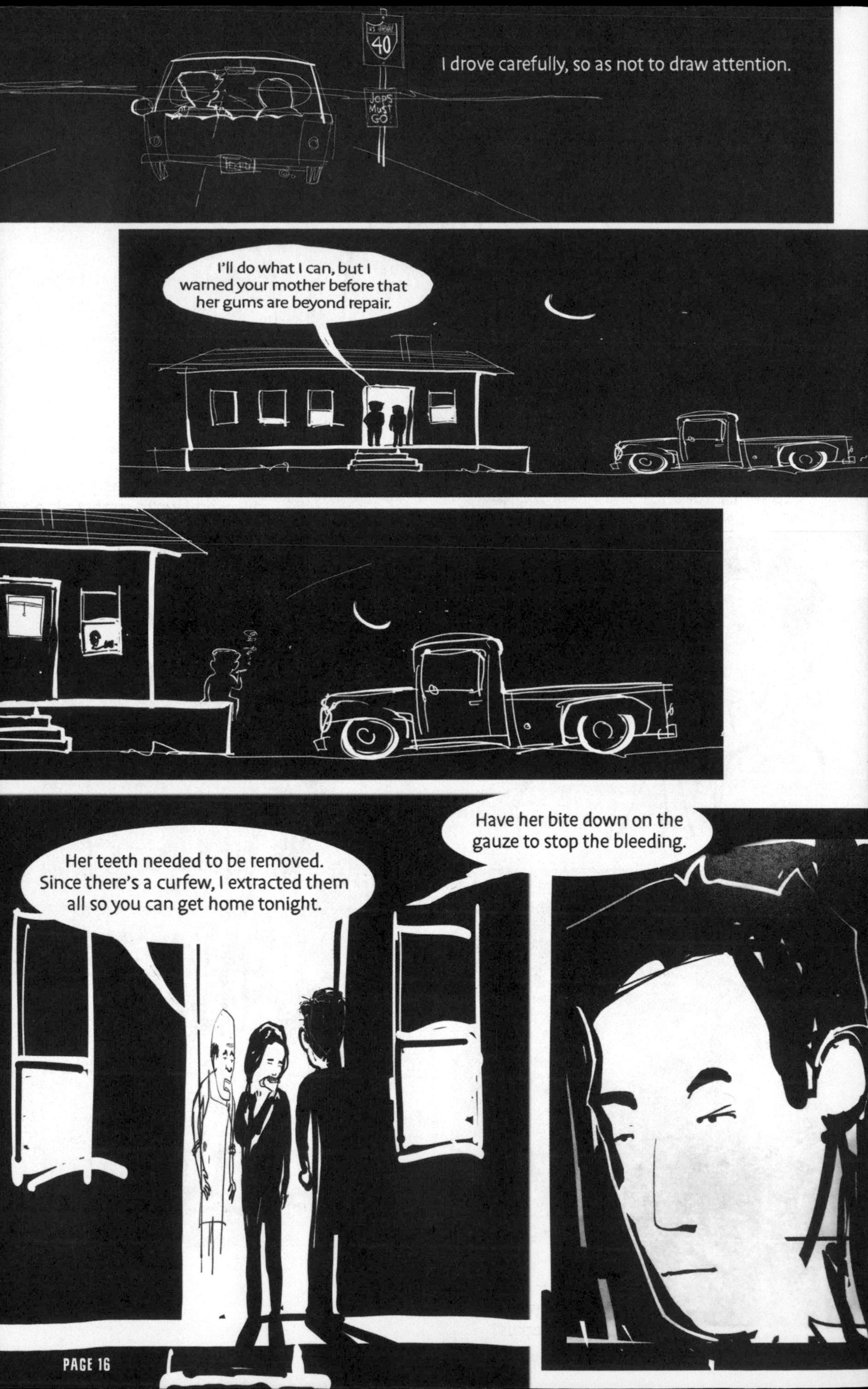
40
JAPS MUST GO
I drove carefully, so as not to draw attention.
I'll do what I can, but I warned your mother before that her gums are beyond repair.
Her teeth needed to be removed. Since there's a curfew, I extracted them all so you can get home tonight.
Have her bite down on the gauze to stop the bleeding.

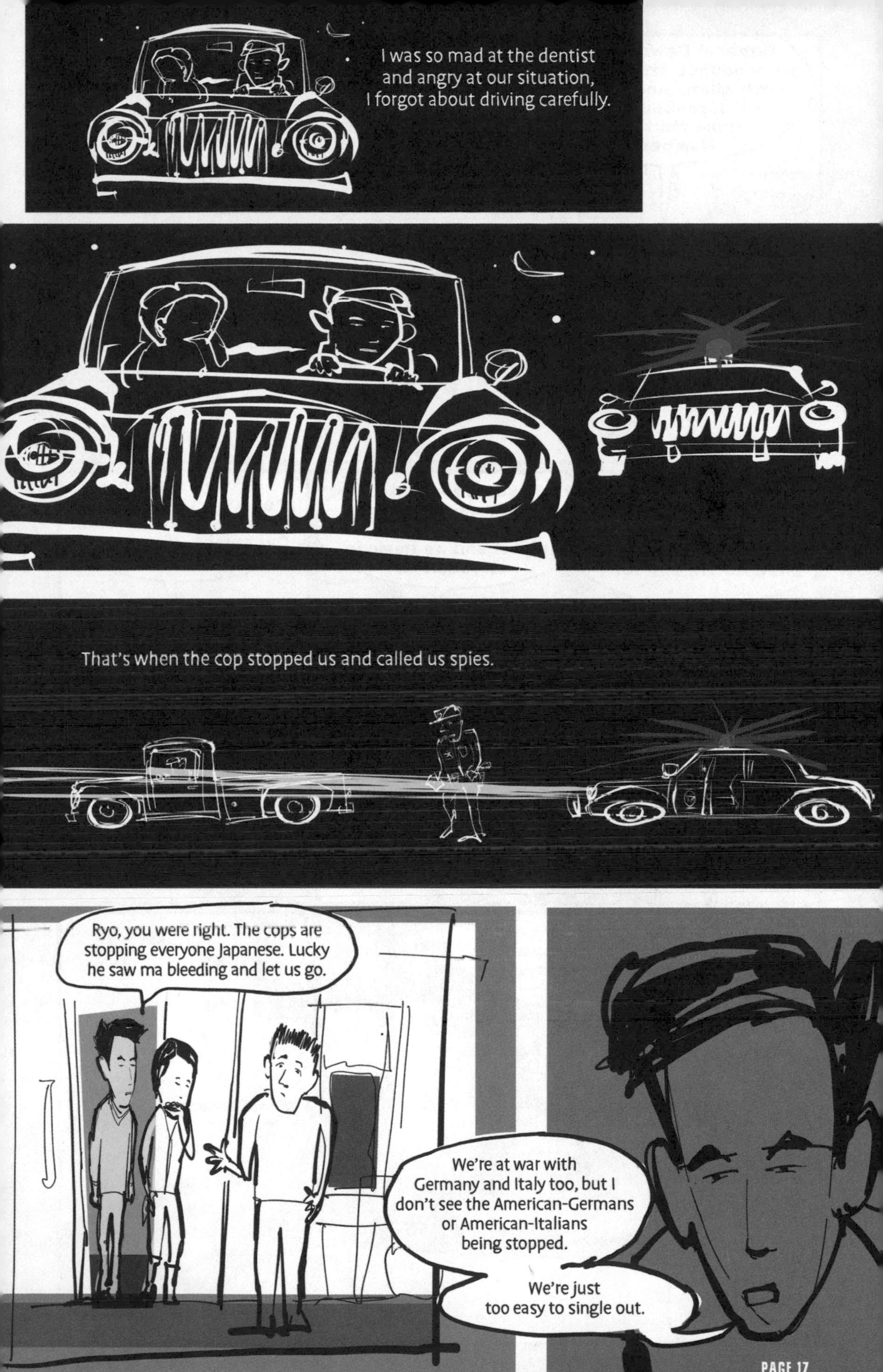

I was so mad at the dentist and angry at our situation, I forgot about driving carefully.
That's when the cop stopped us and called us spies.
Ryo, you were right. The cops are stopping everyone Japanese. Lucky he saw ma bleeding and let us go.
We're at war with Germany and Italy too, but I don't see the American-Germans or American-Italians being stopped.
We're just too easy to single out.

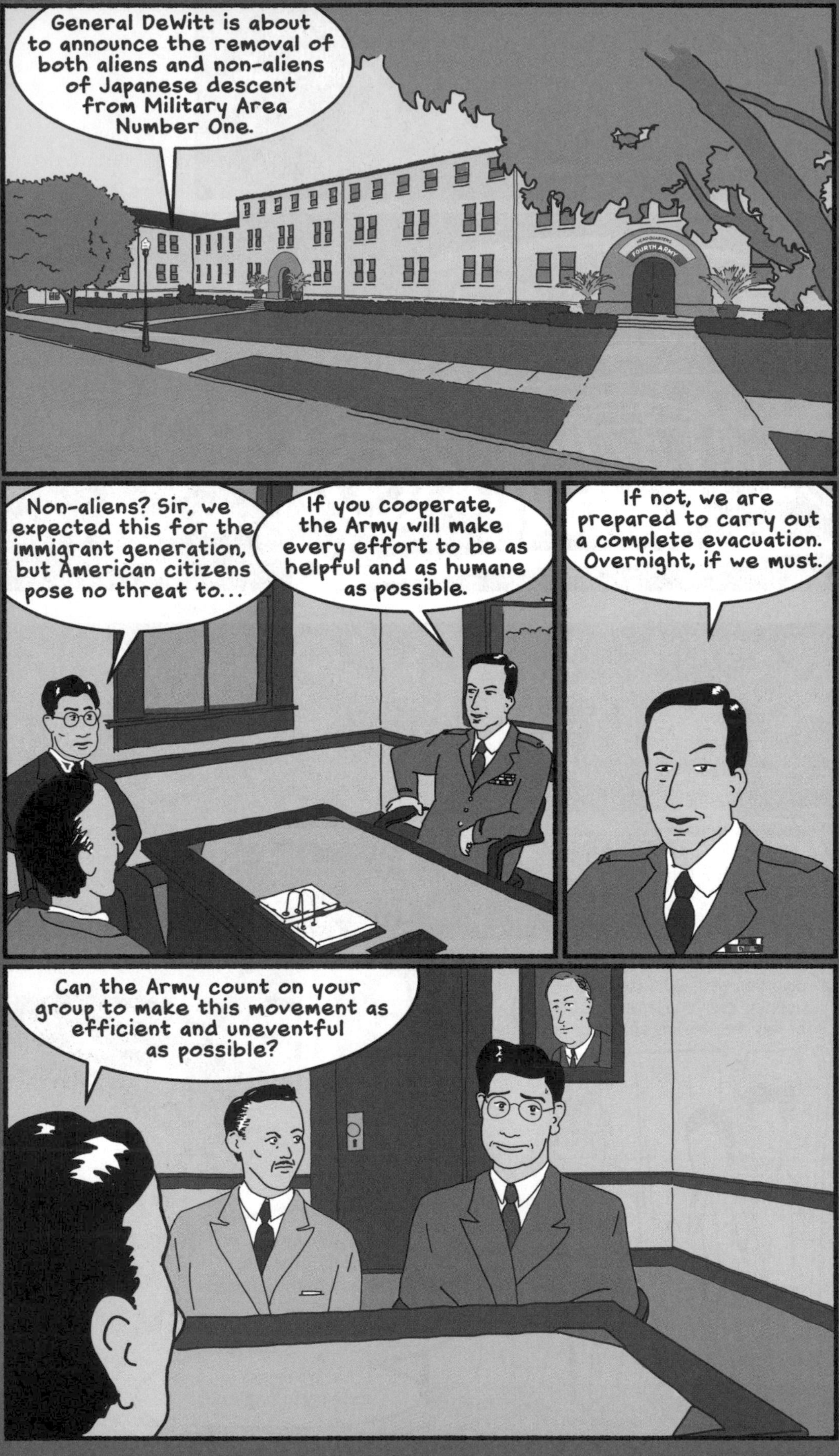

General DeWitt is about to announce the removal of both aliens and non-aliens of Japanese descent from Military Area Number One.
HEADQUARTERS FOURTH ARMY
Non-aliens? Sir, we expected this for the immigrant generation, but American citizens pose no threat to...
If you cooperate, the Army will make every effort to be as helpful and as humane as possible.
If not, we are prepared to carry out a complete evacuation. Overnight, if we must.
Can the Army count on your group to make this movement as efficient and uneventful as possible?

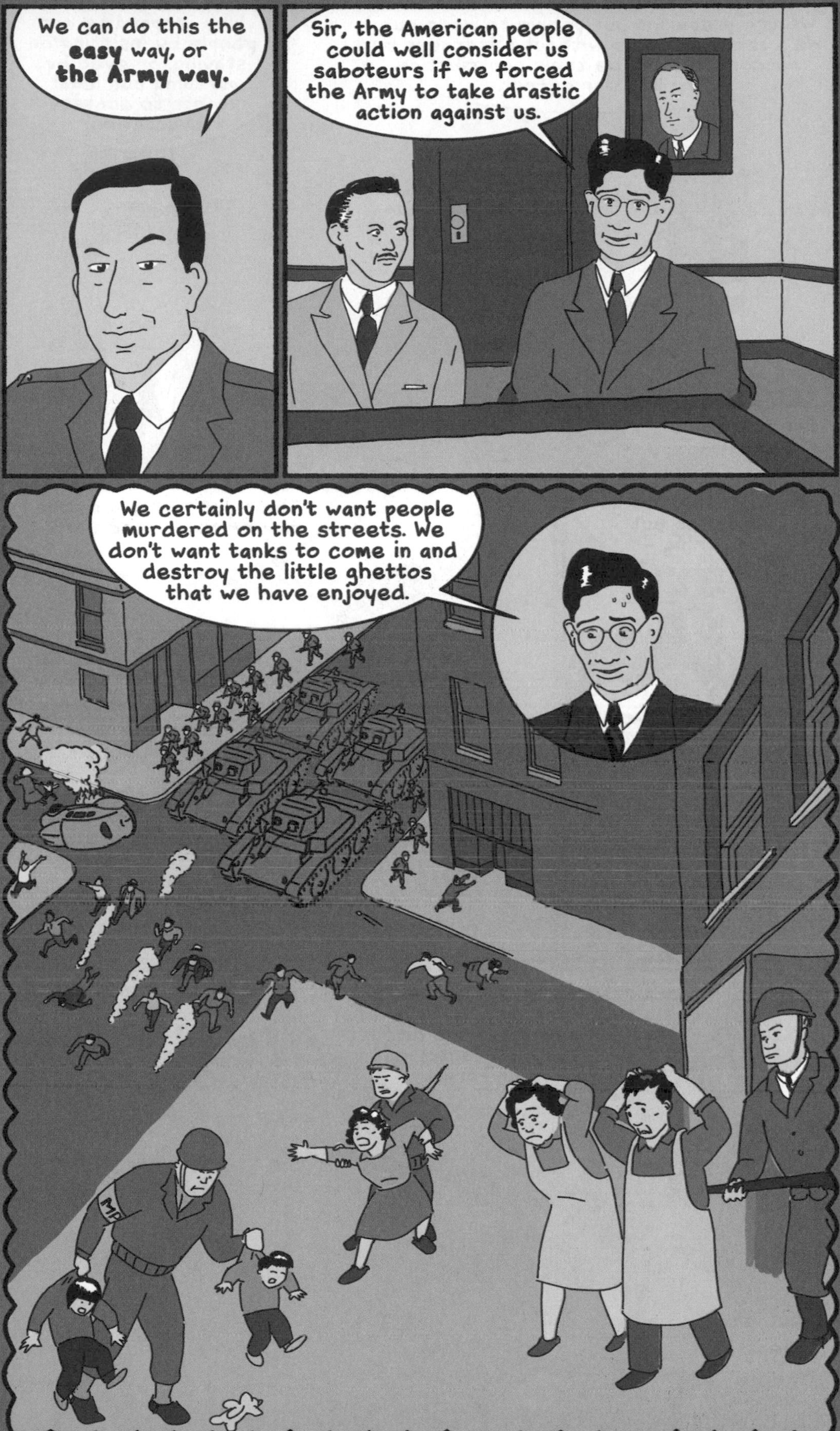
We can do this the easy way, or the Army way.
Sir, the American people could well consider us saboteurs if we forced the Army to take drastic action against us.
We certainly don't want people murdered on the streets. We don't want tanks to come in and destroy the little ghettos that we have enjoyed.
MP

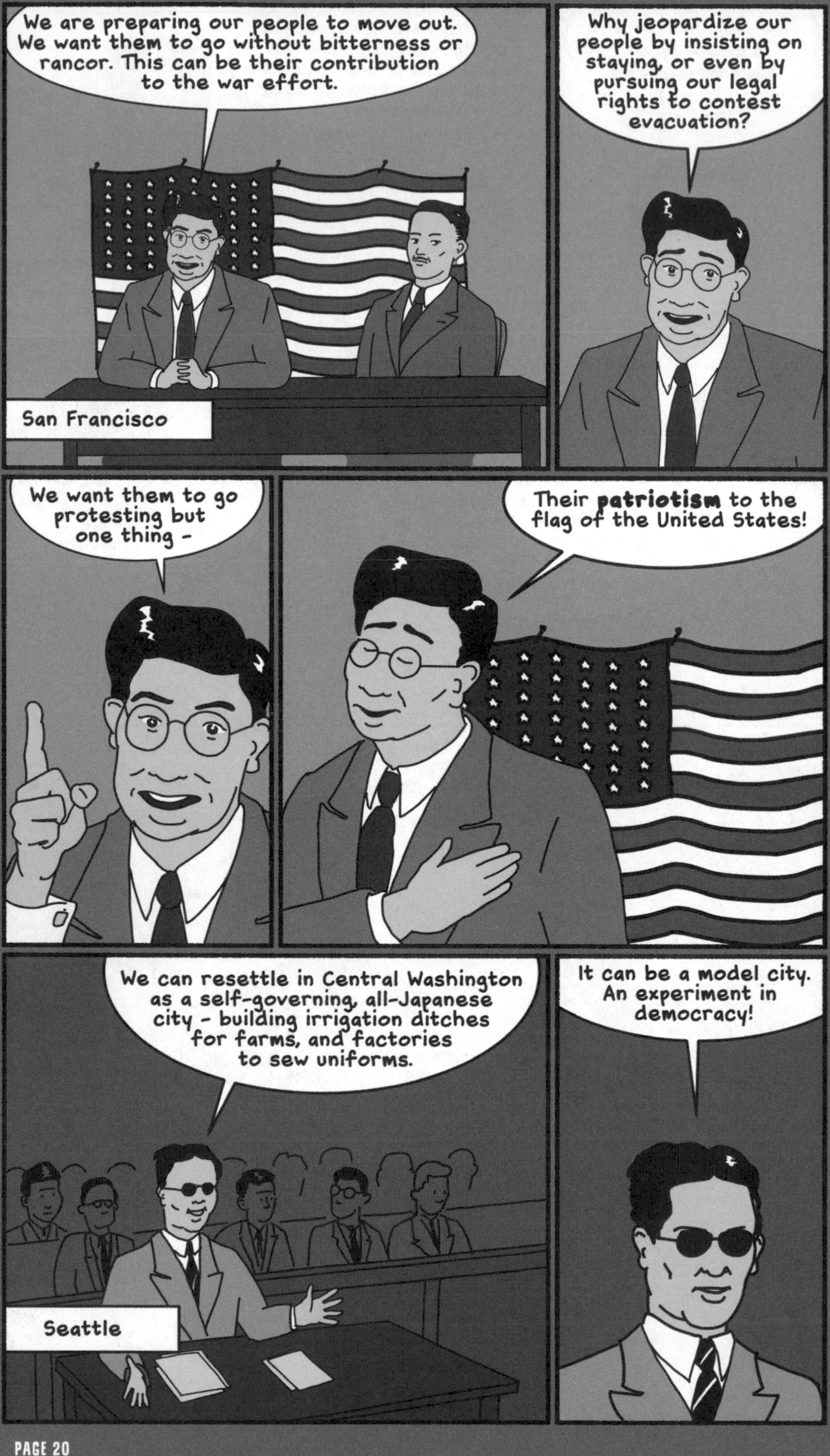
We are preparing our people to move out. We want them to go without bitterness or rancor. This can be their contribution to the war effort.
San Francisco
Why jeopardize our people by insisting on staying, or even by pursuing our legal rights to contest evacuation?
We want them to go protesting but one thing -
Their **patriotism** to the flag of the United States!
We can resettle in Central Washington as a self-governing, all-Japanese city - building irrigation ditches for farms, and factories to sew uniforms.
Seattle
It can be a model city. An experiment in democracy!

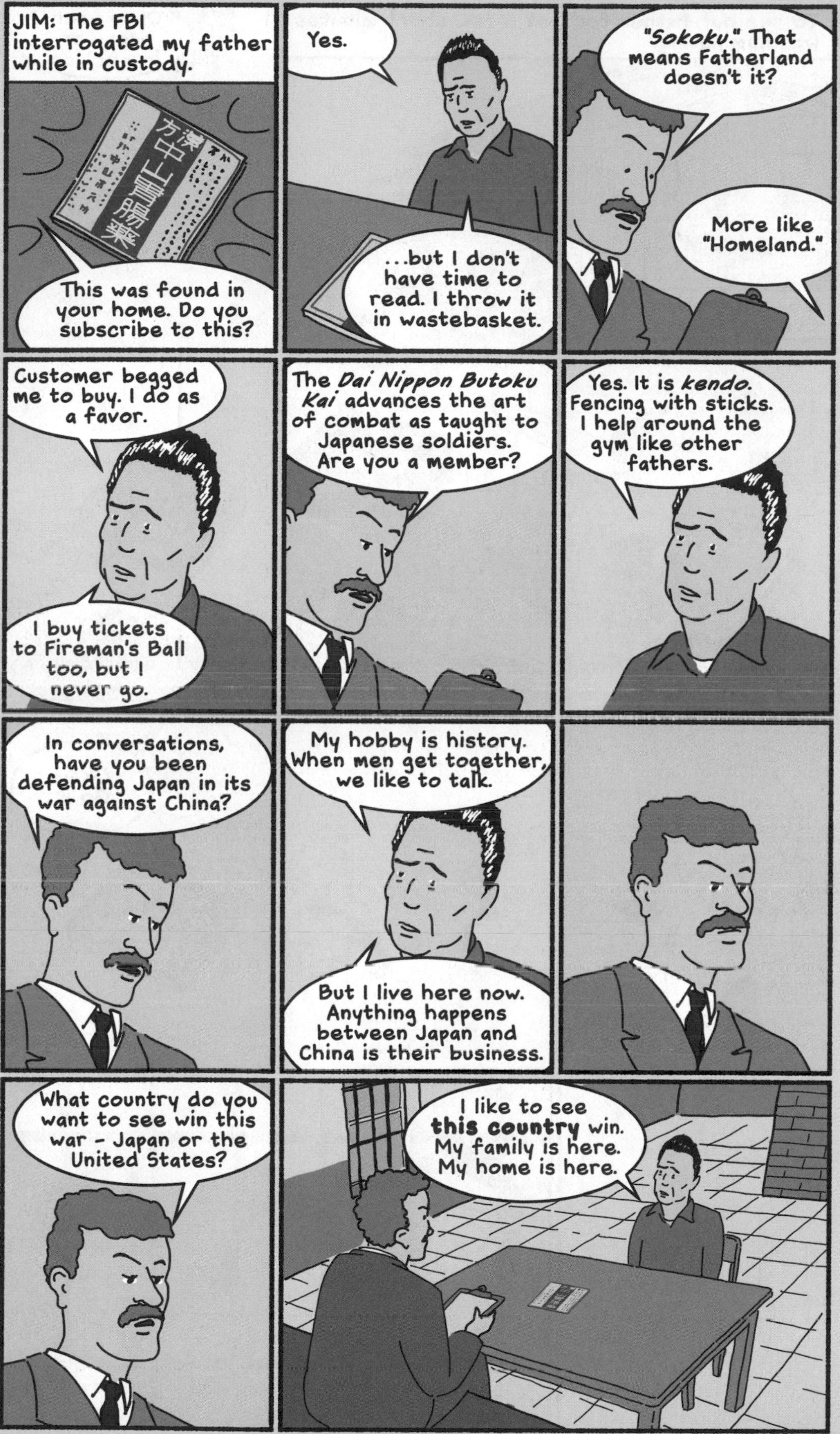
JIM: The FBI interrogated my father while in custody.
This was found in your home. Do you subscribe to this?
Yes.
...but I don't have time to read. I throw it in wastebasket.
"*Sokoku*." That means Fatherland doesn't it?
More like "Homeland."
Customer begged me to buy. I do as a favor.
I buy tickets to Fireman's Ball too, but I never go.
The *Dai Nippon Butoku Kai* advances the art of combat as taught to Japanese soldiers. Are you a member?
Yes. It is *kendo*. Fencing with sticks. I help around the gym like other fathers.
In conversations, have you been defending Japan in its war against China?
My hobby is history. When men get together, we like to talk.
But I live here now. Anything happens between Japan and China is their business.
What country do you want to see win this war - Japan or the United States?
I like to see **this country** win. My family is here. My home is here.

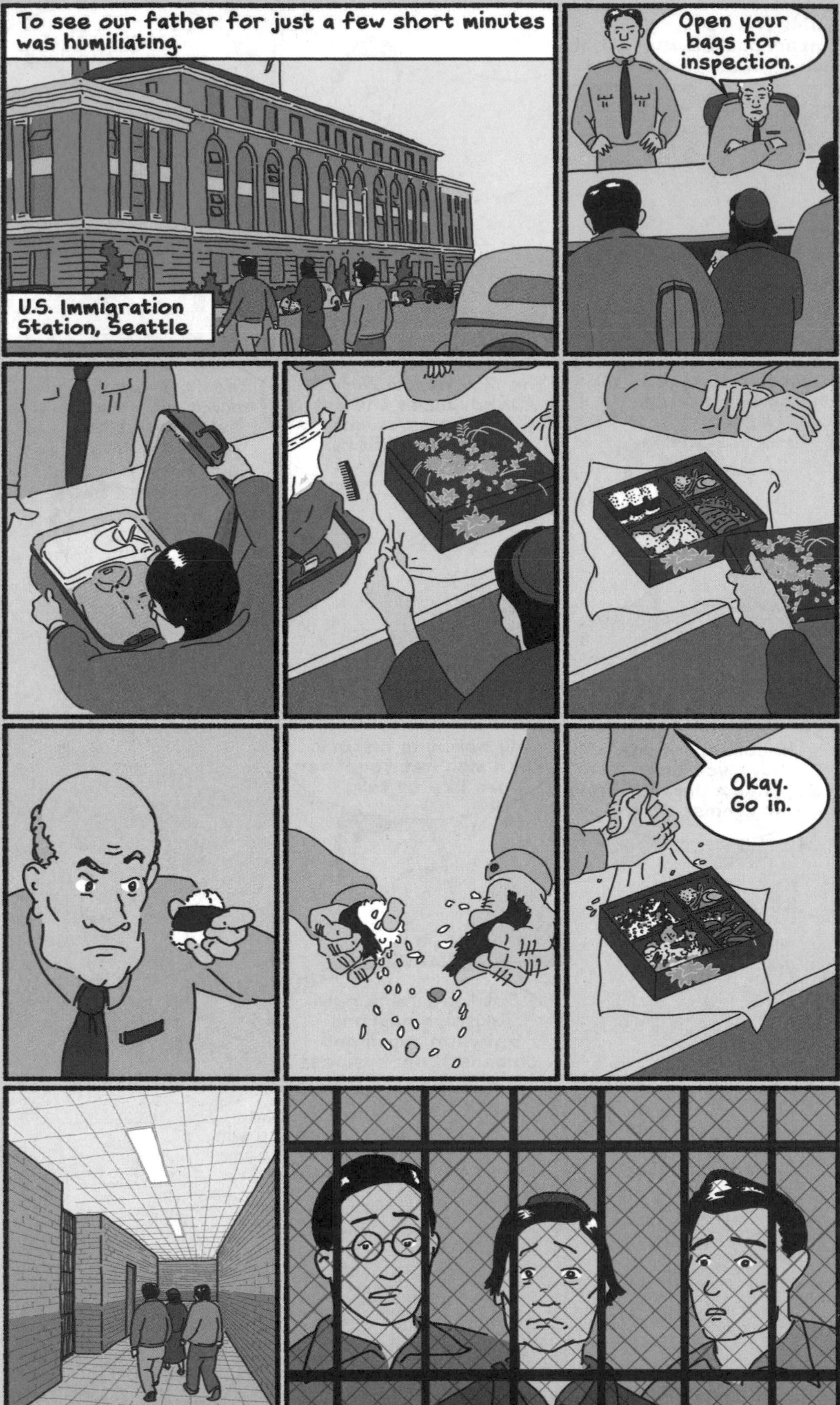
To see our father for just a few short minutes was humiliating.
U.S. Immigration Station, Seattle
Open your bags for inspection.
Okay. Go in.

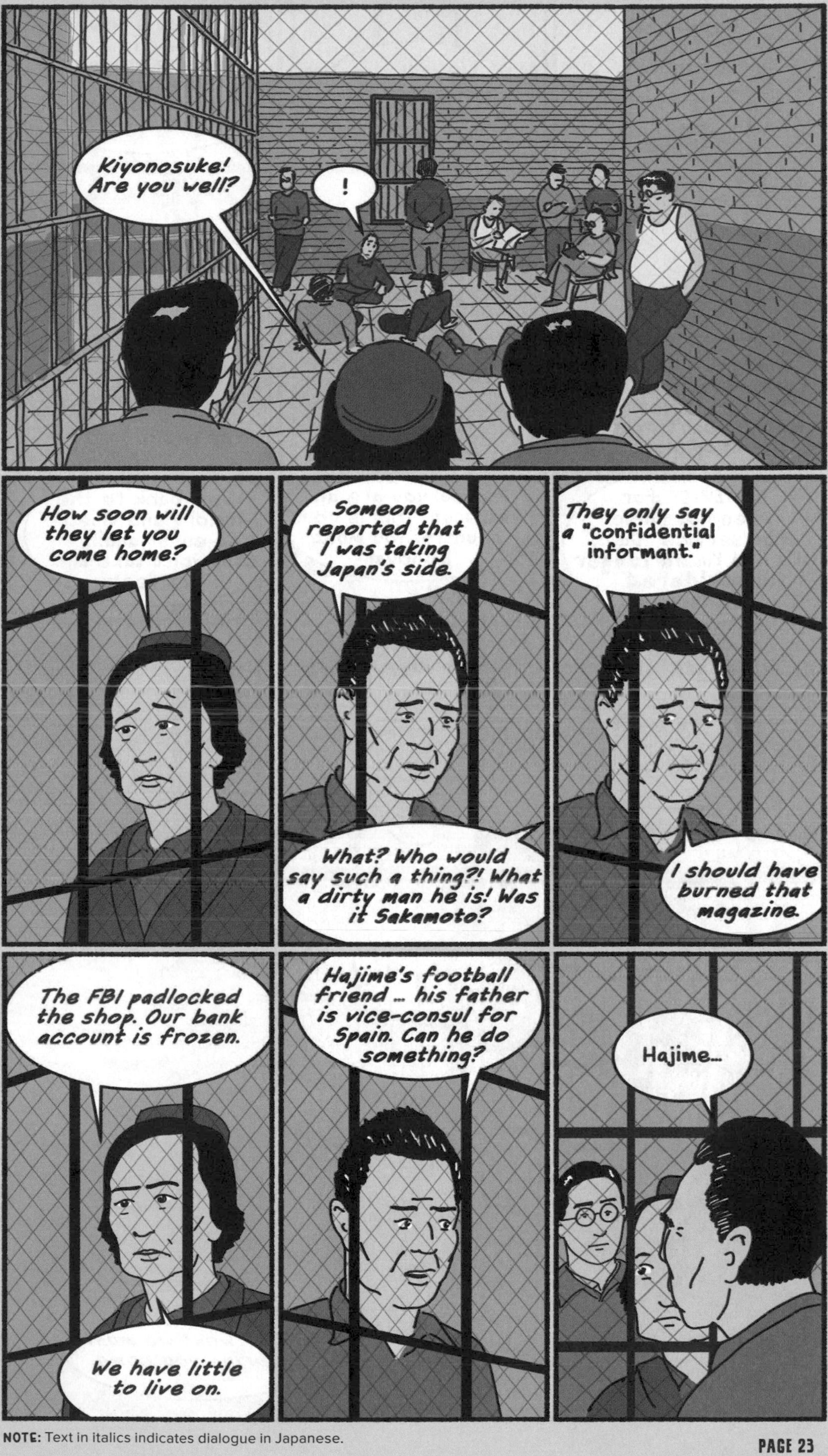
Kiyonosuke! Are you well?
!
How soon will they let you come home?
Someone reported that I was taking Japan's side.
What? Who would say such a thing?! What a dirty man he is! Was it Sakamoto?
They only say a "confidential informant."
I should have burned that magazine.
The FBI padlocked the shop. Our bank account is frozen.
We have little to live on.
Hajime's football friend ... his father is vice-consul for Spain. Can he do something?
Hajime...

NOTE: Text in italics indicates dialogue in Japanese.

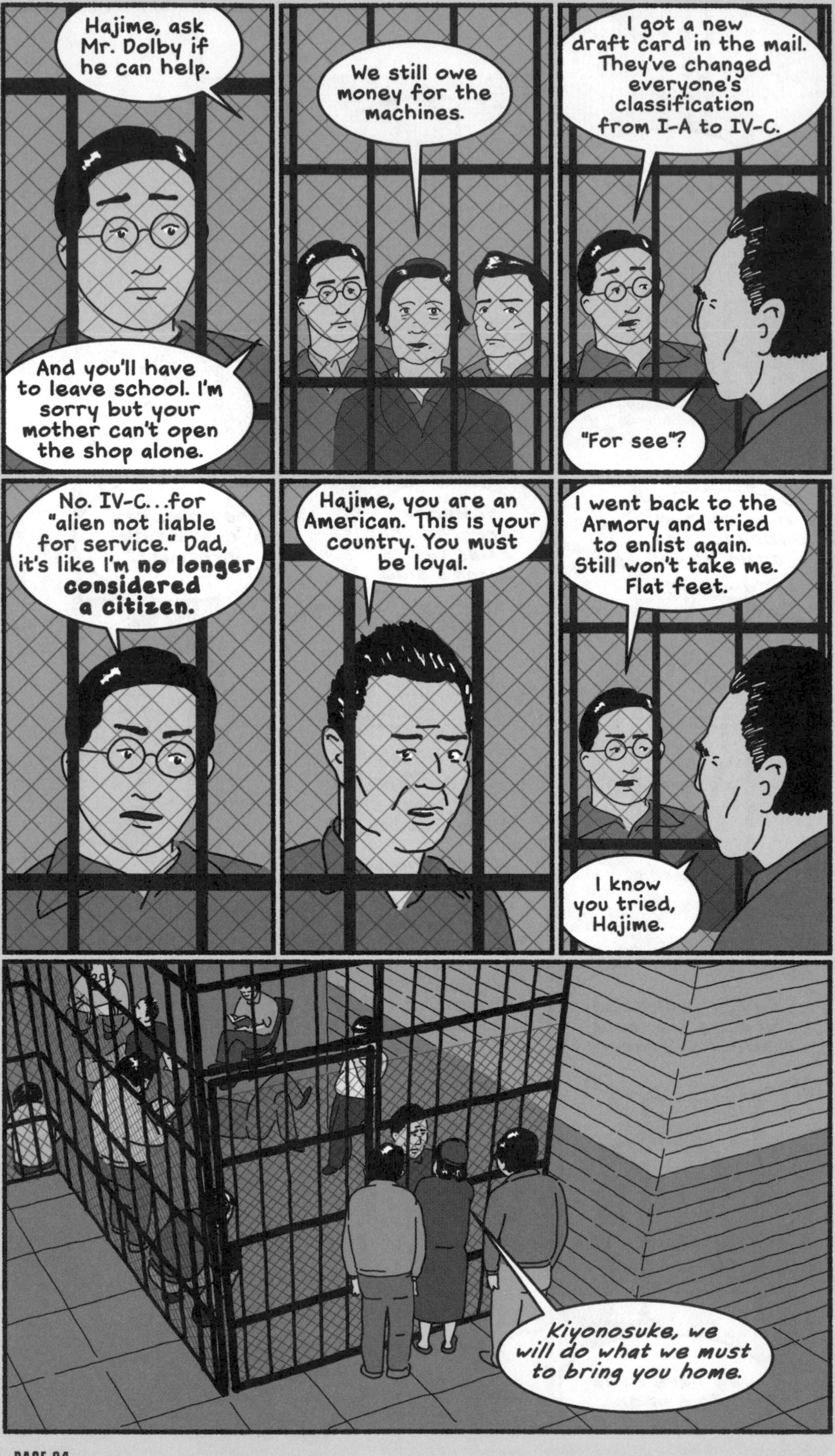
Hajime, ask Mr. Dolby if he can help.
And you'll have to leave school. I'm sorry but your mother can't open the shop alone.
We still owe money for the machines.
I got a new draft card in the mail. They've changed everyone's classification from I-A to IV-C.
"For see"?
No. IV-C...for "alien not liable for service." Dad, it's like I'm **no longer considered a citizen.**
Hajime, you are an American. This is your country. You must be loyal.
I went back to the Armory and tried to enlist again. Still won't take me. Flat feet.
I know you tried, Hajime.
Kiyonosuke, we will do what we must to bring you home.

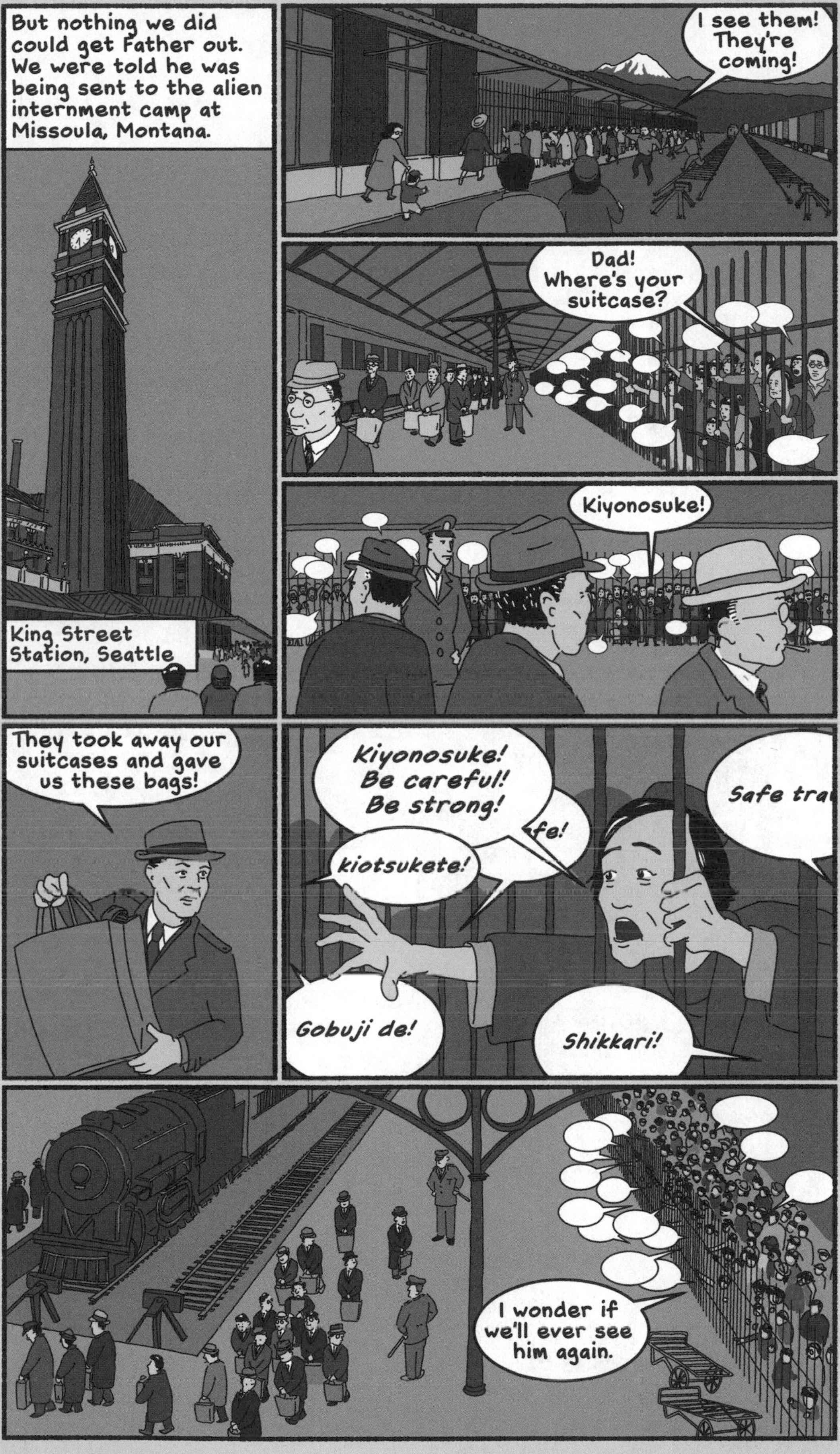

But nothing we did could get Father out. We were told he was being sent to the alien internment camp at Missoula, Montana.
King Street Station, Seattle
I see them! They're coming!
Dad! Where's your suitcase?
Kiyonosuke!
They took away our suitcases and gave us these bags!
Kiyonosuke! Be careful! Be strong!
kiotsukete!
Gobuji de!
Shikkari!
I wonder if we'll ever see him again.

KIDO
ENT
TSUMOTO
ECRETARY
SUGIOKA

KADA

SECRETARY AND
CUTIVE
M. MASAOKA

April 6, 1942

OFFICE OF
AND

TWENTY
SAN F

Mr. Milton S. Eisenhower, Director
War Relocation Authority
Western Defense Command and Fourth Army Headquarte
Whitcomb Hotel
San Francisco, California

Dear Mr. Eisenhower:

Before submitting our recommendations f
sideration, may I, on behalf of the members of ou
and the 20,000 members of the Japanese American C
extend to you and the members of your staff our h
ciation for the privilege and opportunity of meet
and discussing our mutual problems regarding the
Japanese evacuees from the Pacific Coast. Your
understanding and vision of the tremendous force
convinced us of your sincerity and ability. We
that our Federal Government has appointed a man
to direct the humane and democratic resettlement
tunate people who have been called upon to leave
businesses in order that the military defenses o
may be strengthened. We are hopeful that our su
recommendations will be given the utmost conside
frank and reasoned opinions of a number of repr
can citizens of Japanese extraction who are leg
sincerely interested in cooperating with our Go
successful and happy solution to this tragedy.

BACKGROUND

Before introducing various suggestio
might and ought to be done, may we mention a f
which we feel will be helpful to you as backgr
your study of this problem.

the entire evacu

— PART TWO —

WHO PUT THEM IN CHARGE?

APRIL 1942

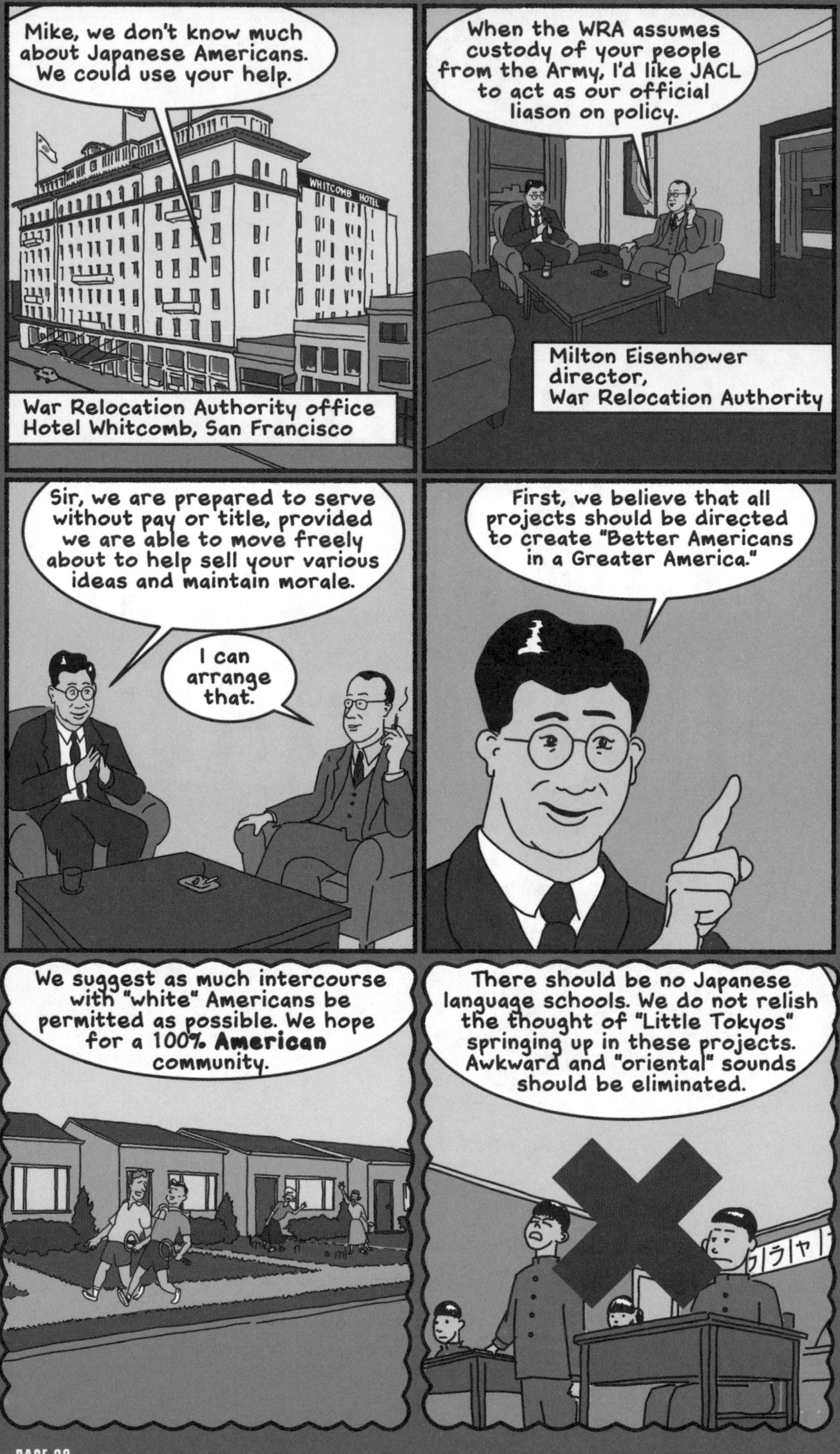
Mike, we don't know much about Japanese Americans. We could use your help.
War Relocation Authority office Hotel Whitcomb, San Francisco
WHITCOMB HOTEL
When the WRA assumes custody of your people from the Army, I'd like JACL to act as our official liason on policy.
Milton Eisenhower director, War Relocation Authority
Sir, we are prepared to serve without pay or title, provided we are able to move freely about to help sell your various ideas and maintain morale.
I can arrange that.
First, we believe that all projects should be directed to create "Better Americans in a Greater America."
We suggest as much intercourse with "white" Americans be permitted as possible. We hope for a 100% **American** community.
There should be no Japanese language schools. We do not relish the thought of "Little Tokyos" springing up in these projects. Awkward and "oriental" sounds should be eliminated.

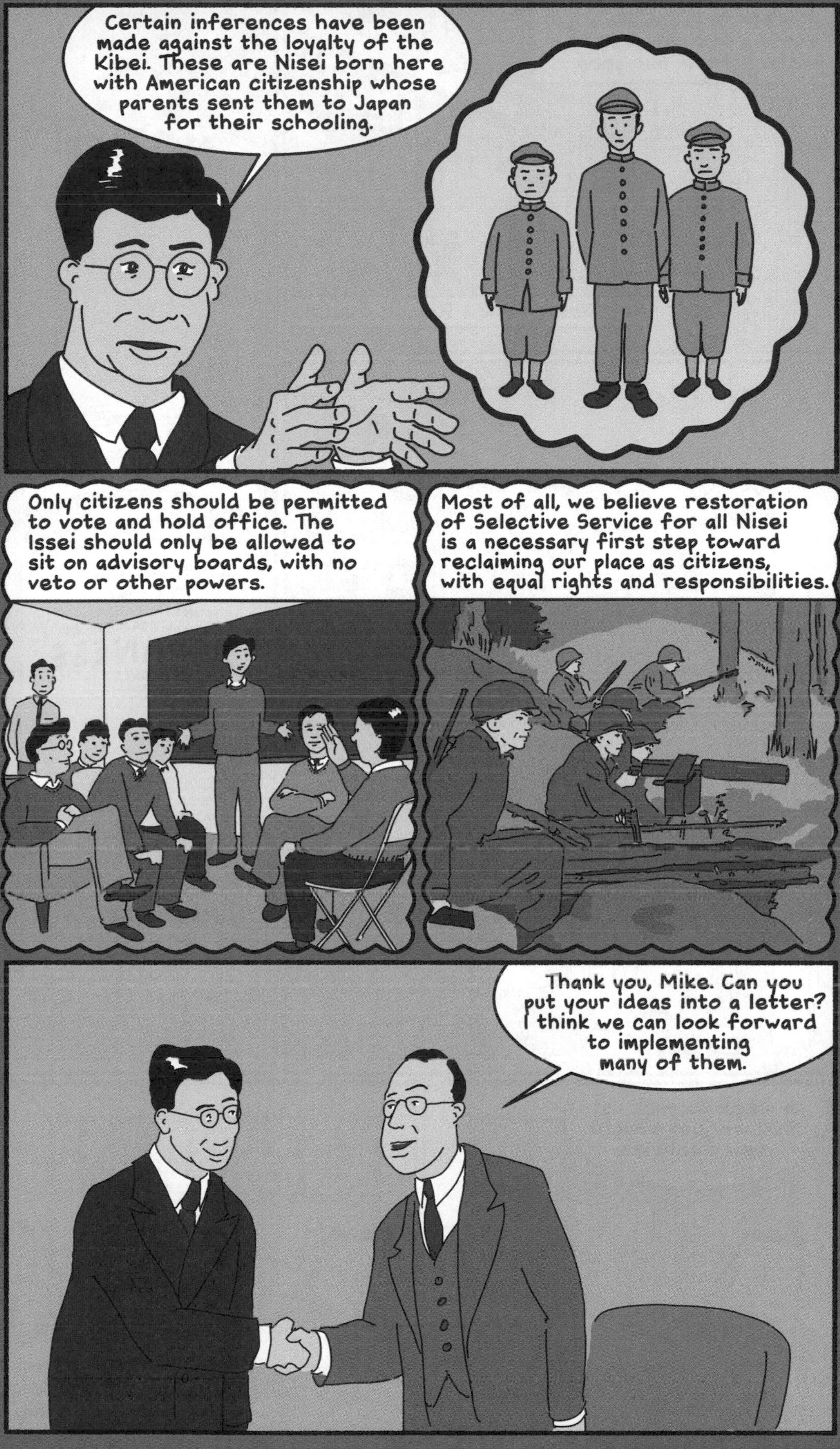
Certain inferences have been made against the loyalty of the Kibei. These are Nisei born here with American citizenship whose parents sent them to Japan for their schooling.
Only citizens should be permitted to vote and hold office. The Issei should only be allowed to sit on advisory boards, with no veto or other powers.
Most of all, we believe restoration of Selective Service for all Nisei is a necessary first step toward reclaiming our place as citizens, with equal rights and responsibilities.
Thank you, Mike. Can you put your ideas into a letter? I think we can look forward to implementing many of them.

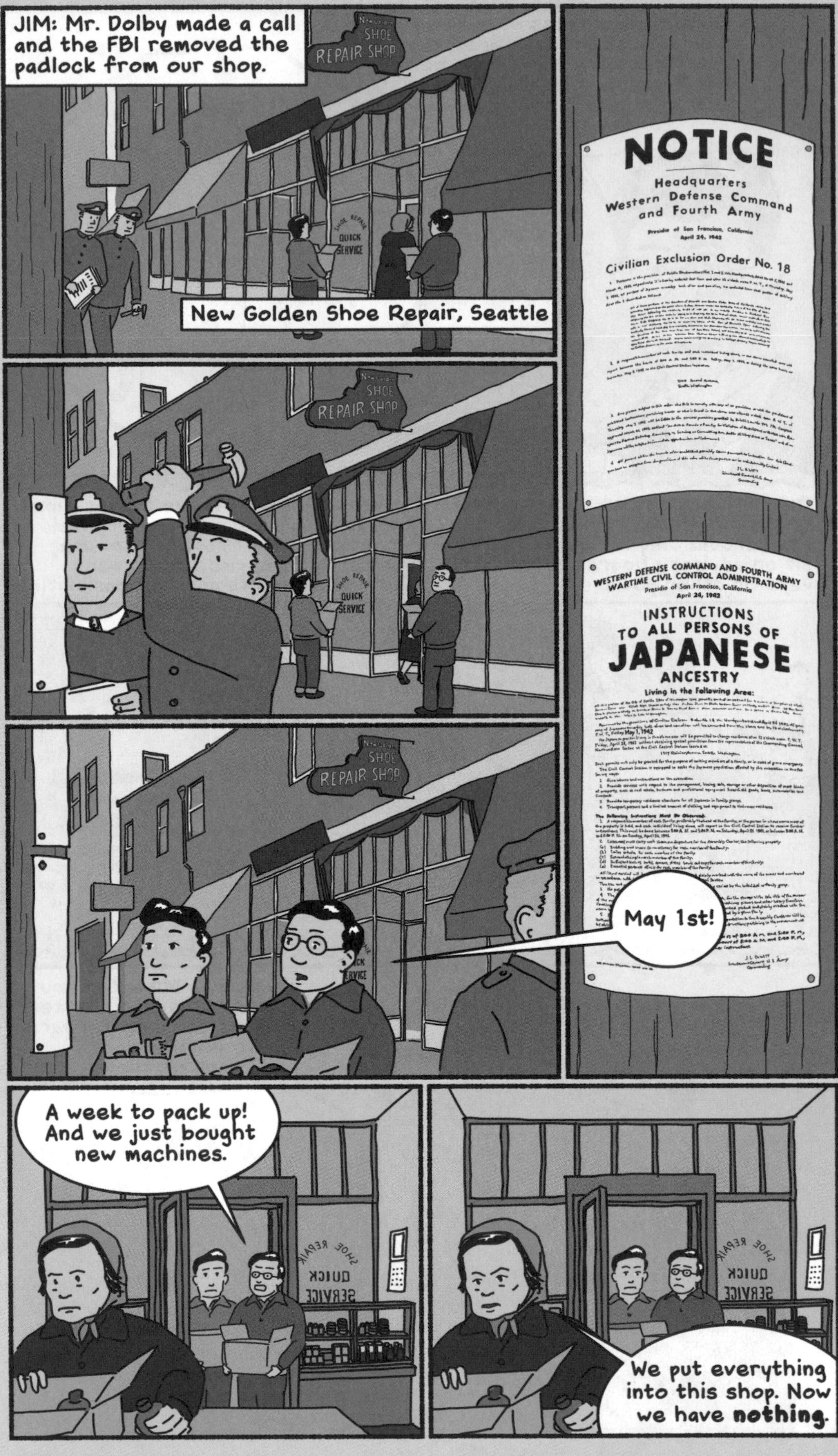
JIM: Mr. Dolby made a call and the FBI removed the padlock from our shop.
SHOE REPAIR SHOP
SHOE REPAIR QUICK SERVICE
New Golden Shoe Repair, Seattle
NOTICE
Headquarters Western Defense Command and Fourth Army
Presidio of San Francisco, California
April 24, 1942
Civilian Exclusion Order No. 18
WESTERN DEFENSE COMMAND AND FOURTH ARMY WARTIME CIVIL CONTROL ADMINISTRATION
Presidio of San Francisco, California
April 24, 1942
INSTRUCTIONS TO ALL PERSONS OF JAPANESE ANCESTRY
Living in the Following Area:
May 1st!
A week to pack up! And we just bought new machines.
We put everything into this shop. Now we have **nothing**.

HIROSHI: Our mother sewed us canvas duffel bags for the trip. The order said we could only bring what we could carry. It left out the part about having to leave everything else behind.

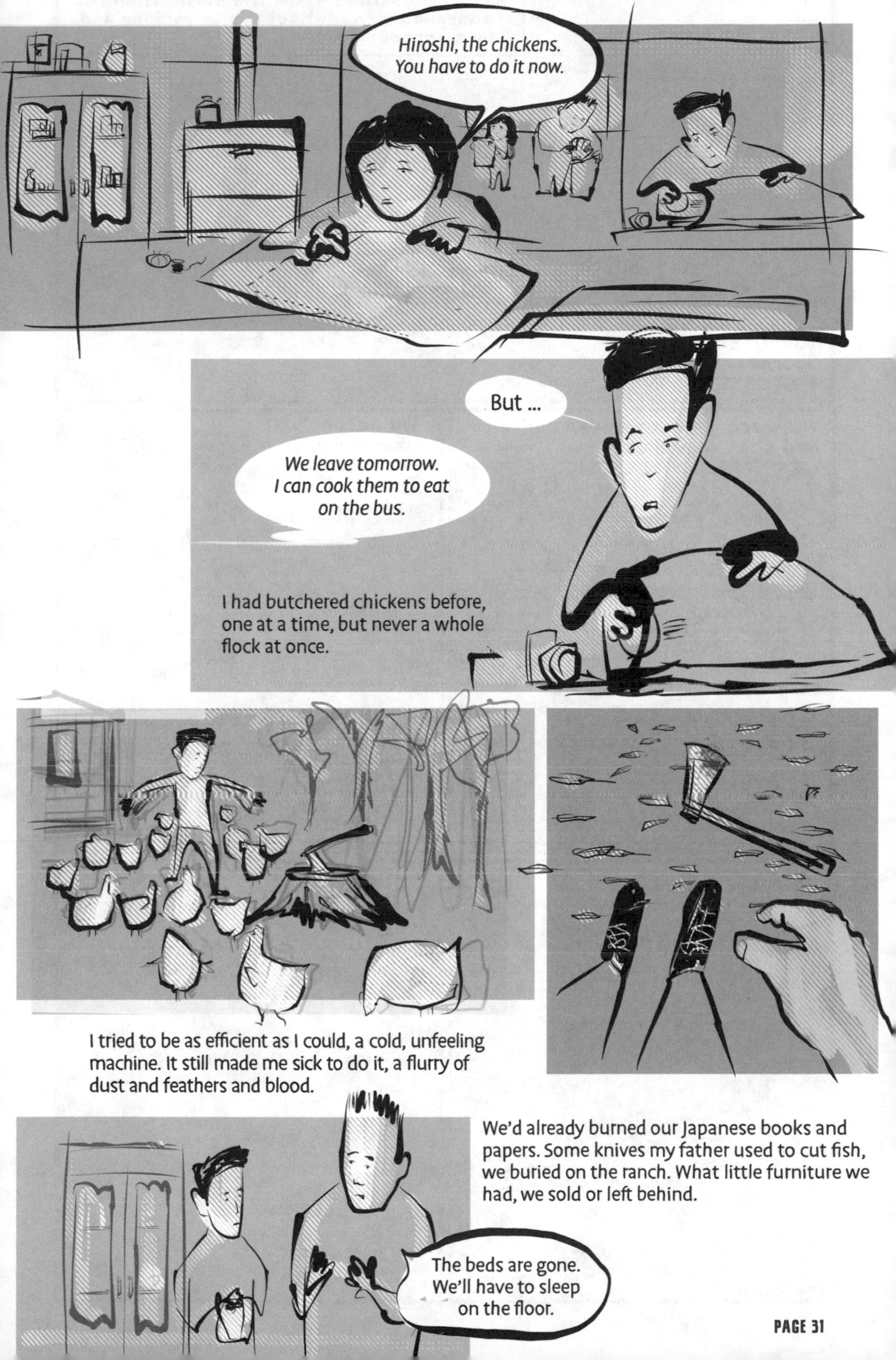
Hiroshi, the chickens. You have to do it now.
But ...
We leave tomorrow. I can cook them to eat on the bus.
I had butchered chickens before, one at a time, but never a whole flock at once.
I tried to be as efficient as I could, a cold, unfeeling machine. It still made me sick to do it, a flurry of dust and feathers and blood.
We'd already burned our Japanese books and papers. Some knives my father used to cut fish, we buried on the ranch. What little furniture we had, we sold or left behind.
The beds are gone. We'll have to sleep on the floor.

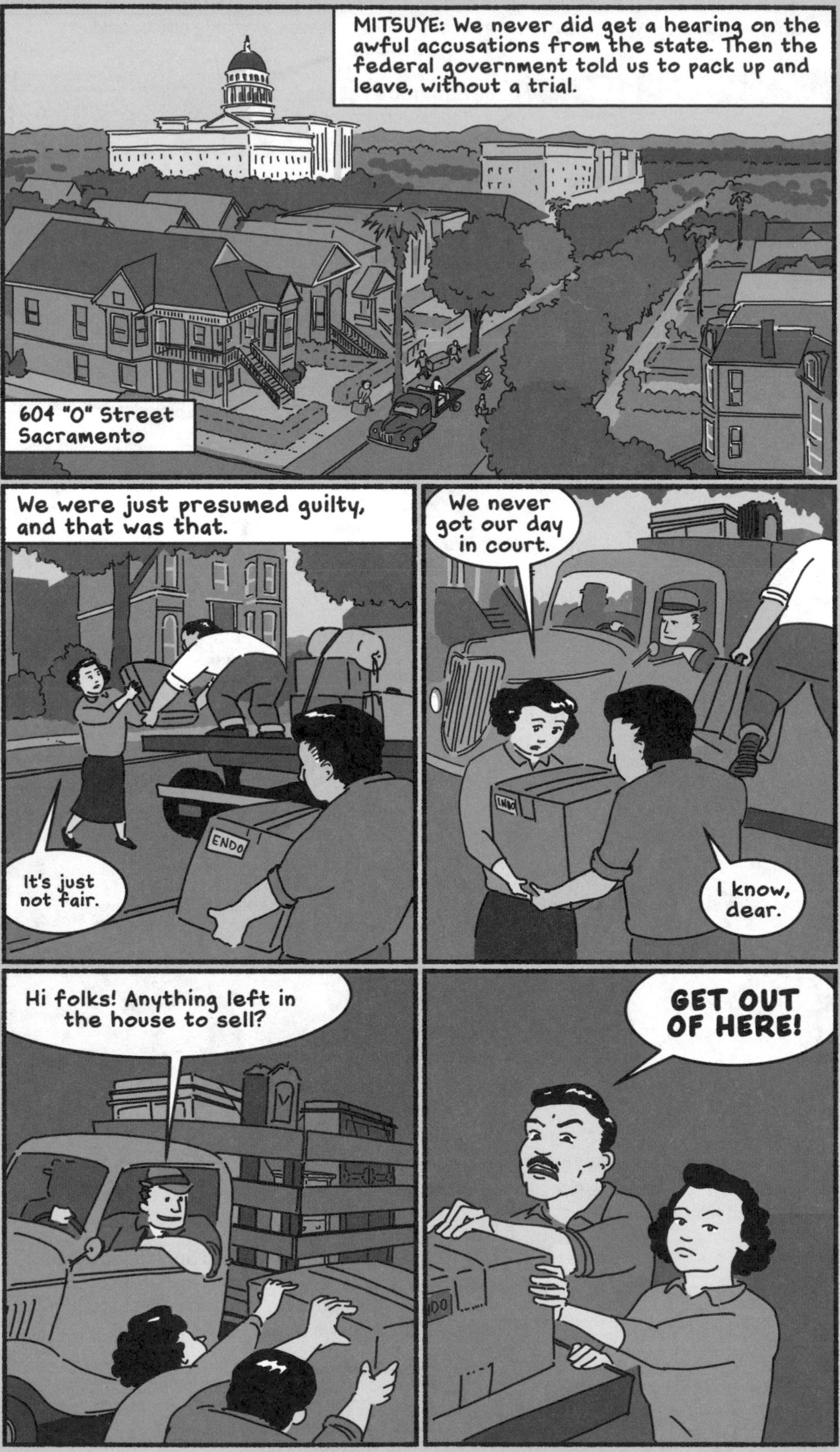

MITSUYE: We never did get a hearing on the awful accusations from the state. Then the federal government told us to pack up and leave, without a trial.
604 "O" Street Sacramento
We were just presumed guilty, and that was that.
ENDO
It's just not fair.
We never got our day in court.
I know, dear.
Hi folks! Anything left in the house to sell?
GET OUT OF HERE!

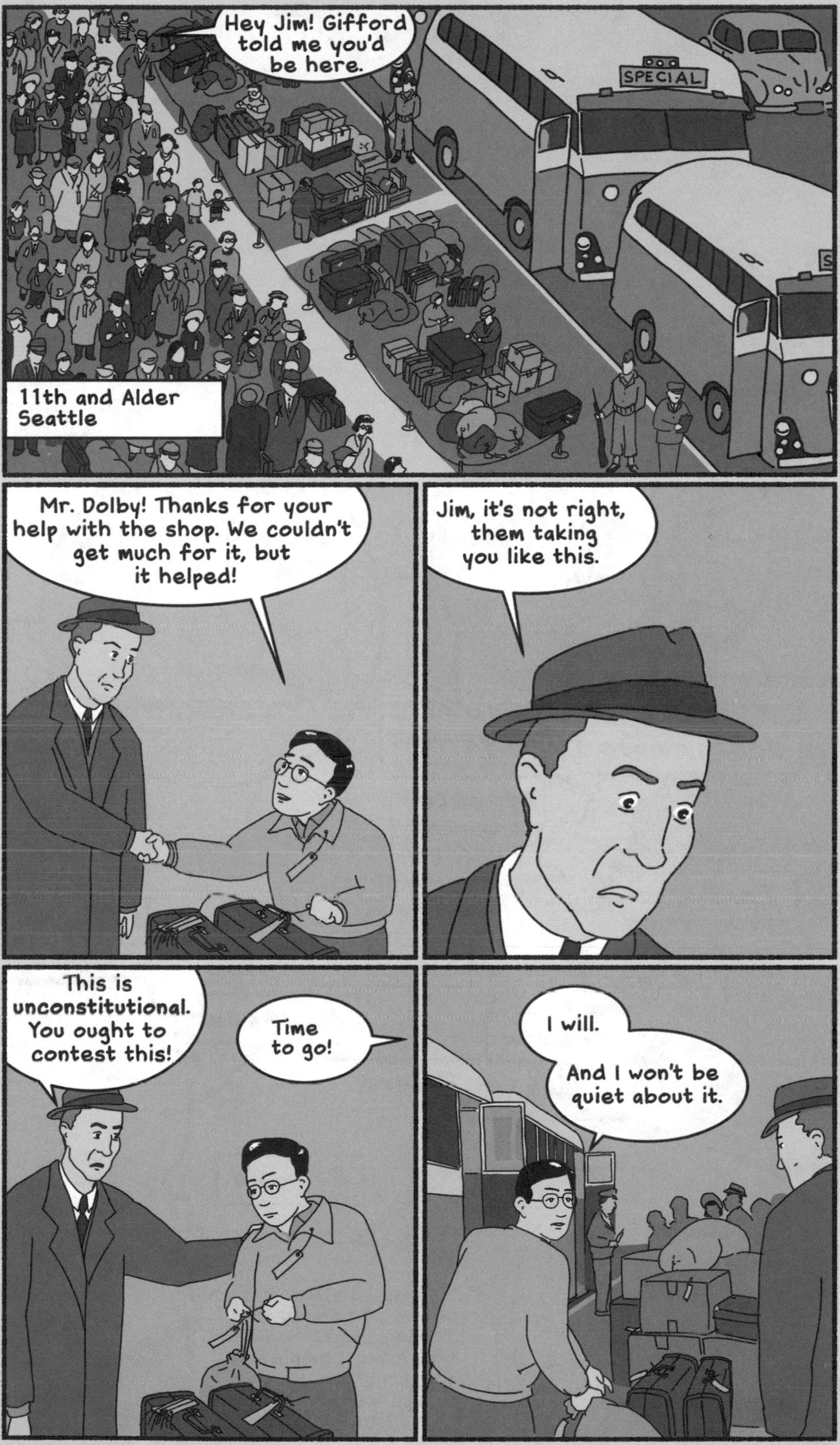
Hey Jim! Gifford told me you'd be here.
SPECIAL
11th and Alder Seattle
Mr. Dolby! Thanks for your help with the shop. We couldn't get much for it, but it helped!
Jim, it's not right, them taking you like this.
This is unconstitutional. You ought to contest this!
Time to go!
I will.
And I won't be quiet about it.

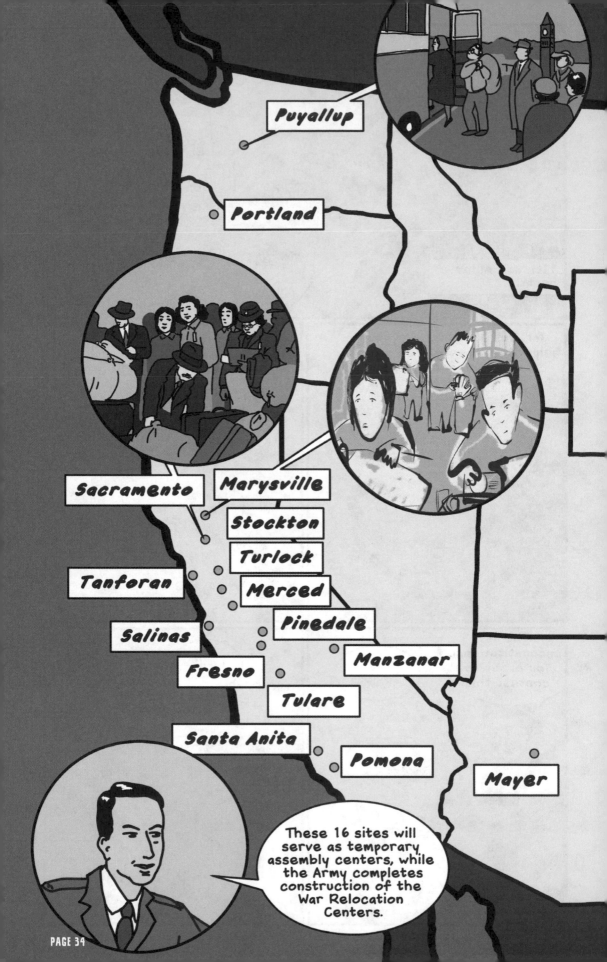

Puyallup

Portland

Sacramento

Marysville

Stockton

Turlock

Tanforan

Merced

Pinedale

Salinas

Fresno

Manzanar

Tulare

Santa Anita

Pomona

Mayer

These 16 sites will serve as temporary assembly centers, while the Army completes construction of the War Relocation Centers.

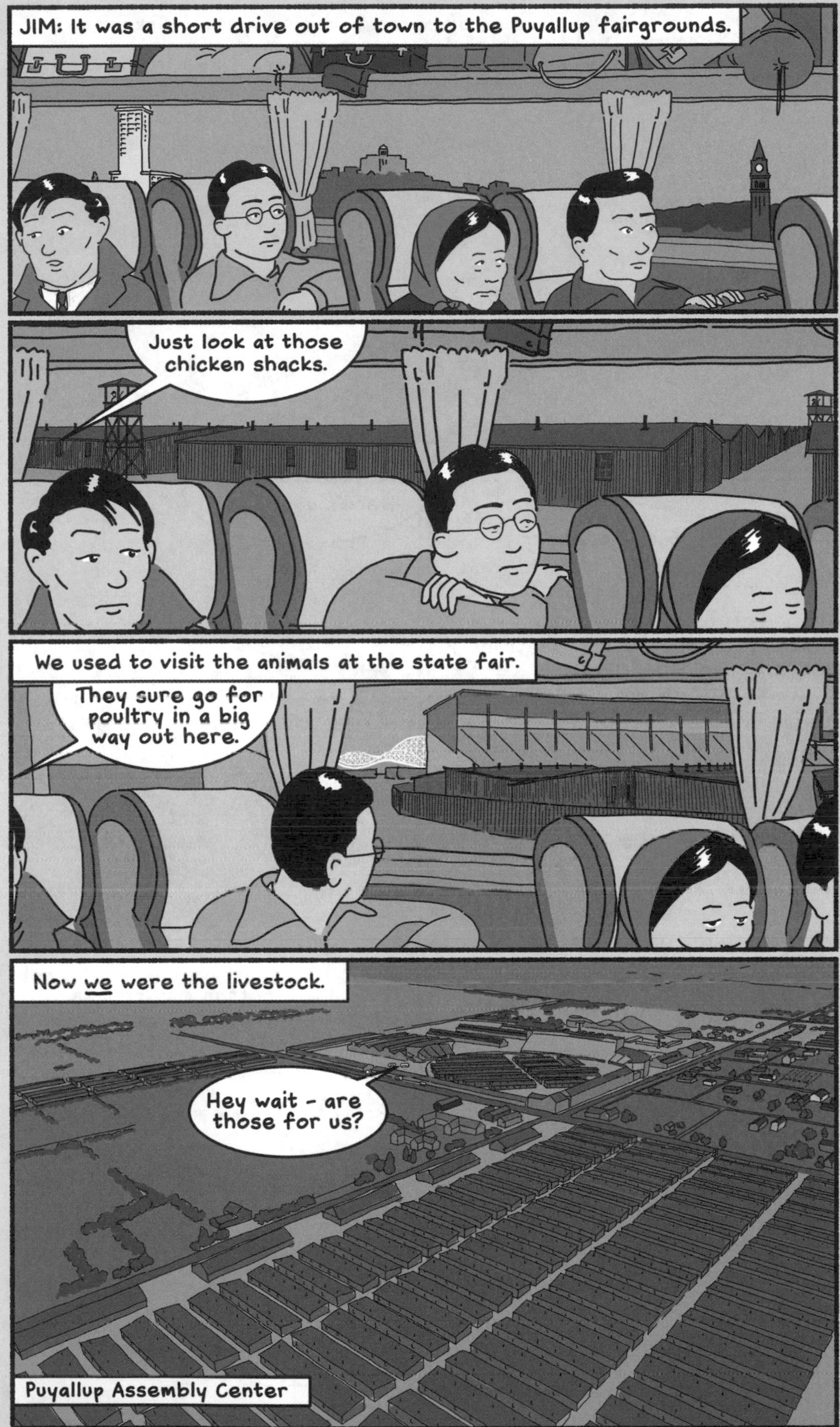
JIM: It was a short drive out of town to the Puyallup fairgrounds.
Just look at those chicken shacks.
We used to visit the animals at the state fair.
They sure go for poultry in a big way out here.
Now we were the livestock.
Hey wait - are those for us?
Puyallup Assembly Center

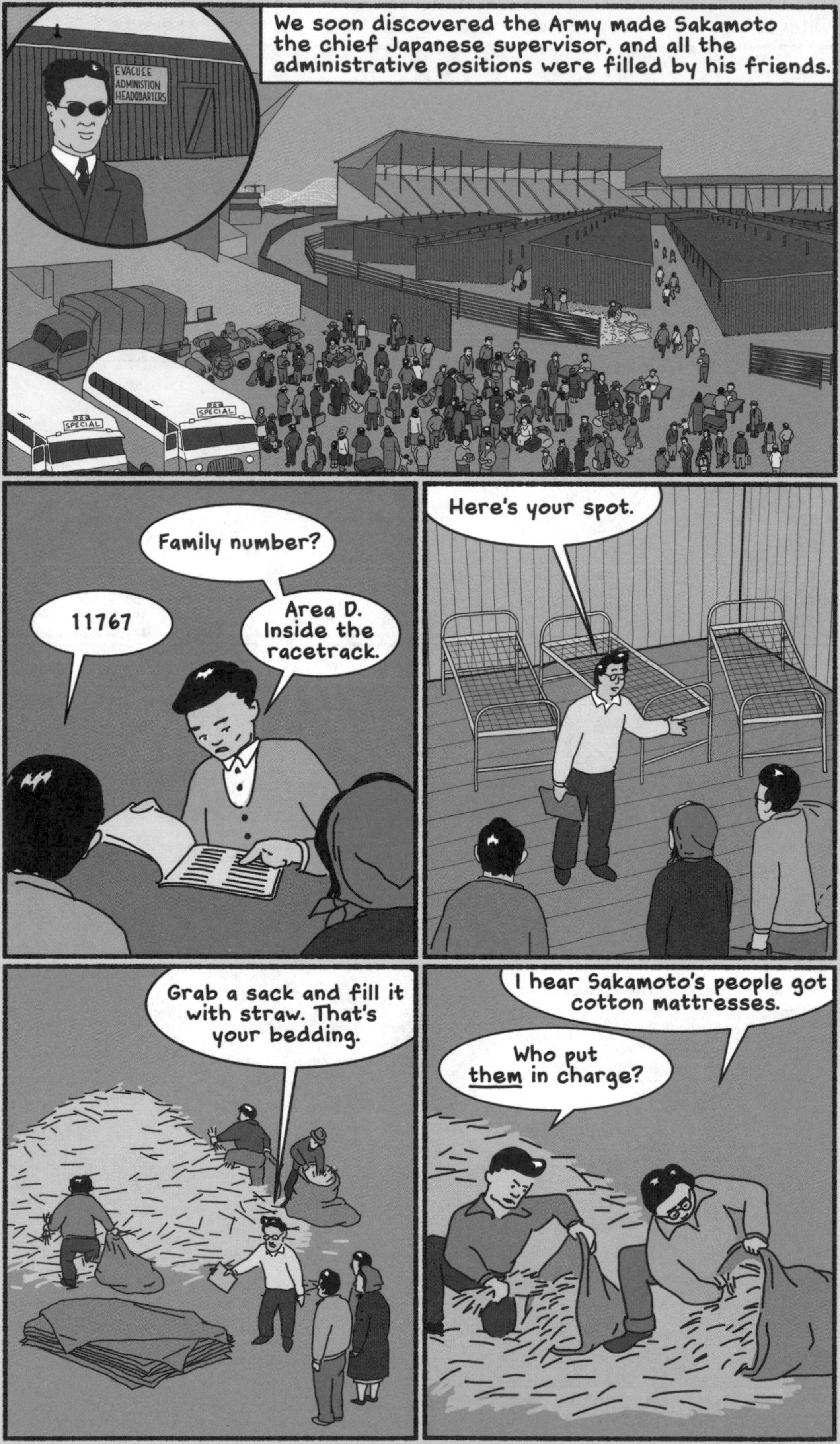
We soon discovered the Army made Sakamoto the chief Japanese supervisor, and all the administrative positions were filled by his friends.
EVACUEE ADMINISTION HEADQUARTERS
SPECIAL
SPECIAL
Family number?
11767
Area D. Inside the racetrack.
Here's your spot.
Grab a sack and fill it with straw. That's your bedding.
I hear Sakamoto's people got cotton mattresses.
Who put them in charge?

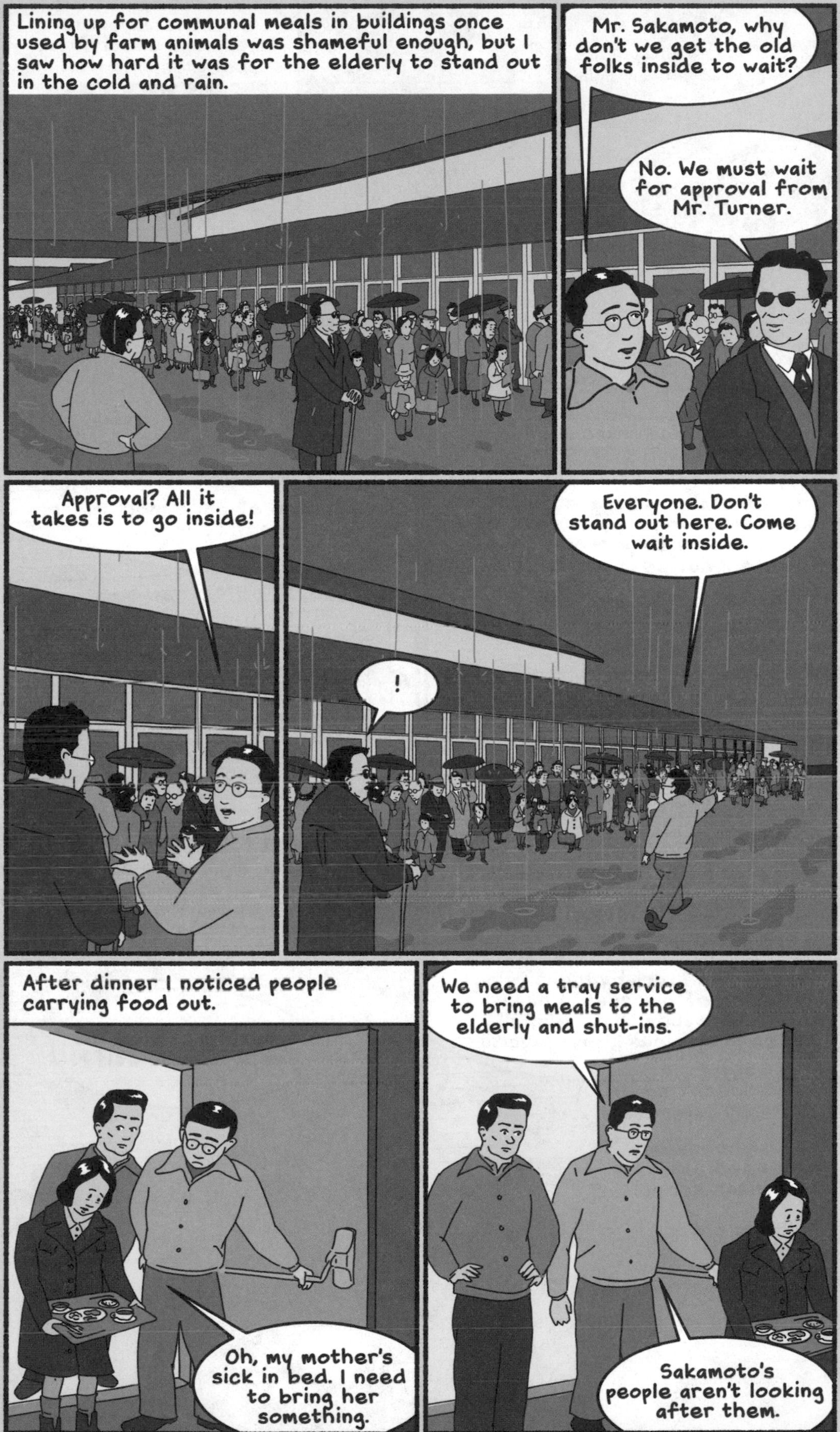
Lining up for communal meals in buildings once used by farm animals was shameful enough, but I saw how hard it was for the elderly to stand out in the cold and rain.
Mr. Sakamoto, why don't we get the old folks inside to wait?
No. We must wait for approval from Mr. Turner.
Approval? All it takes is to go inside!
!
Everyone. Don't stand out here. Come wait inside.
After dinner I noticed people carrying food out.
Oh, my mother's sick in bed. I need to bring her something.
We need a tray service to bring meals to the elderly and shut-ins.
Sakamoto's people aren't looking after them.

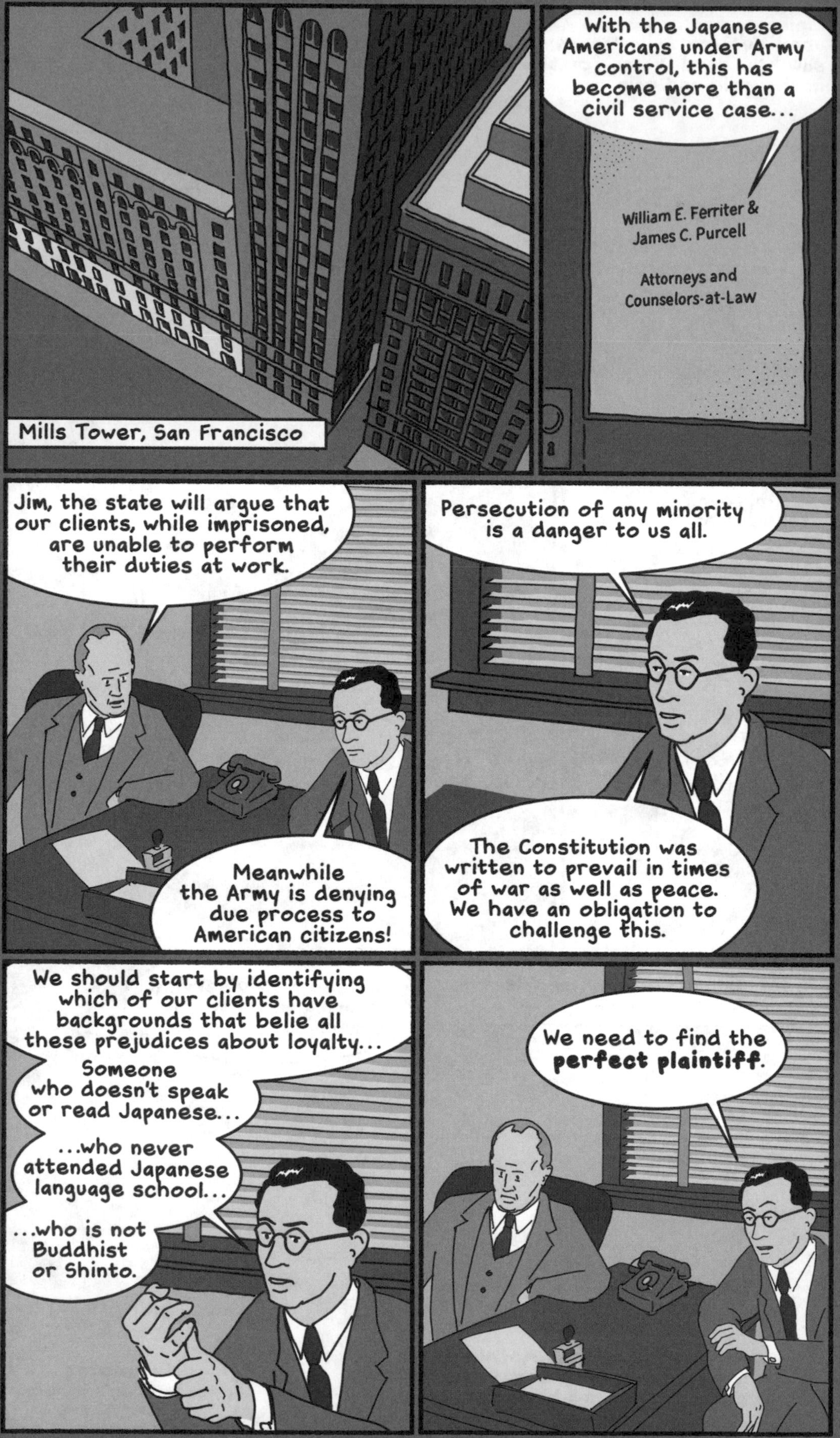

Mills Tower, San Francisco
With the Japanese Americans under Army control, this has become more than a civil service case...
William E. Ferriter & James C. Purcell
Attorneys and Counselors-at-Law
Jim, the state will argue that our clients, while imprisoned, are unable to perform their duties at work.
Meanwhile the Army is denying due process to American citizens!
Persecution of any minority is a danger to us all.
The Constitution was written to prevail in times of war as well as peace. We have an obligation to challenge this.
We should start by identifying which of our clients have backgrounds that belie all these prejudices about loyalty...
Someone who doesn't speak or read Japanese...
...who never attended Japanese language school...
...who is not Buddhist or Shinto.
We need to find the **perfect plaintiff**.

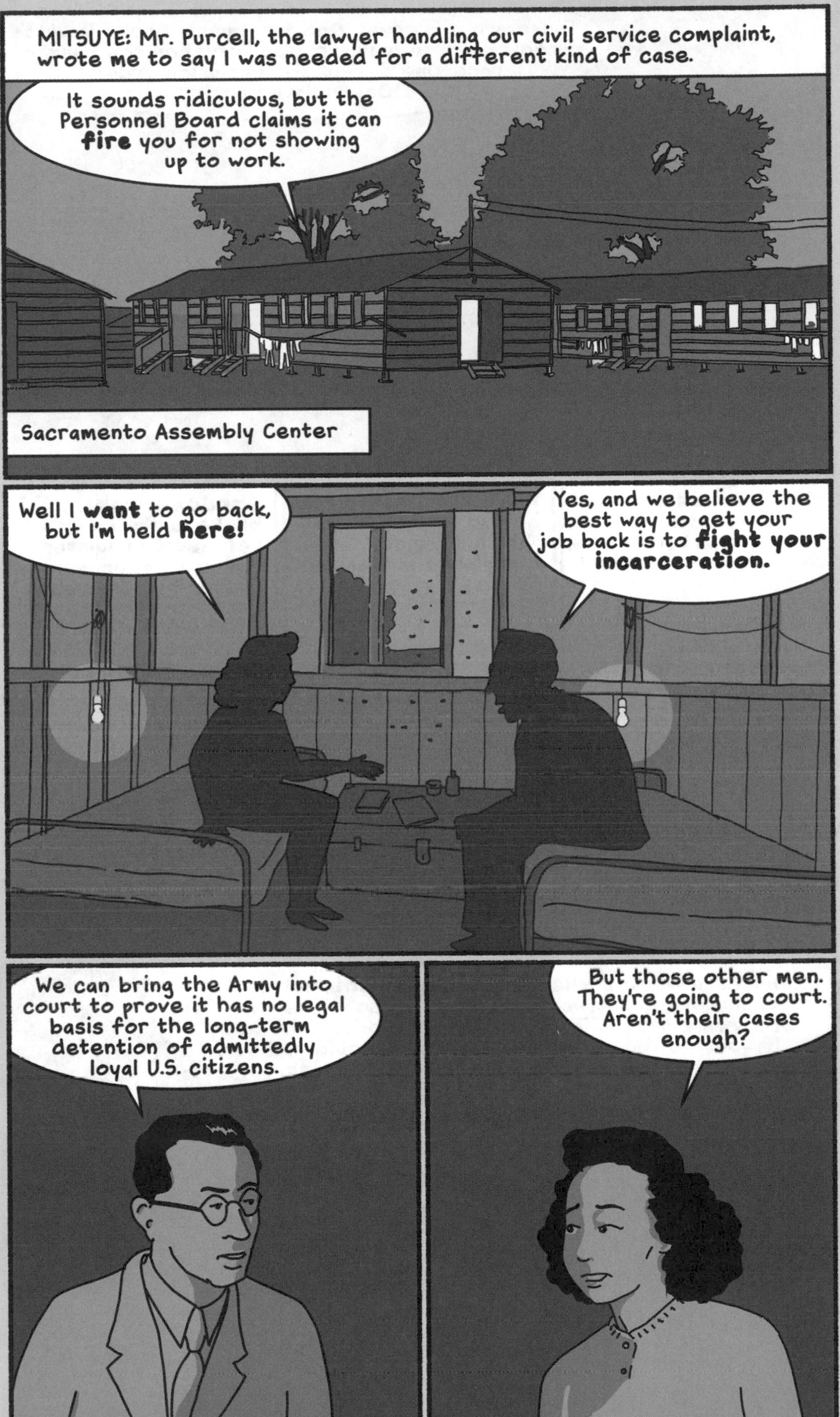
MITSUYE: Mr. Purcell, the lawyer handling our civil service complaint, wrote me to say I was needed for a different kind of case.
It sounds ridiculous, but the Personnel Board claims it can **fire** you for not showing up to work.
Sacramento Assembly Center
Well I **want** to go back, but I'm held **here!**
Yes, and we believe the best way to get your job back is to **fight your incarceration.**
We can bring the Army into court to prove it has no legal basis for the long-term detention of admittedly loyal U.S. citizens.
But those other men. They're going to court. Aren't their cases enough?

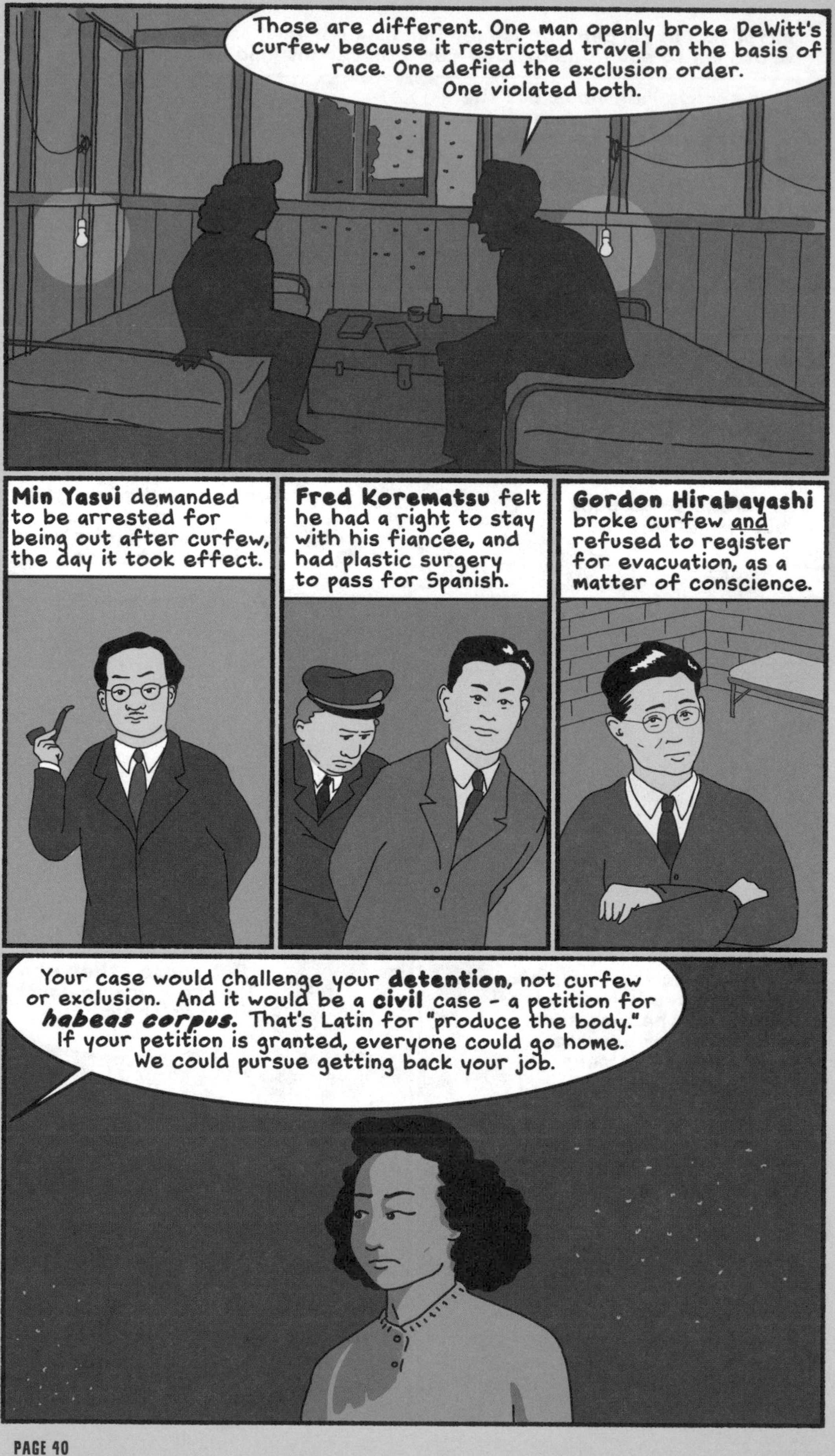

Those are different. One man openly broke DeWitt's curfew because it restricted travel on the basis of race. One defied the exclusion order. One violated both.
Min Yasui demanded to be arrested for being out after curfew, the day it took effect.
Fred Korematsu felt he had a right to stay with his fiancée, and had plastic surgery to pass for Spanish.
Gordon Hirabayashi broke curfew and refused to register for evacuation, as a matter of conscience.
Your case would challenge your detention, not curfew or exclusion. And it would be a civil case - a petition for habeas corpus. That's Latin for "produce the body." If your petition is granted, everyone could go home. We could pursue getting back your job.

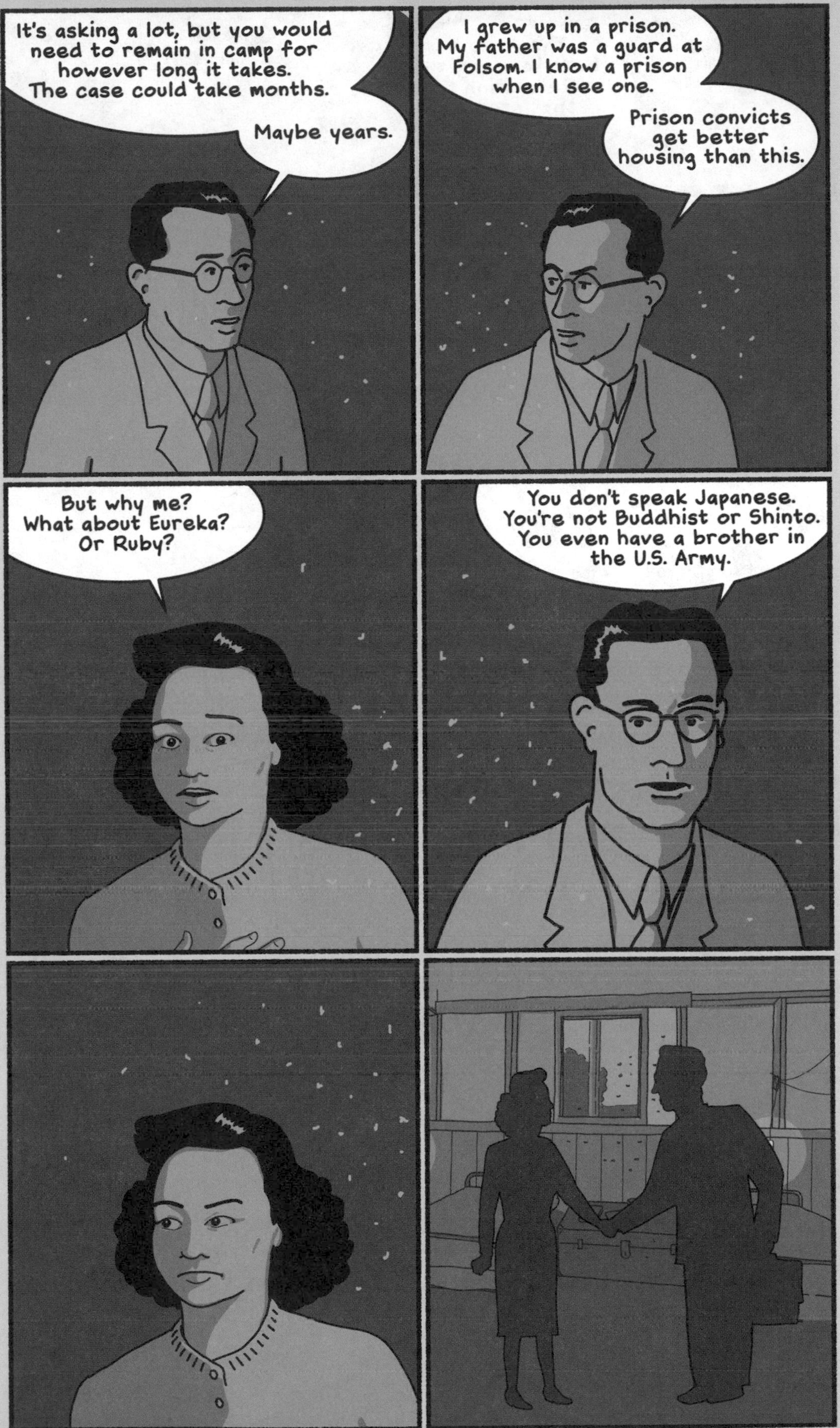
It's asking a lot, but you would need to remain in camp for however long it takes. The case could take months.
Maybe years.
I grew up in a prison. My father was a guard at Folsom. I know a prison when I see one.
Prison convicts get better housing than this.
But why me? What about Eureka? Or Ruby?
You don't speak Japanese. You're not Buddhist or Shinto. You even have a brother in the U.S. Army.

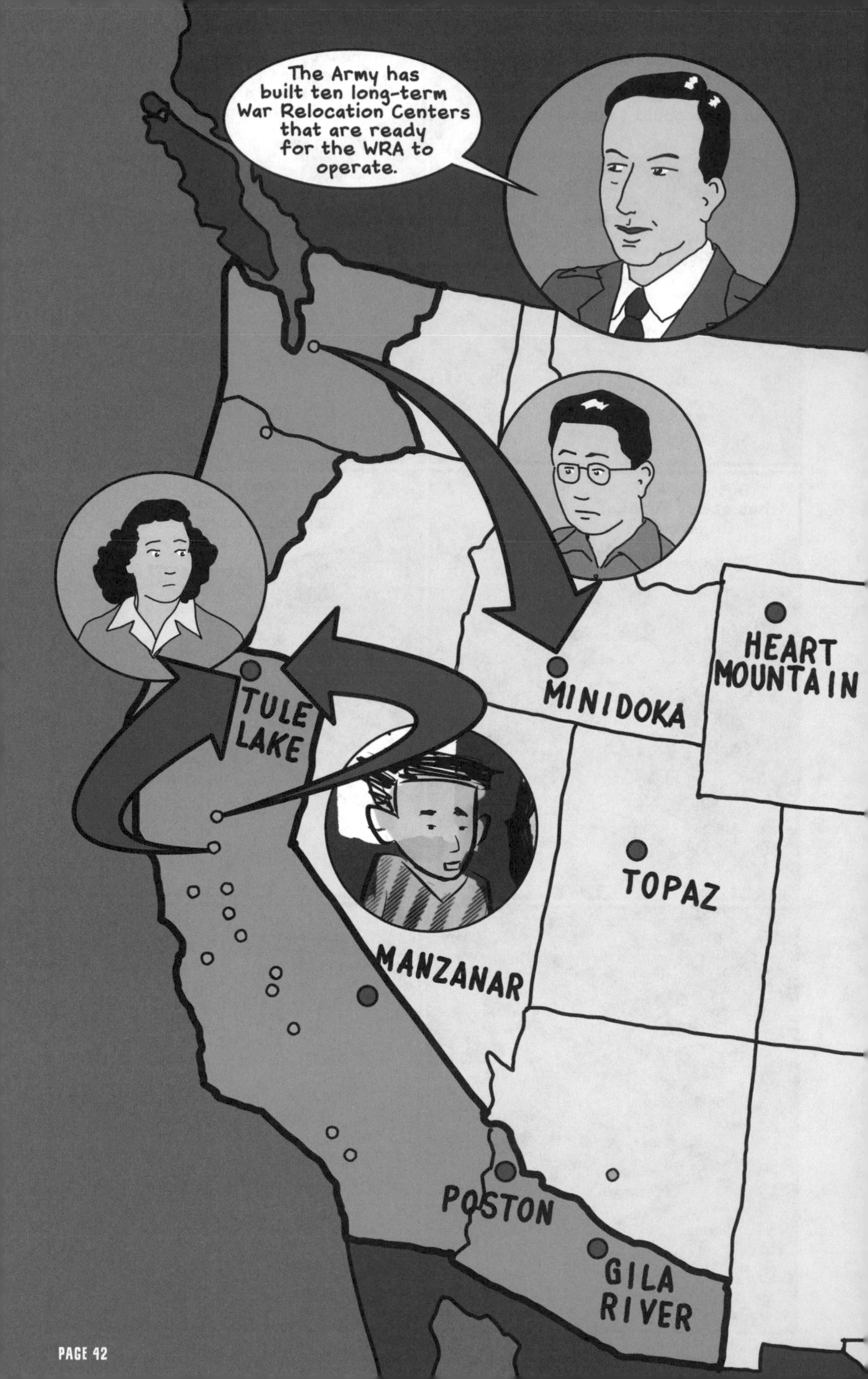
The Army has built ten long-term War Relocation Centers that are ready for the WRA to operate.
HEART MOUNTAIN
MINIDOKA
TULE LAKE
TOPAZ
MANZANAR
POSTON
GILA RIVER

HIROSHI: Everyone sat grim-looking on the train to Tule Lake. A soldier armed with a rifle watched us from each end of a shabby old coach that had just been taken out of mothballs. It was hot and muggy, and the wooden benches made it impossible to sleep.

I volunteered as a car monitor. My job was to pass out sandwiches and milk to the passengers and baby food to the mothers of infants, and to stop people from lifting the window shades to see where we were going. The WRA apparently didn't want people on the outside to see who was riding inside.

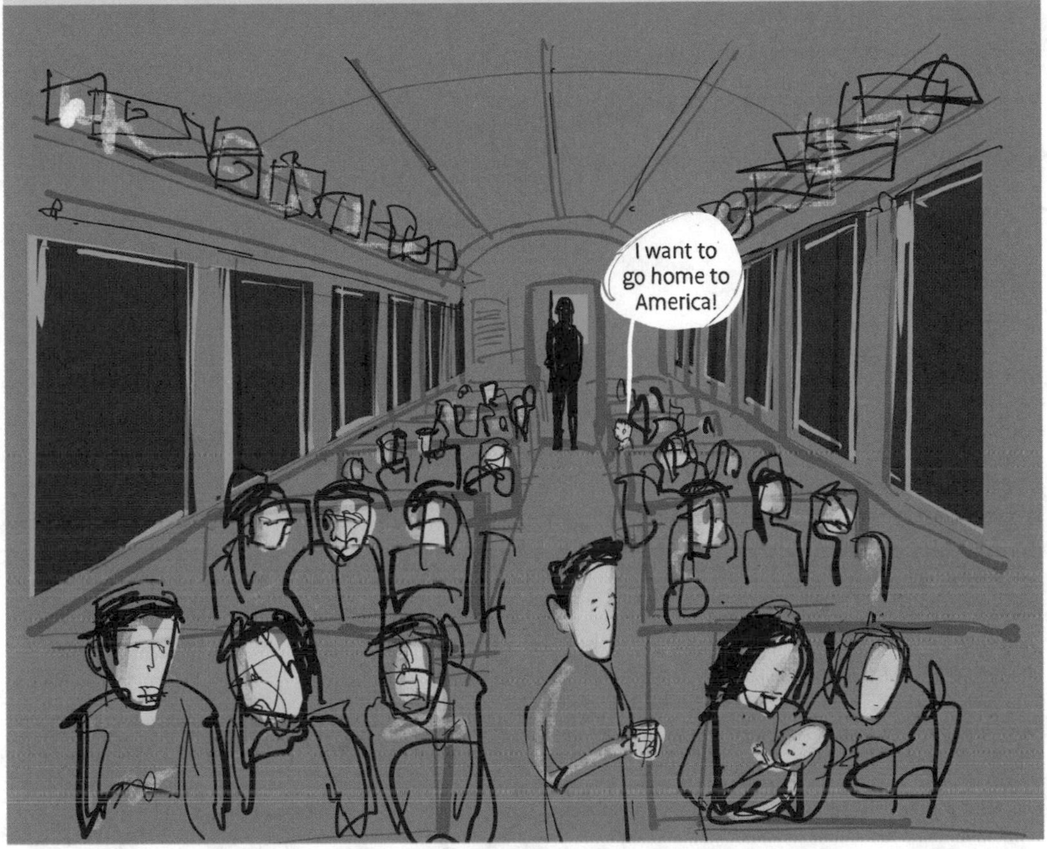
I want to go home to America!

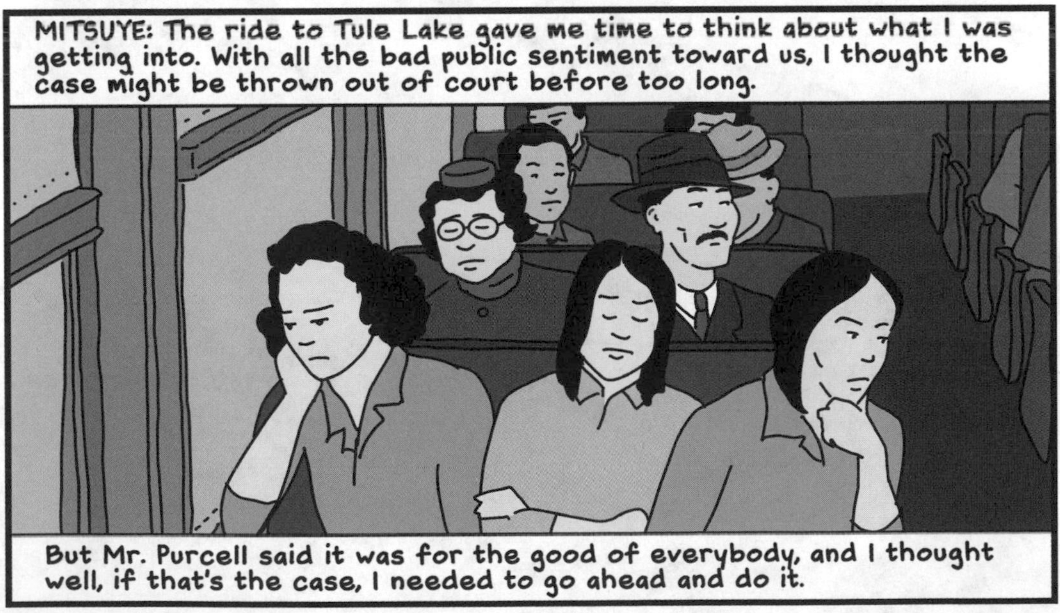
MITSUYE: The ride to Tule Lake gave me time to think about what I was getting into. With all the bad public sentiment toward us, I thought the case might be thrown out of court before too long.
But Mr. Purcell said it was for the good of everybody, and I thought well, if that's the case, I needed to go ahead and do it.

HIROSHI: The train stopped just short of the Oregon border at a wretched, flat, treeless terrain with nothing but grass and sagebrush.

Sixty-four blocks of wooden barracks were laid out to house 15,000 of us, surrounded by six watch towers and a barbed-wire fence.

To the south was a flat mountain shaped like an abalone shell.

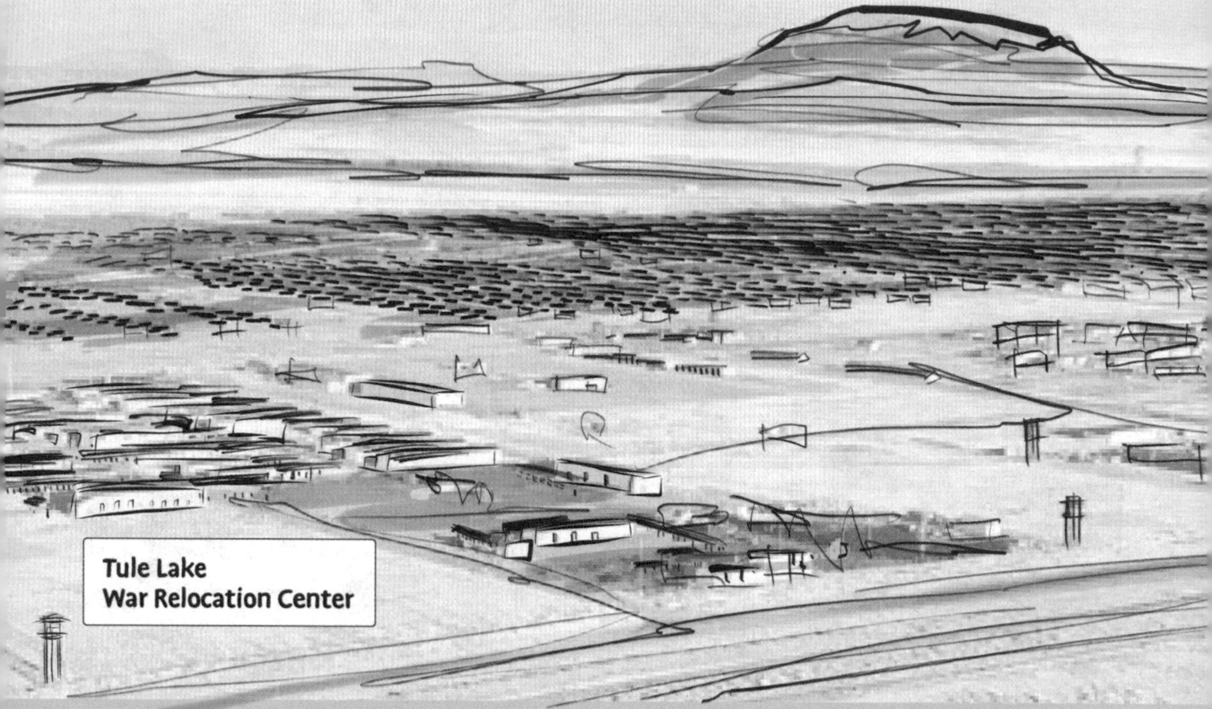
Tule Lake
War Relocation Center

To the west, a highway and a bluff with a distinct formation we quickly dubbed "Castle Rock." The Military Police and WRA staff lived on that side, apart from us.

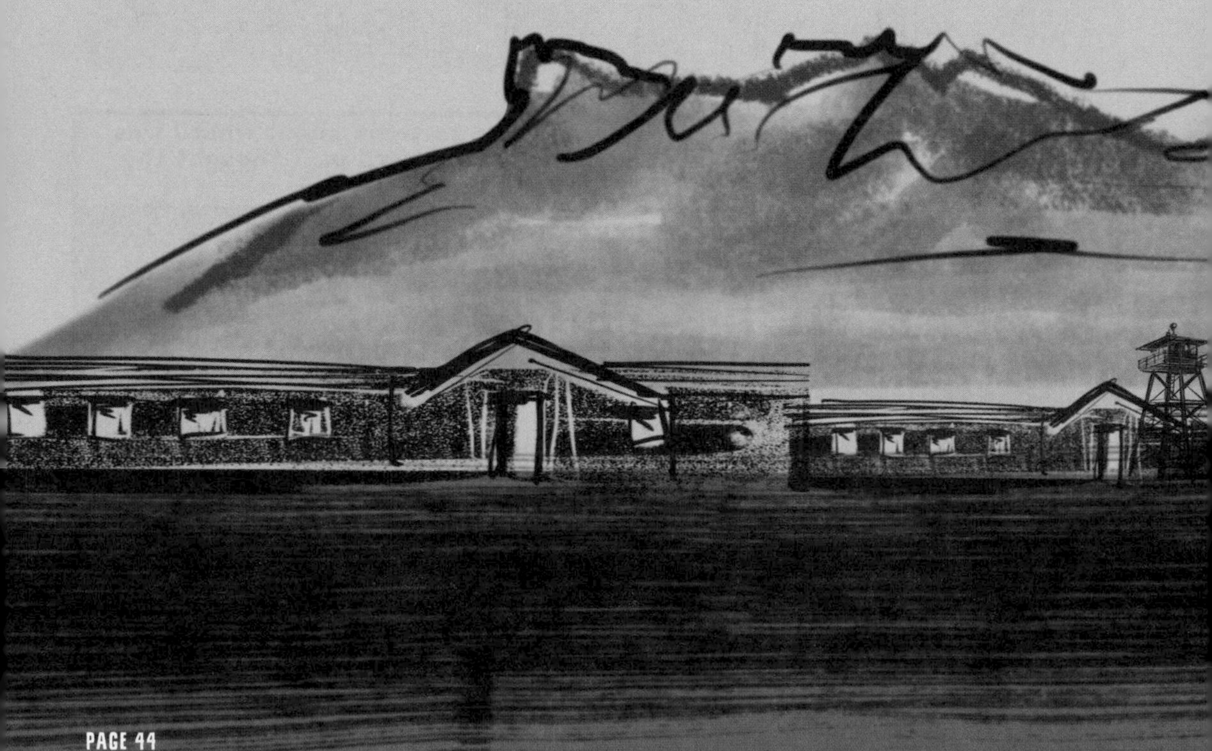

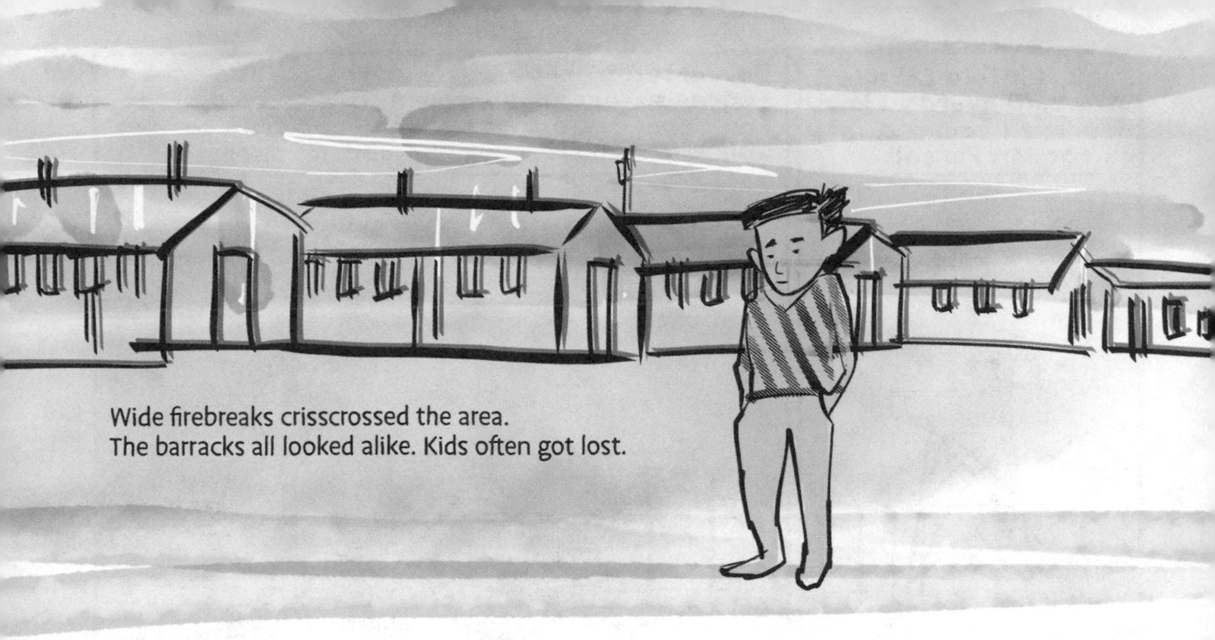
Wide firebreaks crisscrossed the area.
The barracks all looked alike. Kids often got lost.

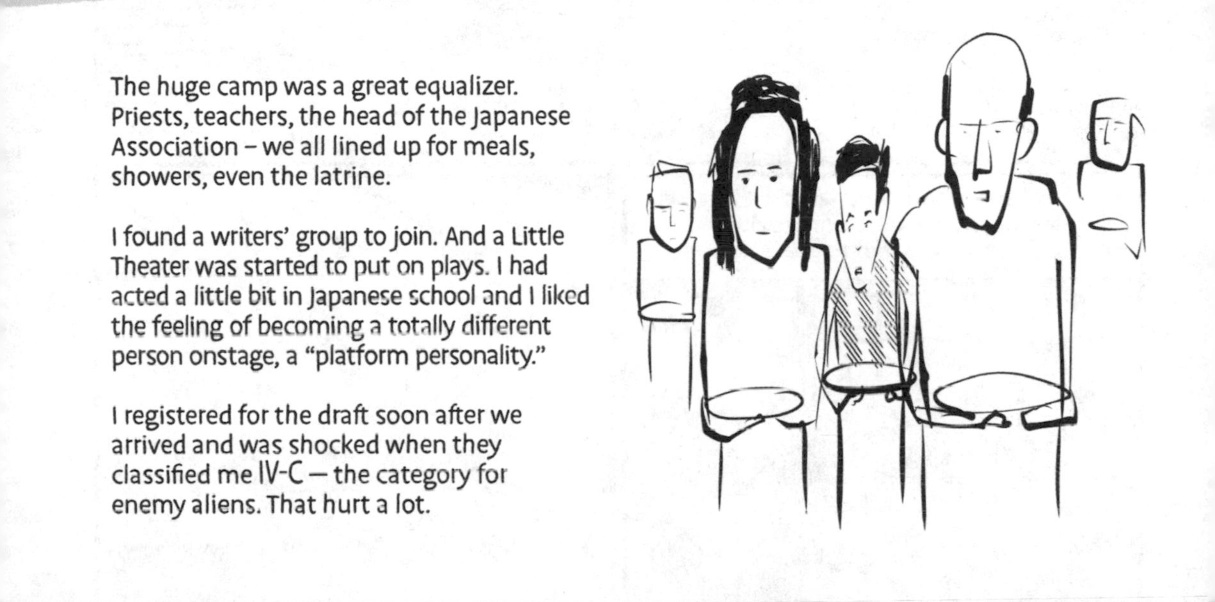
The huge camp was a great equalizer. Priests, teachers, the head of the Japanese Association – we all lined up for meals, showers, even the latrine.
I found a writers' group to join. And a Little Theater was started to put on plays. I had acted a little bit in Japanese school and I liked the feeling of becoming a totally different person onstage, a "platform personality."
I registered for the draft soon after we arrived and was shocked when they classified me IV-C – the category for enemy aliens. That hurt a lot.

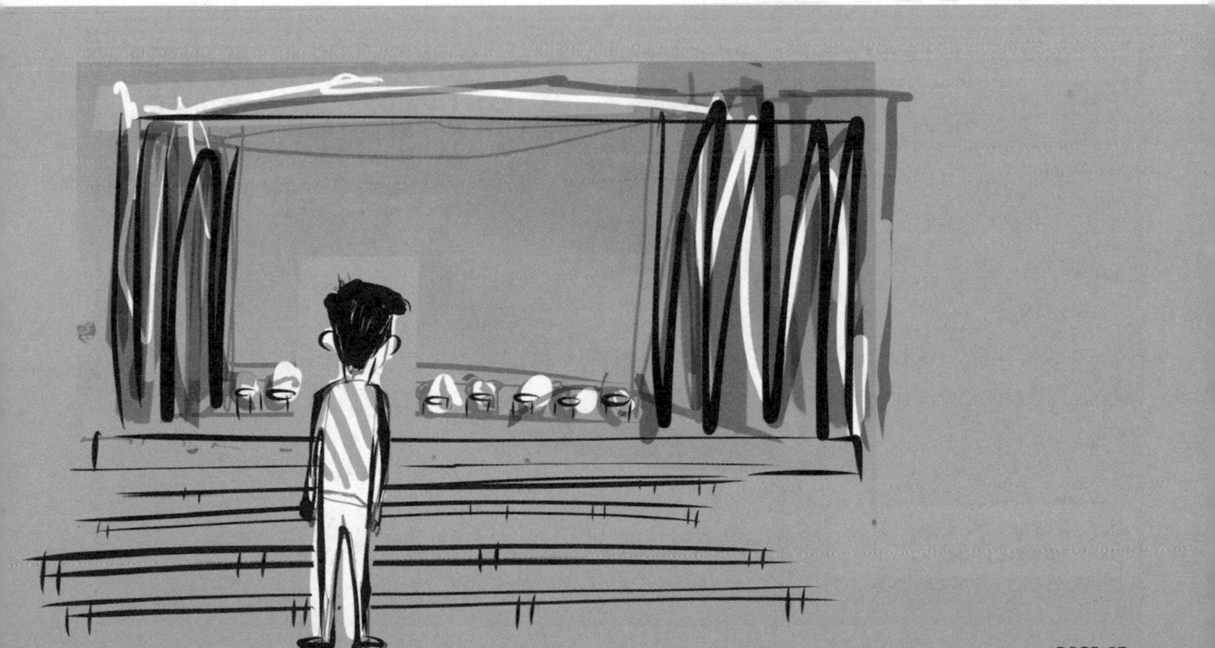

MITSUYE: Tule Lake had 52 armed guards. I know because I counted them all for Mr. Purcell.

He wanted to know whether the barbed-wire fences extended all around. They sure did. And I confirmed that we were not free to walk out without being stopped, or shot.

Mr. Purcell filed the writ of *habeas corpus* as soon as I arrived. Then he said he got a surprise.

LAW OFFICES
FERRITER AND PURCE
MILLS TOWER
220 BUSH STREET
SAN FRANCISCO

Miss Mitsuye Endo
Block 5, Bldg. 2916, Apt. C
Tule Lake Relocation Center
Newell, California

Dear Miss Endo,

I appeared before the federal judge in San Francisco for what I thought was a calendar hearing. Instead, he asked to hear my argument.

"Instead, he asked to hear my argument."

...Throwing into concentration camps people whose sole offense is their ancestry is to follow the example of Nazi Germany...

U.S. District Court
San Francisco

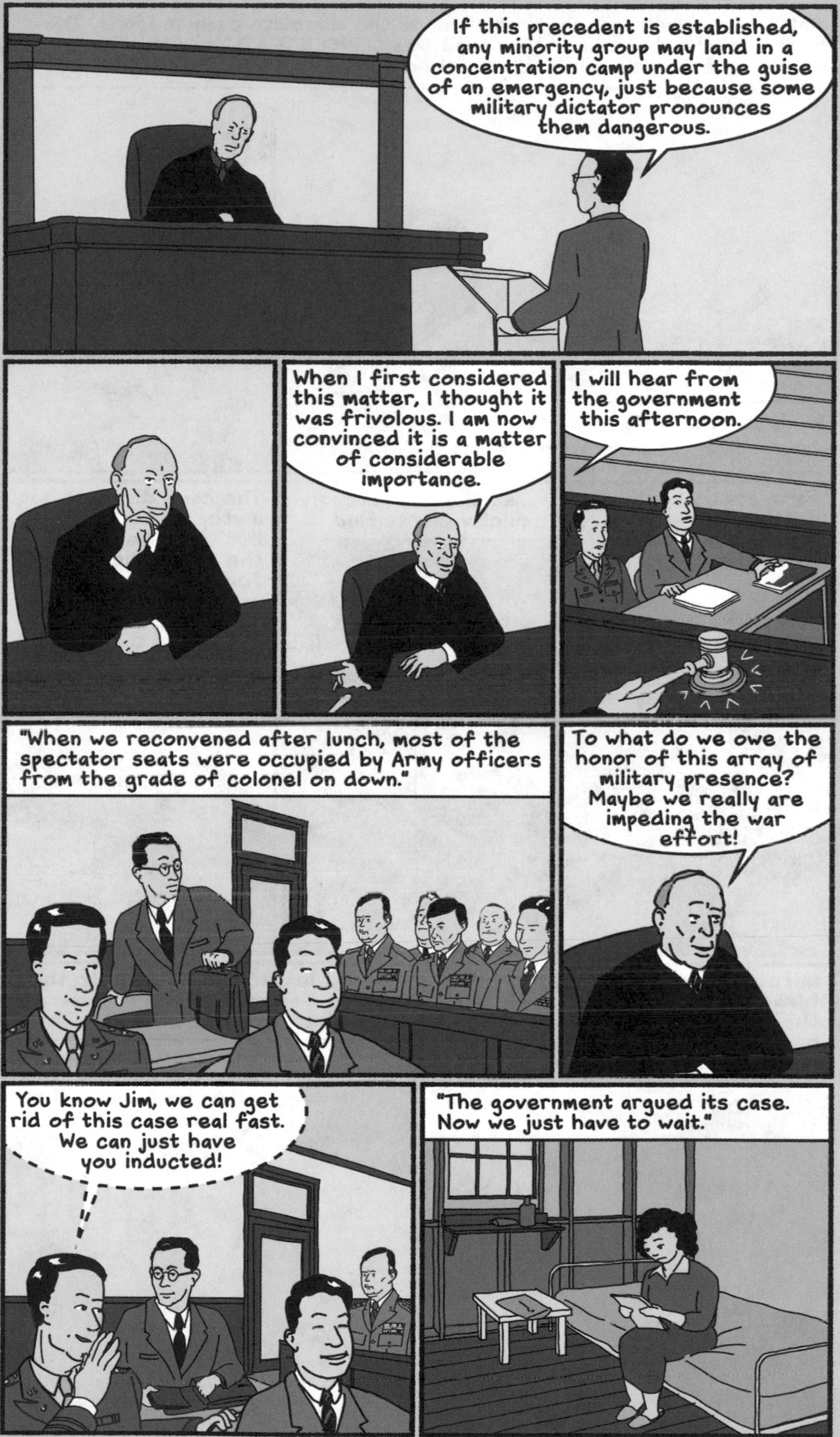

If this precedent is established, any minority group may land in a concentration camp under the guise of an emergency, just because some military dictator pronounces them dangerous.
When I first considered this matter, I thought it was frivolous. I am now convinced it is a matter of considerable importance.
I will hear from the government this afternoon.
"When we reconvened after lunch, most of the spectator seats were occupied by Army officers from the grade of colonel on down."
To what do we owe the honor of this array of military presence? Maybe we really are impeding the war effort!
You know Jim, we can get rid of this case real fast. We can just have you inducted!
"The government argued its case. Now we just have to wait."

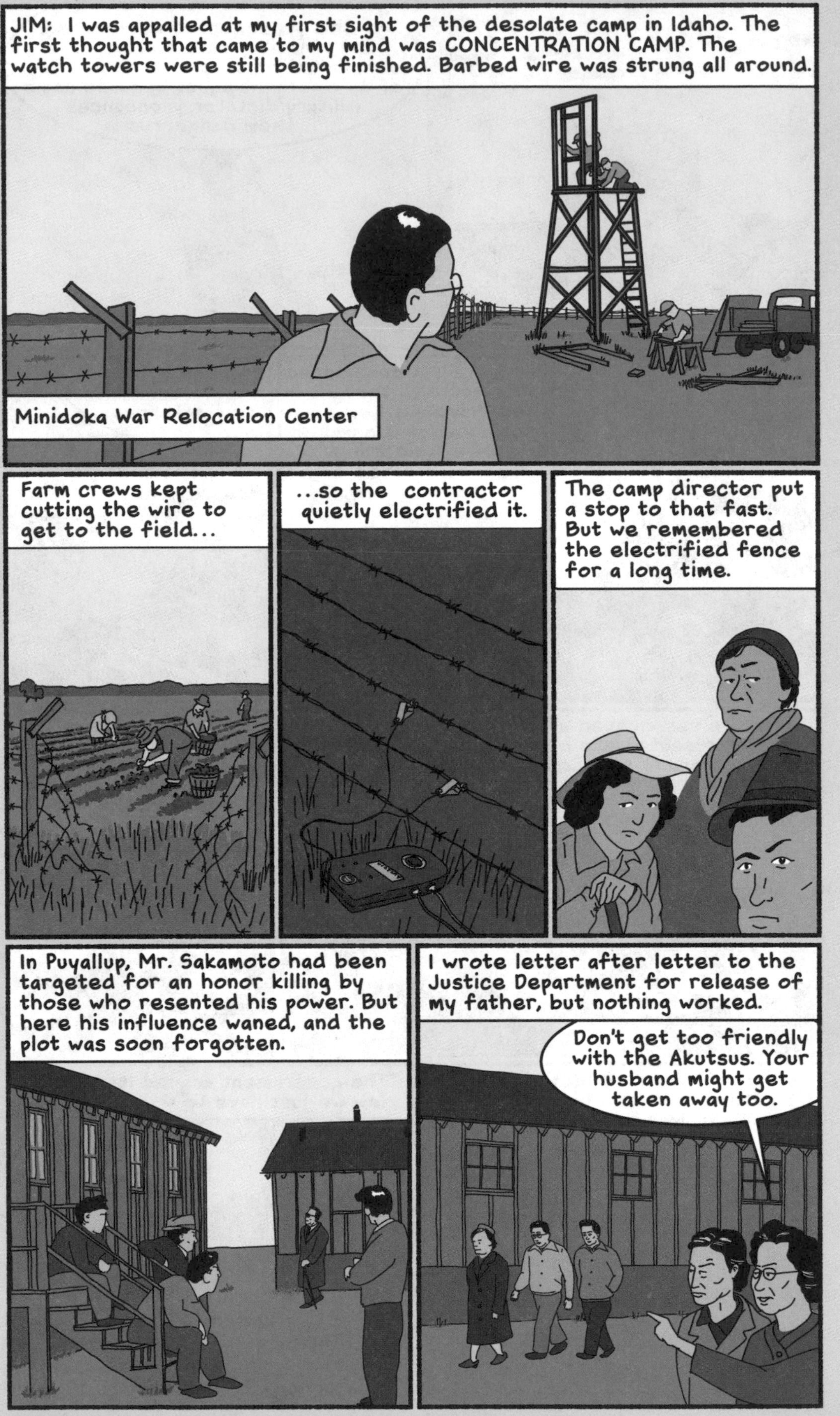

JIM: I was appalled at my first sight of the desolate camp in Idaho. The first thought that came to my mind was CONCENTRATION CAMP. The watch towers were still being finished. Barbed wire was strung all around.
Minidoka War Relocation Center
Farm crews kept cutting the wire to get to the field...
...so the contractor quietly electrified it.
The camp director put a stop to that fast. But we remembered the electrified fence for a long time.
In Puyallup, Mr. Sakamoto had been targeted for an honor killing by those who resented his power. But here his influence waned, and the plot was soon forgotten.
I wrote letter after letter to the Justice Department for release of my father, but nothing worked.
Don't get too friendly with the Akutsus. Your husband might get taken away too.

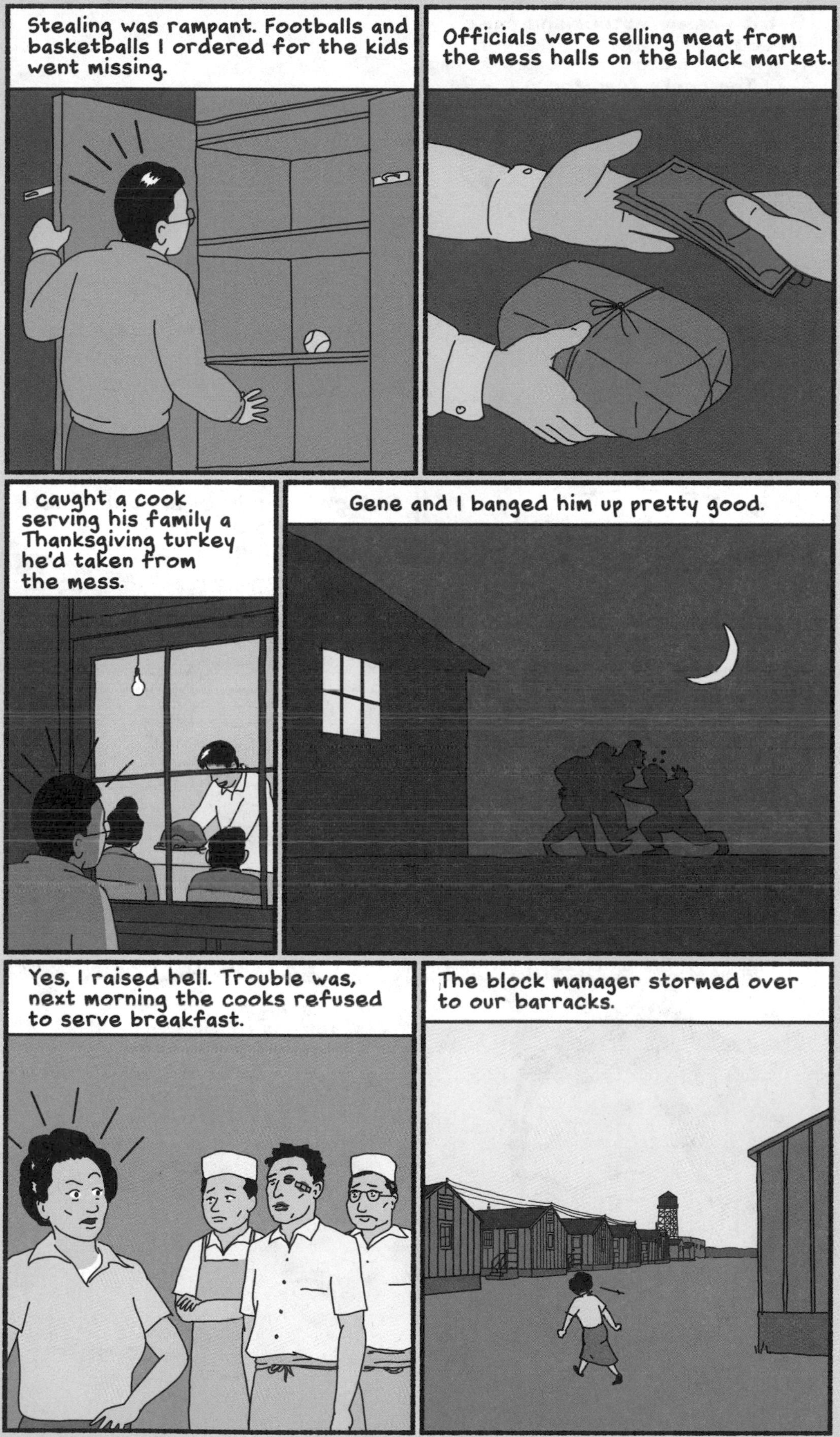
Stealing was rampant. Footballs and basketballs I ordered for the kids went missing.
Officials were selling meat from the mess halls on the black market.
I caught a cook serving his family a Thanksgiving turkey he'd taken from the mess.
Gene and I banged him up pretty good.
Yes, I raised hell. Trouble was, next morning the cooks refused to serve breakfast.
The block manager stormed over to our barracks.

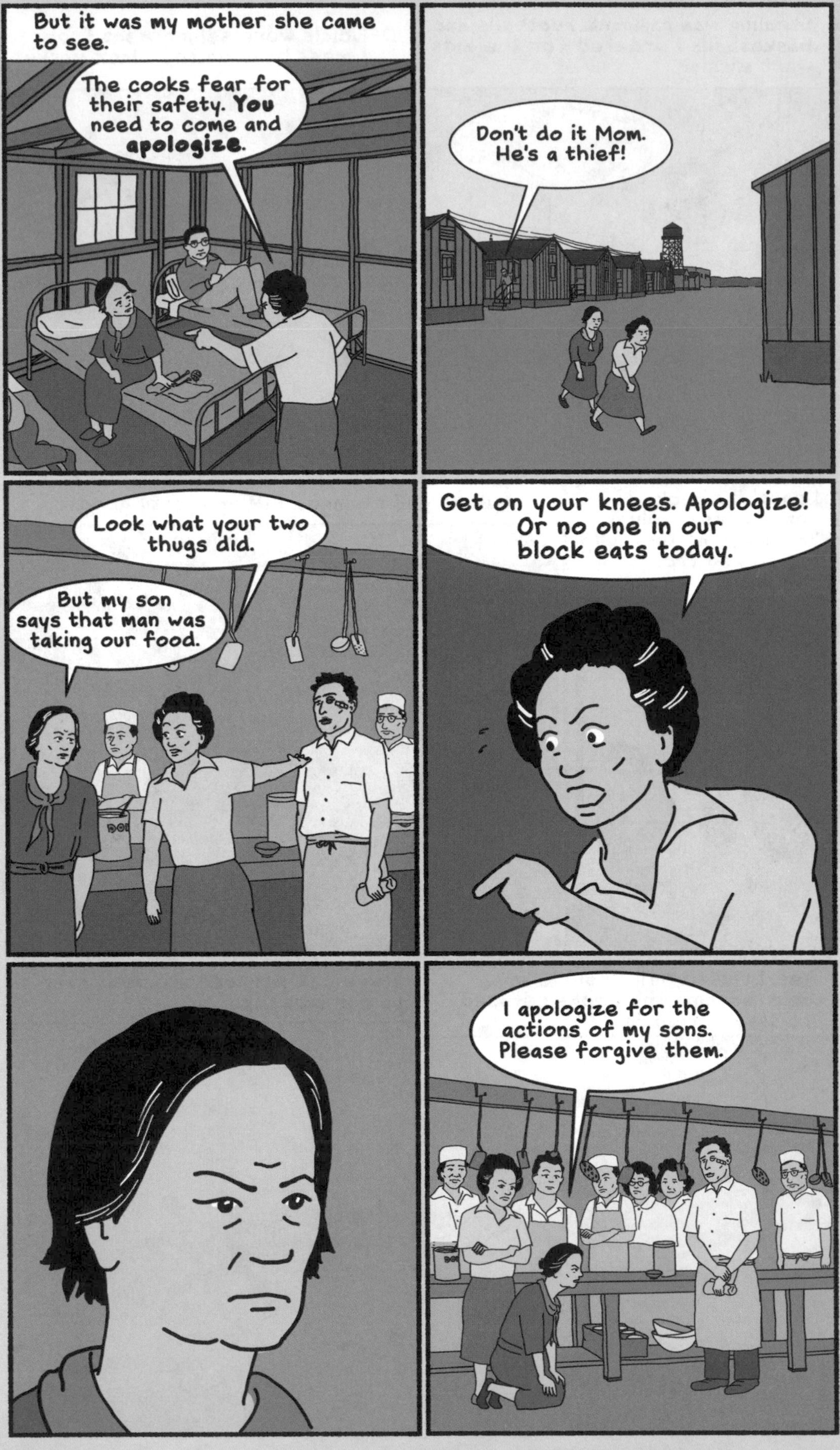

But it was my mother she came to see.
The cooks fear for their safety. **You** need to come and **apologize**.
Don't do it Mom. He's a thief!
Look what your two thugs did.
But my son says that man was taking our food.
Get on your knees. Apologize! Or no one in our block eats today.
I apologize for the actions of my sons. Please forgive them.

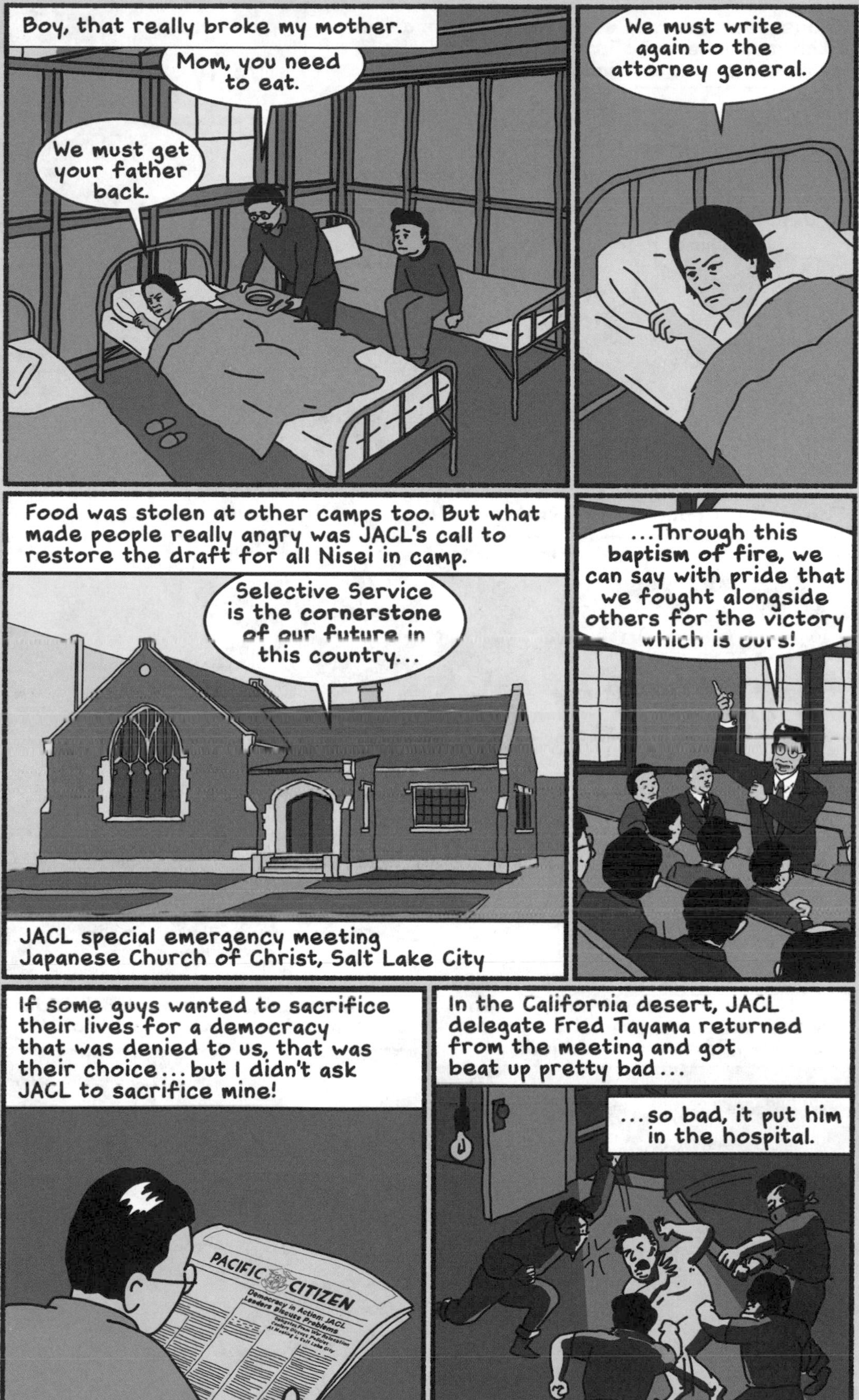
Boy, that really broke my mother.
Mom, you need to eat.
We must get your father back.
We must write again to the attorney general.
Food was stolen at other camps too. But what made people really angry was JACL's call to restore the draft for all Nisei in camp.
Selective Service is the cornerstone of our future in this country...
JACL special emergency meeting Japanese Church of Christ, Salt Lake City
...Through this baptism of fire, we can say with pride that we fought alongside others for the victory which is ours!
If some guys wanted to sacrifice their lives for a democracy that was denied to us, that was their choice... but I didn't ask JACL to sacrifice mine!
PACIFIC CITIZEN
Democracy in Action: JACL Leaders Discuss Problems
In the California desert, JACL delegate Fred Tayama returned from the meeting and got beat up pretty bad...
...so bad, it put him in the hospital.
Manzanar War Relocation Center

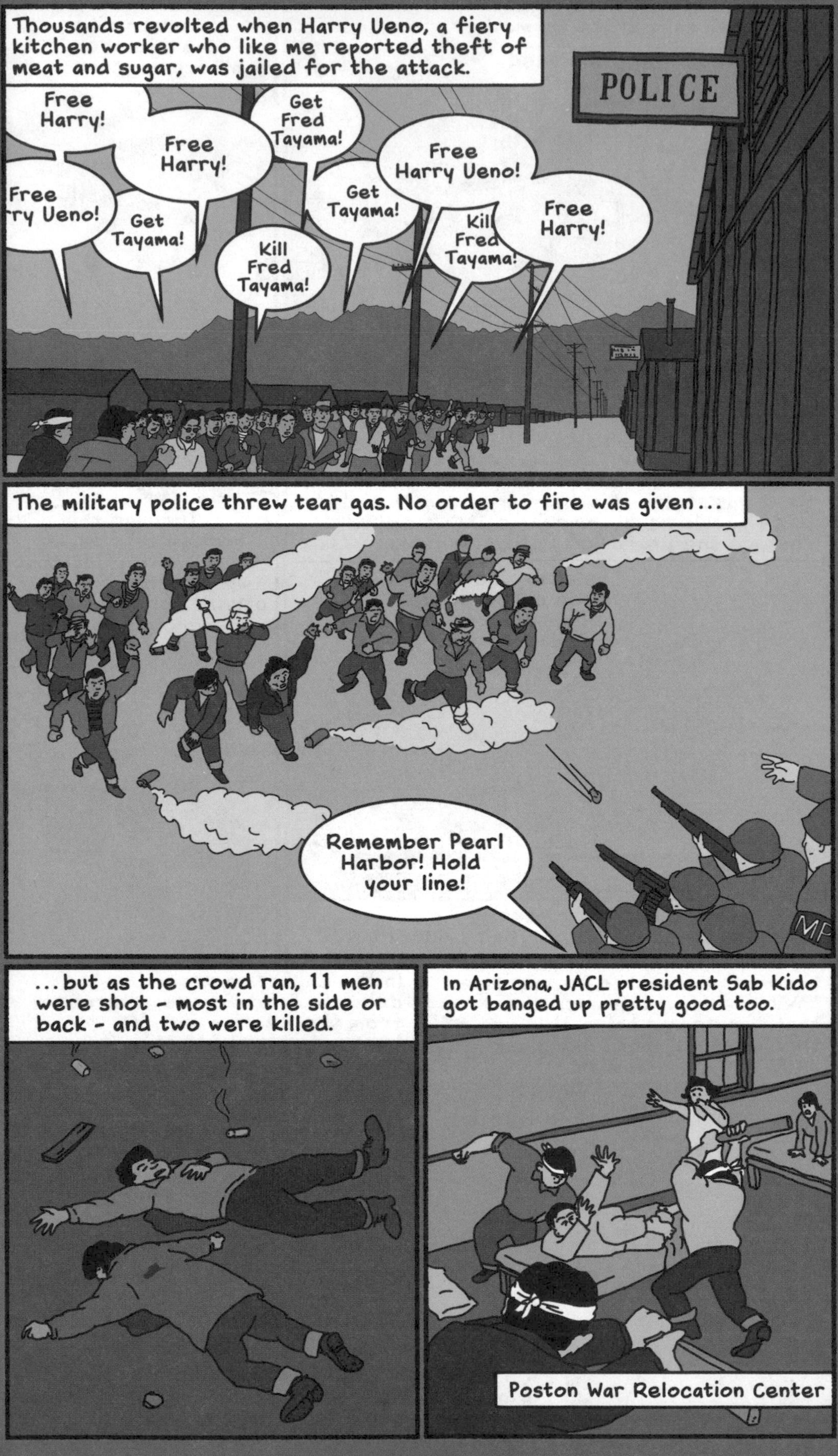

Thousands revolted when Harry Ueno, a fiery kitchen worker who like me reported theft of meat and sugar, was jailed for the attack.
POLICE
Free Harry!
Free Harry!
Get Fred Tayama!
Free rry Ueno!
Get Tayama!
Kill Fred Tayama!
Get Tayama!
Free Harry Ueno!
Kil Fred Tayama!
Free Harry!
The military police threw tear gas. No order to fire was given...
Remember Pearl Harbor! Hold your line!
MP
...but as the crowd ran, 11 men were shot - most in the side or back - and two were killed.
In Arizona, JACL president Sab Kido got banged up pretty good too.
Poston War Relocation Center

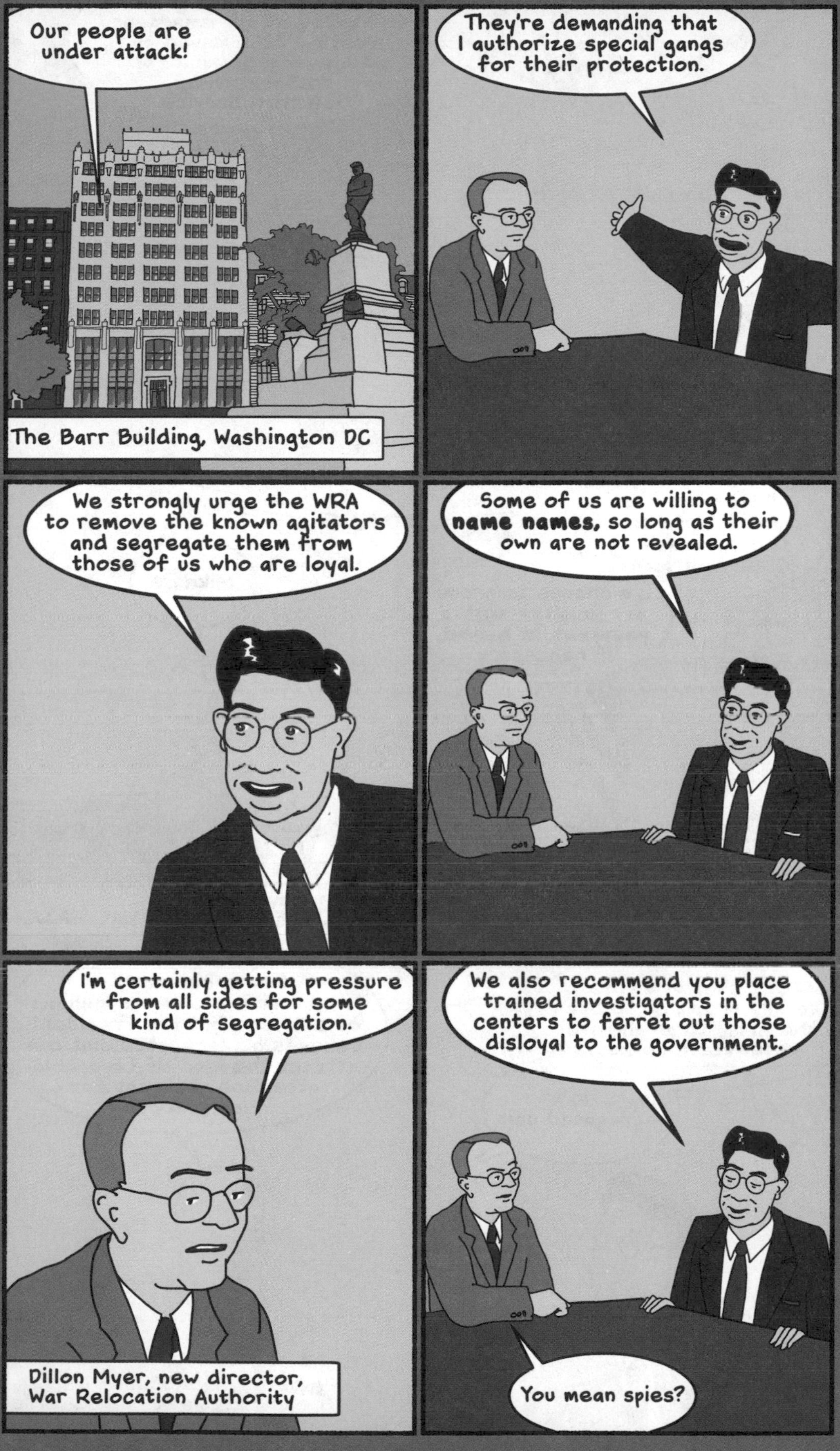
Our people are under attack!
The Barr Building, Washington DC
They're demanding that I authorize special gangs for their protection.
We strongly urge the WRA to remove the known agitators and segregate them from those of us who are loyal.
Some of us are willing to **name names**, so long as their own are not revealed.
I'm certainly getting pressure from all sides for some kind of segregation.
Dillon Myer, new director, War Relocation Authority
We also recommend you place trained investigators in the centers to ferret out those disloyal to the government.
You mean spies?

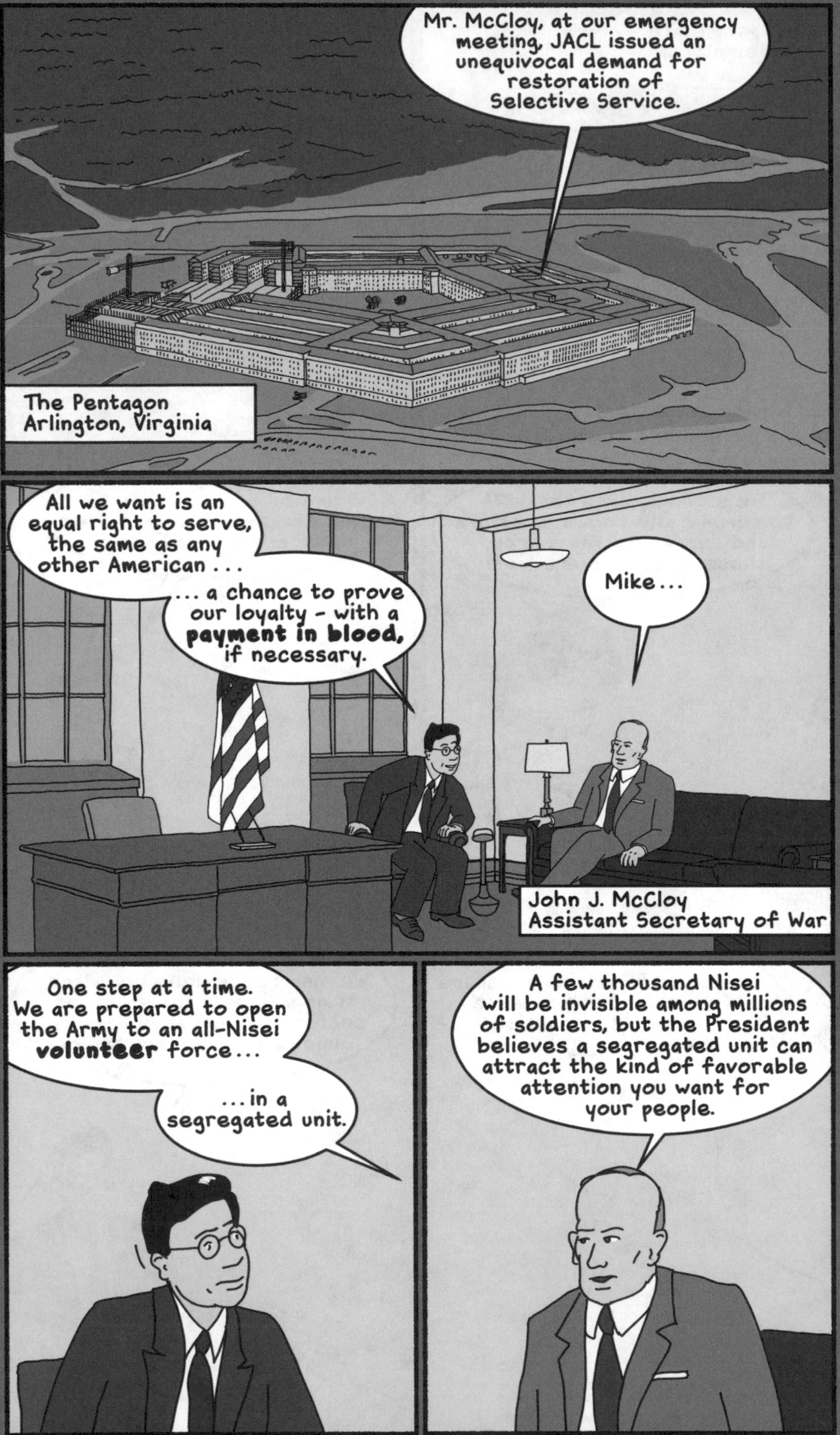
Mr. McCloy, at our emergency meeting, JACL issued an unequivocal demand for restoration of Selective Service.
The Pentagon
Arlington, Virginia
All we want is an equal right to serve, the same as any other American . . .
. . . a chance to prove our loyalty - with a **payment in blood,** if necessary.
Mike . . .
John J. McCloy
Assistant Secretary of War
One step at a time. We are prepared to open the Army to an all-Nisei **volunteer** force . . .
. . . in a segregated unit.
A few thousand Nisei will be invisible among millions of soldiers, but the President believes a segregated unit can attract the kind of favorable attention you want for your people.

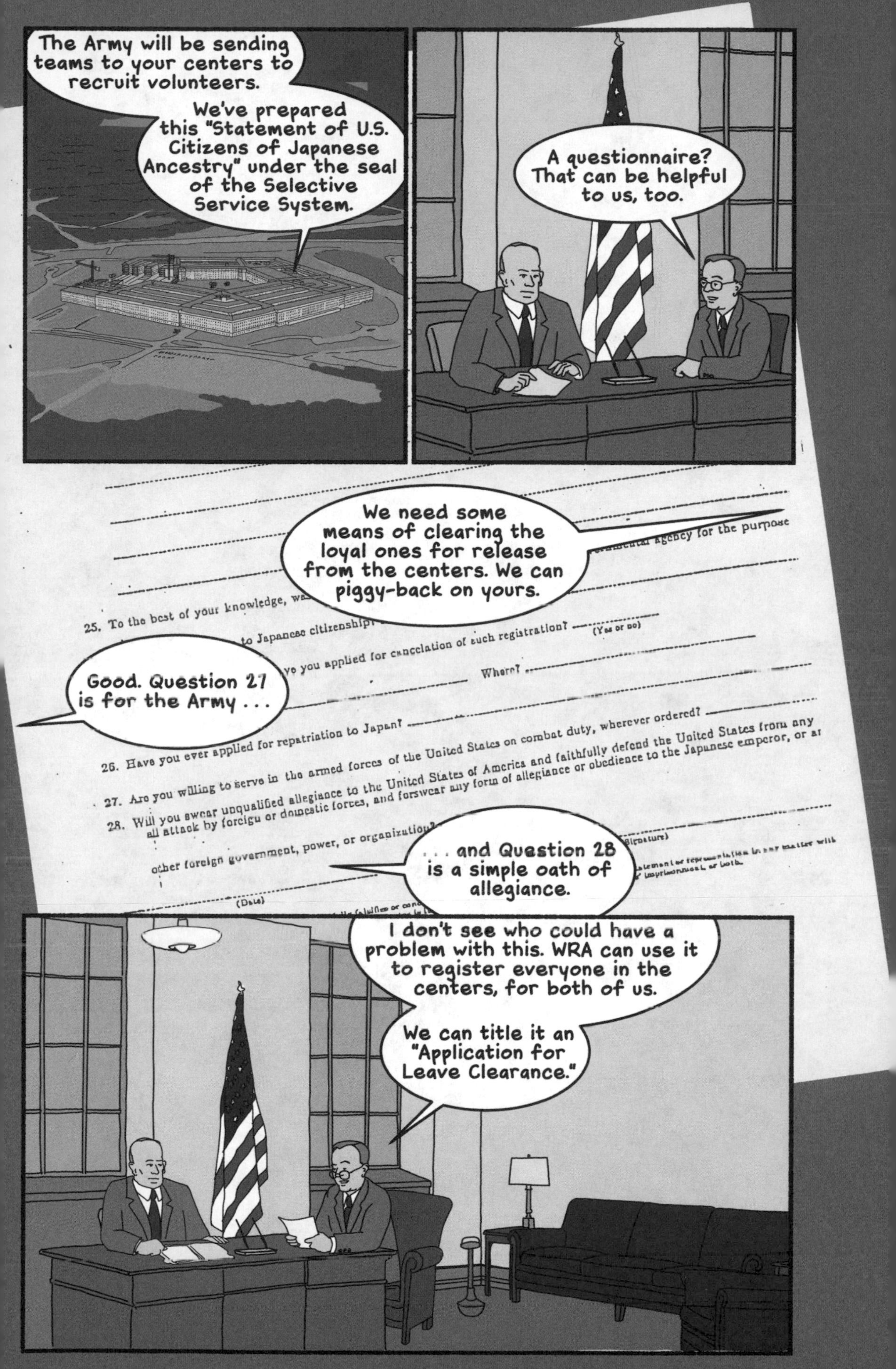
The Army will be sending teams to your centers to recruit volunteeers.
We've prepared this "Statement of U.S. Citizens of Japanese Ancestry" under the seal of the Selective Service System.
A questionnaire? That can be helpful to us, too.
We need some means of clearing the loyal ones for release from the centers. We can piggy-back on yours.
25. To the best of your knowledge, wa
to Japanese citizenship
ve you applied for cancelation of such registration?
(Yes or no)
Where?
Good. Question 27 is for the Army . . .
26. Have you ever applied for repatriation to Japan?
27. Are you willing to serve in the armed forces of the United States on combat duty, wherever ordered?
28. Will you swear unqualified allegiance to the United States of America and faithfully defend the United States from any all attack by foreign or domestic forces, and forswear any form of allegiance or obedience to the Japanese emperor, or any other foreign government, power, or organization?
(Signature)
(Date)
. . . and Question 28 is a simple oath of allegiance.
I don't see who could have a problem with this. WRA can use it to register everyone in the centers, for both of us.
We can title it an "Application for Leave Clearance."

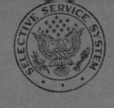

. BOARD DATE STAMP WITH CODE)

TATEMENT OF UNITED STATES CITIZEN OF JAPANESE A

(Surname) (English given name) (Japa

lias

elective service board (Number)

(City) (County)

of birth Place of birth

nt address (Street) (City)

two addresses at which you lived 3 months or more (exclude residence at relocation center

From

From

Height Weight

e you a registered voter? Year first registered

Where? Party

Marital status Citizenship of wife Race c

(Father's Name) (Town or Ken) (Birthplace) (State or Country)

(Mother's Name) (Town or Ken) (Birthplace) (State or Country)

In items 11 and 12, you need not list relatives other than your parents, your children,
For each person give name; relationship to you (such as father); citizenship; comple

Relatives in the United States (if in military service, indicate whether a selectee or voluntee

(Name) (Relationship to you)

PART THREE

IT'S THE COUNTRY THAT'S NOT LOYAL TO US

1943

HIROSHI: The Army sent recruiters to us at Tule Lake with a prepared statement on military registration, but little else.

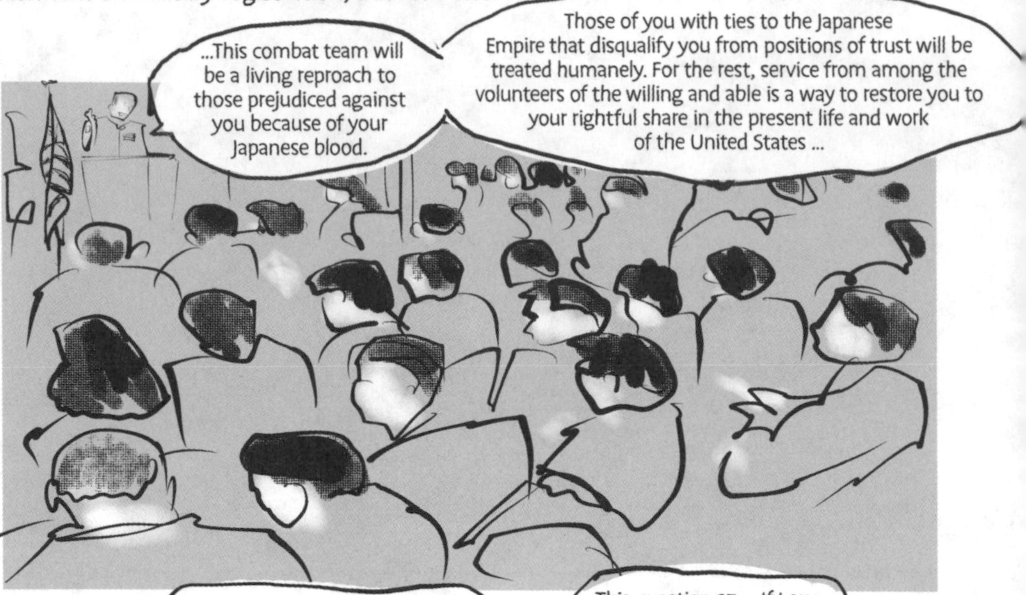
...This combat team will be a living reproach to those prejudiced against you because of your Japanese blood.
Those of you with ties to the Japanese Empire that disqualify you from positions of trust will be treated humanely. For the rest, service from among the volunteers of the willing and able is a way to restore you to your rightful share in the present life and work of the United States ...

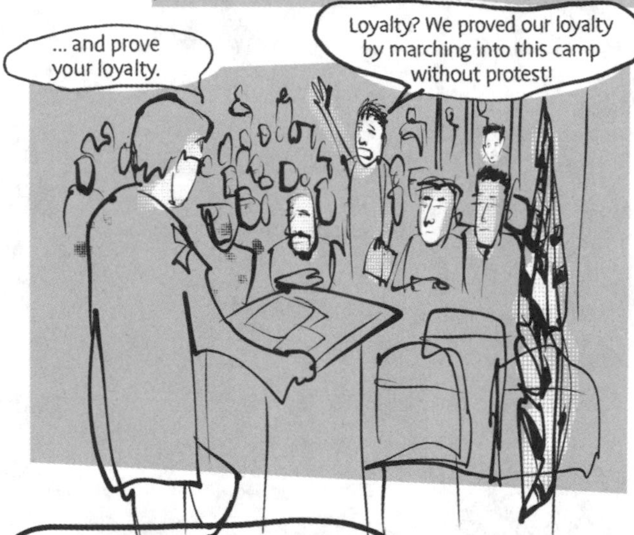
... and prove your loyalty.
Loyalty? We proved our loyalty by marching into this camp without protest!

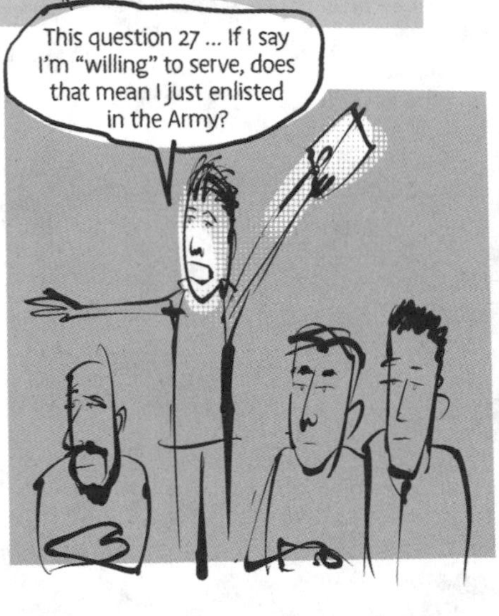
This question 27 ... If I say I'm "willing" to serve, does that mean I just enlisted in the Army?

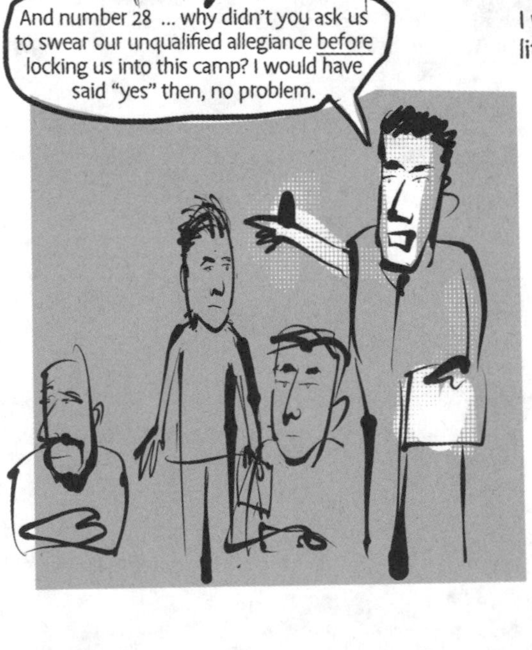
And number 28 ... why didn't you ask us to swear our unqualified allegiance before locking us into this camp? I would have said "yes" then, no problem.

I was surprised to see Rocky stand to speak. I knew him a little bit from before and had never seen him so agitated.

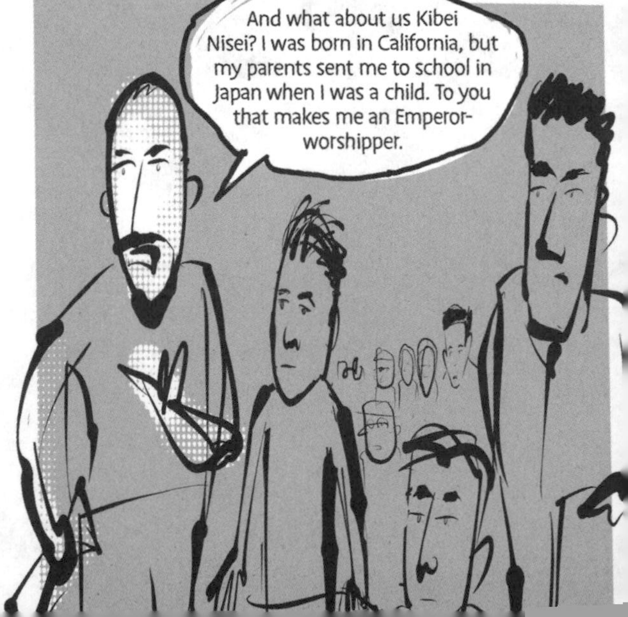
And what about us Kibei Nisei? I was born in California, but my parents sent me to school in Japan when I was a child. To you that makes me an Emperor-worshipper.

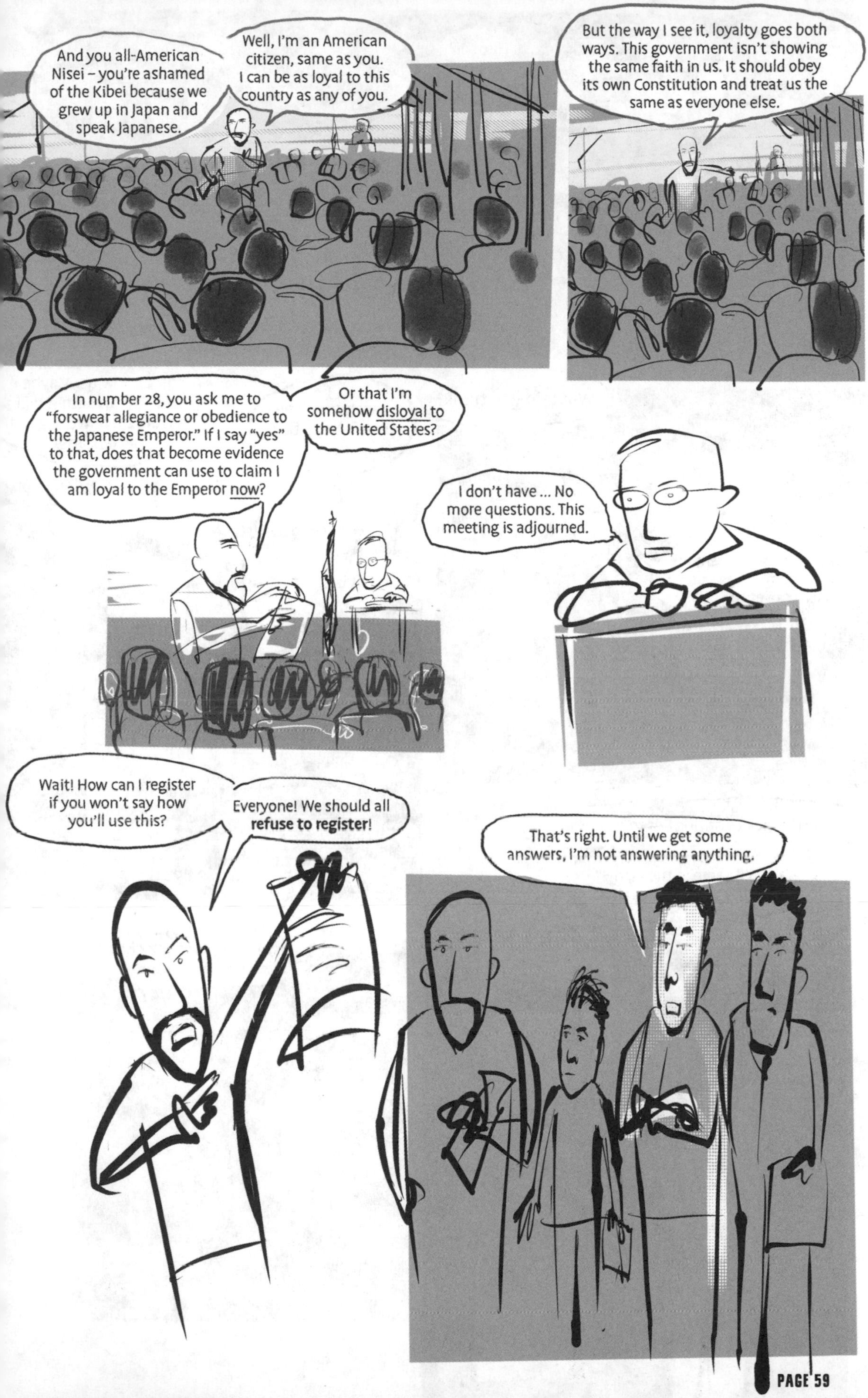
And you all-American Nisei – you're ashamed of the Kibei because we grew up in Japan and speak Japanese.
Well, I'm an American citizen, same as you. I can be as loyal to this country as any of you.
But the way I see it, loyalty goes both ways. This government isn't showing the same faith in us. It should obey its own Constitution and treat us the same as everyone else.
In number 28, you ask me to "forswear allegiance or obedience to the Japanese Emperor." If I say "yes" to that, does that become evidence the government can use to claim I am loyal to the Emperor now?
Or that I'm somehow disloyal to the United States?
I don't have ... No more questions. This meeting is adjourned.
Wait! How can I register if you won't say how you'll use this?
Everyone! We should all **refuse to register**!
That's right. Until we get some answers, I'm not answering anything.

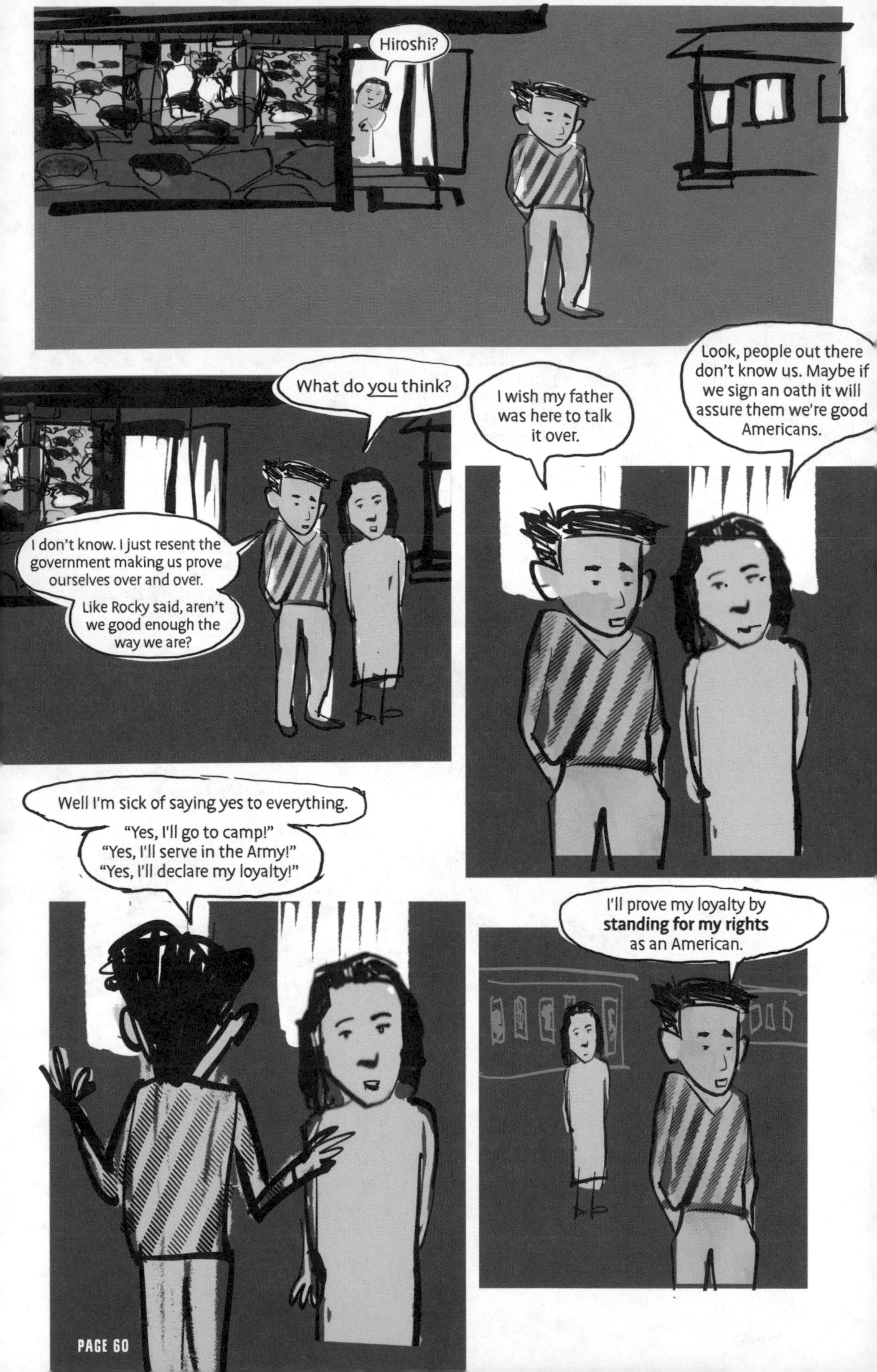
Hiroshi?
What do you think?
I don't know. I just resent the government making us prove ourselves over and over.
Like Rocky said, aren't we good enough the way we are?
I wish my father was here to talk it over.
Look, people out there don't know us. Maybe if we sign an oath it will assure them we're good Americans.
Well I'm sick of saying yes to everything.
"Yes, I'll go to camp!" "Yes, I'll serve in the Army!" "Yes, I'll declare my loyalty!"
I'll prove my loyalty by **standing for my rights** as an American.

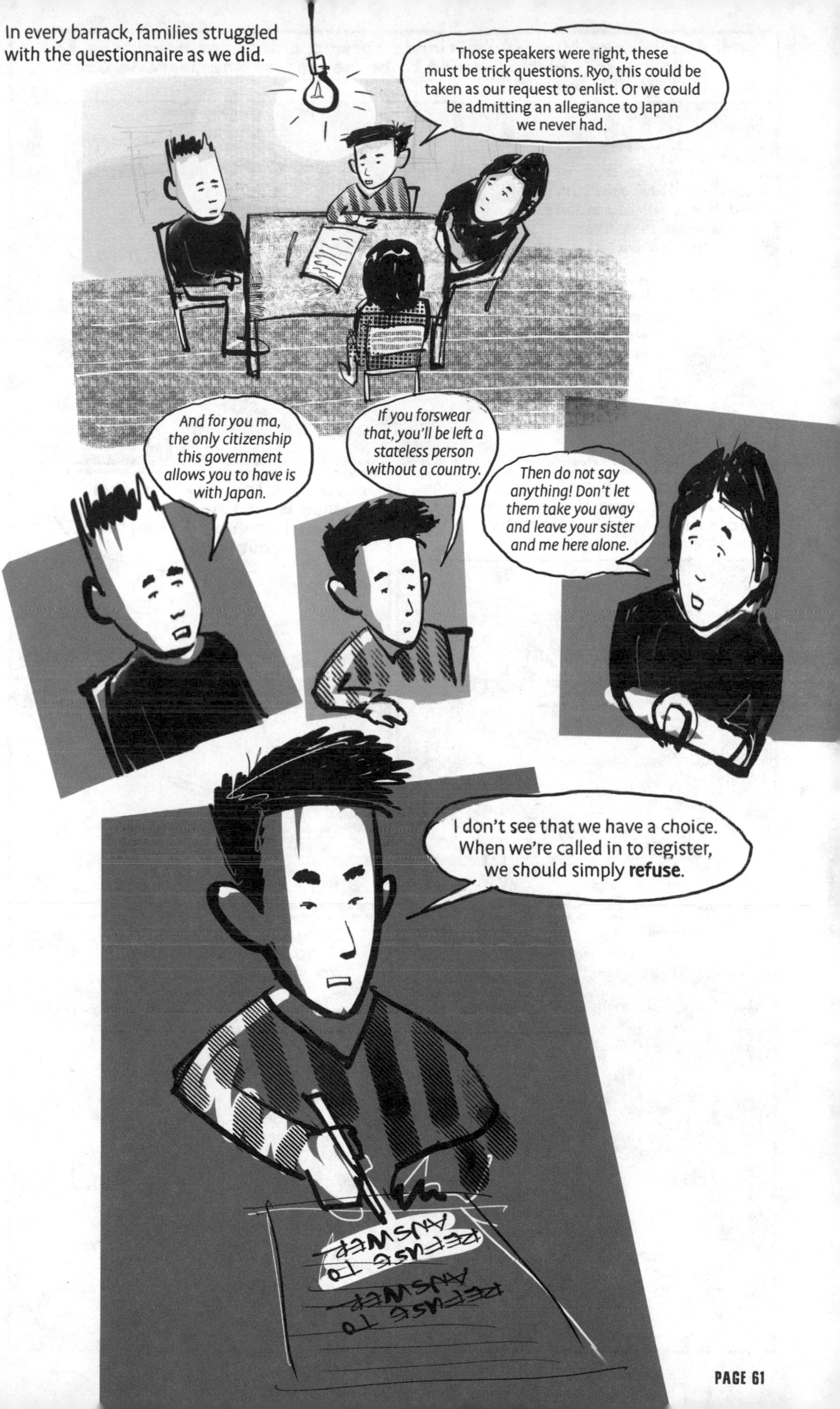
In every barrack, families struggled with the questionnaire as we did.
Those speakers were right, these must be trick questions. Ryo, this could be taken as our request to enlist. Or we could be admitting an allegiance to Japan we never had.
And for you ma, the only citizenship this government allows you to have is with Japan.
If you forswear that, you'll be left a stateless person without a country.
Then do not say anything! Don't let them take you away and leave your sister and me here alone.
I don't see that we have a choice. When we're called in to register, we should simply **refuse**.
REFUSE TO ANSWER
REFUSE TO ANSWER

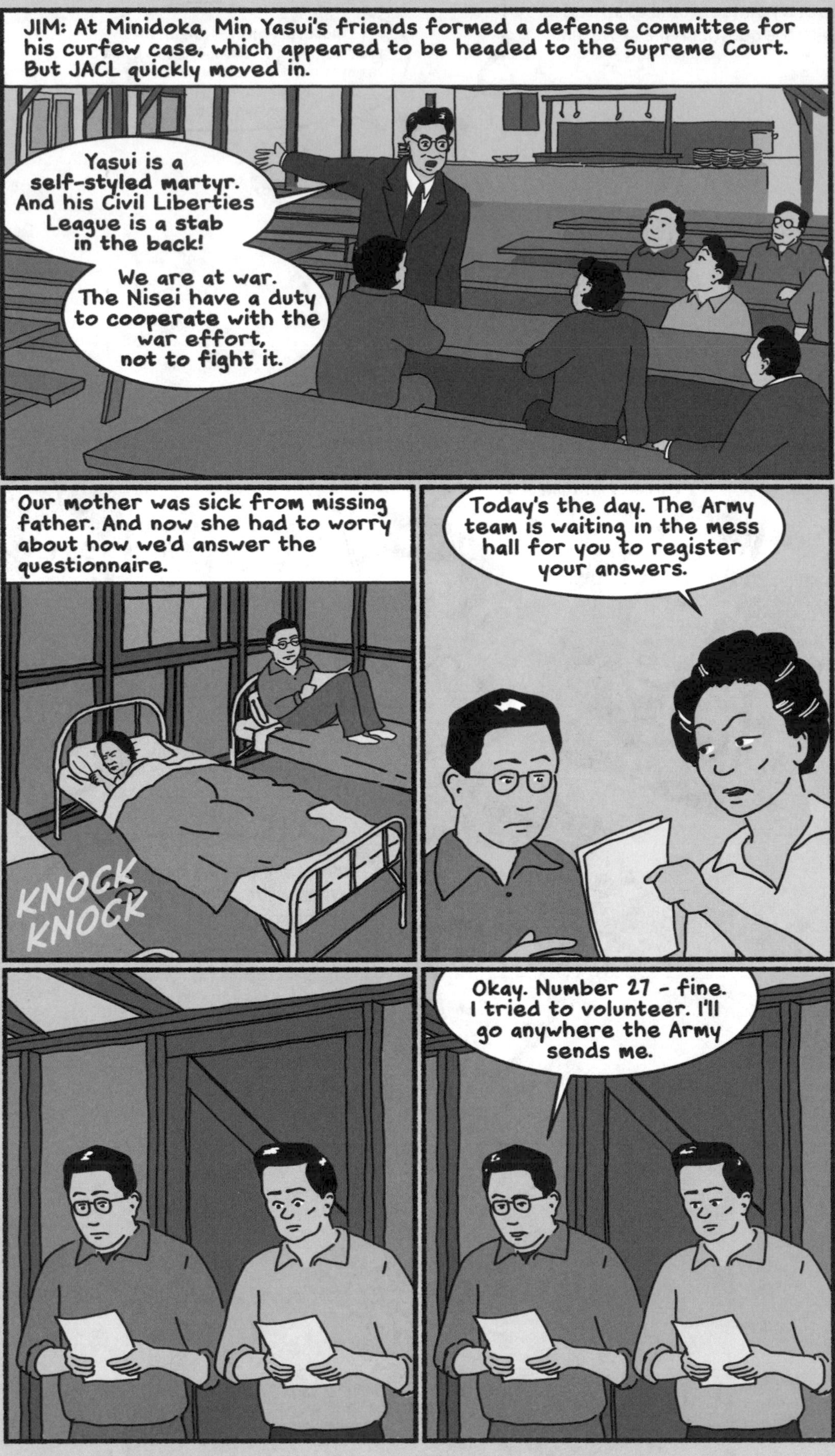
JIM: At Minidoka, Min Yasui's friends formed a defense committee for his curfew case, which appeared to be headed to the Supreme Court. But JACL quickly moved in.
Yasui is a self-styled martyr. And his Civil Liberties League is a stab in the back!
We are at war. The Nisei have a duty to cooperate with the war effort, not to fight it.
Our mother was sick from missing father. And now she had to worry about how we'd answer the questionnaire.
KNOCK KNOCK
Today's the day. The Army team is waiting in the mess hall for you to register your answers.
Okay. Number 27 - fine. I tried to volunteer. I'll go anywhere the Army sends me.

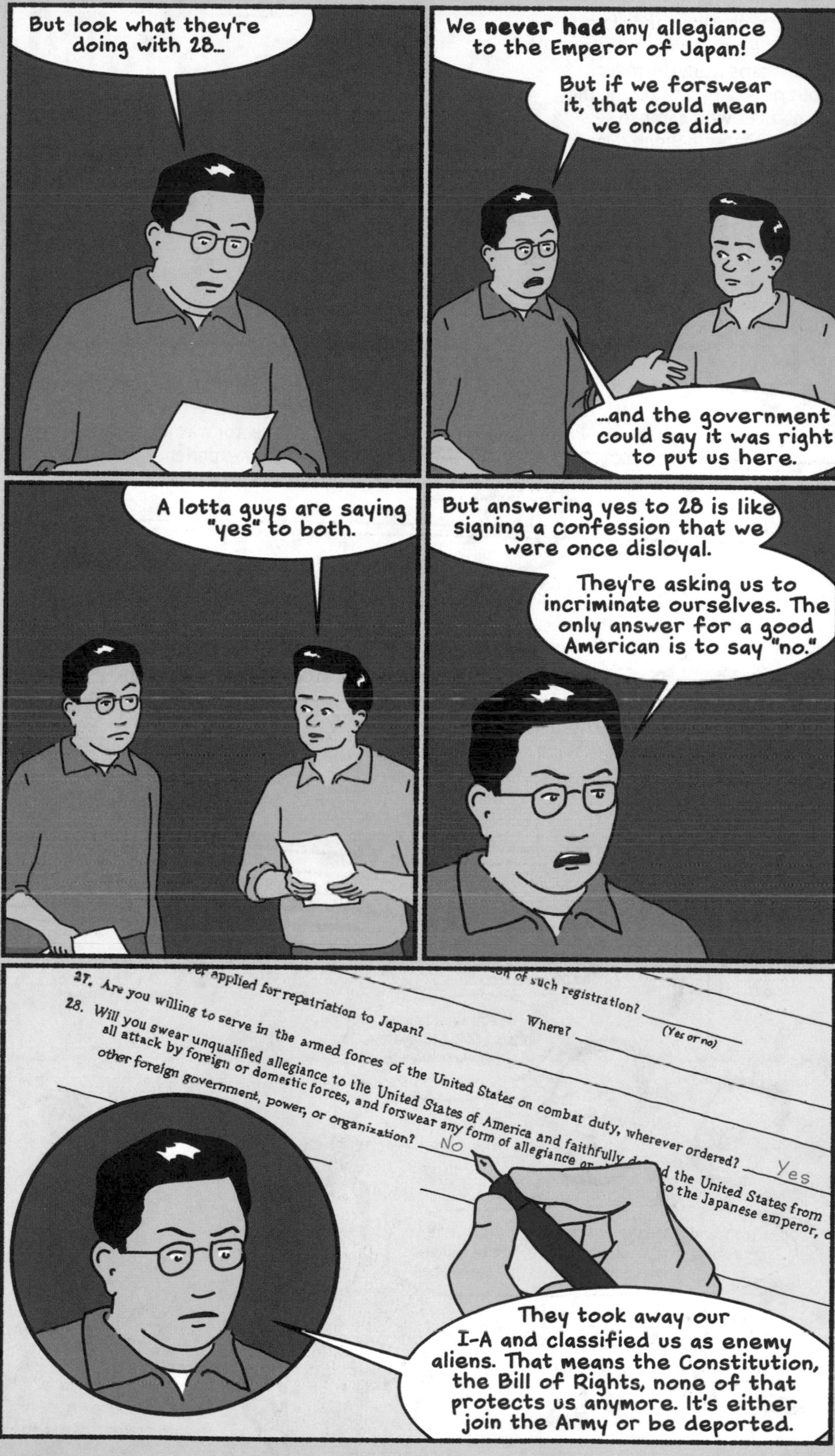

But look what they're doing with 28...
We **never had** any allegiance to the Emperor of Japan!
But if we forswear it, that could mean we once did...
...and the government could say it was right to put us here.
A lotta guys are saying "yes" to both.
But answering yes to 28 is like signing a confession that we were once disloyal.
They're asking us to incriminate ourselves. The only answer for a good American is to say "no."
applied for repatriation to Japan?
of such registration?
Where?
(Yes or no)
27. Are you willing to serve in the armed forces of the United States on combat duty, wherever ordered? Yes
28. Will you swear unqualified allegiance to the United States of America and faithfully defend the United States from all attack by foreign or domestic forces, and forswear any form of allegiance or obedience to the Japanese emperor, or other foreign government, power, or organization? No
They took away our I-A and classified us as enemy aliens. That means the Constitution, the Bill of Rights, none of that protects us anymore. It's either join the Army or be deported.

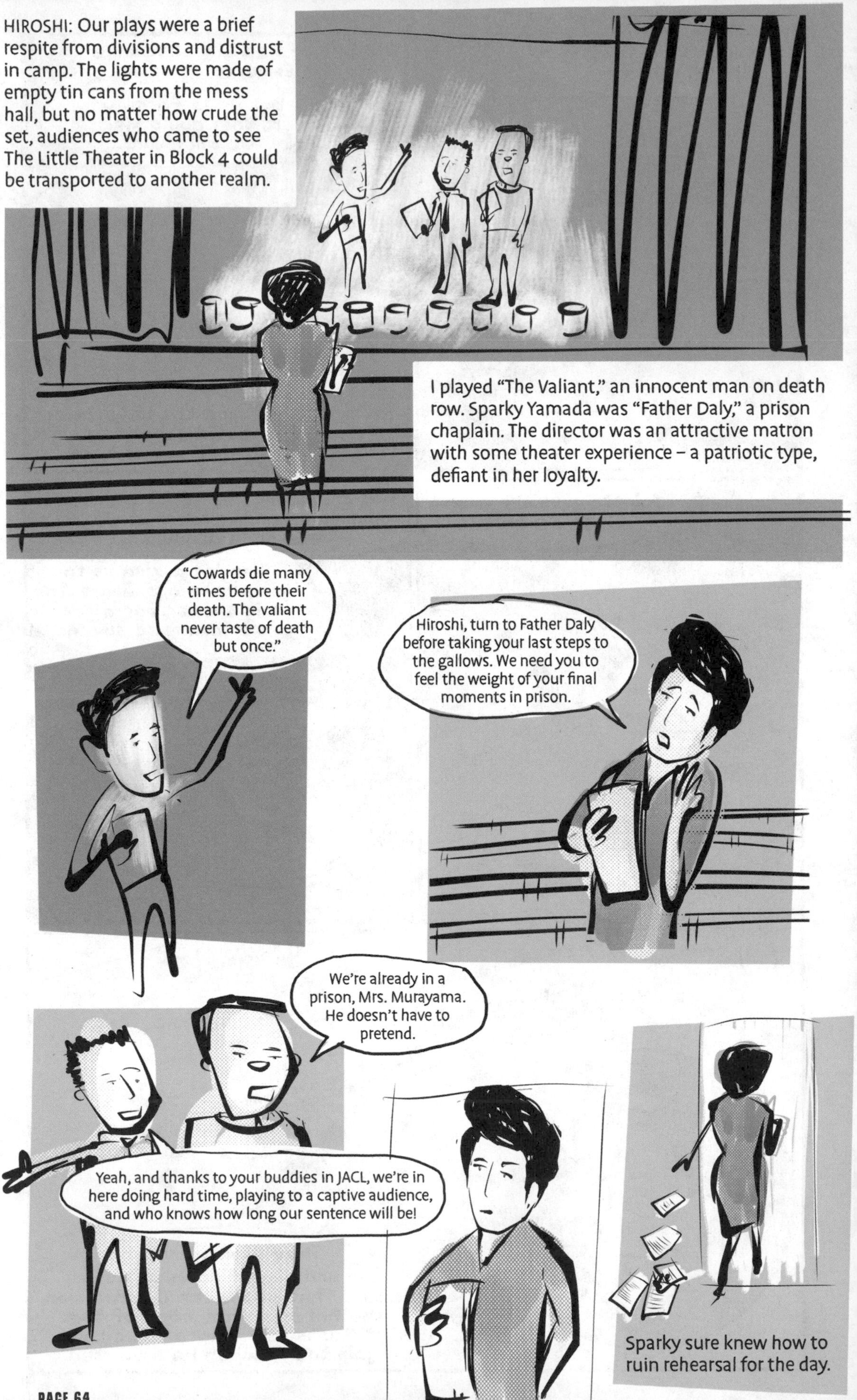
HIROSHI: Our plays were a brief respite from divisions and distrust in camp. The lights were made of empty tin cans from the mess hall, but no matter how crude the set, audiences who came to see The Little Theater in Block 4 could be transported to another realm.
I played "The Valiant," an innocent man on death row. Sparky Yamada was "Father Daly," a prison chaplain. The director was an attractive matron with some theater experience – a patriotic type, defiant in her loyalty.
"Cowards die many times before their death. The valiant never taste of death but once."
Hiroshi, turn to Father Daly before taking your last steps to the gallows. We need you to feel the weight of your final moments in prison.
We're already in a prison, Mrs. Murayama. He doesn't have to pretend.
Yeah, and thanks to your buddies in JACL, we're in here doing hard time, playing to a captive audience, and who knows how long our sentence will be!
Sparky sure knew how to ruin rehearsal for the day.

In another part of Block 4, Rocky was also onstage – at a meeting of Kibei Nisei, reading back a statement of principles *in Japanese* to present to the project director.

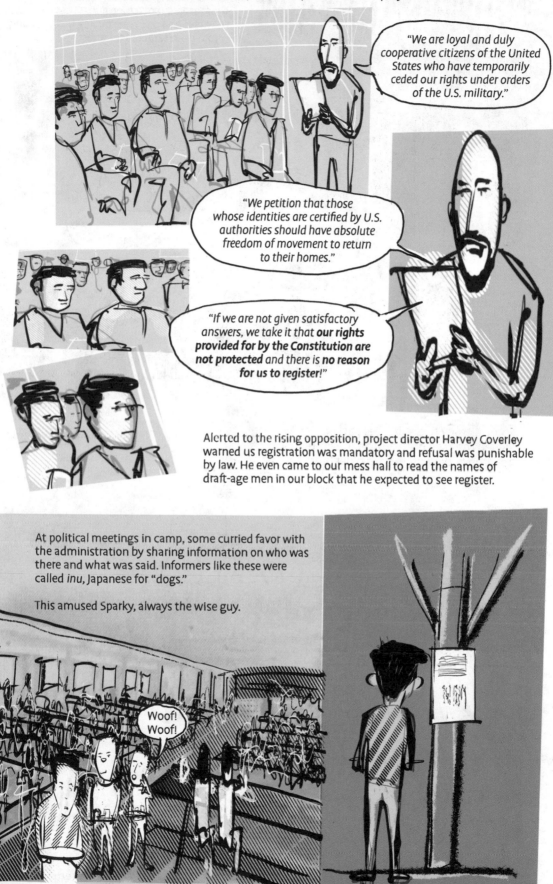

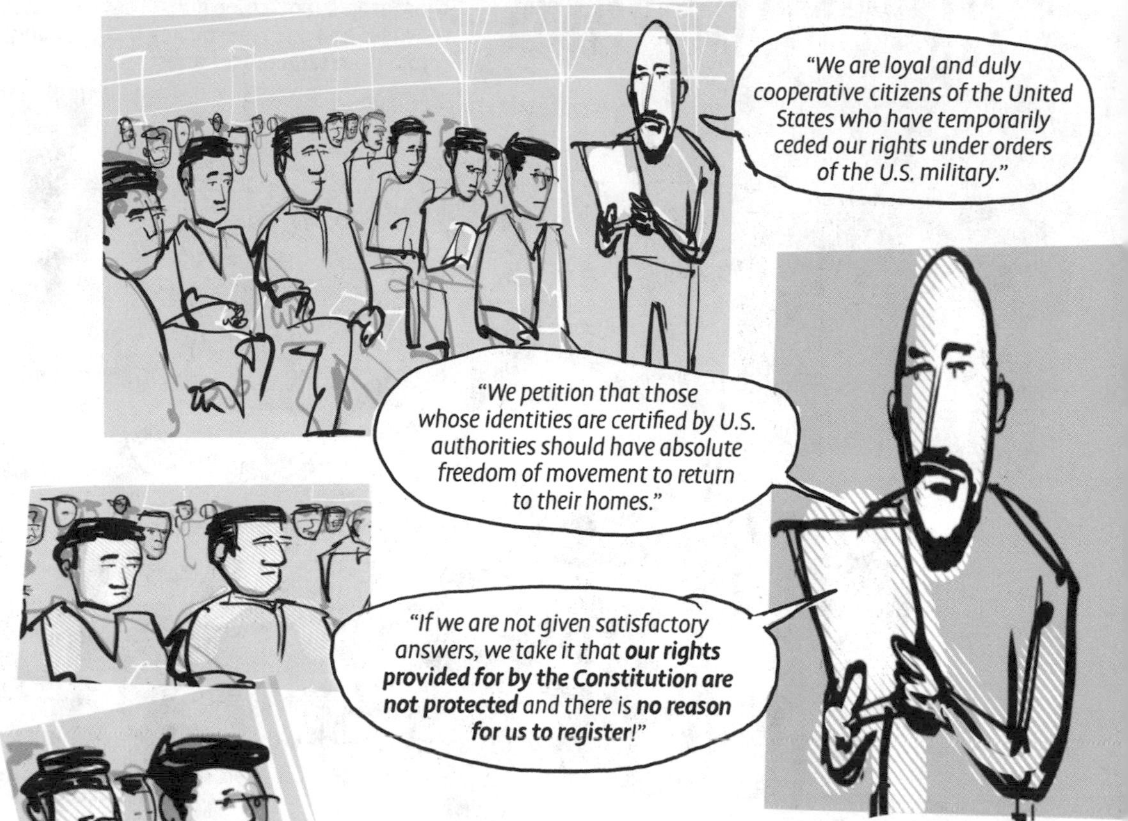
"We are loyal and duly cooperative citizens of the United States who have temporarily ceded our rights under orders of the U.S. military."
"We petition that those whose identities are certified by U.S. authorities should have absolute freedom of movement to return to their homes."
"If we are not given satisfactory answers, we take it that **our rights provided for by the Constitution are not protected** and there is **no reason for us to register**!"

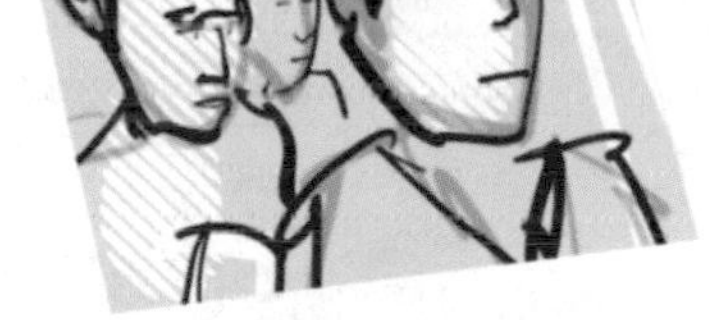

Alerted to the rising opposition, project director Harvey Coverley warned us registration was mandatory and refusal was punishable by law. He even came to our mess hall to read the names of draft-age men in our block that he expected to see register.

At political meetings in camp, some curried favor with the administration by sharing information on who was there and what was said. Informers like these were called *inu*, Japanese for "dogs."

This amused Sparky, always the wise guy.

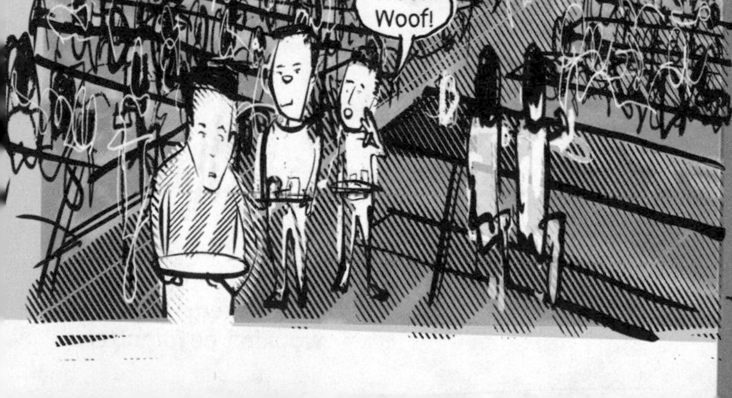
Woof!
Woof!

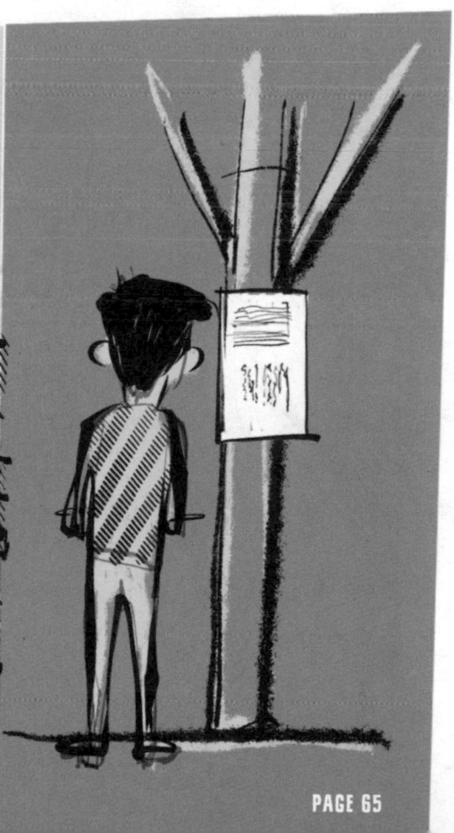

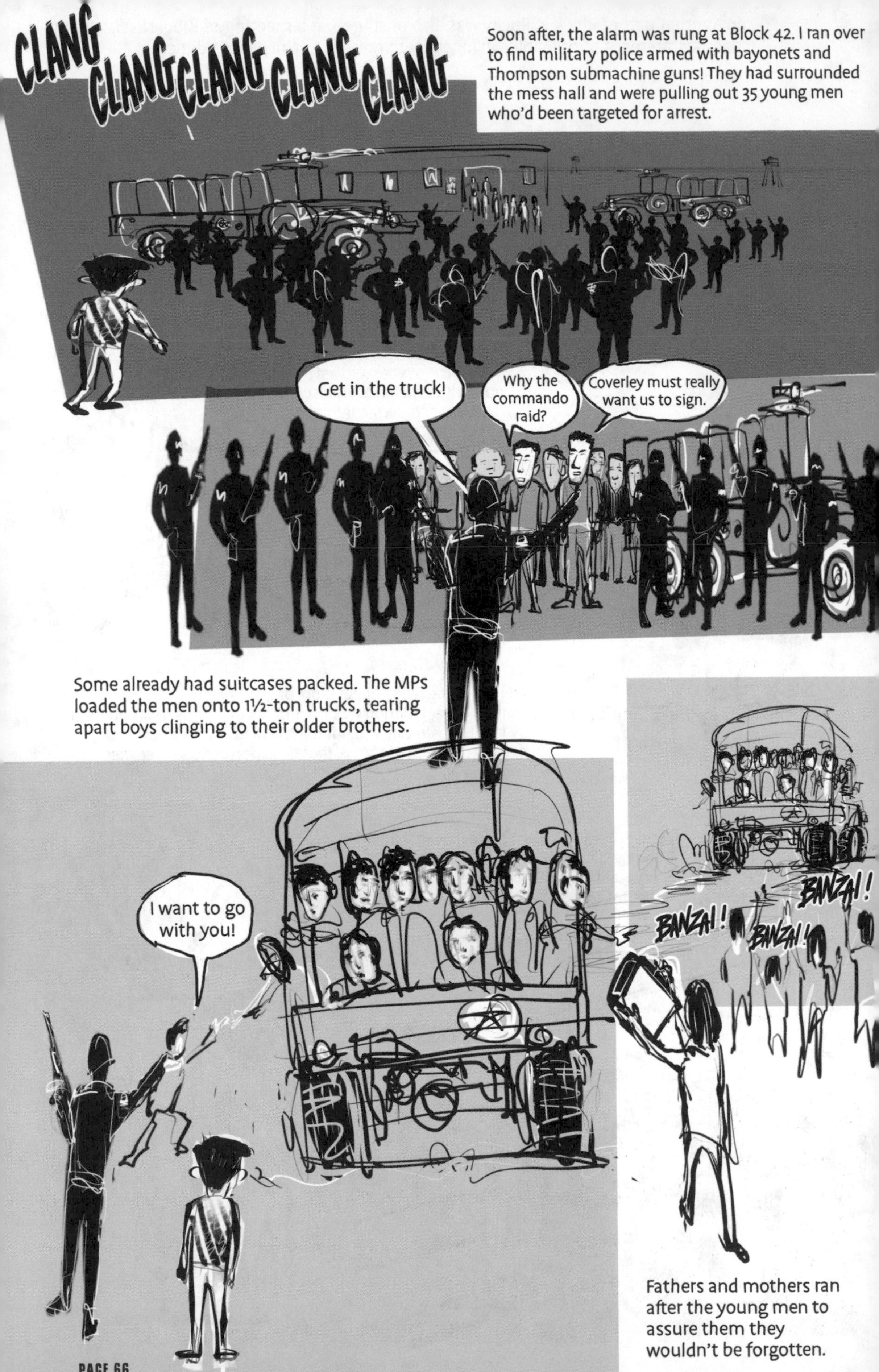
CLANG CLANG CLANG CLANG CLANG
Soon after, the alarm was rung at Block 42. I ran over to find military police armed with bayonets and Thompson submachine guns! They had surrounded the mess hall and were pulling out 35 young men who'd been targeted for arrest.
Get in the truck!
Why the commando raid?
Coverley must really want us to sign.
Some already had suitcases packed. The MPs loaded the men onto 1½-ton trucks, tearing apart boys clinging to their older brothers.
I want to go with you!
BANZAI!
BANZAI!
BANZAI!
Fathers and mothers ran after the young men to assure them they wouldn't be forgotten.

The show of force only hardened everyone's resolve.

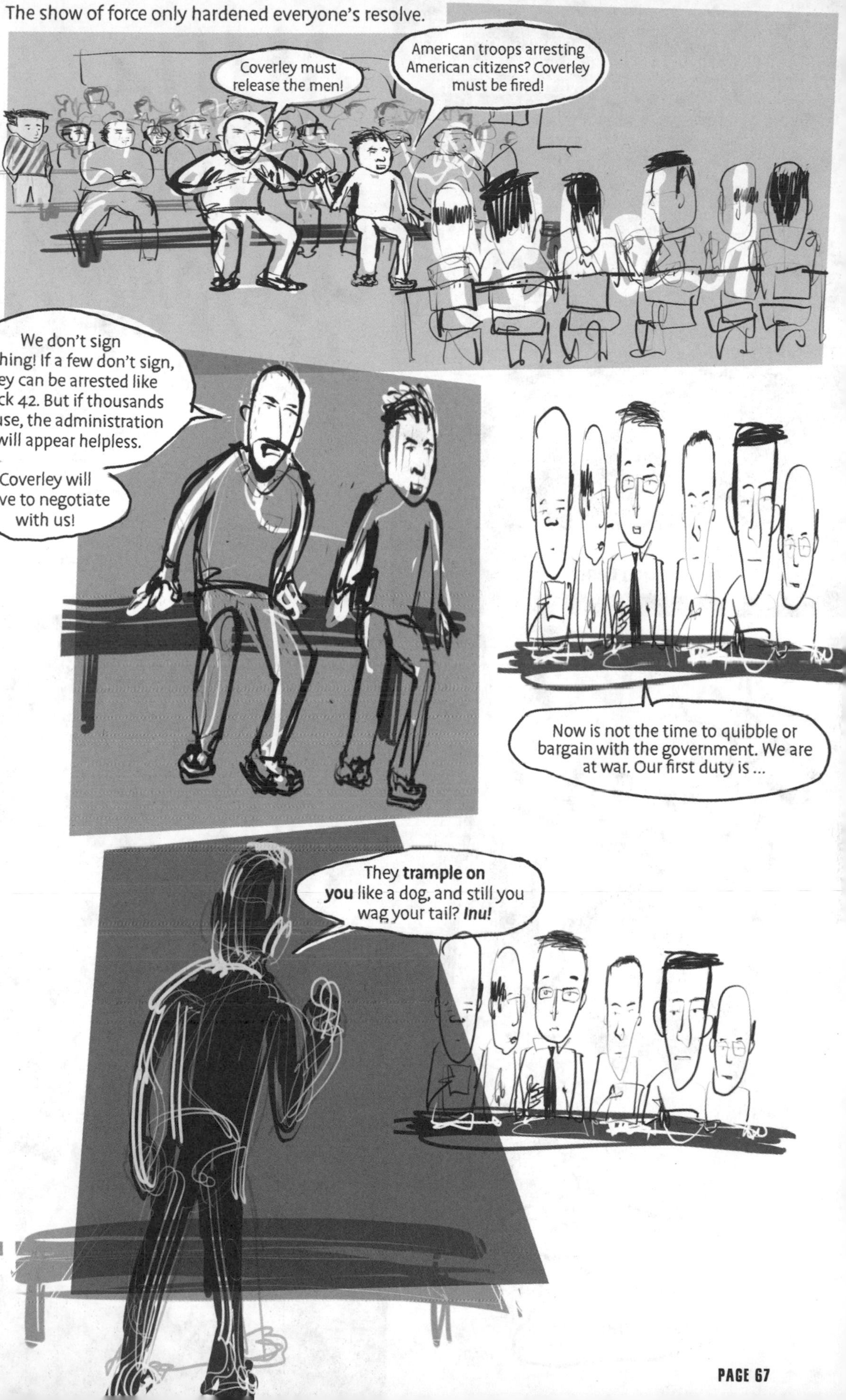

Coverley must release the men!
American troops arresting American citizens? Coverley must be fired!
We don't sign anything! If a few don't sign, they can be arrested like Block 42. But if thousands refuse, the administration will appear helpless.
Coverley will have to negotiate with us!
Now is not the time to quibble or bargain with the government. We are at war. Our first duty is ...
They **trample on you** like a dog, and still you wag your tail? ***Inu!***

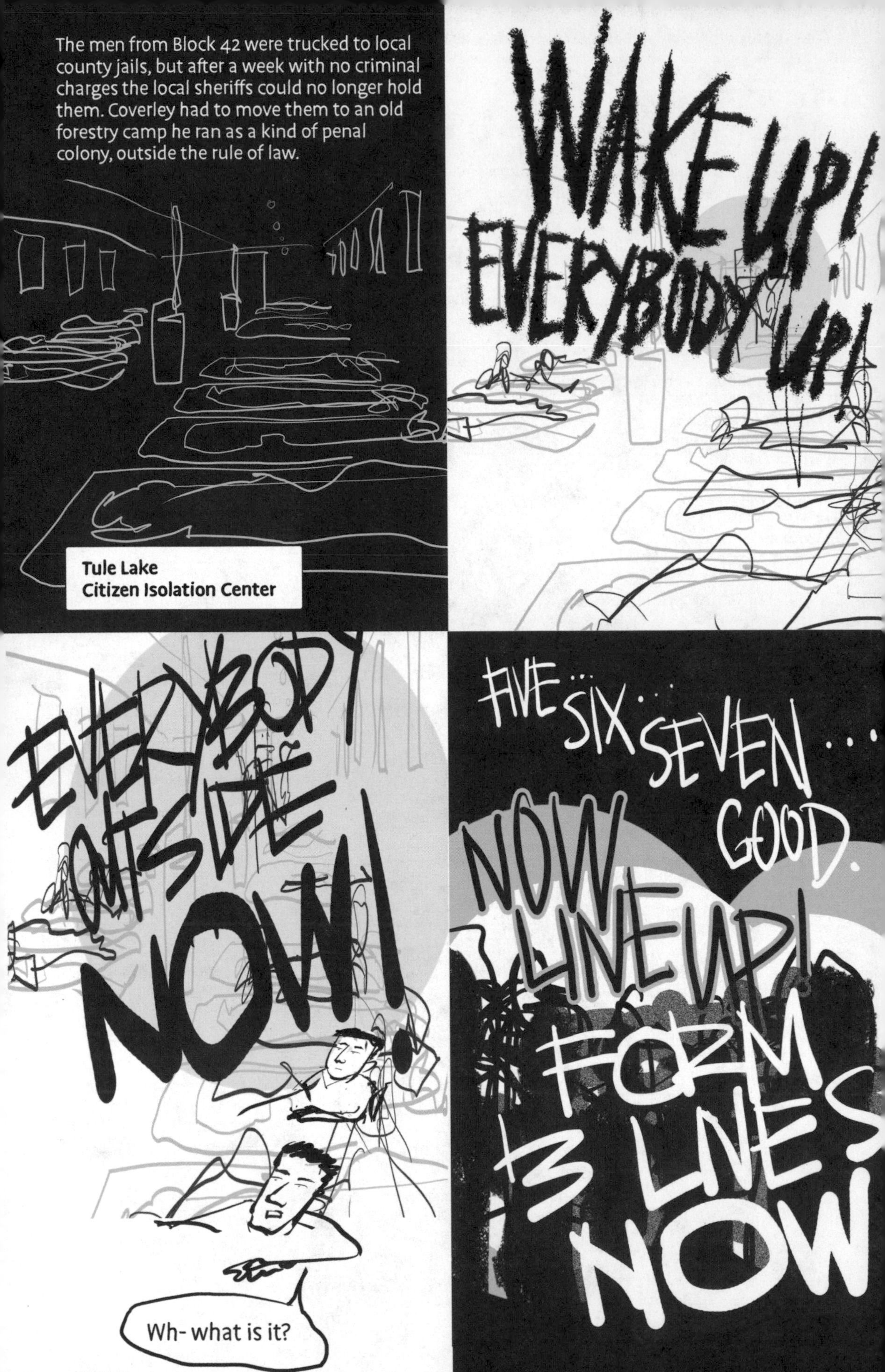
The men from Block 42 were trucked to local county jails, but after a week with no criminal charges the local sheriffs could no longer hold them. Coverley had to move them to an old forestry camp he ran as a kind of penal colony, outside the rule of law.
Tule Lake
Citizen Isolation Center
WAKE UP! EVERYBODY UP!
EVERYBODY OUTSIDE NOW!
Wh- what is it?
FIVE... SIX... SEVEN...
GOOD.
NOW LINE UP!
FORM 3 LINES NOW

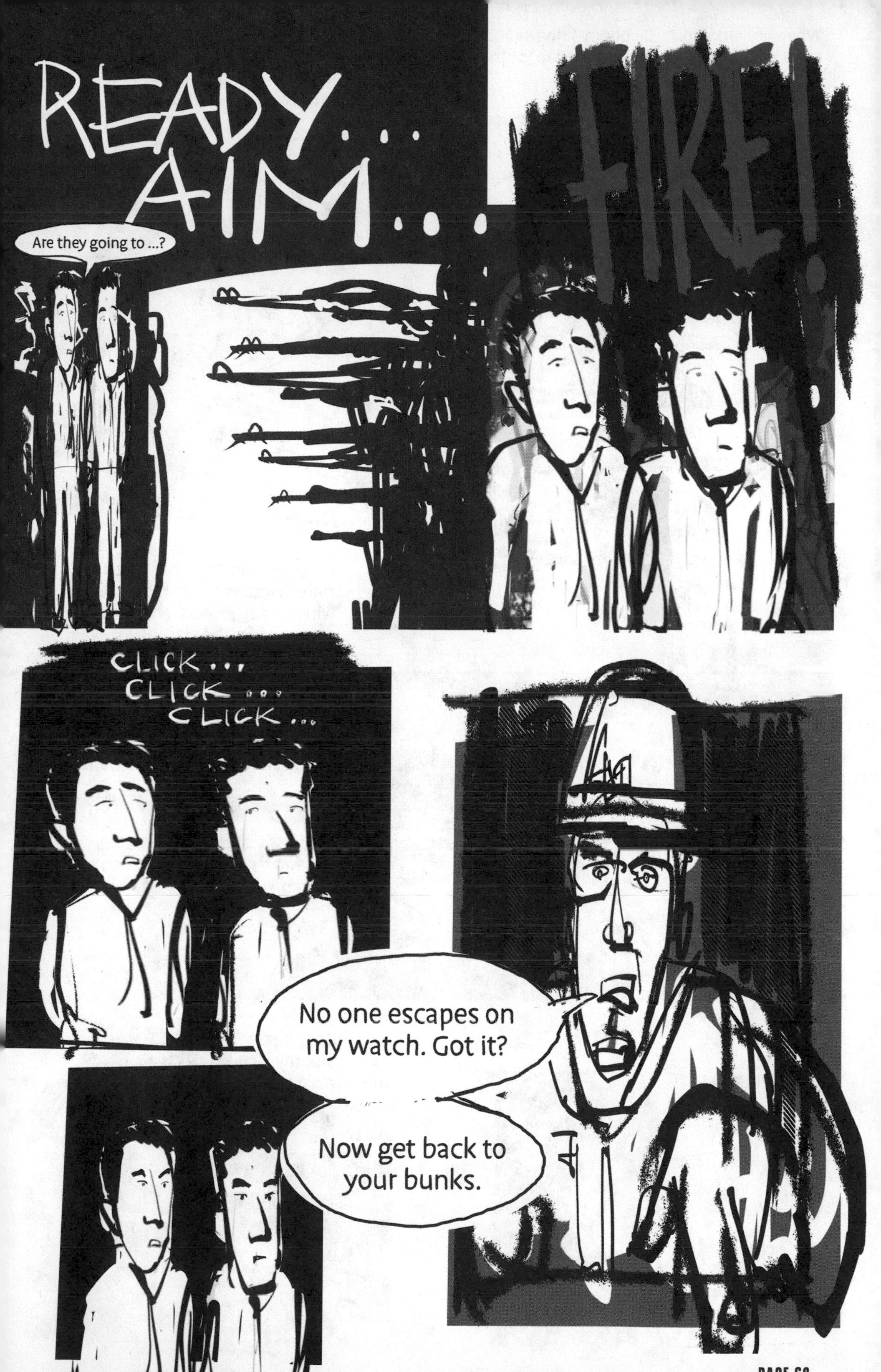
READY...
AIM...
FIRE!
Are they going to ...?
CLICK...
CLICK...
CLICK...
No one escapes on my watch. Got it?
Now get back to your bunks.

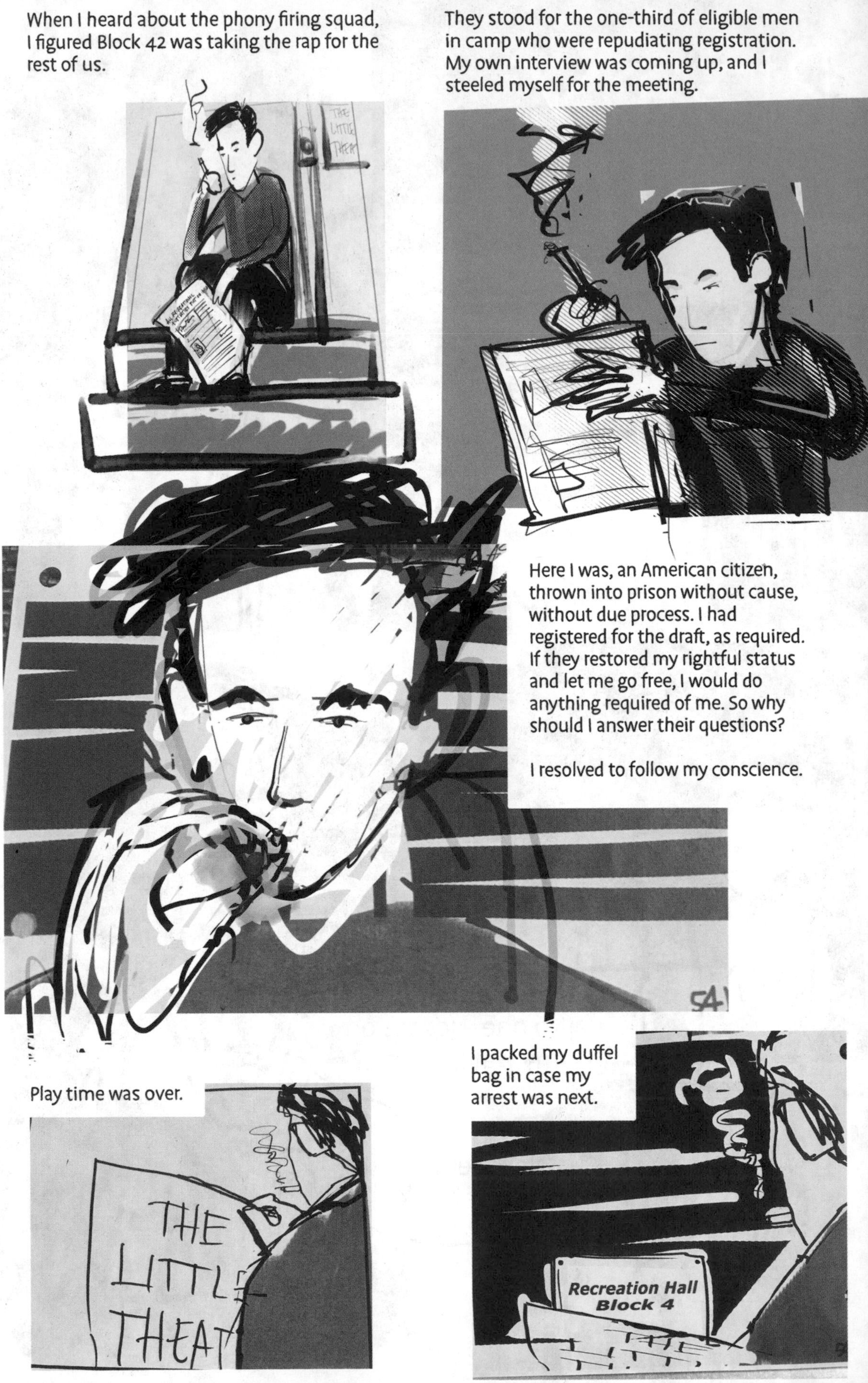
When I heard about the phony firing squad, I figured Block 42 was taking the rap for the rest of us.
They stood for the one-third of eligible men in camp who were repudiating registration. My own interview was coming up, and I steeled myself for the meeting.
Here I was, an American citizen, thrown into prison without cause, without due process. I had registered for the draft, as required. If they restored my rightful status and let me go free, I would do anything required of me. So why should I answer their questions?
I resolved to follow my conscience.
Play time was over.
THE LITTLE THEAT
I packed my duffel bag in case my arrest was next.
Recreation Hall Block 4

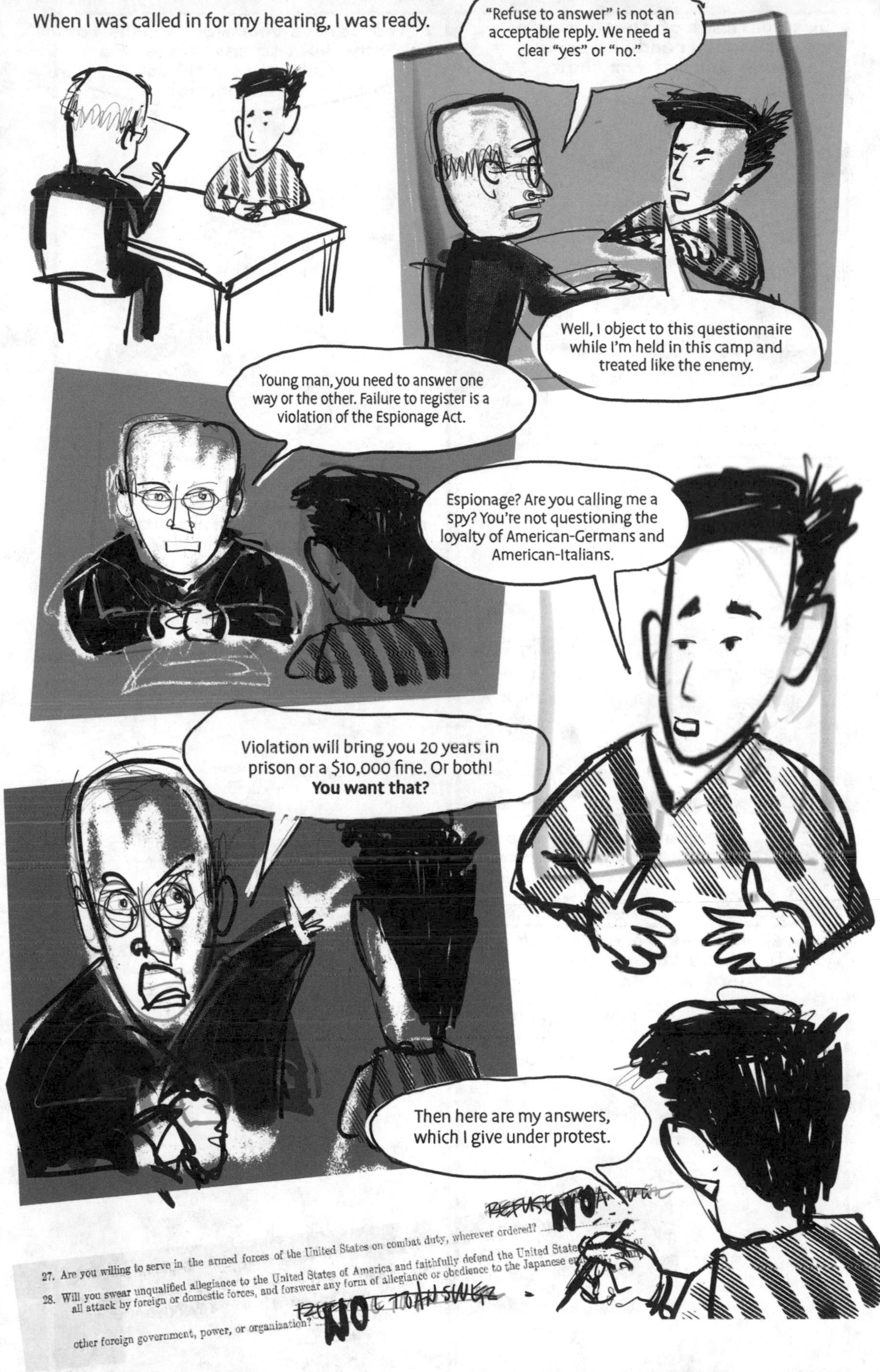
When I was called in for my hearing, I was ready.
"Refuse to answer" is not an acceptable reply. We need a clear "yes" or "no."
Well, I object to this questionnaire while I'm held in this camp and treated like the enemy.
Young man, you need to answer one way or the other. Failure to register is a violation of the Espionage Act.
Espionage? Are you calling me a spy? You're not questioning the loyalty of American-Germans and American-Italians.
Violation will bring you 20 years in prison or a $10,000 fine. Or both! **You want that?**
Then here are my answers, which I give under protest.
27. Are you willing to serve in the armed forces of the United States on combat duty, wherever ordered?
REFUSE NO
28. Will you swear unqualified allegiance to the United States of America and faithfully defend the United States
all attack by foreign or domestic forces, and forswear any form of allegiance or obedience to the Japanese
other foreign government, power, or organization?
NO

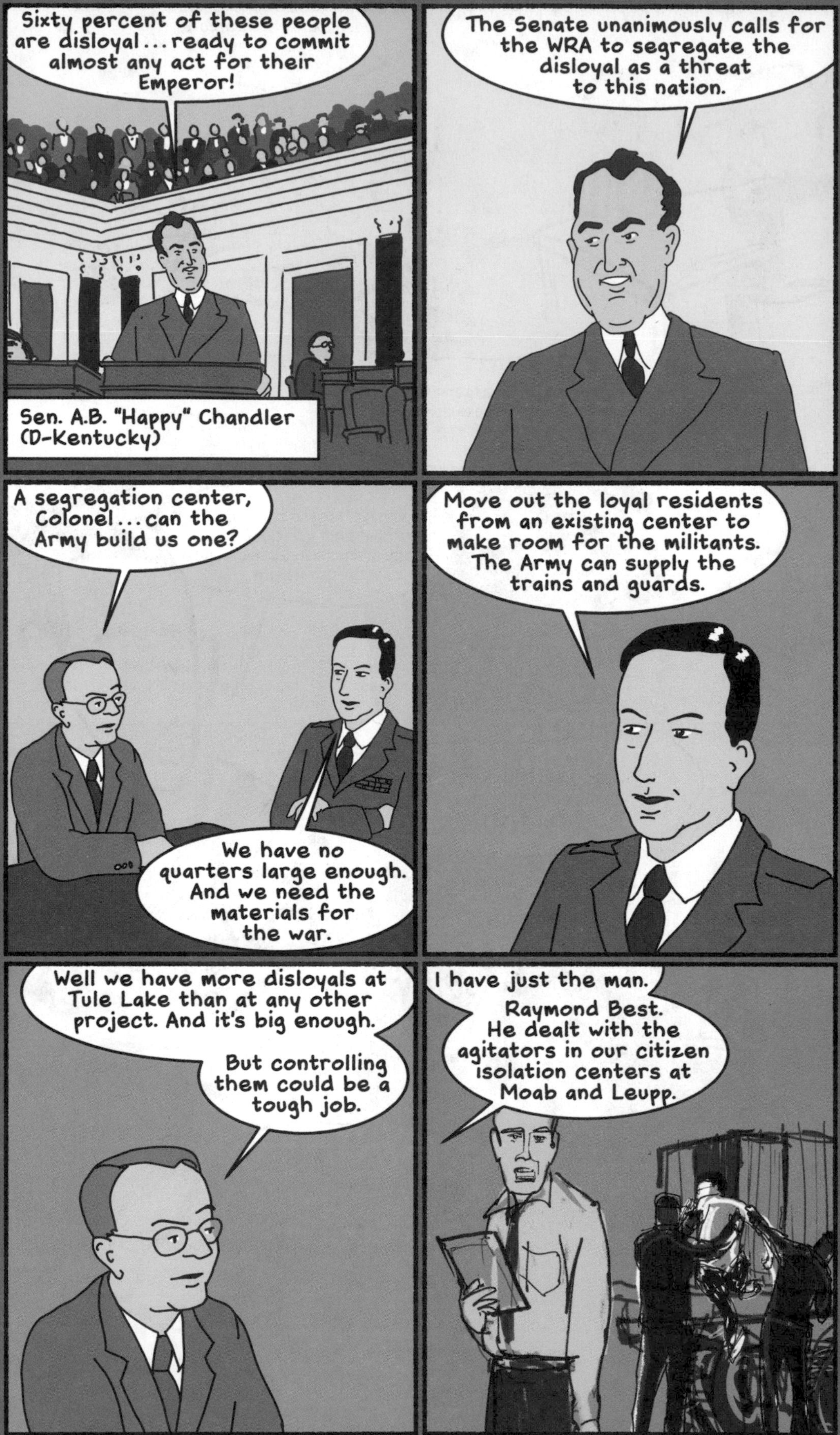
Sixty percent of these people are disloyal... ready to commit almost any act for their Emperor!
Sen. A.B. "Happy" Chandler (D-Kentucky)
The Senate unanimously calls for the WRA to segregate the disloyal as a threat to this nation.
A segregation center, Colonel... can the Army build us one?
We have no quarters large enough. And we need the materials for the war.
Move out the loyal residents from an existing center to make room for the militants. The Army can supply the trains and guards.
Well we have more disloyals at Tule Lake than at any other project. And it's big enough.
But controlling them could be a tough job.
I have just the man.
Raymond Best. He dealt with the agitators in our citizen isolation centers at Moab and Leupp.

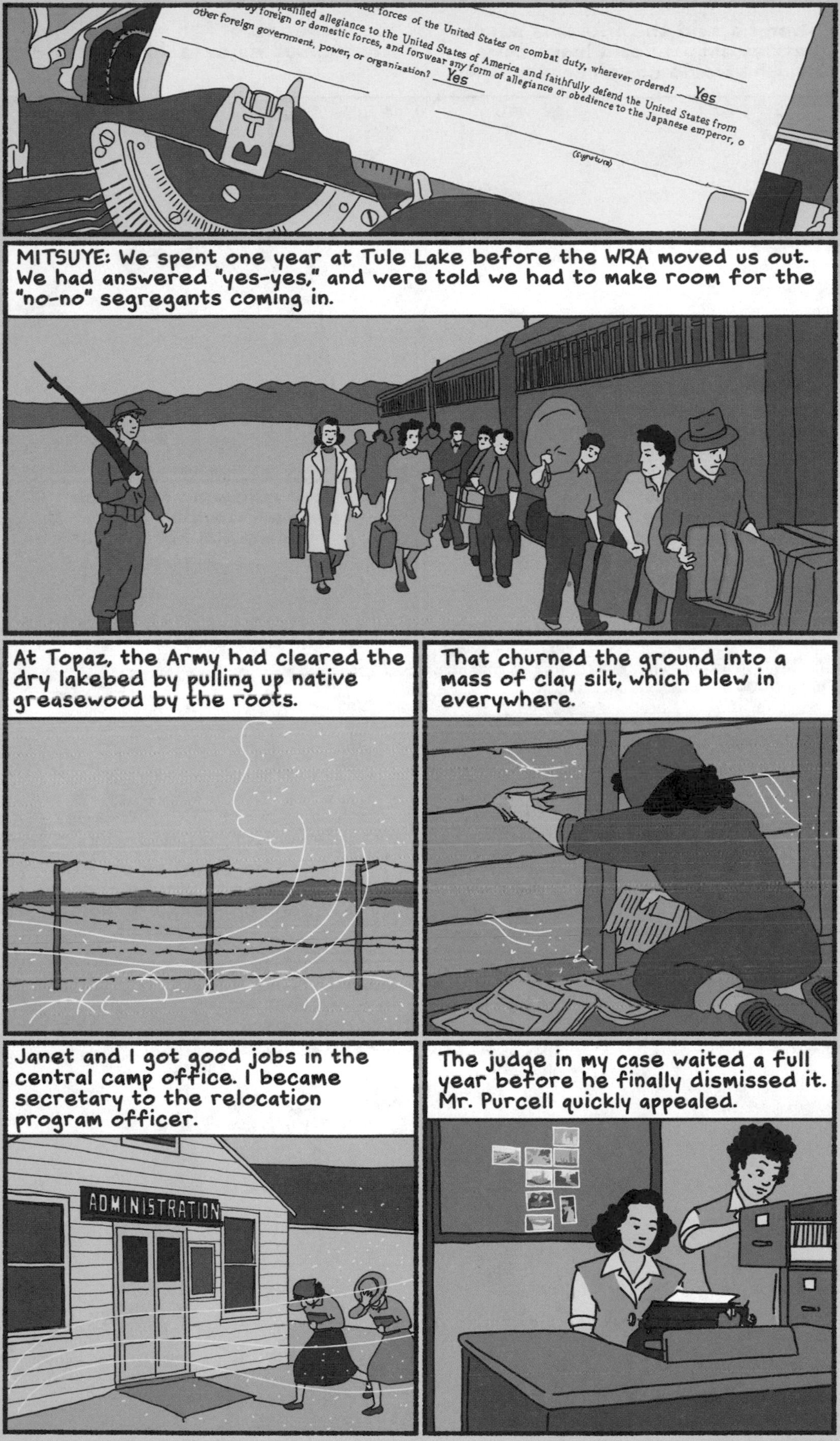

forces of the United States on combat duty, wherever ordered? Yes
allegiance to the United States of America and faithfully defend the United States from
foreign or domestic forces, and forswear any form of allegiance or obedience to the Japanese emperor, o
other foreign government, power, or organization? Yes
(signature)
MITSUYE: We spent one year at Tule Lake before the WRA moved us out. We had answered "yes-yes," and were told we had to make room for the "no-no" segregants coming in.
At Topaz, the Army had cleared the dry lakebed by pulling up native greasewood by the roots.
That churned the ground into a mass of clay silt, which blew in everywhere.
Janet and I got good jobs in the central camp office. I became secretary to the relocation program officer.
ADMINISTRATION
The judge in my case waited a full year before he finally dismissed it. Mr. Purcell quickly appealed.

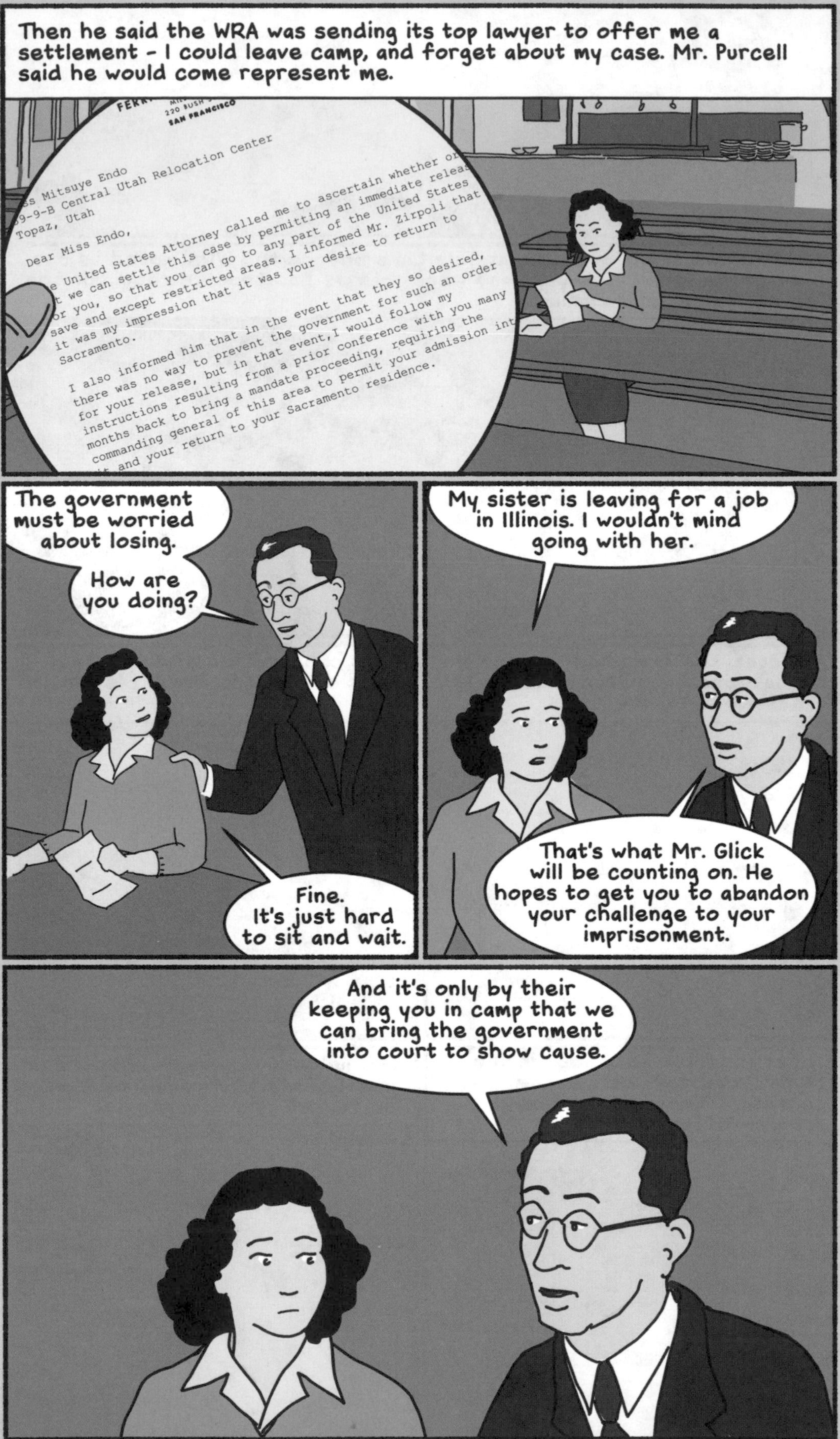
Then he said the WRA was sending its top lawyer to offer me a settlement - I could leave camp, and forget about my case. Mr. Purcell said he would come represent me.
220 BUSH
SAN FRANCISCO
ss Mitsuye Endo
39-9-B Central Utah Relocation Center
Topaz, Utah
Dear Miss Endo,
e United States Attorney called me to ascertain whether or
t we can settle this case by permitting an immediate releas
or you, so that you can go to any part of the United States
save and except restricted areas. I informed Mr. Zirpoli that
it was my impression that it was your desire to return to
Sacramento.
I also informed him that in the event that they so desired,
there was no way to prevent the government for such an order
for your release, but in that event, I would follow my
instructions resulting from a prior conference with you many
months back to bring a mandate proceeding, requiring the
commanding general of this area to permit your admission int
and your return to your Sacramento residence.
The government must be worried about losing.
How are you doing?
Fine. It's just hard to sit and wait.
My sister is leaving for a job in Illinois. I wouldn't mind going with her.
That's what Mr. Glick will be counting on. He hopes to get you to abandon your challenge to your imprisonment.
And it's only by their keeping you in camp that we can bring the government into court to show cause.

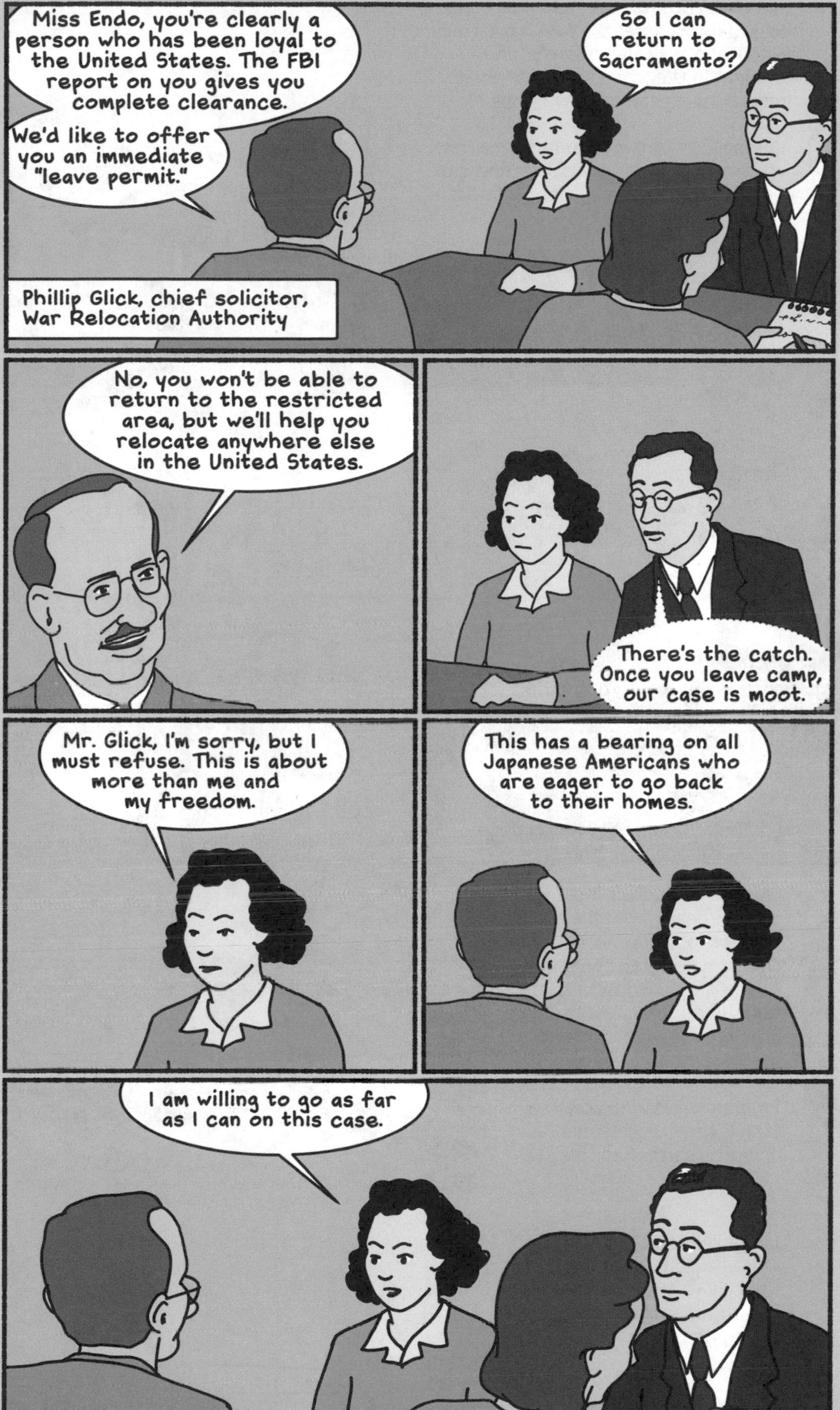

Miss Endo, you're clearly a person who has been loyal to the United States. The FBI report on you gives you complete clearance.
We'd like to offer you an immediate "leave permit."
So I can return to Sacramento?
Phillip Glick, chief solicitor, War Relocation Authority
No, you won't be able to return to the restricted area, but we'll help you relocate anywhere else in the United States.
There's the catch. Once you leave camp, our case is moot.
Mr. Glick, I'm sorry, but I must refuse. This is about more than me and my freedom.
This has a bearing on all Japanese Americans who are eager to go back to their homes.
I am willing to go as far as I can on this case.

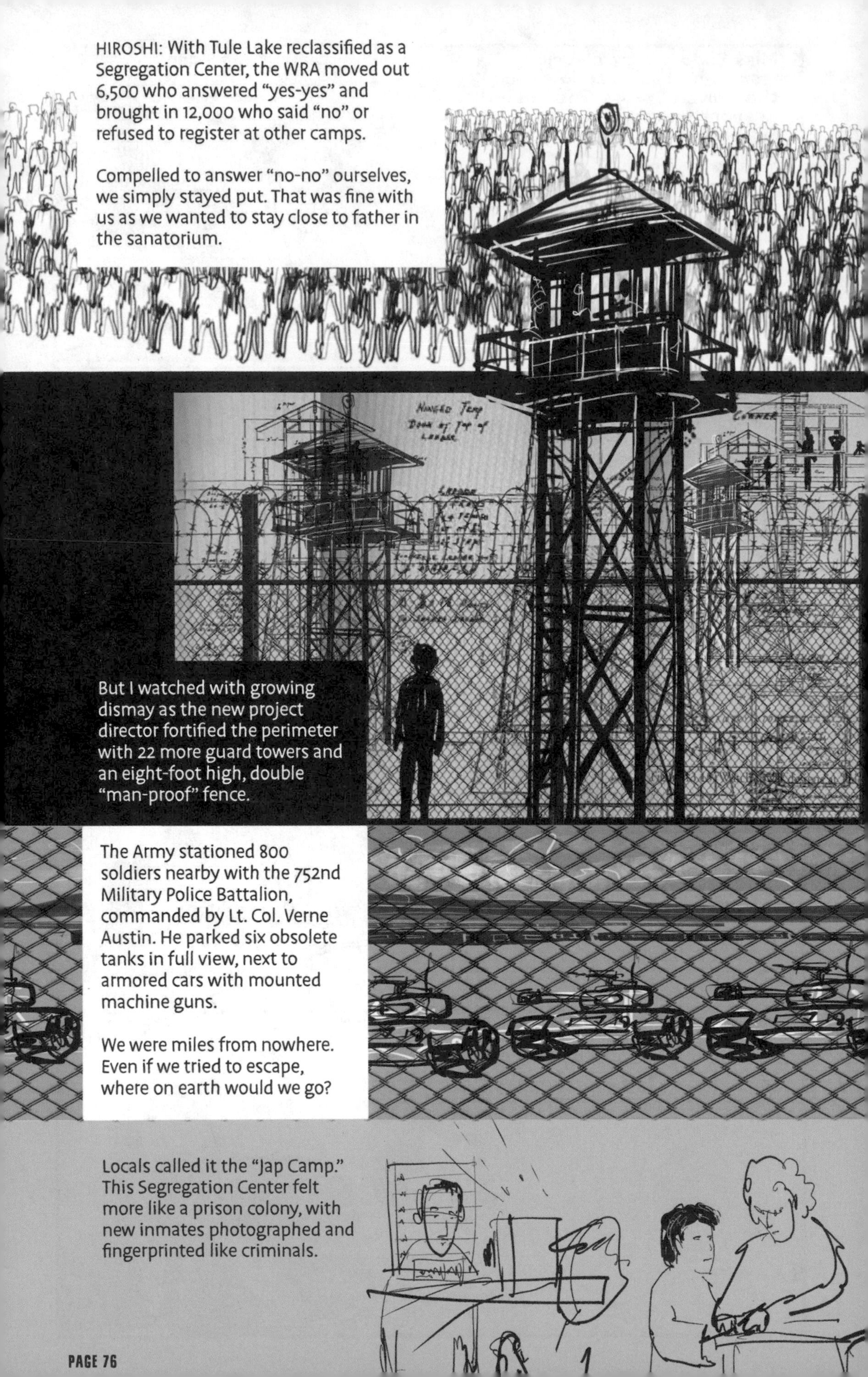
HIROSHI: With Tule Lake reclassified as a Segregation Center, the WRA moved out 6,500 who answered "yes-yes" and brought in 12,000 who said "no" or refused to register at other camps.
Compelled to answer "no-no" ourselves, we simply stayed put. That was fine with us as we wanted to stay close to father in the sanatorium.
But I watched with growing dismay as the new project director fortified the perimeter with 22 more guard towers and an eight-foot high, double "man-proof" fence.
The Army stationed 800 soldiers nearby with the 752nd Military Police Battalion, commanded by Lt. Col. Verne Austin. He parked six obsolete tanks in full view, next to armored cars with mounted machine guns.
We were miles from nowhere. Even if we tried to escape, where on earth would we go?
Locals called it the "Jap Camp." This Segregation Center felt more like a prison colony, with new inmates photographed and fingerprinted like criminals.

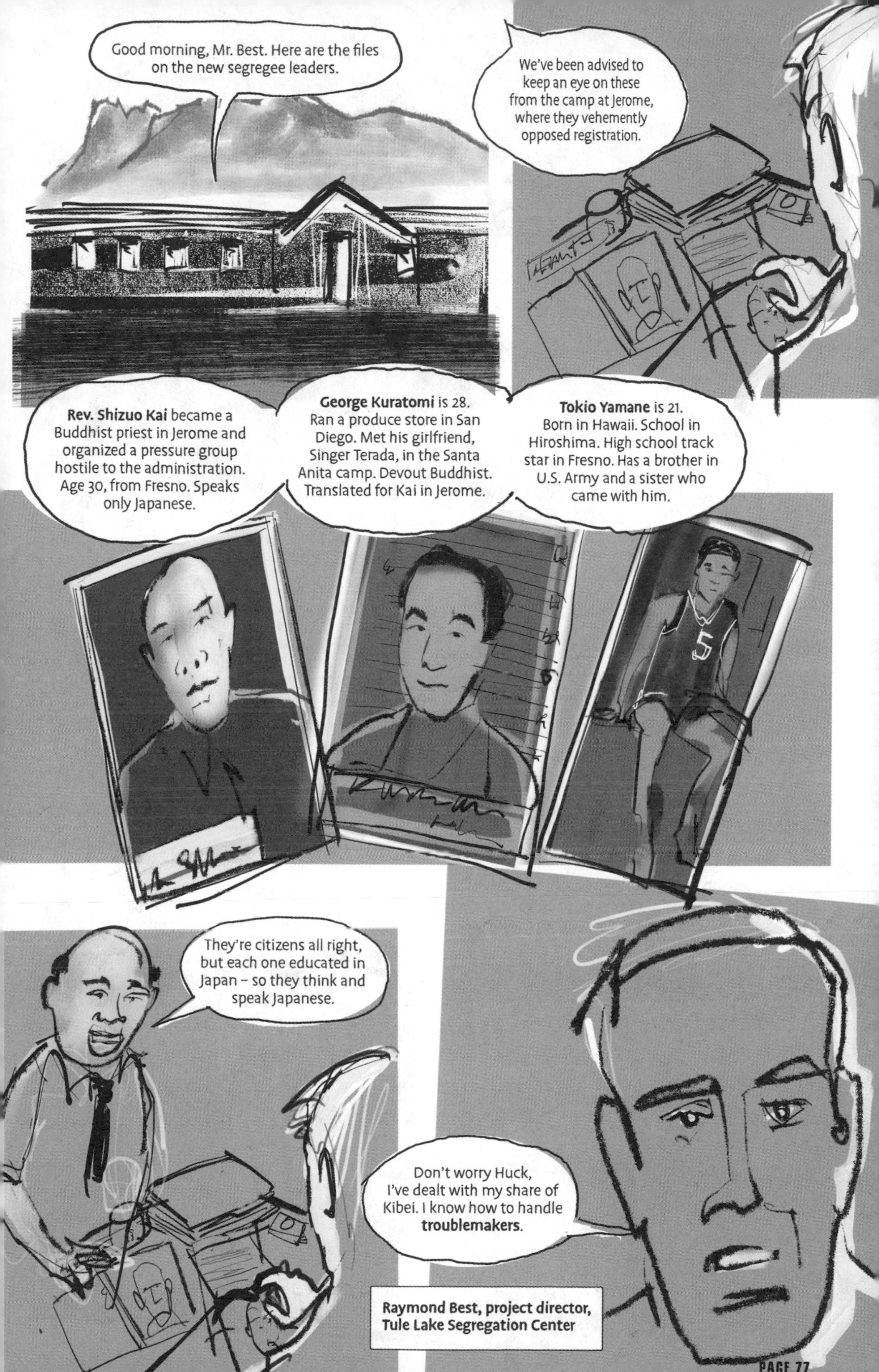

Good morning, Mr. Best. Here are the files on the new segregee leaders.
We've been advised to keep an eye on these from the camp at Jerome, where they vehemently opposed registration.
Rev. Shizuo Kai became a Buddhist priest in Jerome and organized a pressure group hostile to the administration. Age 30, from Fresno. Speaks only Japanese.
George Kuratomi is 28. Ran a produce store in San Diego. Met his girlfriend, Singer Terada, in the Santa Anita camp. Devout Buddhist. Translated for Kai in Jerome.
Tokio Yamane is 21. Born in Hawaii. School in Hiroshima. High school track star in Fresno. Has a brother in U.S. Army and a sister who came with him.
They're citizens all right, but each one educated in Japan – so they think and speak Japanese.
Don't worry Huck, I've dealt with my share of Kibei. I know how to handle troublemakers.
Raymond Best, project director, Tule Lake Segregation Center

The newcomers from Jerome came in and acted like they owned the place.

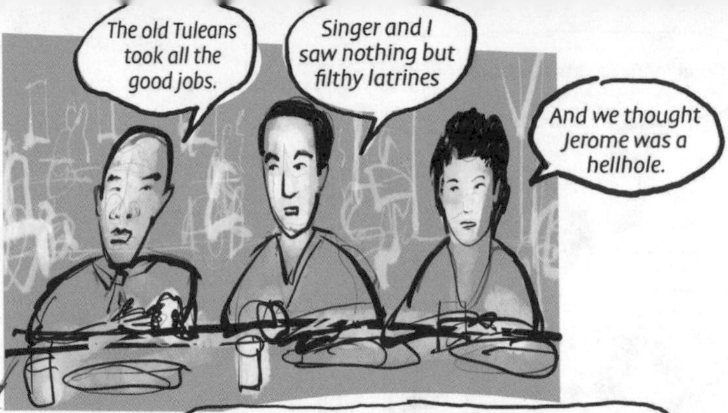
The old Tuleans took all the good jobs.
Singer and I saw nothing but filthy latrines
And we thought Jerome was a hellhole.

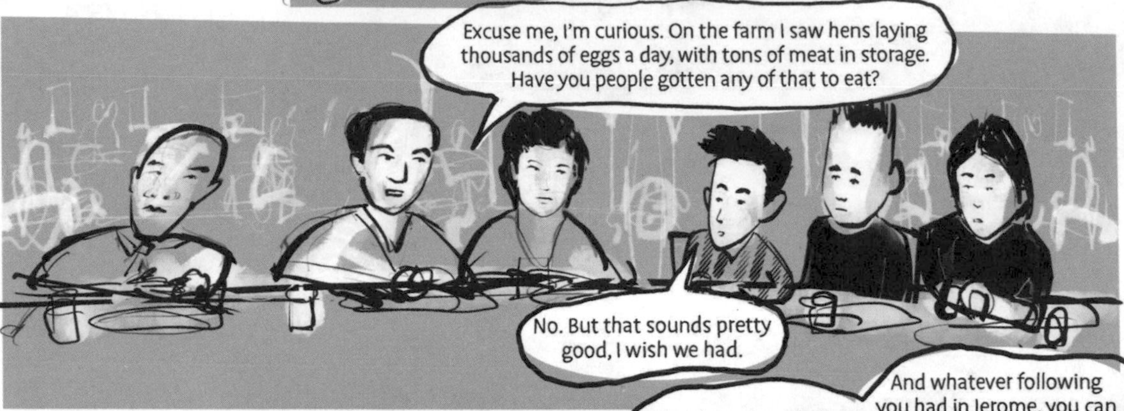
Excuse me, I'm curious. On the farm I saw hens laying thousands of eggs a day, with tons of meat in storage. Have you people gotten any of that to eat?
No. But that sounds pretty good, I wish we had.

We soon learned Kuratomi and Kai had no fear of confronting Mr. Best.

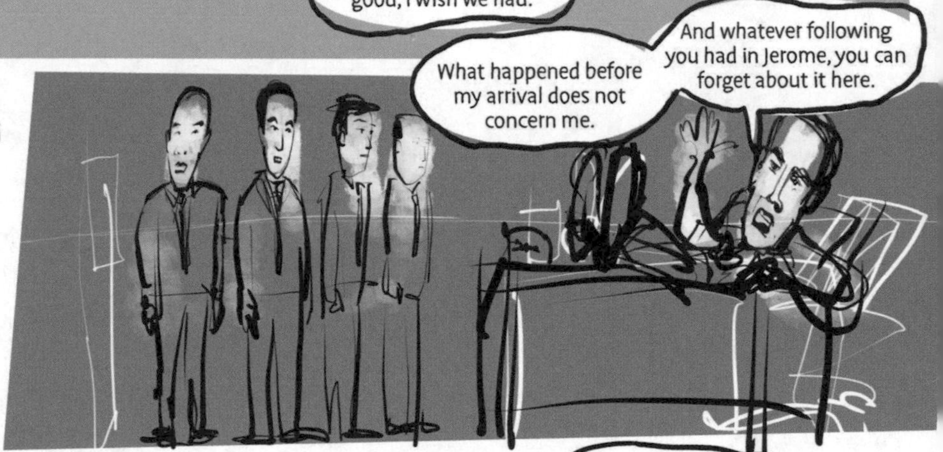
What happened before my arrival does not concern me.
And whatever following you had in Jerome, you can forget about it here.

I wasn't much for dancing, but Alice showed me how, and the parties gave us a way to pass the time. Crusaders among the new arrivals, like Tokio Yamane, saw it differently.

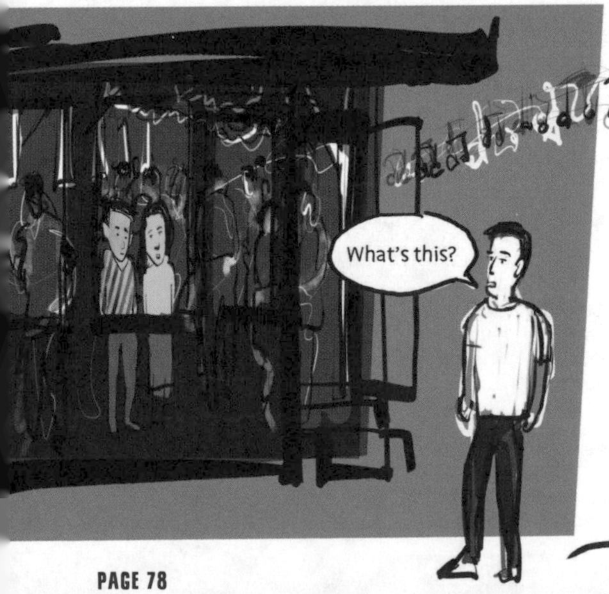
What's this?

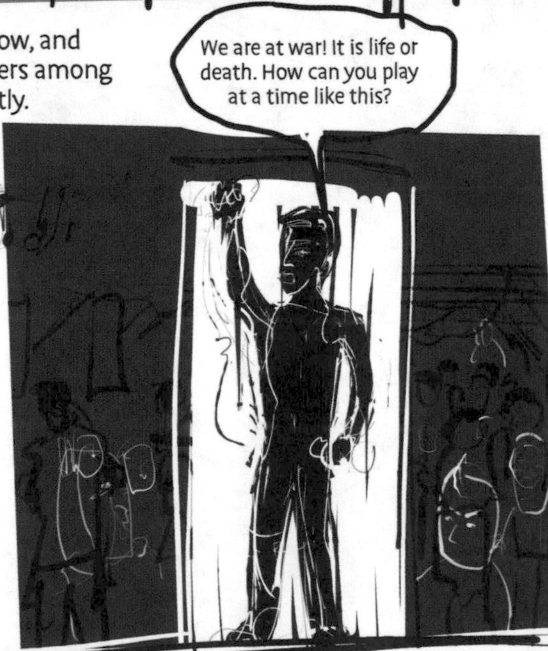
We are at war! It is life or death. How can you play at a time like this?

That was the last dance we had at Tule Lake.

Vegetables in the field were ready for harvest when a farm truck driven by a teenager flipped over and killed one worker. All 800 farmhands in camp refused to work.

The death of Mr. Kashima came to symbolize the injustice we all felt.

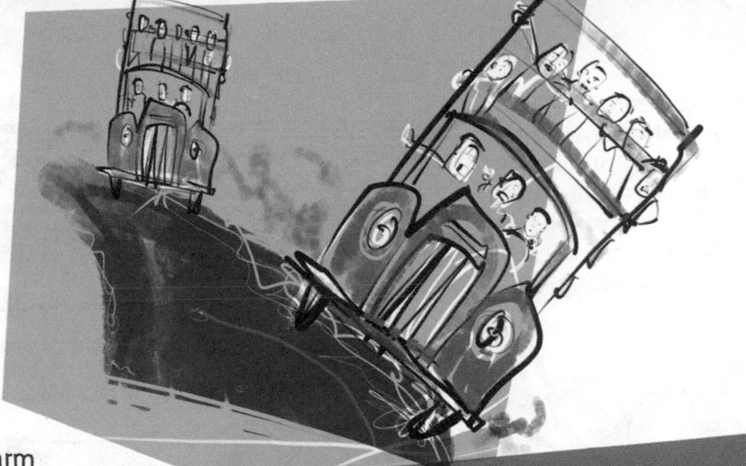

Mr. Best denied permission for a funeral ceremony. The farm workers held one anyway in the firebreak and thousands attended, including me. But we couldn't hear anything after Best turned off power to the entire camp just to kill the loudspeakers.

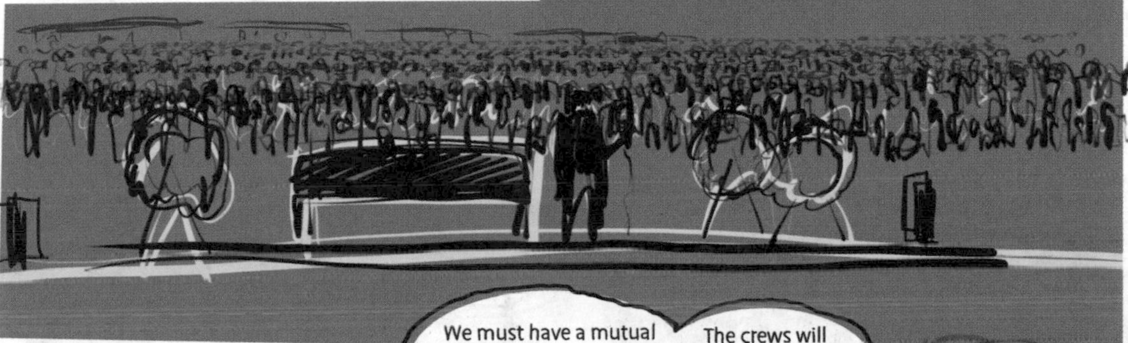

To demand better living and working conditions, each block elected one member to form a Representative Body, the Daihyo Sha Kai. George Kuratomi spoke for its Negotiating Committee.

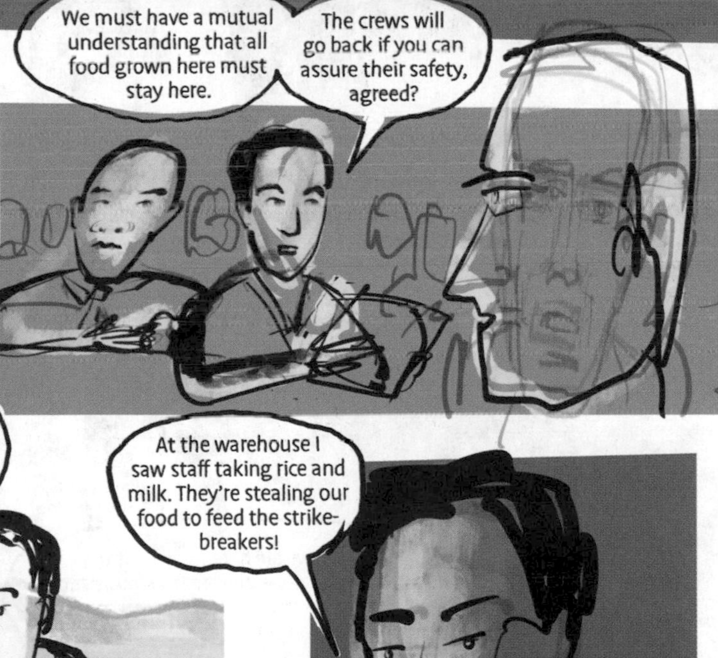
We must have a mutual understanding that all food grown here must stay here.
The crews will go back if you can assure their safety, agreed?

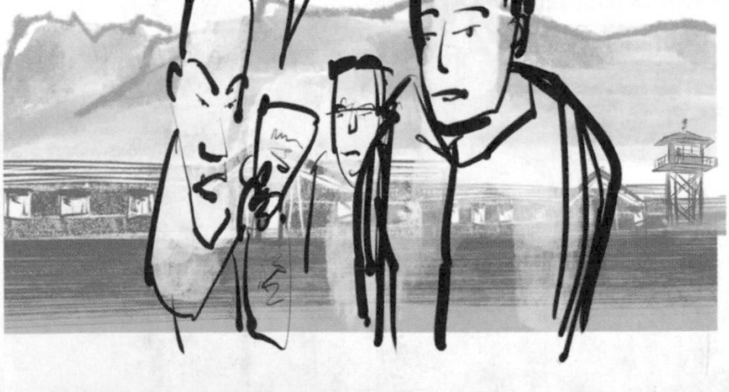
Best double-crossed us! He's bringing in strikebreakers from Poston and Topaz. Our people get $16 a month. These scabs are getting $1 an hour!

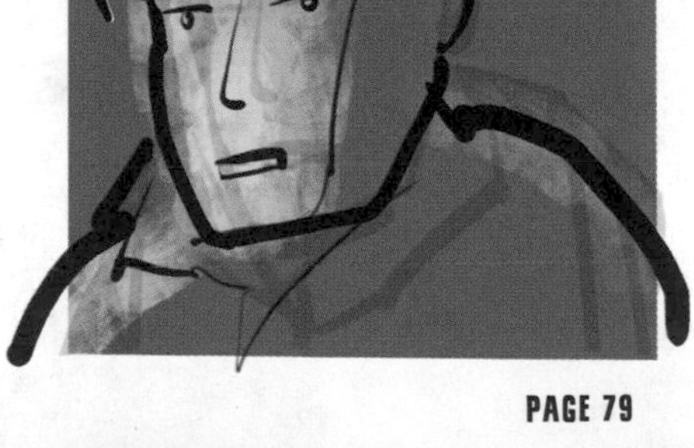
At the warehouse I saw staff taking rice and milk. They're stealing our food to feed the strike-breakers!

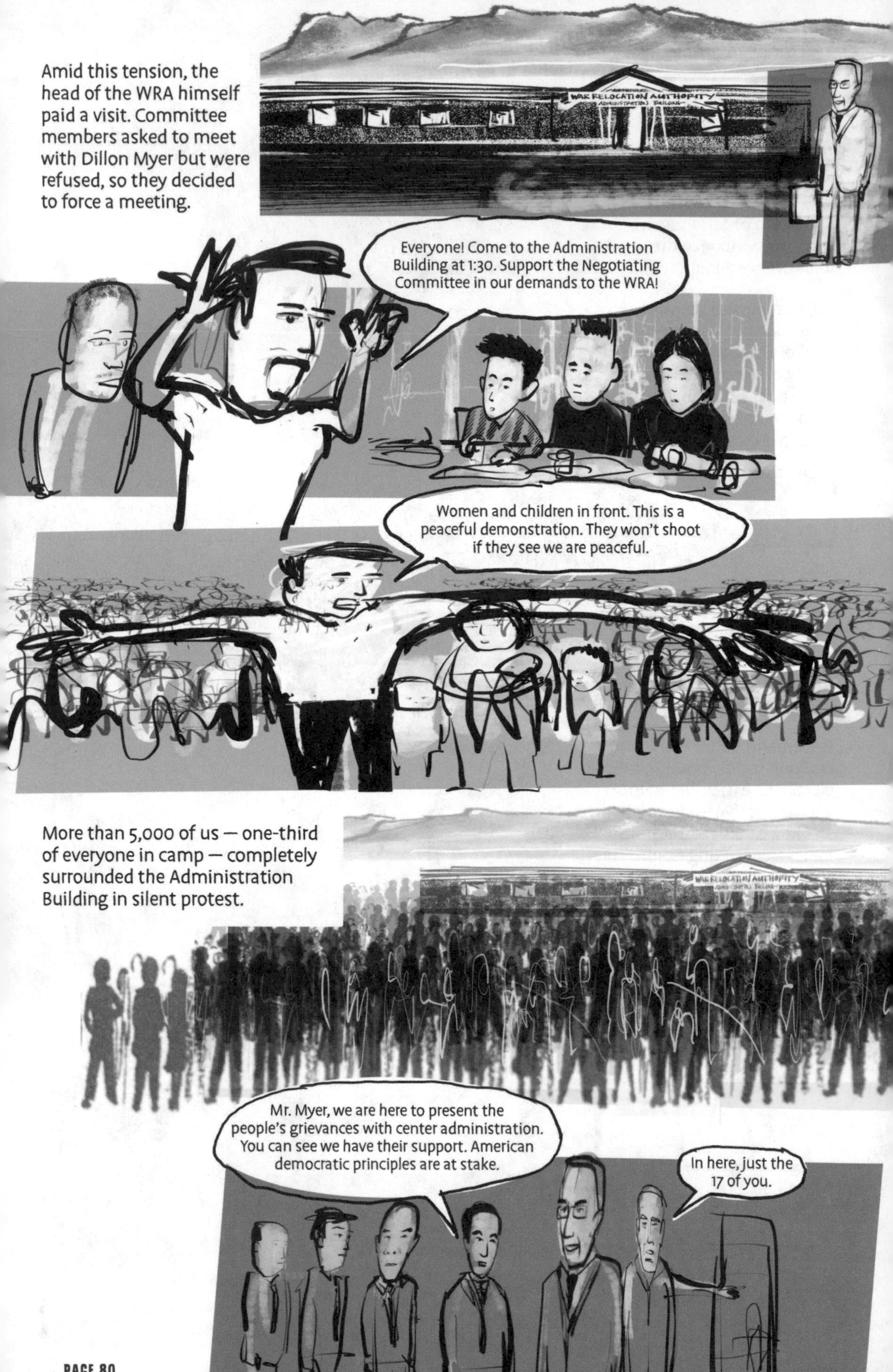
Amid this tension, the head of the WRA himself paid a visit. Committee members asked to meet with Dillon Myer but were refused, so they decided to force a meeting.
WAR RELOCATION AUTHORITY
Everyone! Come to the Administration Building at 1:30. Support the Negotiating Committee in our demands to the WRA!
Women and children in front. This is a peaceful demonstration. They won't shoot if they see we are peaceful.
More than 5,000 of us — one-third of everyone in camp — completely surrounded the Administration Building in silent protest.
WAR RELOCATION AUTHORITY
Mr. Myer, we are here to present the people's grievances with center administration. You can see we have their support. American democratic principles are at stake.
In here, just the 17 of you.

WRA workers inside the building were terrified at the size of the crowd.

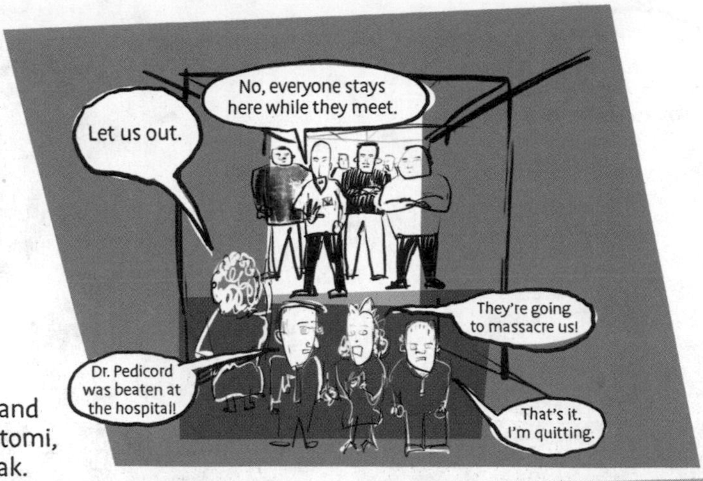
Let us out.
No, everyone stays here while they meet.
They're going to massacre us!
Dr. Pedicord was beaten at the hospital!
That's it. I'm quitting.

I stood outside with everyone and waited. After three hours, Kuratomi, Myer, and Kai came out to speak. Myer promised to investigate our complaints. I didn't expect what came next.

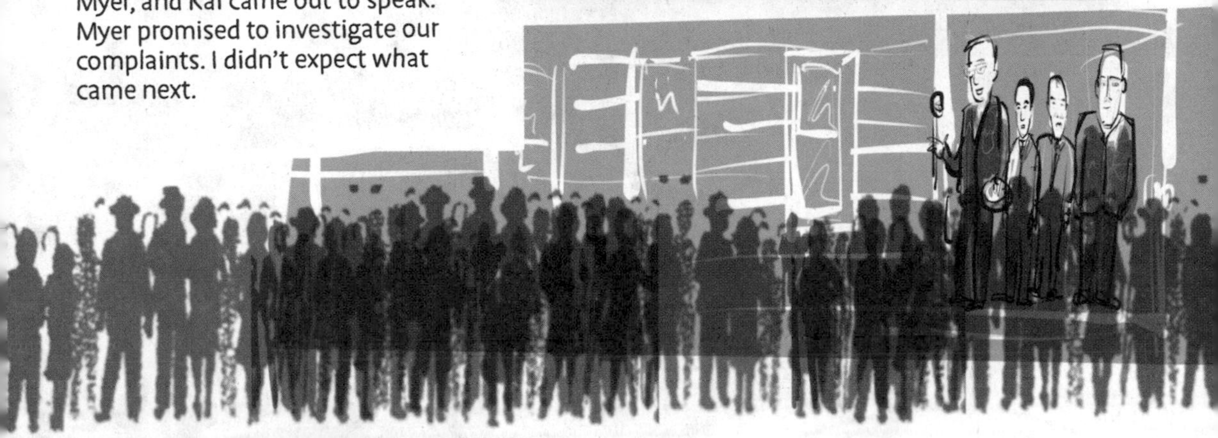

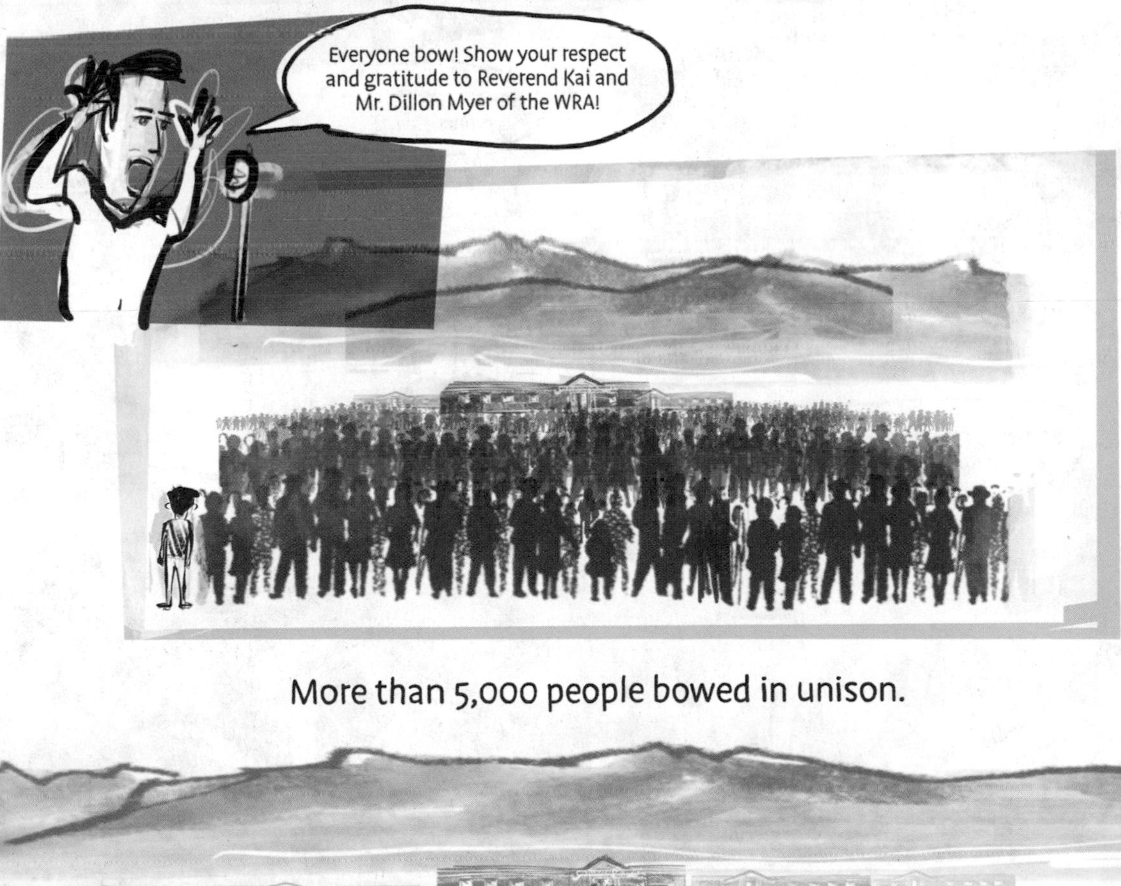
Everyone bow! Show your respect and gratitude to Reverend Kai and Mr. Dillon Myer of the WRA!

More than 5,000 people bowed in unison.

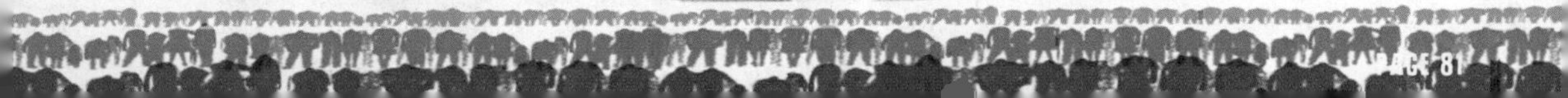

Kobayashi, we insisted in there that the food is for our people, not the strikebreakers. Set up a watch at night, just in case.

Huck, better have your boys start nightly patrols.

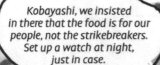

Three nights later, the Negotiating Committee was meeting after dark when trucks were spotted driving away from the warehouse.

Trucks are taking our food to the strikebreakers!

Yamane, you're a fast runner. Go see.

Best won't recognize our committee unless we elect permanent officers. Let's keep going ...

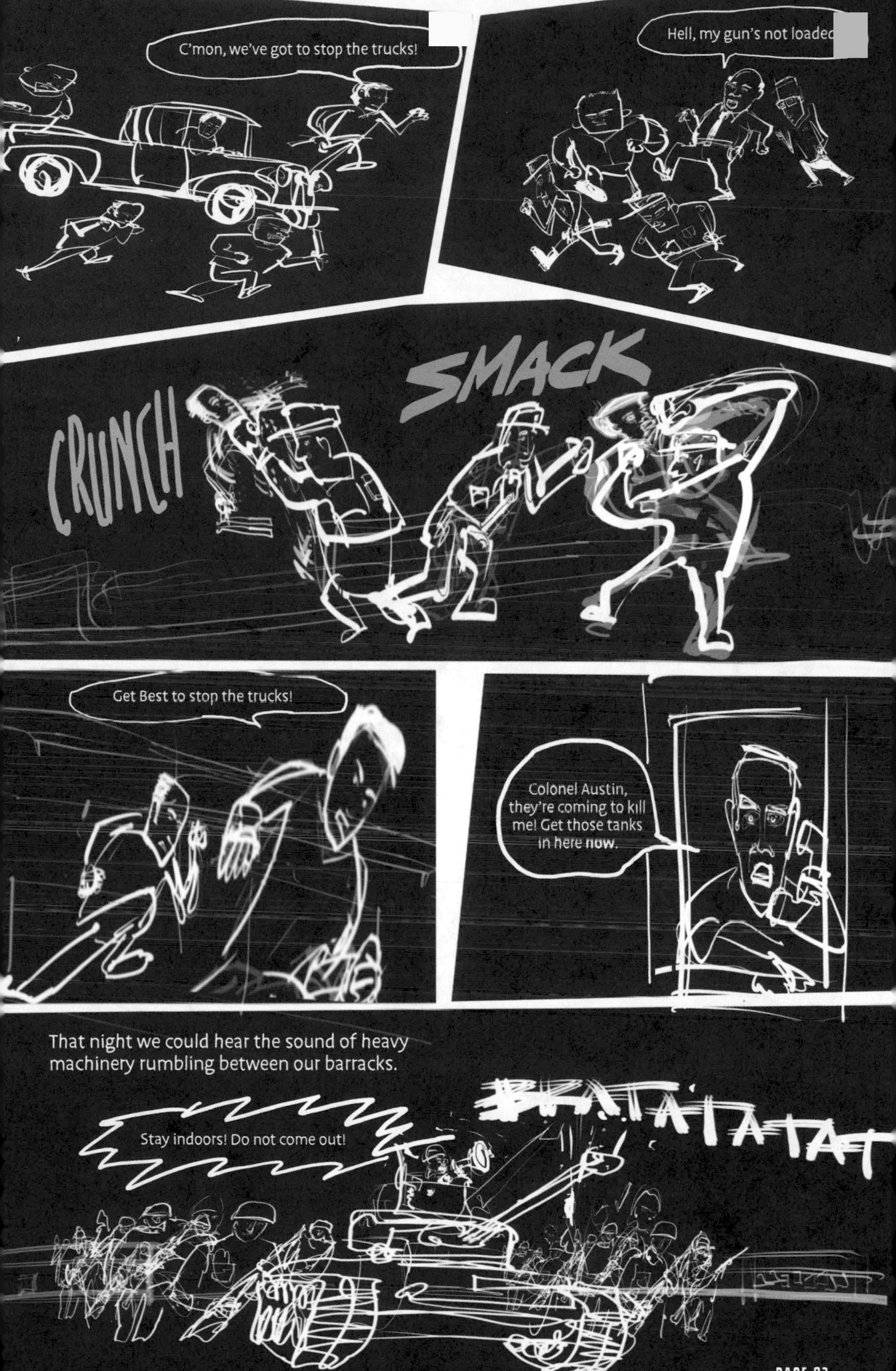
C'mon, we've got to stop the trucks!
Hell, my gun's not loaded
SMACK
CRUNCH
Get Best to stop the trucks!
Colonel Austin, they're coming to kill me! Get those tanks in here **now**.
That night we could hear the sound of heavy machinery rumbling between our barracks.
Stay indoors! Do not come out!
TATATAT

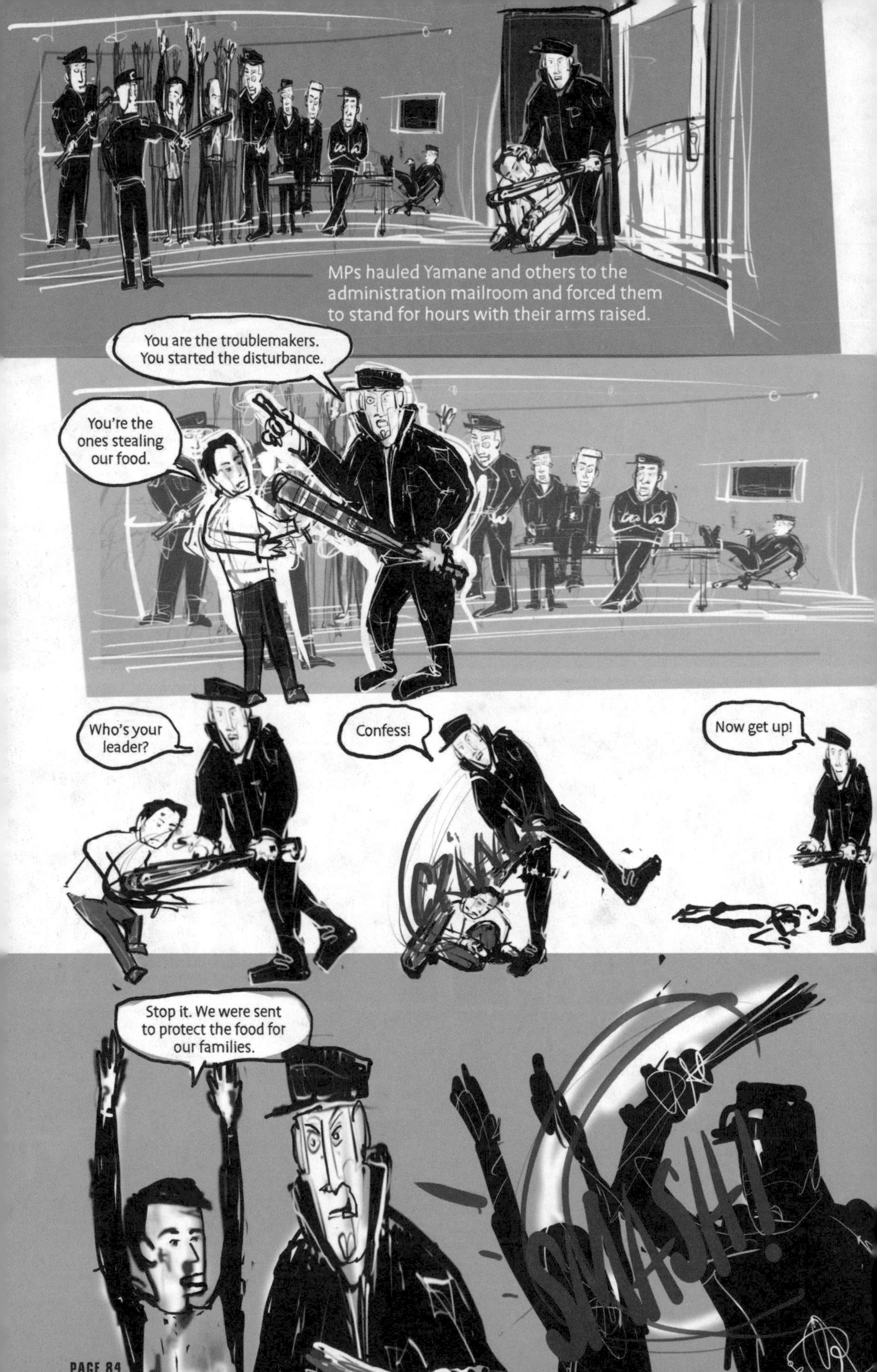
MPs hauled Yamane and others to the administration mailroom and forced them to stand for hours with their arms raised.
You are the troublemakers. You started the disturbance.
You're the ones stealing our food.
Who's your leader?
Confess!
Now get up!
Stop it. We were sent to protect the food for our families.
SMASH!

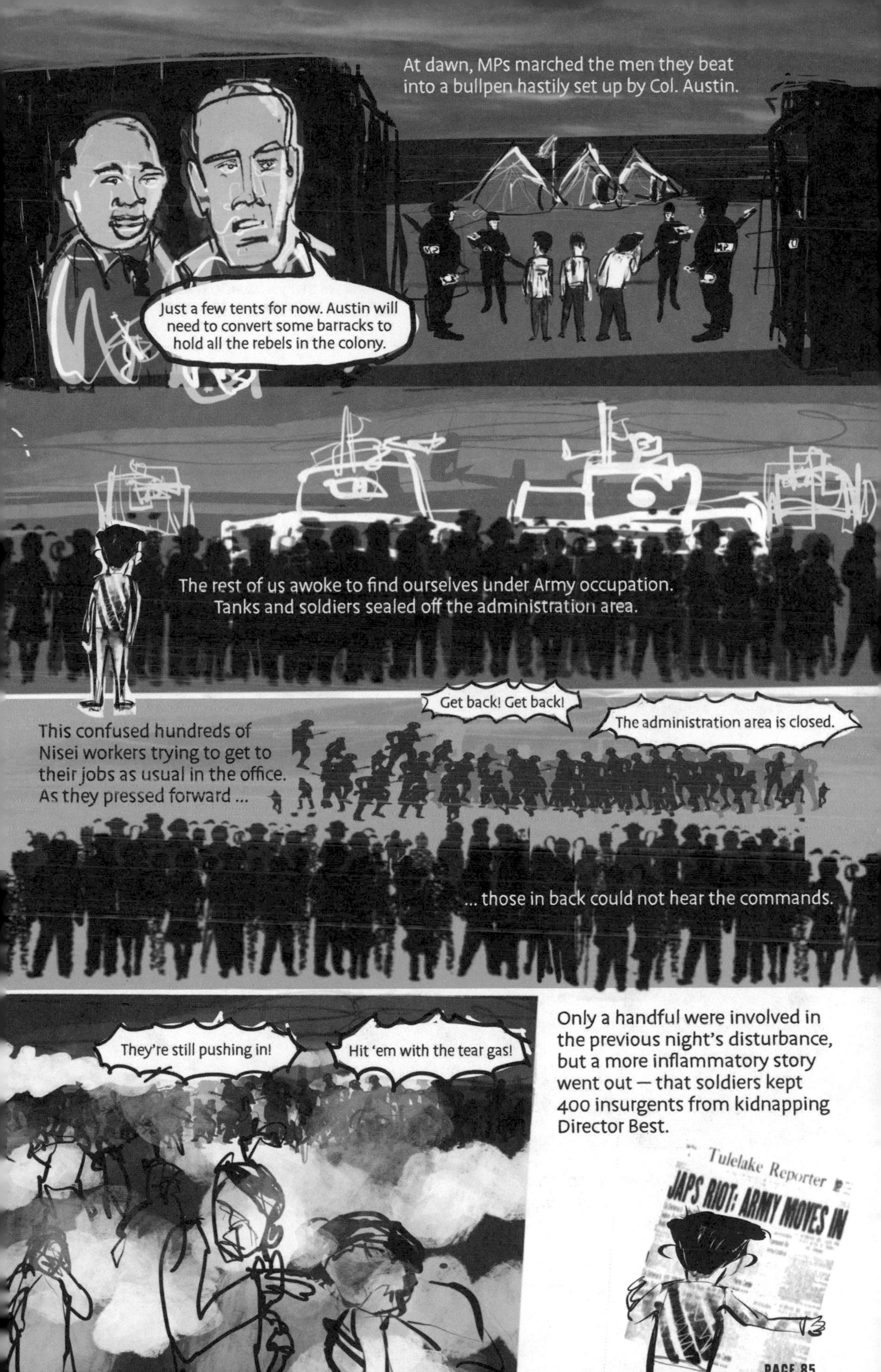

At dawn, MPs marched the men they beat into a bullpen hastily set up by Col. Austin.
Just a few tents for now. Austin will need to convert some barracks to hold all the rebels in the colony.
MP
MP
The rest of us awoke to find ourselves under Army occupation. Tanks and soldiers sealed off the administration area.
This confused hundreds of Nisei workers trying to get to their jobs as usual in the office. As they pressed forward ...
Get back! Get back!
The administration area is closed.
... those in back could not hear the commands.
They're still pushing in!
Hit 'em with the tear gas!
Only a handful were involved in the previous night's disturbance, but a more inflammatory story went out — that soldiers kept 400 insurgents from kidnapping Director Best.
Tulelake Reporter
JAPS RIOT; ARMY MOVES IN

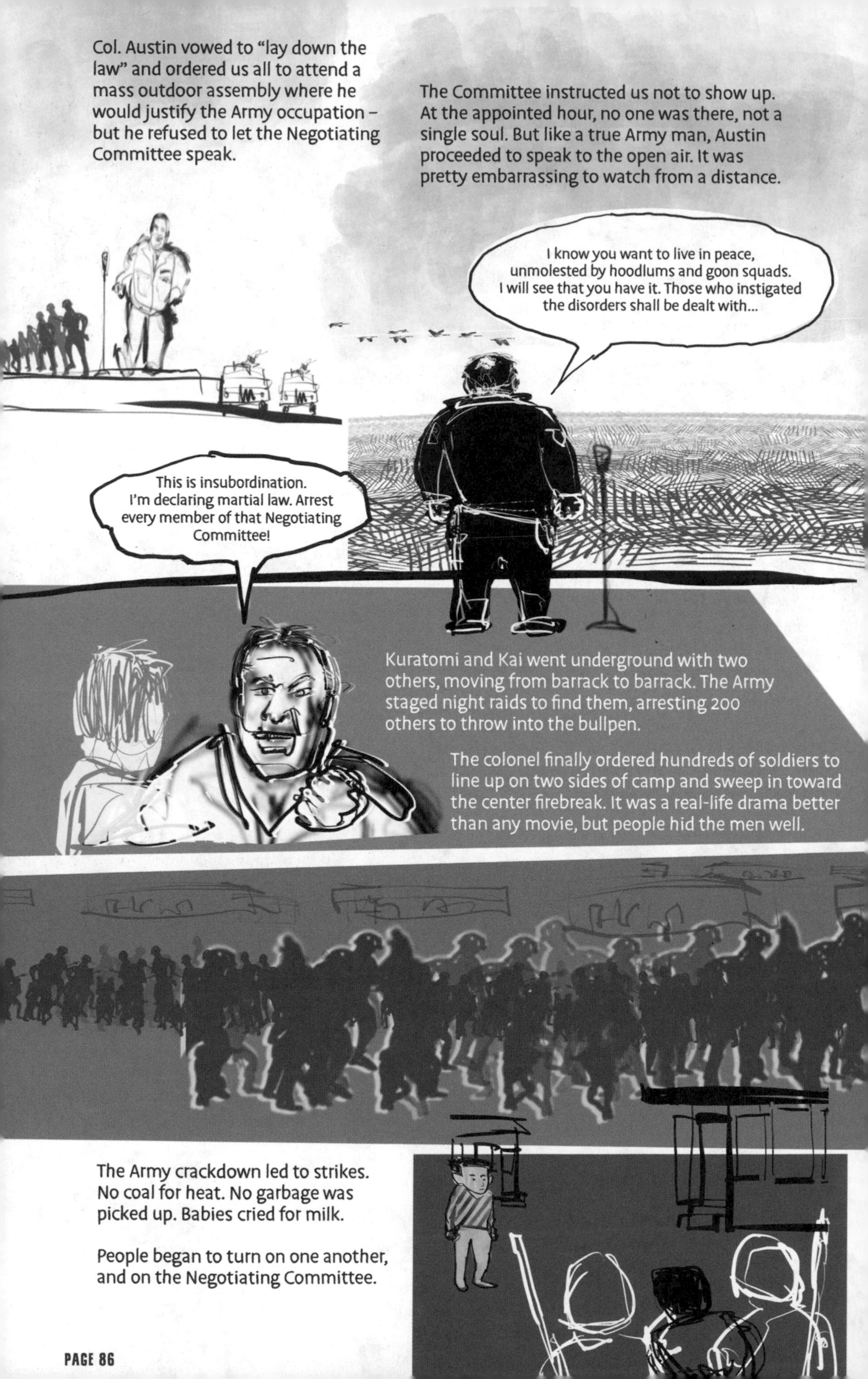
Col. Austin vowed to "lay down the law" and ordered us all to attend a mass outdoor assembly where he would justify the Army occupation – but he refused to let the Negotiating Committee speak.
The Committee instructed us not to show up. At the appointed hour, no one was there, not a single soul. But like a true Army man, Austin proceeded to speak to the open air. It was pretty embarrassing to watch from a distance.
I know you want to live in peace, unmolested by hoodlums and goon squads. I will see that you have it. Those who instigated the disorders shall be dealt with...
This is insubordination. I'm declaring martial law. Arrest every member of that Negotiating Committee!
Kuratomi and Kai went underground with two others, moving from barrack to barrack. The Army staged night raids to find them, arresting 200 others to throw into the bullpen.
The colonel finally ordered hundreds of soldiers to line up on two sides of camp and sweep in toward the center firebreak. It was a real-life drama better than any movie, but people hid the men well.
The Army crackdown led to strikes. No coal for heat. No garbage was picked up. Babies cried for milk.
People began to turn on one another, and on the Negotiating Committee.

Seeing no end to it, the leaders arranged for a meeting of the *Daihyo Sha Kai* where they could surrender with honor. As they entered, they were greeted with thunderous applause.

We surrender only to the FBI, with a complete record of our activities so it can investigate the WRA for neglect, incompetence, and corruption.

We demand the wholesale resignation of WRA administrators, and we hereby appoint an Acting Negotiating Committee to carry on the demands of the people during our absence.

All injustices done since the disturbance are the responsibility of the Army. Together with the WRA they have created an international incident, and the Japanese government is well aware of what happened here.

We are being sent into confinement for disturbing the peace of the center whose very peace we were striving to maintain. Ironic, isn't it?

MPs marched the leaders into the Army bullpen to join the others. Kuratomi surrendered knowing his fiancée was expecting their baby.

Austin immediately refused to recognize the Acting Committee, and the camp dissolved into competing factions. Rumors spread and people were ready to believe them all ...

... including a family friend, Mr. Yoshida, who secretly listened to shortwave broadcasts from Radio Tokyo.

"... heed not the lies of your traitorous countrymen, the day of glory is close at hand. The victorious government will send ships to return the true Japanese to an island of their own ..."

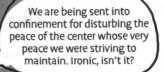

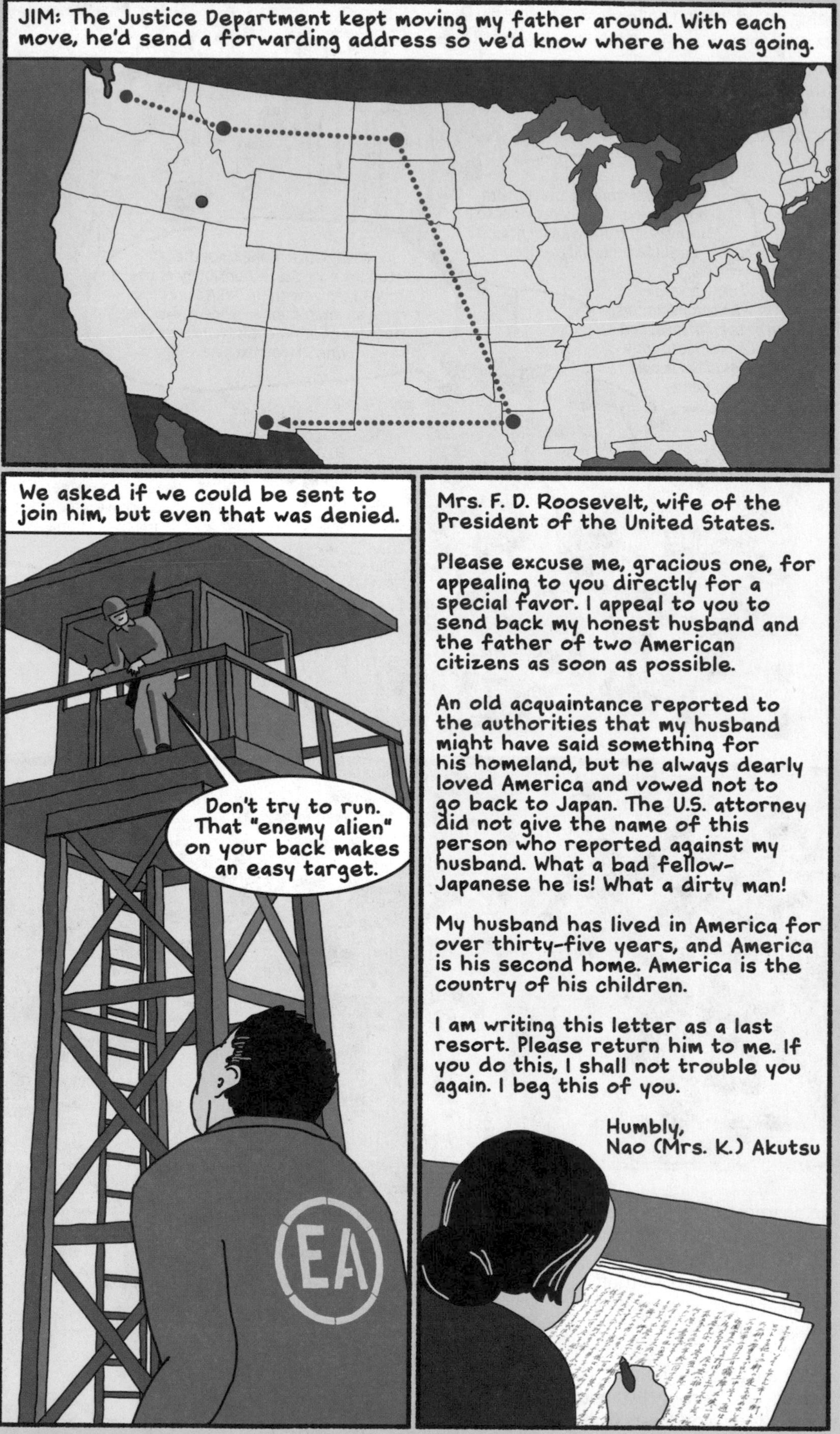

JIM: The Justice Department kept moving my father around. With each move, he'd send a forwarding address so we'd know where he was going.

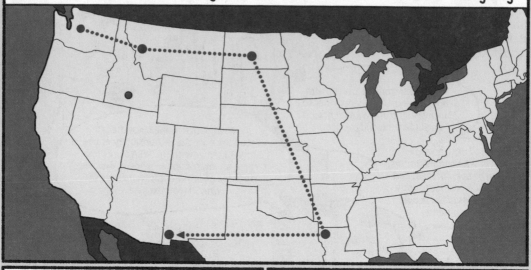

We asked if we could be sent to join him, but even that was denied.

Don't try to run. That "enemy alien" on your back makes an easy target.

Mrs. F. D. Roosevelt, wife of the President of the United States.

Please excuse me, gracious one, for appealing to you directly for a special favor. I appeal to you to send back my honest husband and the father of two American citizens as soon as possible.

An old acquaintance reported to the authorities that my husband might have said something for his homeland, but he always dearly loved America and vowed not to go back to Japan. The U.S. attorney did not give the name of this person who reported against my husband. What a bad fellow-Japanese he is! What a dirty man!

My husband has lived in America for over thirty-five years, and America is his second home. America is the country of his children.

I am writing this letter as a last resort. Please return him to me. If you do this, I shall not trouble you again. I beg this of you.

Humbly,
Nao (Mrs. K.) Akutsu

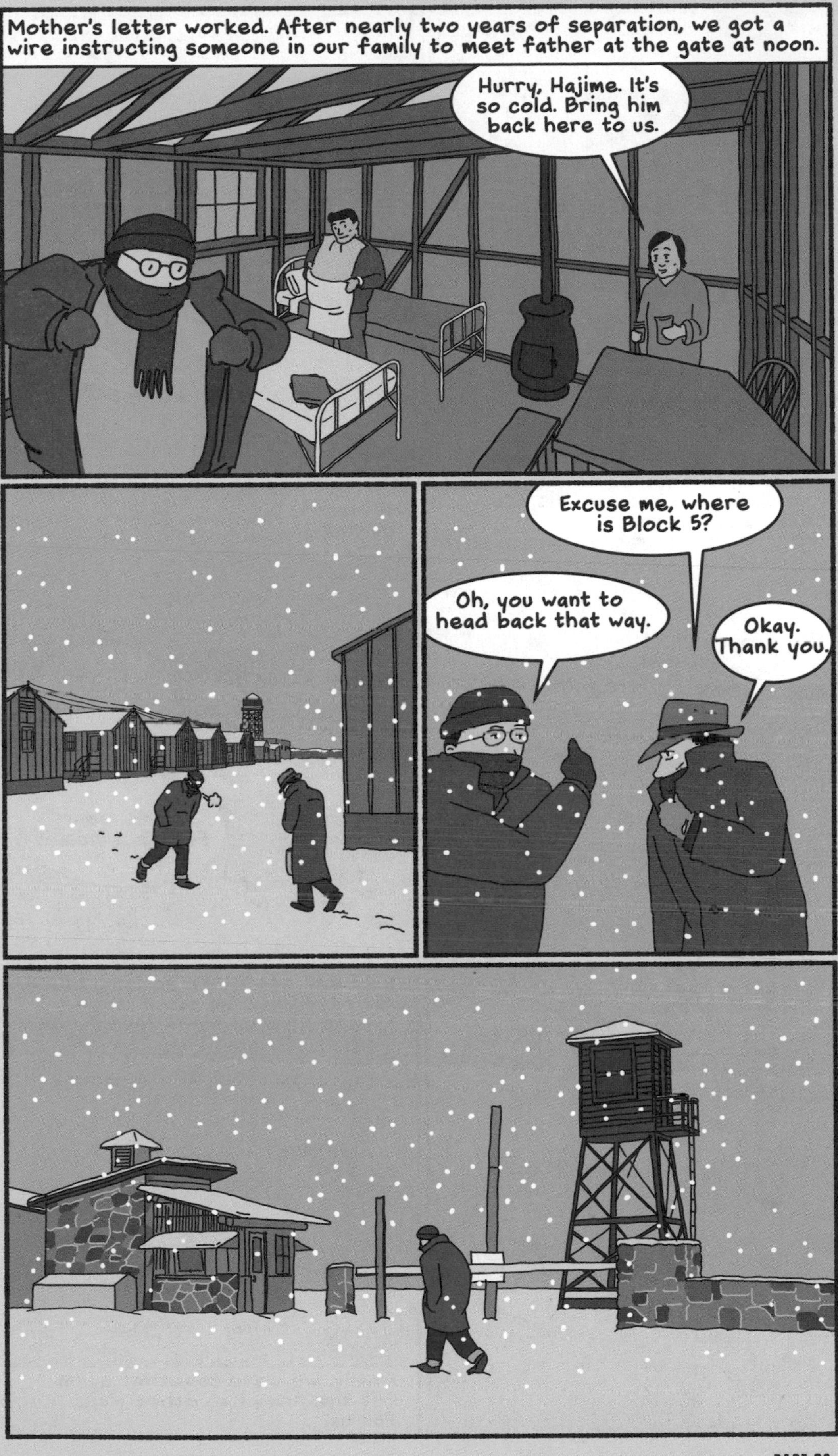
Mother's letter worked. After nearly two years of separation, we got a wire instructing someone in our family to meet father at the gate at noon.
Hurry, Hajime. It's so cold. Bring him back here to us.
Excuse me, where is Block 5?
Oh, you want to head back that way.
Okay. Thank you.

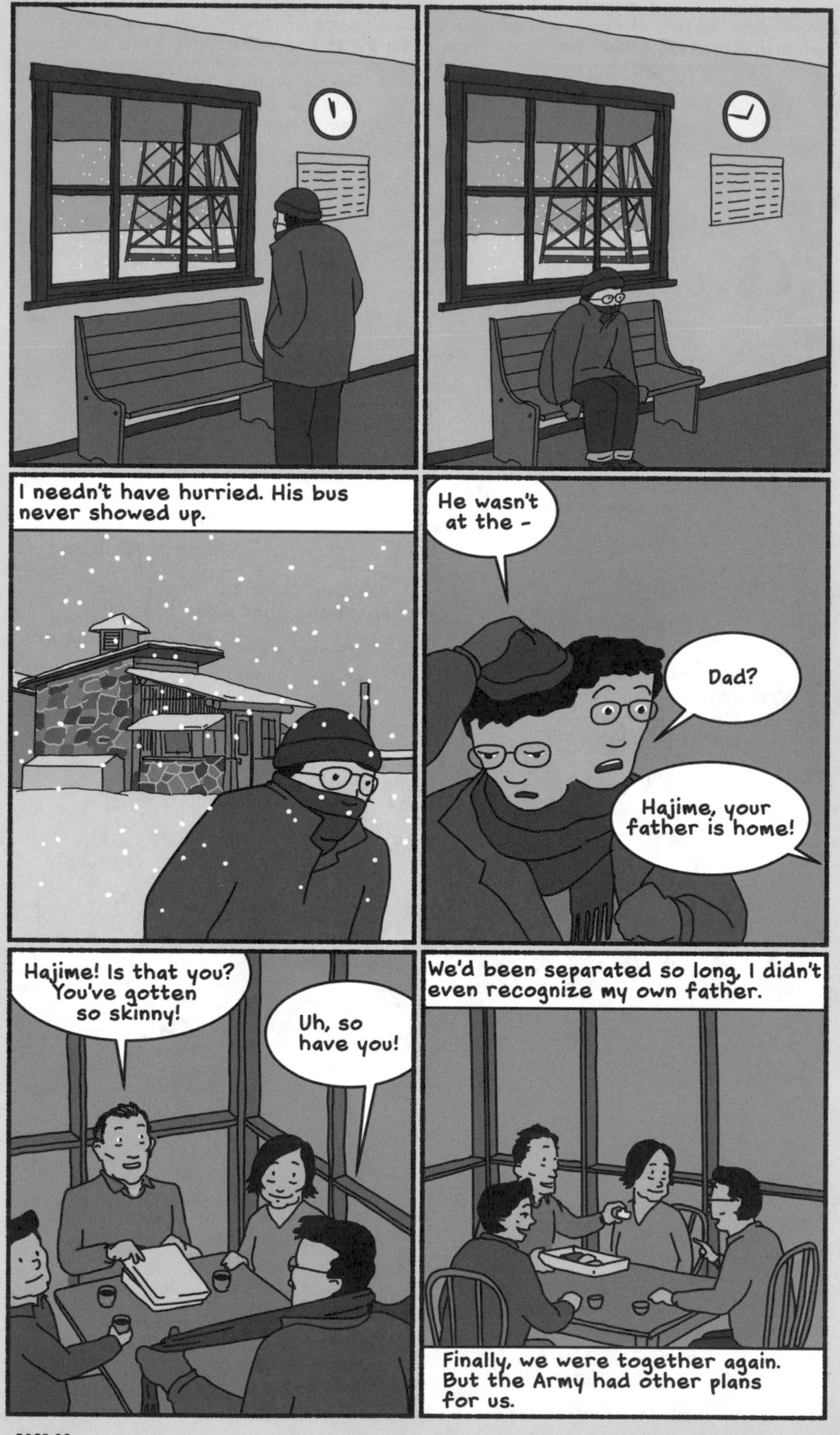
I needn't have hurried. His bus never showed up.
He wasn't at the -
Dad?
Hajime, your father is home!
Hajime! Is that you? You've gotten so skinny!
Uh, so have you!
We'd been separated so long, I didn't even recognize my own father.
Finally, we were together again. But the Army had other plans for us.

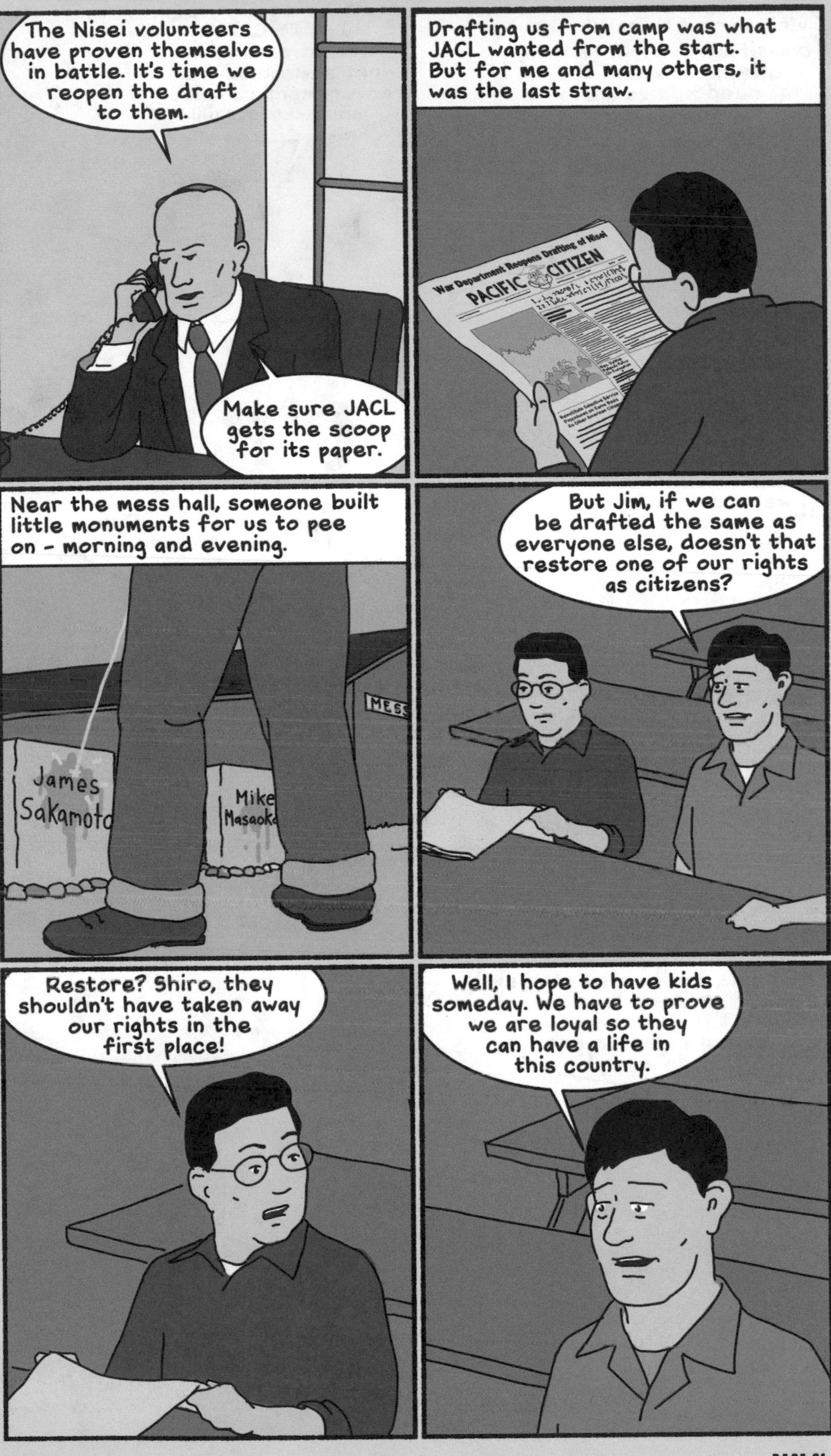
The Nisei volunteers have proven themselves in battle. It's time we reopen the draft to them.
Make sure JACL gets the scoop for its paper.
Drafting us from camp was what JACL wanted from the start. But for me and many others, it was the last straw.
War Department Reopens Drafting of Nisei
PACIFIC CITIZEN
Near the mess hall, someone built little monuments for us to pee on - morning and evening.
MESS
James Sakamoto
Mike Masaoka
But Jim, if we can be drafted the same as everyone else, doesn't that restore one of our rights as citizens?
Restore? Shiro, they shouldn't have taken away our rights in the first place!
Well, I hope to have kids someday. We have to prove we are loyal so they can have a life in this country.

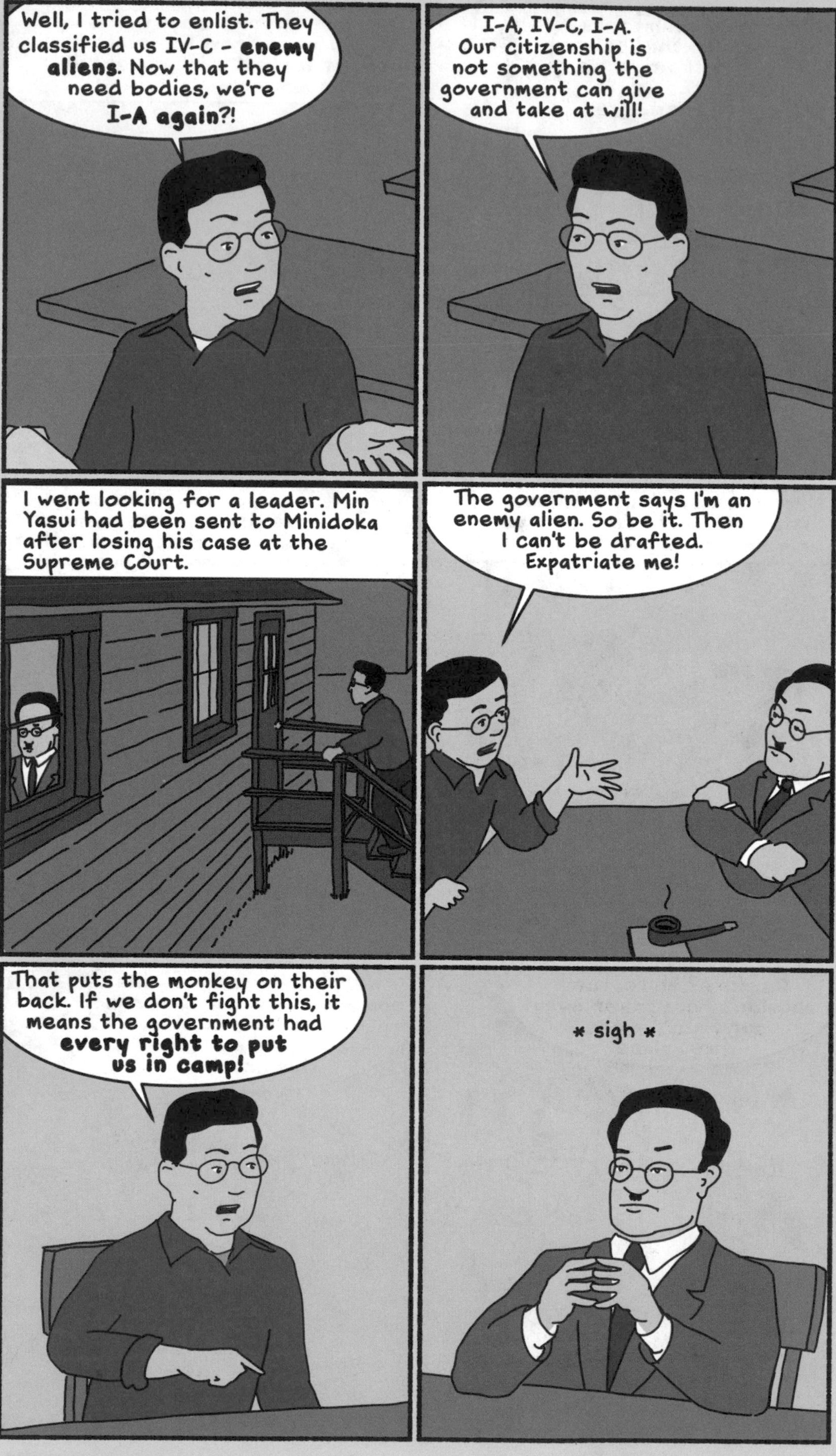
Well, I tried to enlist. They classified us IV-C - **enemy aliens**. Now that they need bodies, we're **I-A again**?!
I-A, IV-C, I-A. Our citizenship is not something the government can give and take at will!
I went looking for a leader. Min Yasui had been sent to Minidoka after losing his case at the Supreme Court.
The government says I'm an enemy alien. So be it. Then I can't be drafted. Expatriate me!
That puts the monkey on their back. If we don't fight this, it means the government had **every right to put us in camp!**
* sigh *

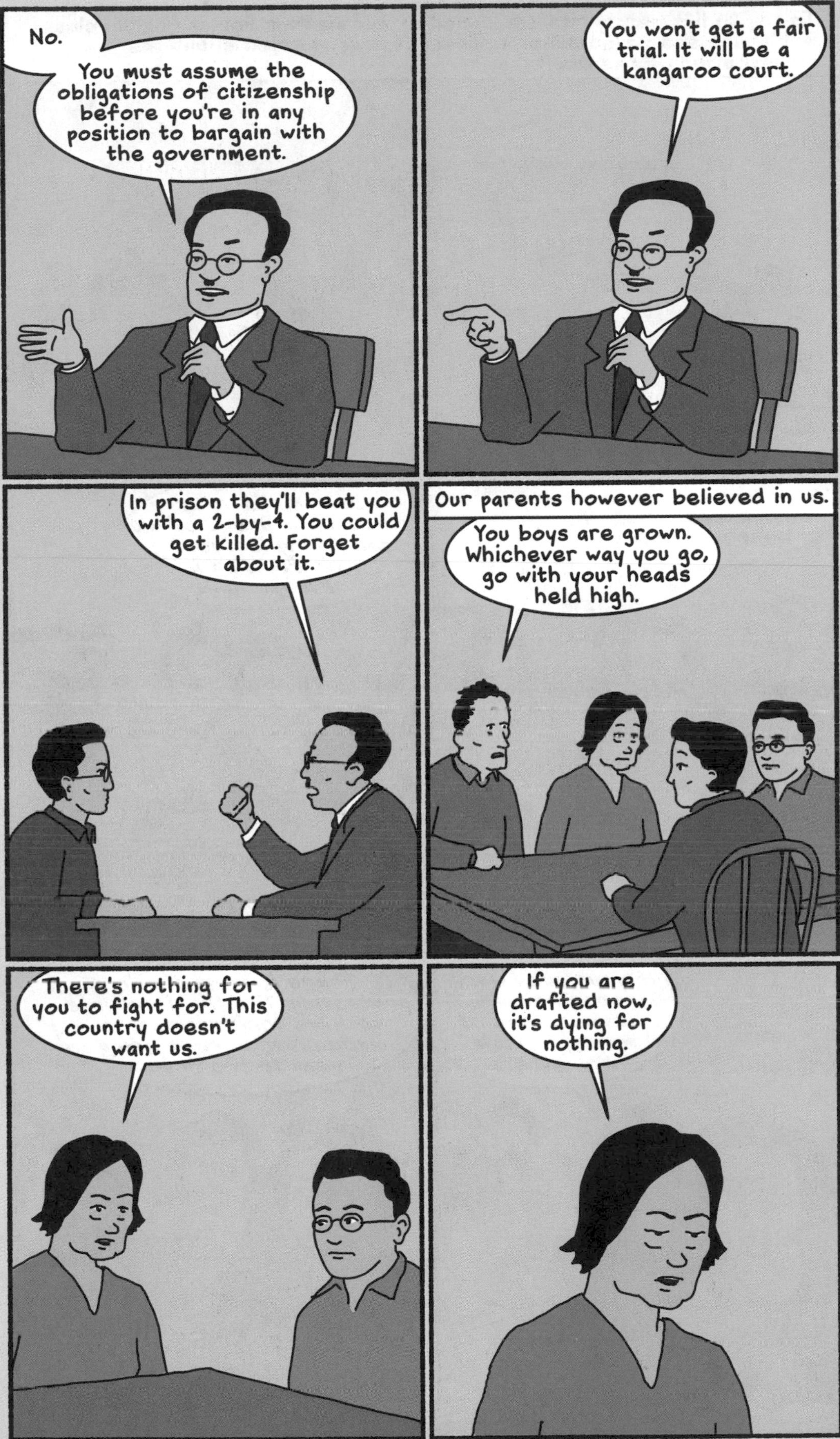
No.
You must assume the obligations of citizenship before you're in any position to bargain with the government.
You won't get a fair trial. It will be a kangaroo court.
In prison they'll beat you with a 2-by-4. You could get killed. Forget about it.
Our parents however believed in us.
You boys are grown. Whichever way you go, go with your heads held high.
There's nothing for you to fight for. This country doesn't want us.
If you are drafted now, it's dying for nothing.

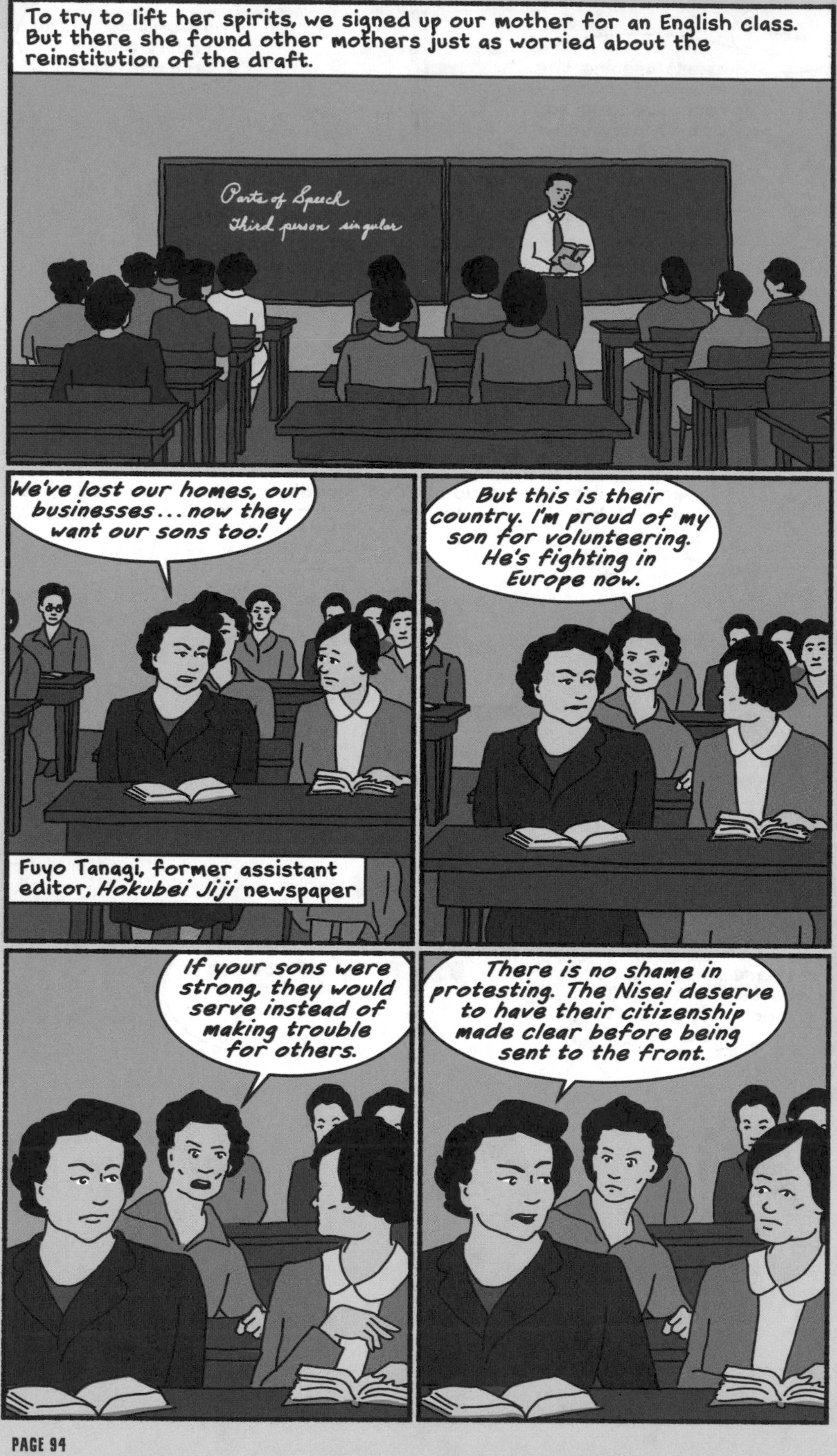

To try to lift her spirits, we signed up our mother for an English class. But there she found other mothers just as worried about the reinstitution of the draft.
Parts of Speech
Third person singular
We've lost our homes, our businesses... now they want our sons too!
Fuyo Tanagi, former assistant editor, *Hokubei Jiji* newspaper
But this is their country. I'm proud of my son for volunteering. He's fighting in Europe now.
If your sons were strong, they would serve instead of making trouble for others.
There is no shame in protesting. The Nisei deserve to have their citizenship made clear before being sent to the front.

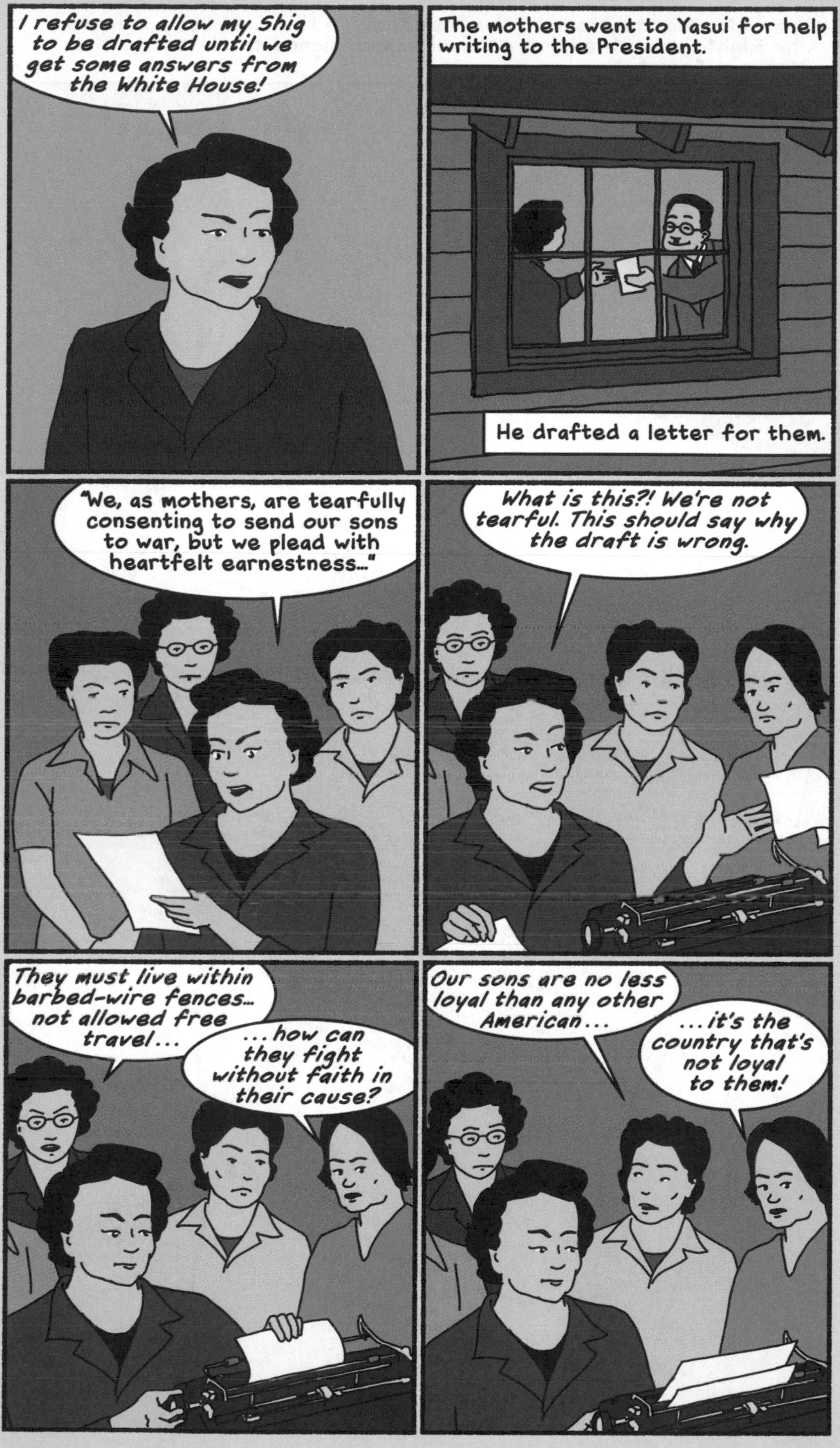
I refuse to allow my Shig to be drafted until we get some answers from the White House!
The mothers went to Yasui for help writing to the President.
He drafted a letter for them.
"We, as mothers, are tearfully consenting to send our sons to war, but we plead with heartfelt earnestness..."
What is this?! We're not tearful. This should say why the draft is wrong.
They must live within barbed-wire fences... not allowed free travel...
...how can they fight without faith in their cause?
Our sons are no less loyal than any other American...
...it's the country that's not loyal to them!

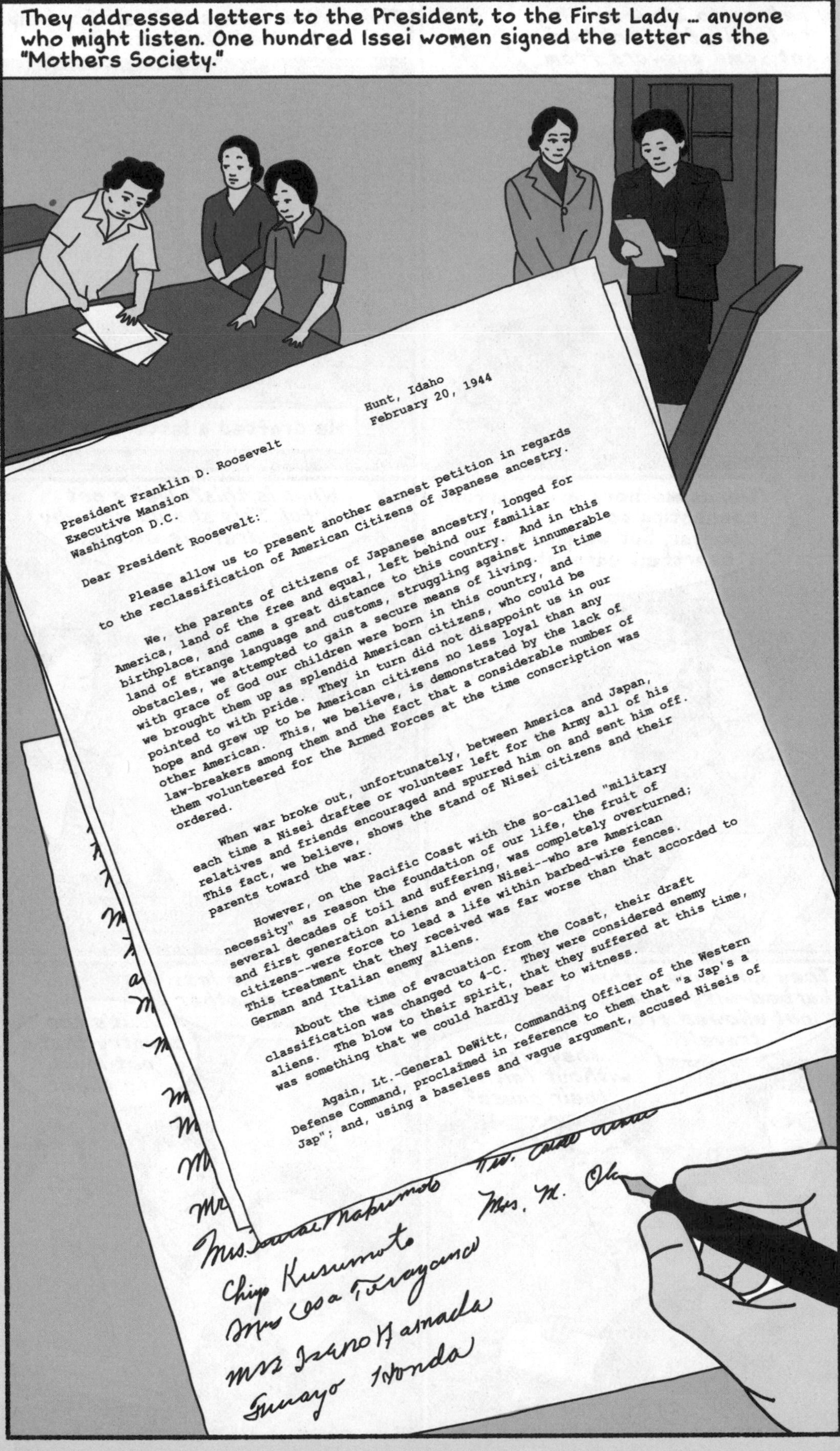
They addressed letters to the President, to the First Lady ... anyone who might listen. One hundred Issei women signed the letter as the "Mothers Society."
Hunt, Idaho
February 20, 1944
President Franklin D. Roosevelt
Executive Mansion
Washington D.C.
Dear President Roosevelt:
Please allow us to present another earnest petition in regards to the reclassification of American Citizens of Japanese ancestry.
We, the parents of citizens of Japanese ancestry, longed for America, land of the free and equal, left behind our familiar birthplace, and came a great distance to this country. And in this land of strange language and customs, struggling against innumerable obstacles, we attempted to gain a secure means of living. In time with grace of God our children were born in this country, and we brought them up as splendid American citizens, who could be pointed to with pride. They in turn did not disappoint us in our hope and grew up to be American citizens no less loyal than any other American. This, we believe, is demonstrated by the lack of law-breakers among them and the fact that a considerable number of them volunteered for the Armed Forces at the time conscription was ordered.
When war broke out, unfortunately, between America and Japan, each time a Nisei draftee or volunteer left for the Army all of his relatives and friends encouraged and spurred him on and sent him off. This fact, we believe, shows the stand of Nisei citizens and their parents toward the war.
However, on the Pacific Coast with the so-called "military necessity" as reason the foundation of our life, the fruit of several decades of toil and suffering, was completely overturned; and first generation aliens and even Nisei--who are American citizens--were force to lead a life within barbed-wire fences. This treatment that they received was far worse than that accorded to German and Italian enemy aliens.
About the time of evacuation from the Coast, their draft classification was changed to 4-C. They were considered enemy aliens. The blow to their spirit, that they suffered at this time, was something that we could hardly bear to witness.
Again, Lt.-General DeWitt, Commanding Officer of the Western Defense Command, proclaimed in reference to them that "a Jap's a Jap"; and, using a baseless and vague argument, accused Niseis of
Chiyo Kusumoto

In Wyoming, the Fair Play Committee was making the same argument - no draft without first clarifying our citizenship - but they took it a step further...

Heart Mountain War Relocation Center

... and crossed the line from protest to resistance.

If we don't take a definite stand, it's not going to do us any good. But once you fail to report, you're breaking the law. That has to be your individual choice.

therefore, WE MEMBERS OF THE FAIR PLAY COMMITTEE HEREBY REFUSE TO GO TO THE PHYSICAL EXAMINATION OR TO THE INDUCTION IF OR WHEN WE ARE CALLED IN ORDER TO CONTEST THE ISSUE.

Frank Emi
Fair Play Committee

Gene and I admired how organized they were - openly violating the Selective Service Act to get a test case into court.

Rocky Shimpo

NISEI AMERICA
Know the Facts
By Jimmie Omura

James M. Omura
Editor
English Section

Largest Circulation
Japanese Vernacular
In Continental U.S.A.

Wyoming Draft Resistance Has Authorities Stumped

Five Fair Play Committee Members at Heart Mt. Oppose Draft; No Action Is Taken

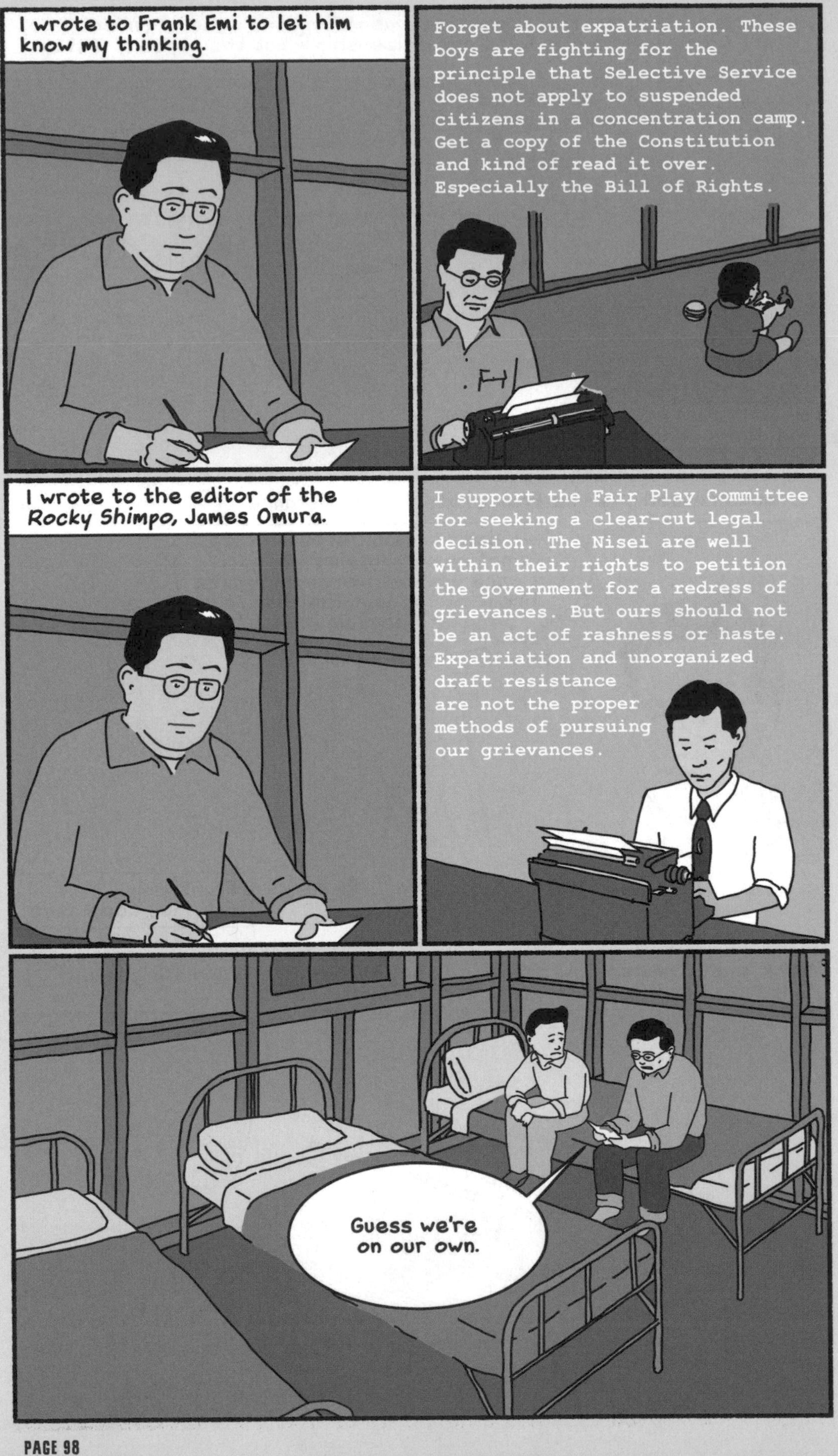
I wrote to Frank Emi to let him know my thinking.
Forget about expatriation. These boys are fighting for the principle that Selective Service does not apply to suspended citizens in a concentration camp. Get a copy of the Constitution and kind of read it over. Especially the Bill of Rights.
I wrote to the editor of the *Rocky Shimpo*, James Omura.
I support the Fair Play Committee for seeking a clear-cut legal decision. The Nisei are well within their rights to petition the government for a redress of grievances. But ours should not be an act of rashness or haste. Expatriation and unorganized draft resistance are not the proper methods of pursuing our grievances.
Guess we're on our own.

PART FOUR

FOR THE FIRST TIME, I FEEL GOOD ABOUT BEING JAPANESE

1944

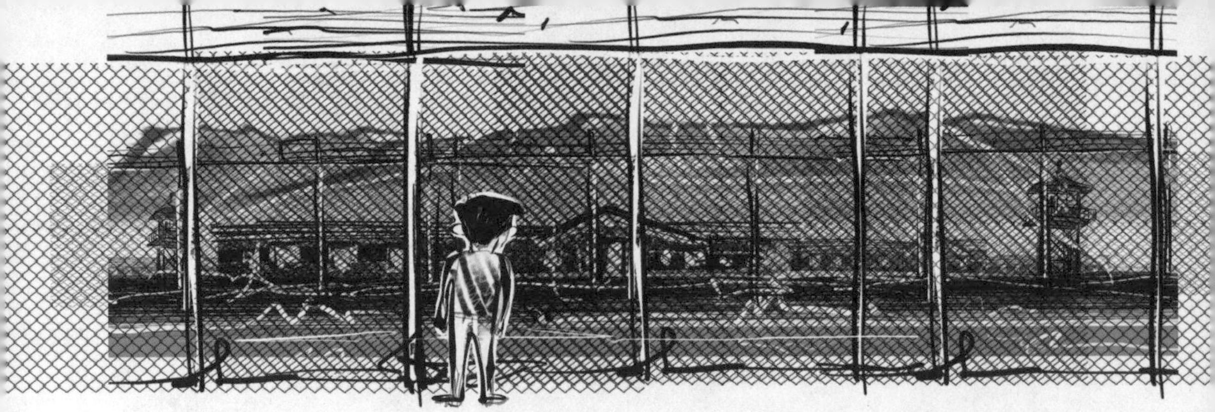

HIROSHI: The Army lifted martial law at Tule Lake two months after the big disturbance. A double man-proof fence now separated us from the administration area. On the other side, near the camp hospital, was the Army's new compound.

Mr. Best called it "Area B." The Army called it the Stockade – a jail within a jail. Around the bullpen tents, Col. Austin converted military barracks to house the men he had arrested – at one point more than 250.

A low watch tower sat on each corner. Powerful searchlights swept the yard at night. Fences were topped with barbed wire all around. And soldiers patrolled with submachine guns.

No visits were allowed and letters were censored – after Army typists copied them for intelligence.

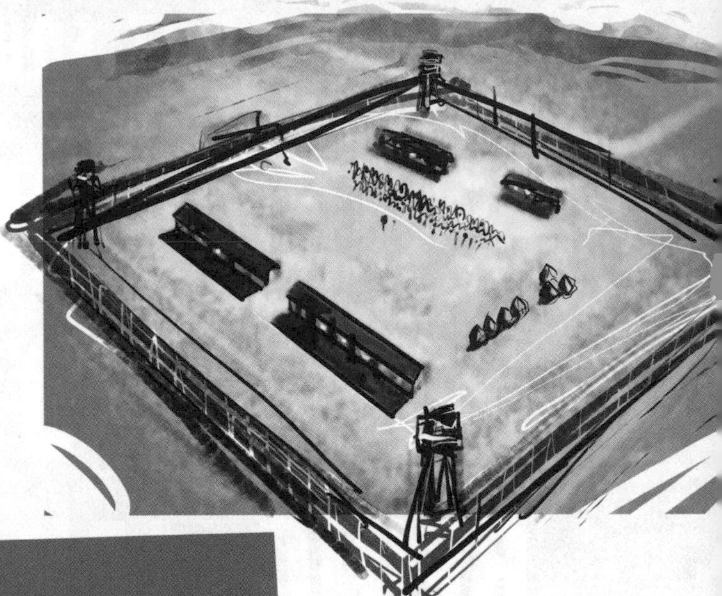

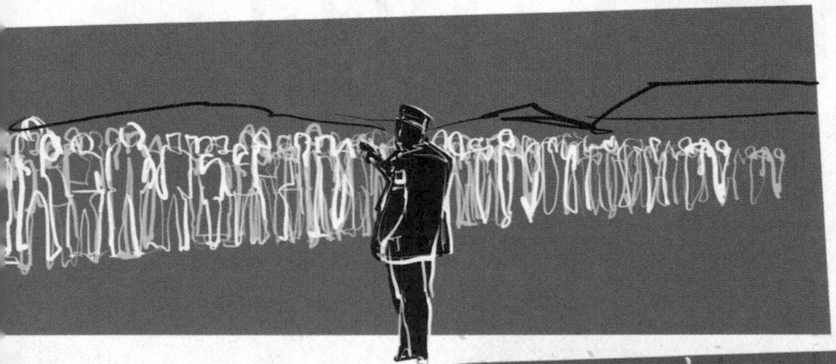

Its captives included the elected leaders of the *Daihyo Sha Kai* and anyone Mr. Best considered to be anti-administration. We all lived on edge, as one word from an *inu* could land you or a loved one in detention.

No charges were ever brought that prisoners could dispute. No reason was ever given for their confinement, nor was any length of term set. They were held at the government's convenience.

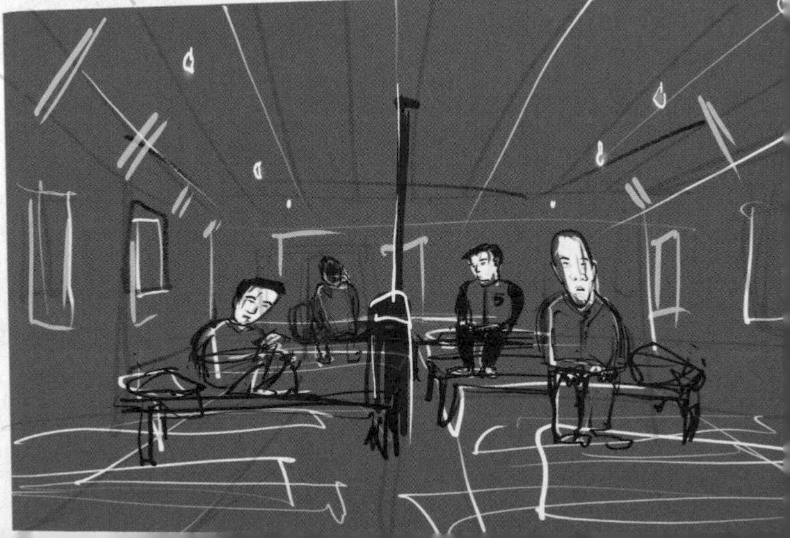

George Kuratomi tried to reason with Mr. Best.

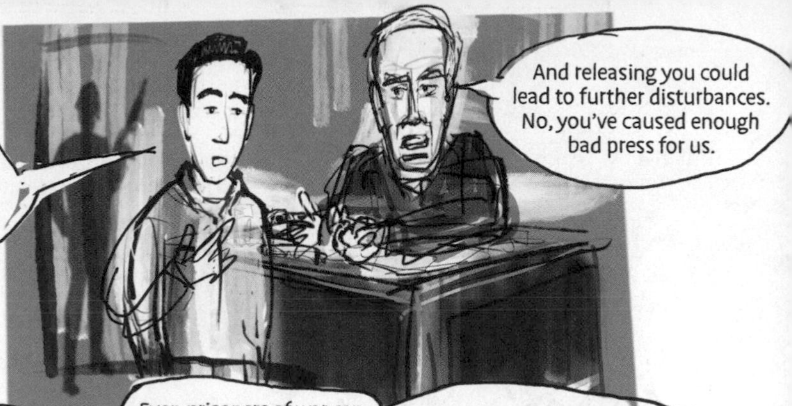
Don't you see? Freeing us would end the feelings of persecution in camp and bring peace and harmony.
And releasing you could lead to further disturbances. No, you've caused enough bad press for us.

Over time, men were transferred out, and by summer only the "Committee of 14" remained — the leaders of the Negotiating Committee and seven others.

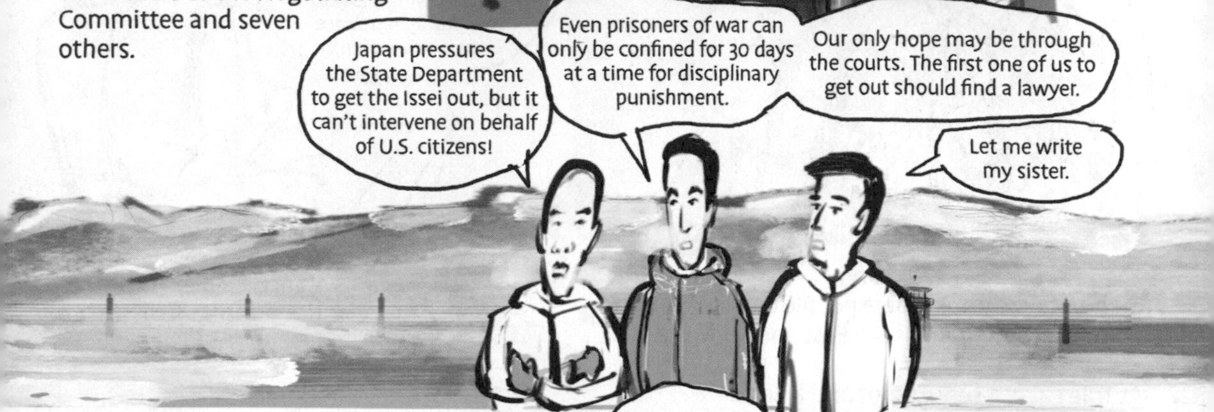
Japan pressures the State Department to get the Issei out, but it can't intervene on behalf of U.S. citizens!
Even prisoners of war can only be confined for 30 days at a time for disciplinary punishment.
Our only hope may be through the courts. The first one of us to get out should find a lawyer.
Let me write my sister.

Singer Terada's baby was due any day. Furious at the interminable wait, she staged her own sit-down strike.

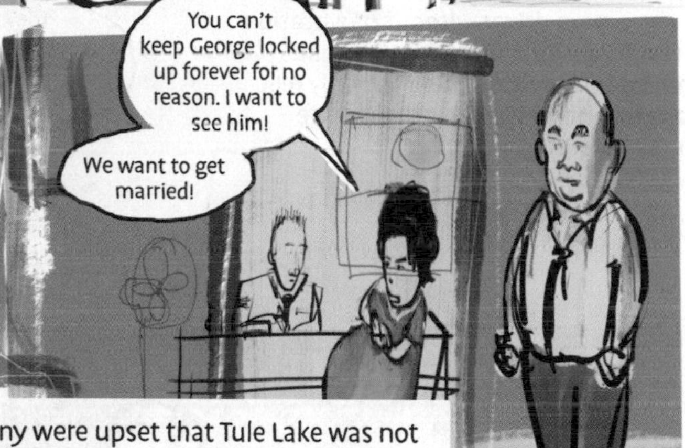
You can't keep George locked up forever for no reason. I want to see him!
We want to get married!

With the leadership vacuum in camp, a new faction emerged to demand immediate repatriation and expatriation to Japan, as a means of reclaiming personal pride and dignity.

Many were upset that Tule Lake was not a true segregation center as promised, but one which mixed those who desired repatriation with those who didn't. They petitioned for a resegregation, a fenced end of camp where like-minded people could live in peace — and no informers.

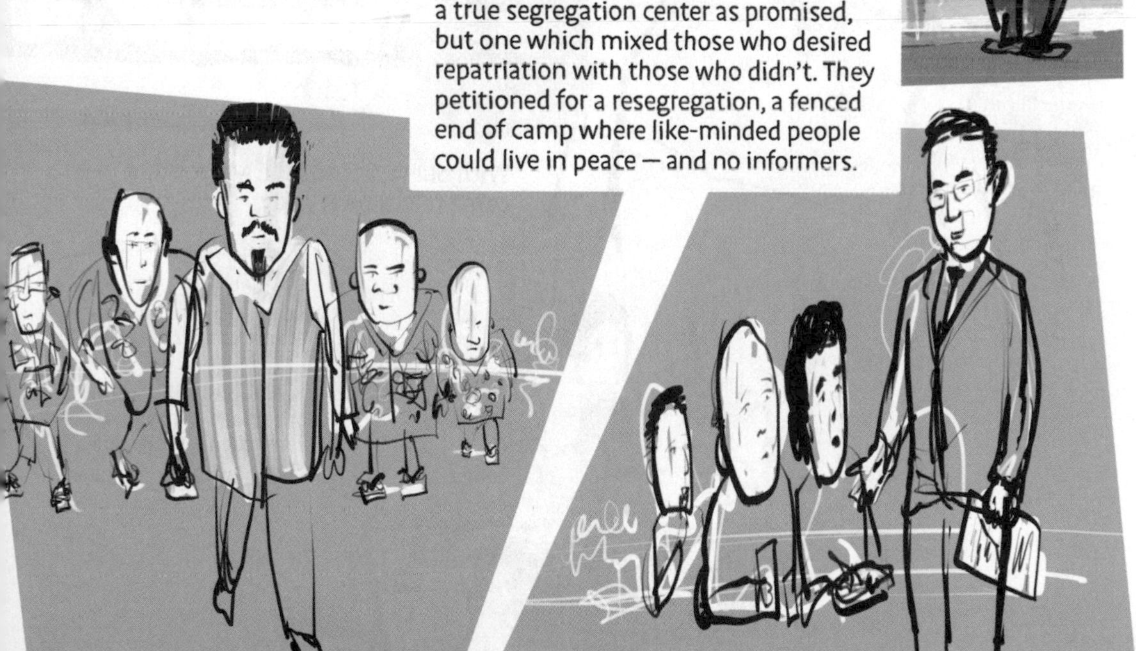

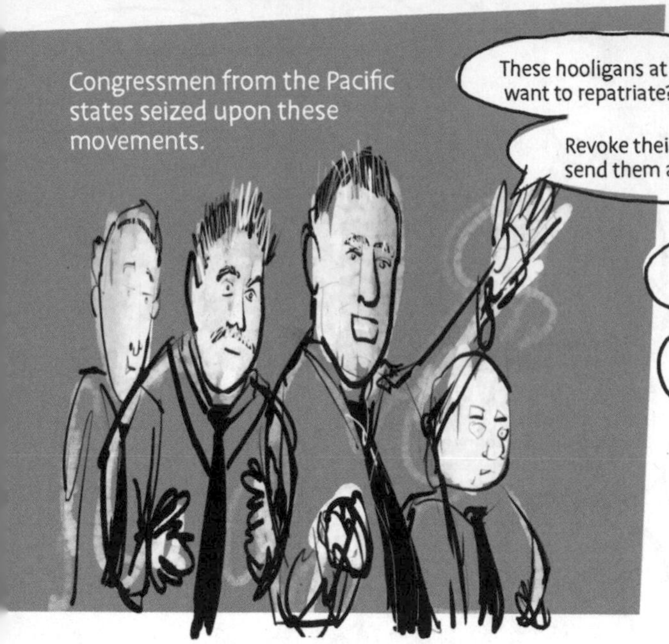
Congressmen from the Pacific states seized upon these movements.
These hooligans at Tule Lake want to repatriate? Let 'em!
Revoke their citizenship and send them all back to Japan!

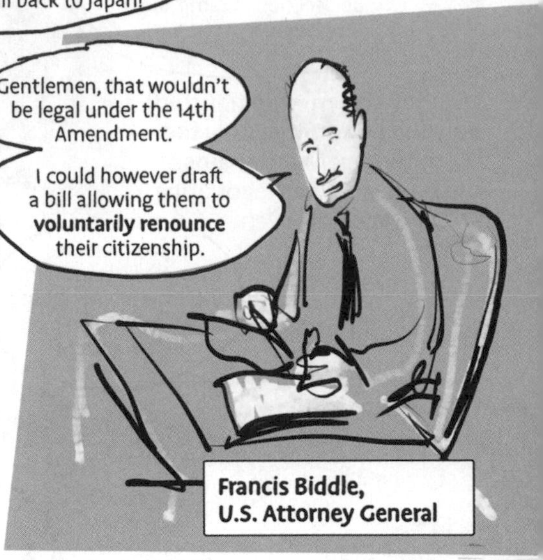
Gentlemen, that wouldn't be legal under the 14th Amendment.
I could however draft a bill allowing them to **voluntarily renounce** their citizenship.
Francis Biddle, U.S. Attorney General

In the other camps where people behaved, the WRA resettled them in the East and Midwest.

At Tule Lake, a sentry shot and killed a construction driver without provocation. A reviled co-op manager had a knife shoved up his throat. And the only relief Congress offered us was the chance to self-deport.

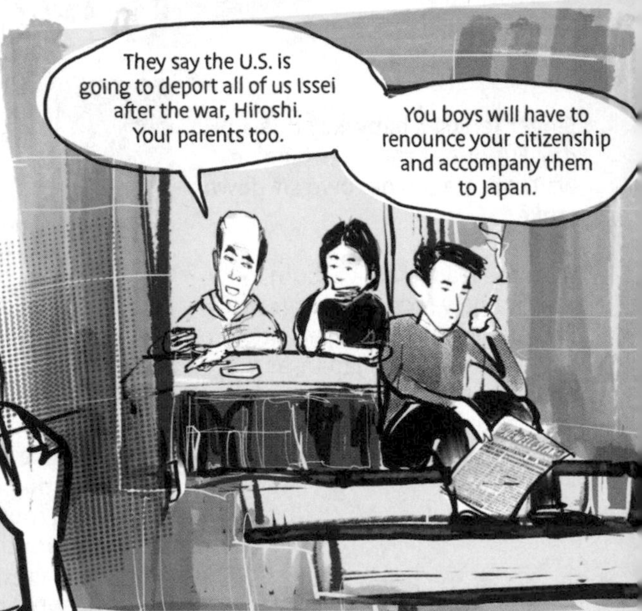
They say the U.S. is going to deport all of us Issei after the war, Hiroshi. Your parents too.
You boys will have to renounce your citizenship and accompany them to Japan.

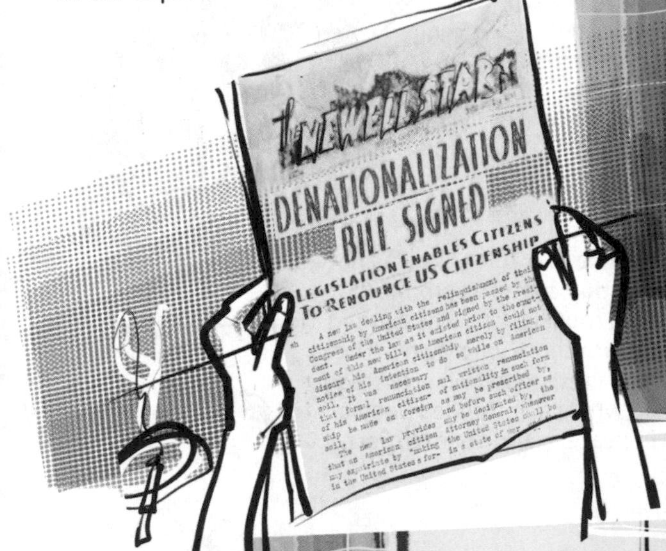
DENATIONALIZATION
BILL SIGNED
LEGISLATION ENABLES CITIZENS TO RENOUNCE US CITIZENSHIP

With our father absent, Mr. Yoshida came to visit every day.

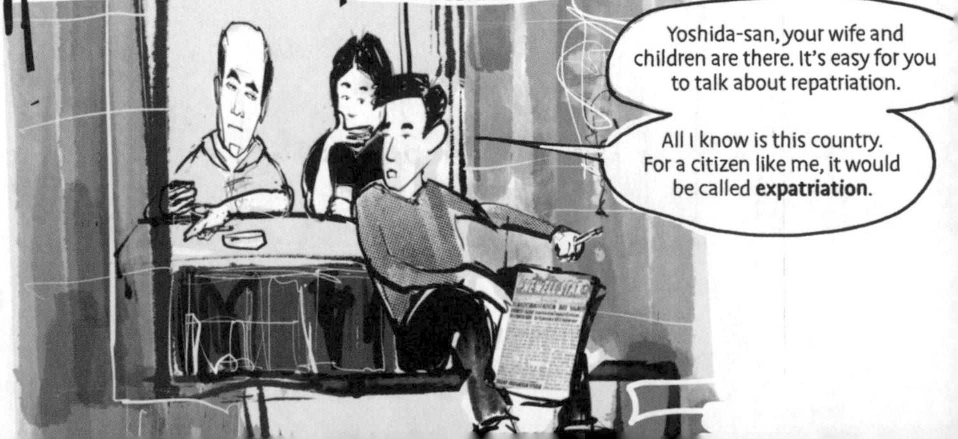
Yoshida-san, your wife and children are there. It's easy for you to talk about repatriation.
All I know is this country. For a citizen like me, it would be called **expatriation**.

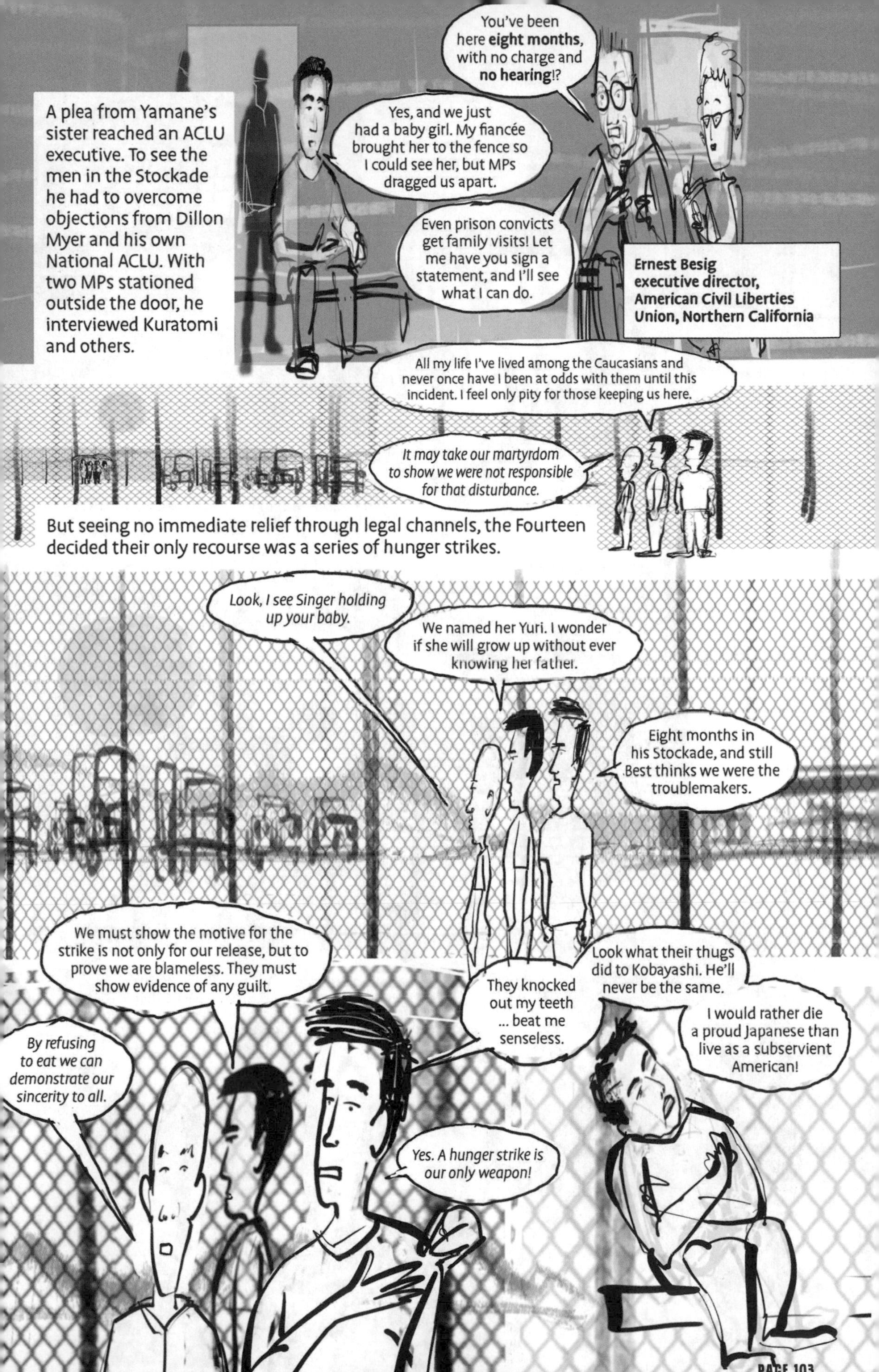

A plea from Yamane's sister reached an ACLU executive. To see the men in the Stockade he had to overcome objections from Dillon Myer and his own National ACLU. With two MPs stationed outside the door, he interviewed Kuratomi and others.
You've been here **eight months**, with no charge and **no hearing**!?
Yes, and we just had a baby girl. My fiancée brought her to the fence so I could see her, but MPs dragged us apart.
Even prison convicts get family visits! Let me have you sign a statement, and I'll see what I can do.
Ernest Besig executive director, American Civil Liberties Union, Northern California
All my life I've lived among the Caucasians and never once have I been at odds with them until this incident. I feel only pity for those keeping us here.
It may take our martyrdom to show we were not responsible for that disturbance.
But seeing no immediate relief through legal channels, the Fourteen decided their only recourse was a series of hunger strikes.
Look, I see Singer holding up your baby.
We named her Yuri. I wonder if she will grow up without ever knowing her father.
Eight months in his Stockade, and still Best thinks we were the troublemakers.
We must show the motive for the strike is not only for our release, but to prove we are blameless. They must show evidence of any guilt.
They knocked out my teeth ... beat me senseless.
Look what their thugs did to Kobayashi. He'll never be the same.
I would rather die a proud Japanese than live as a subservient American!
By refusing to eat we can demonstrate our sincerity to all.
Yes. A hunger strike is our only weapon!

For weeks we heard rumors that several men had collapsed from hunger. Frantic appeals went out, and the resegregationists quickly collected 8,000 names on a petition for release of the inmates.

Singer led a group of wives to crash the Stockade gate and march in to see their husbands.

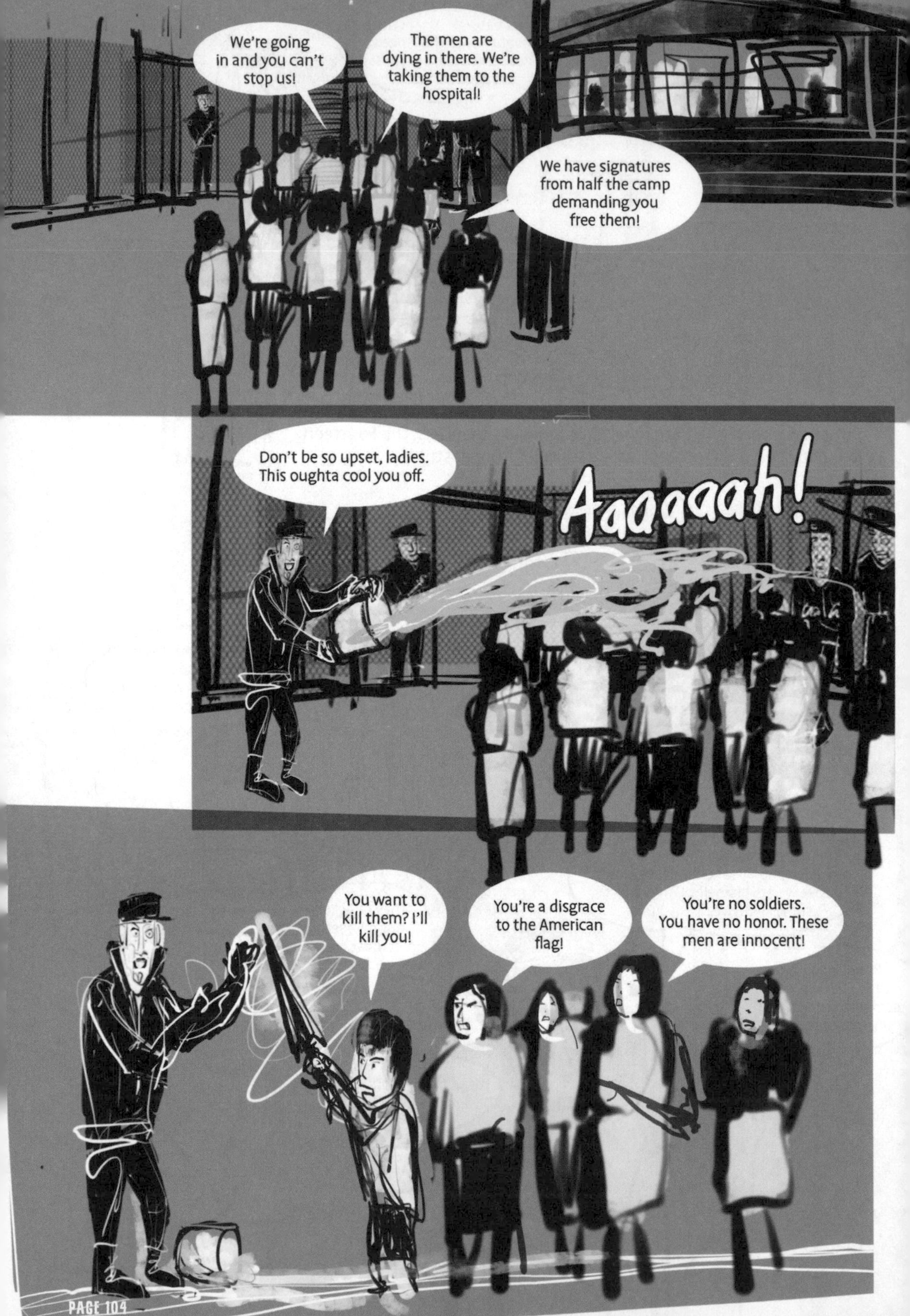

We're going in and you can't stop us!
The men are dying in there. We're taking them to the hospital!
We have signatures from half the camp demanding you free them!
Don't be so upset, ladies. This oughta cool you off.
Aaaaaah!
You want to kill them? I'll kill you!
You're a disgrace to the American flag!
You're no soldiers. You have no honor. These men are innocent!

In the meantime, Ernest Besig had enlisted a lawyer in San Francisco to sue the WRA. Wayne Collins stormed in with the signed affidavits from Kuratomi and others.

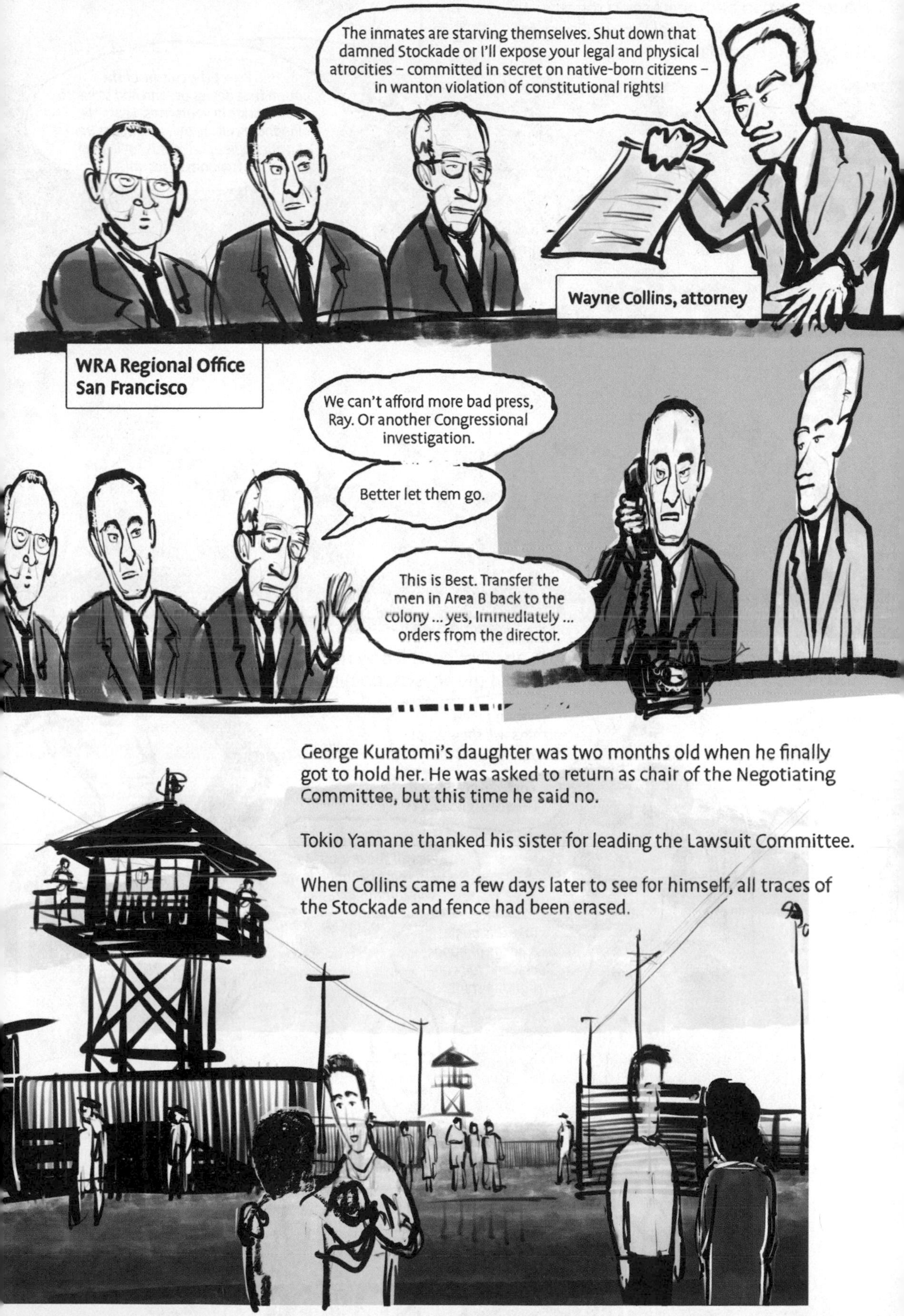

The inmates are starving themselves. Shut down that damned Stockade or I'll expose your legal and physical atrocities – committed in secret on native-born citizens – in wanton violation of constitutional rights!
Wayne Collins, attorney
WRA Regional Office San Francisco
We can't afford more bad press, Ray. Or another Congressional investigation.
Better let them go.
This is Best. Transfer the men in Area B back to the colony ... yes, immediately ... orders from the director.
George Kuratomi's daughter was two months old when he finally got to hold her. He was asked to return as chair of the Negotiating Committee, but this time he said no.
Tokio Yamane thanked his sister for leading the Lawsuit Committee.
When Collins came a few days later to see for himself, all traces of the Stockade and fence had been erased.

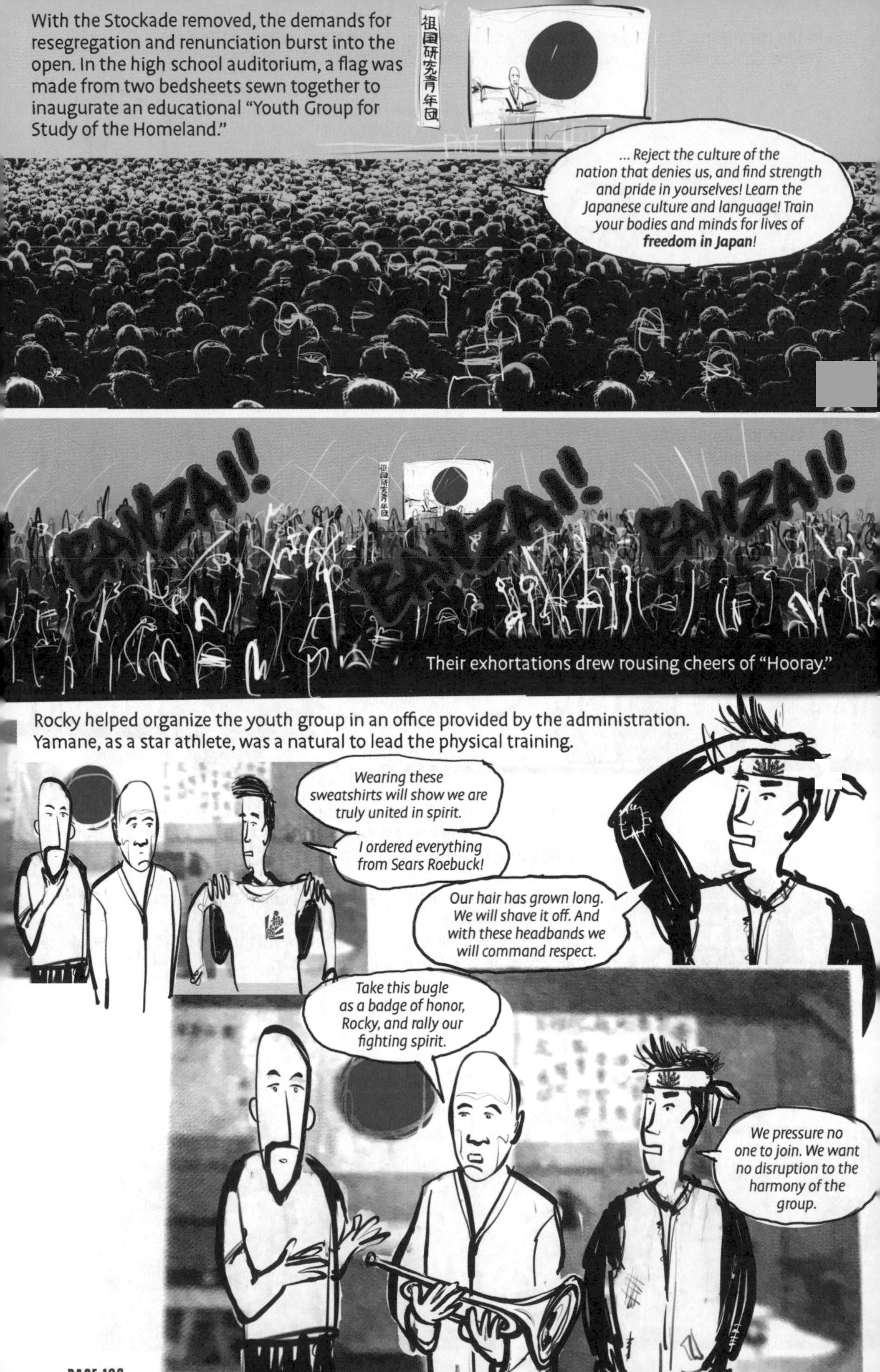
With the Stockade removed, the demands for resegregation and renunciation burst into the open. In the high school auditorium, a flag was made from two bedsheets sewn together to inaugurate an educational "Youth Group for Study of the Homeland."
祖国研究青年団
... Reject the culture of the nation that denies us, and find strength and pride in yourselves! Learn the Japanese culture and language! Train your bodies and minds for lives of **freedom in Japan**!
BANZAI!!
BANZAI!!
BANZAI!!
Their exhortations drew rousing cheers of "Hooray."
Rocky helped organize the youth group in an office provided by the administration. Yamane, as a star athlete, was a natural to lead the physical training.
Wearing these sweatshirts will show we are truly united in spirit.
I ordered everything from Sears Roebuck!
Our hair has grown long. We will shave it off. And with these headbands we will command respect.
Take this bugle as a badge of honor, Rocky, and rally our fighting spirit.
We pressure no one to join. We want no disruption to the harmony of the group.

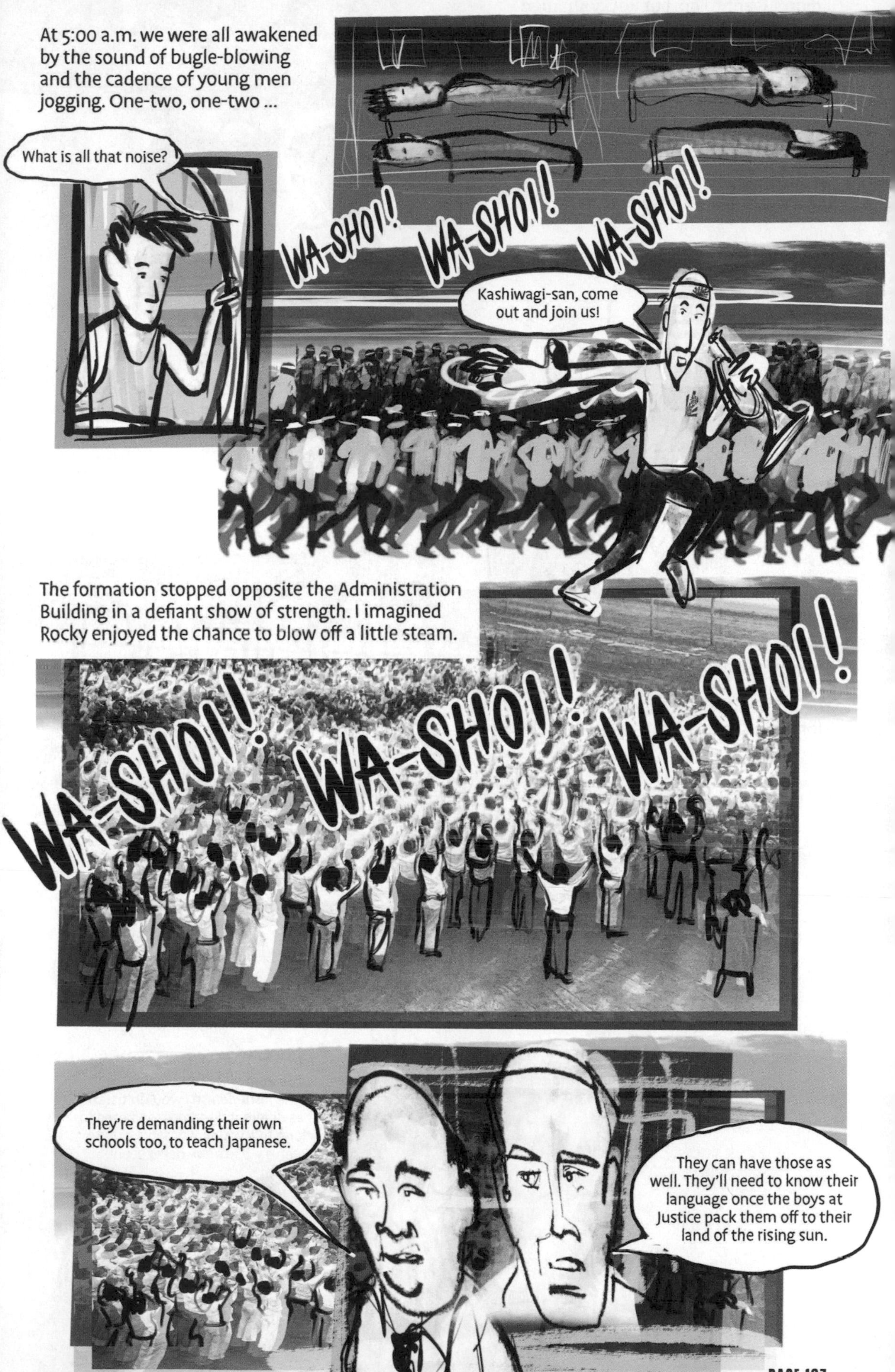
At 5:00 a.m. we were all awakened by the sound of bugle-blowing and the cadence of young men jogging. One-two, one-two ...
What is all that noise?
WA-SHOI!
WA-SHOI!
WA-SHOI!
Kashiwagi-san, come out and join us!
The formation stopped opposite the Administration Building in a defiant show of strength. I imagined Rocky enjoyed the chance to blow off a little steam.
WA-SHOI!
WA-SHOI!
WA-SHOI!
They're demanding their own schools too, to teach Japanese.
They can have those as well. They'll need to know their language once the boys at Justice pack them off to their land of the rising sun.

I didn't want to go, but Rocky shamed me into attending the Peoples' School to learn the real old-style Japanese language and history – which was pretty hard to do!

Alice braided her hair into pigtails to fit in with the other young women, and wore a white shirt in the style of Japanese factory workers.

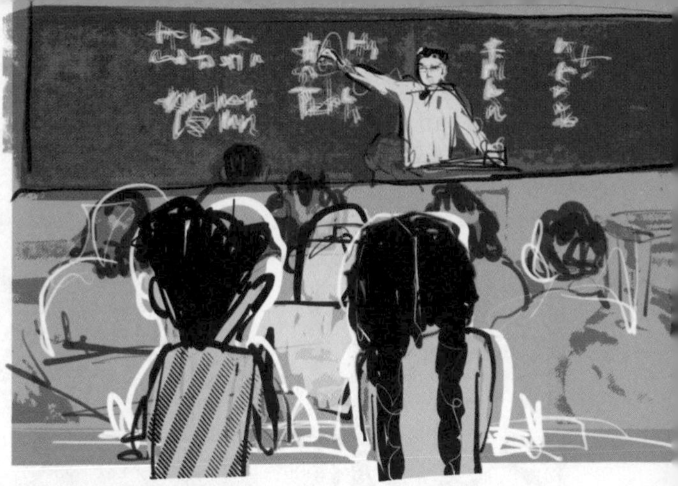

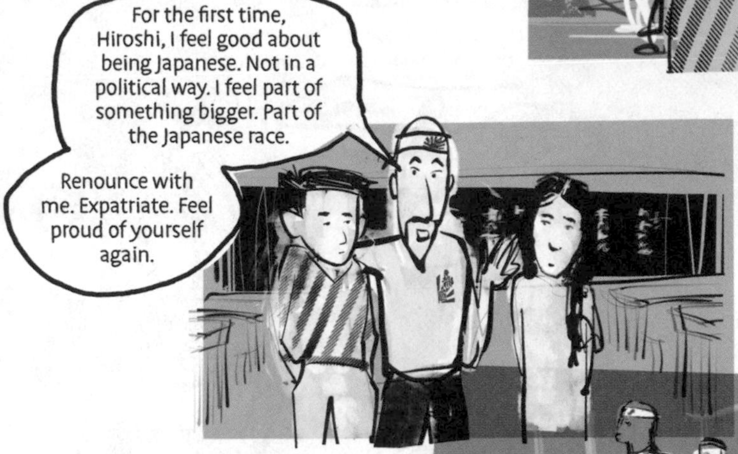
For the first time, Hiroshi, I feel good about being Japanese. Not in a political way. I feel part of something bigger. Part of the Japanese race.
Renounce with me. Expatriate. Feel proud of yourself again.

Rocky had joined the *Hokoku-dan* – the "Young Men's Group for Service to the Homeland" – but I refused.

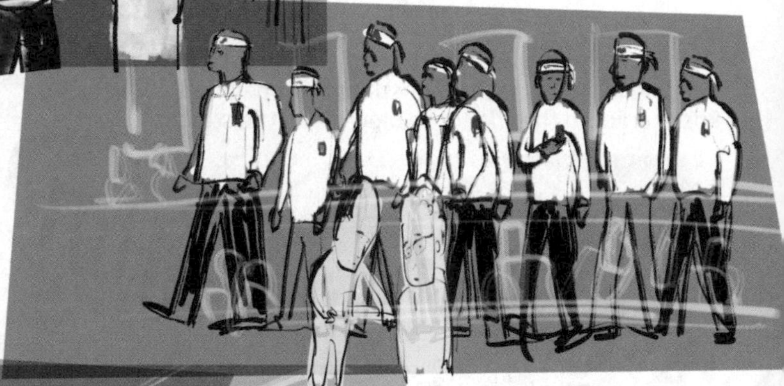

Its parent group was the *Hoshi-dan* – "Volunteers for the Immediate Return to the Homeland to Serve."

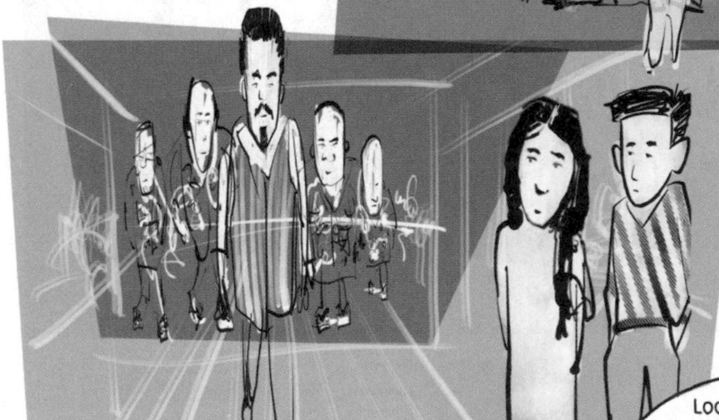

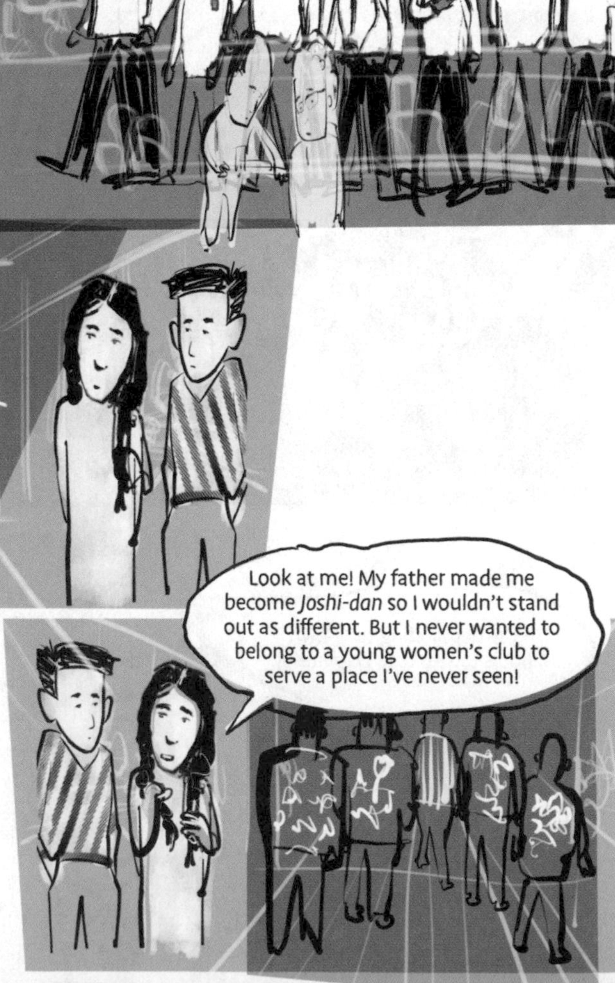
Look at me! My father made me become *Joshi-dan* so I wouldn't stand out as different. But I never wanted to belong to a young women's club to serve a place I've never seen!

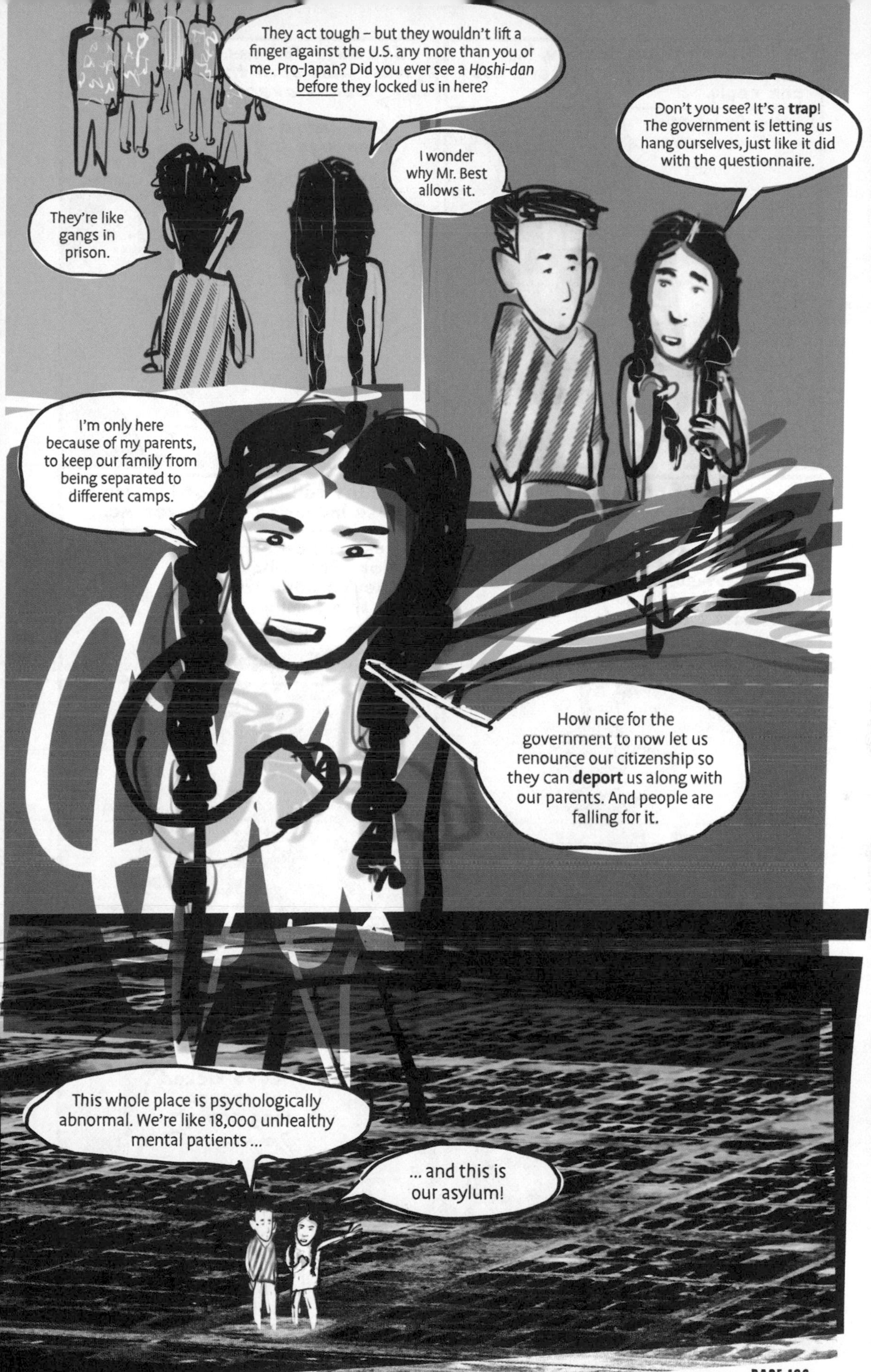
They act tough – but they wouldn't lift a finger against the U.S. any more than you or me. Pro-Japan? Did you ever see a *Hoshi-dan* before they locked us in here?
They're like gangs in prison.
I wonder why Mr. Best allows it.
Don't you see? It's a **trap**! The government is letting us hang ourselves, just like it did with the questionnaire.
I'm only here because of my parents, to keep our family from being separated to different camps.
How nice for the government to now let us renounce our citizenship so they can **deport** us along with our parents. And people are falling for it.
This whole place is psychologically abnormal. We're like 18,000 unhealthy mental patients ...
... and this is our asylum!

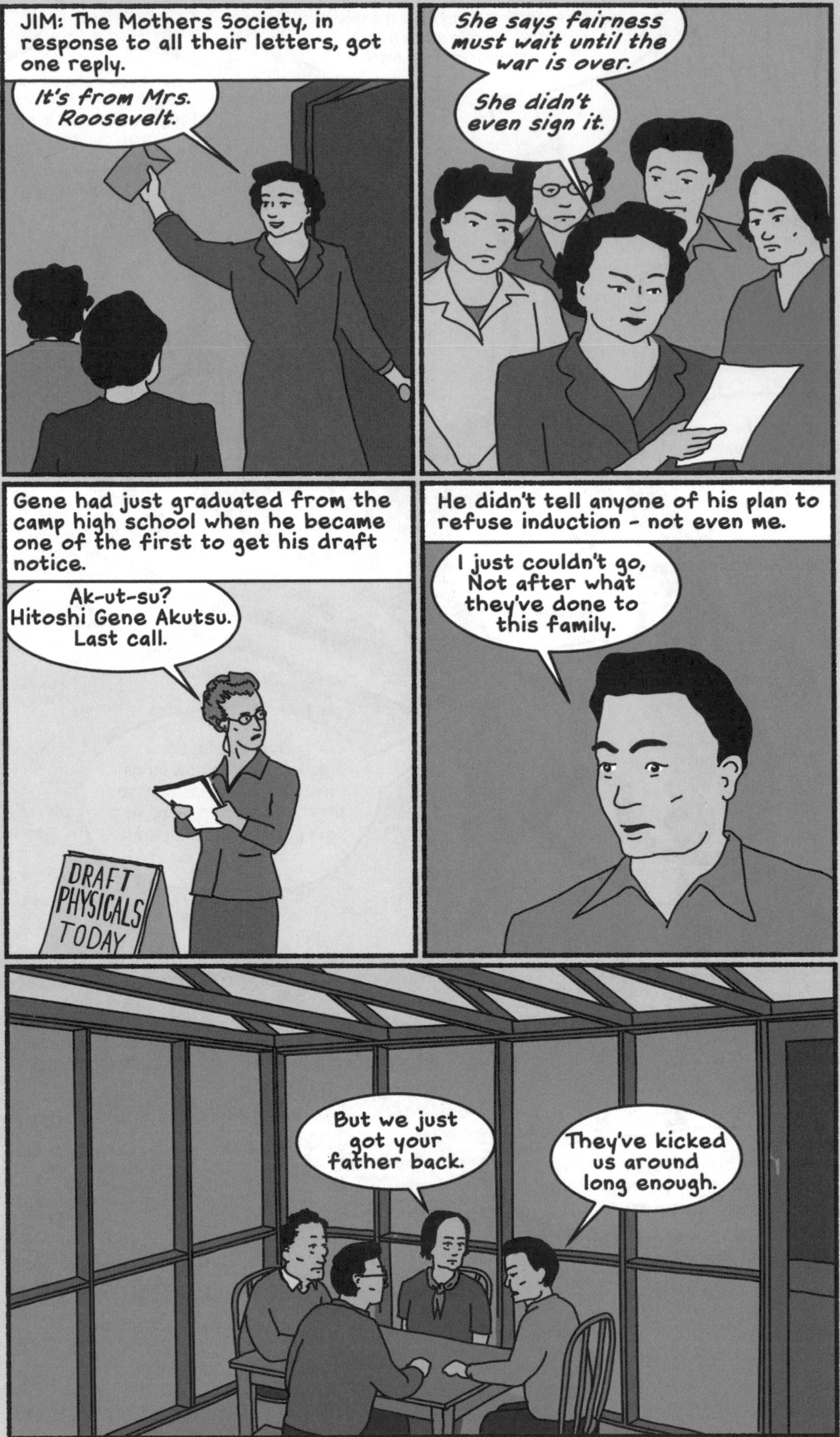
JIM: The Mothers Society, in response to all their letters, got one reply.
It's from Mrs. Roosevelt.
She says fairness must wait until the war is over.
She didn't even sign it.
Gene had just graduated from the camp high school when he became one of the first to get his draft notice.
Ak-ut-su? Hitoshi Gene Akutsu. Last call.
DRAFT PHYSICALS TODAY
He didn't tell anyone of his plan to refuse induction - not even me.
I just couldn't go, Not after what they've done to this family.
But we just got your father back.
They've kicked us around long enough.

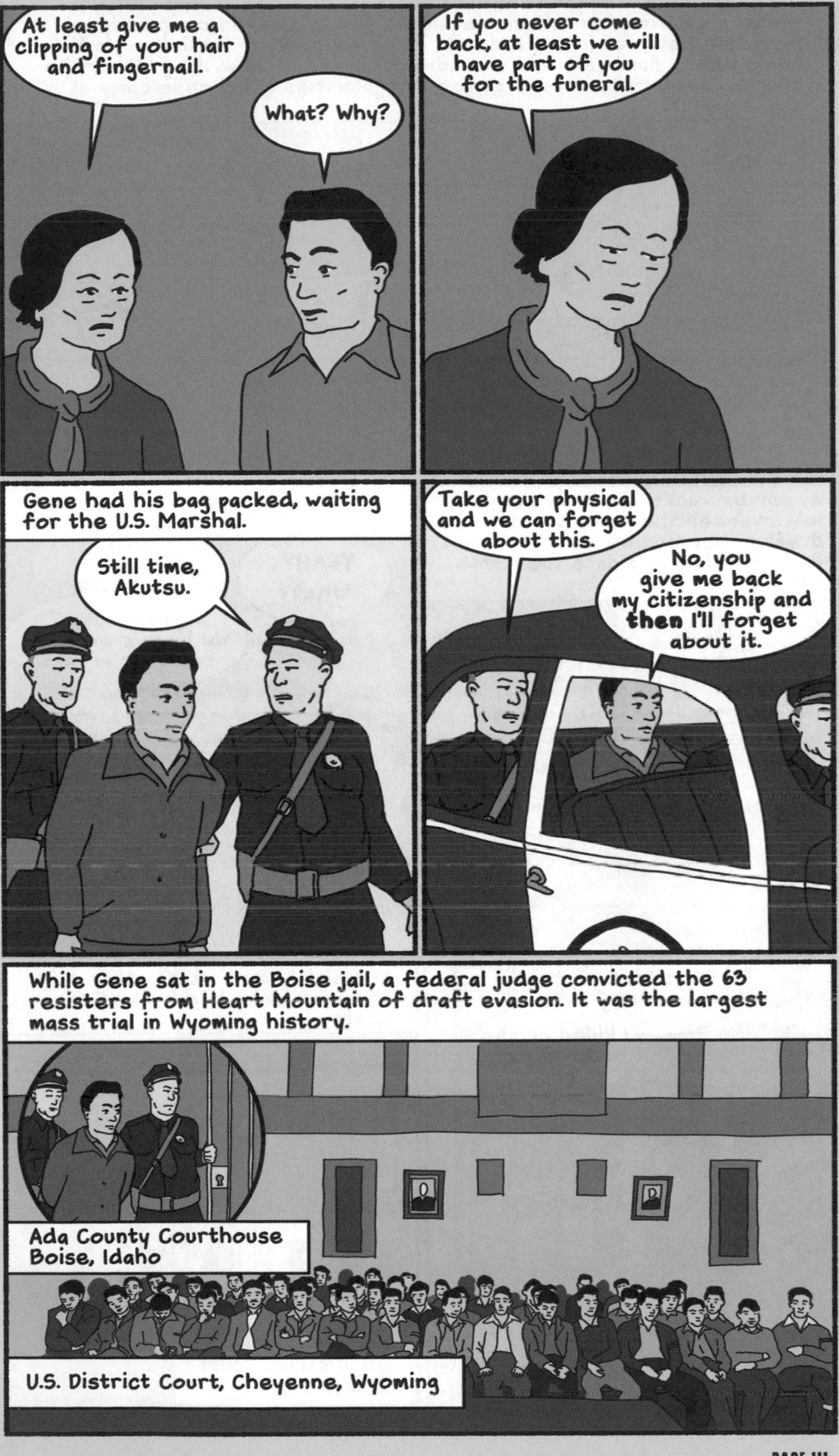
At least give me a clipping of your hair and fingernail.
What? Why?
If you never come back, at least we will have part of you for the funeral.
Gene had his bag packed, waiting for the U.S. Marshal.
Still time, Akutsu.
Take your physical and we can forget about this.
No, you give me back my citizenship and **then** I'll forget about it.
While Gene sat in the Boise jail, a federal judge convicted the 63 resisters from Heart Mountain of draft evasion. It was the largest mass trial in Wyoming history.
Ada County Courthouse Boise, Idaho
U.S. District Court, Cheyenne, Wyoming

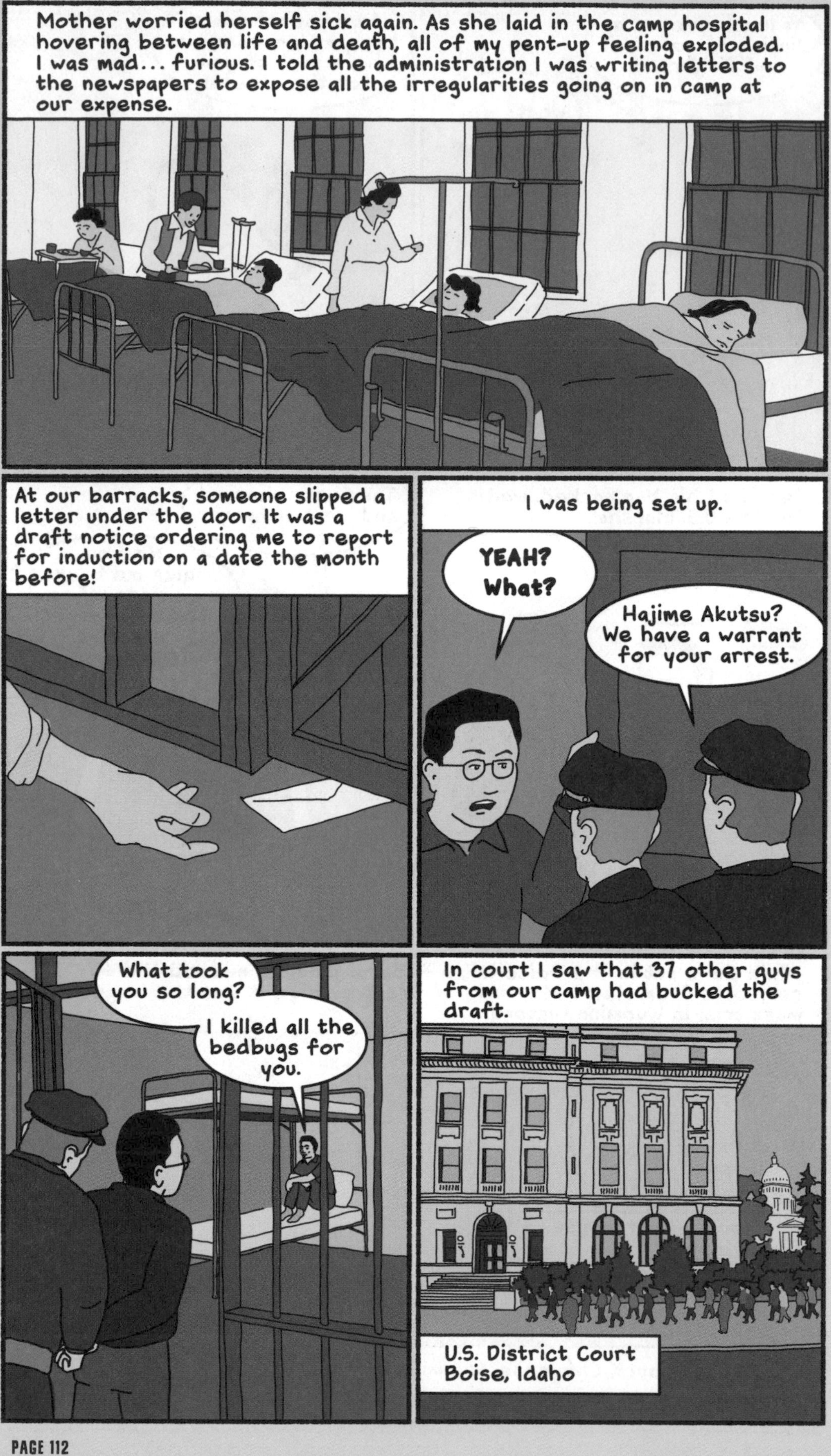
Mother worried herself sick again. As she laid in the camp hospital hovering between life and death, all of my pent-up feeling exploded. I was mad... furious. I told the administration I was writing letters to the newspapers to expose all the irregularities going on in camp at our expense.
At our barracks, someone slipped a letter under the door. It was a draft notice ordering me to report for induction on a date the month before!
I was being set up.
YEAH? What?
Hajime Akutsu? We have a warrant for your arrest.
What took you so long?
I killed all the bedbugs for you.
In court I saw that 37 other guys from our camp had bucked the draft.
U.S. District Court Boise, Idaho

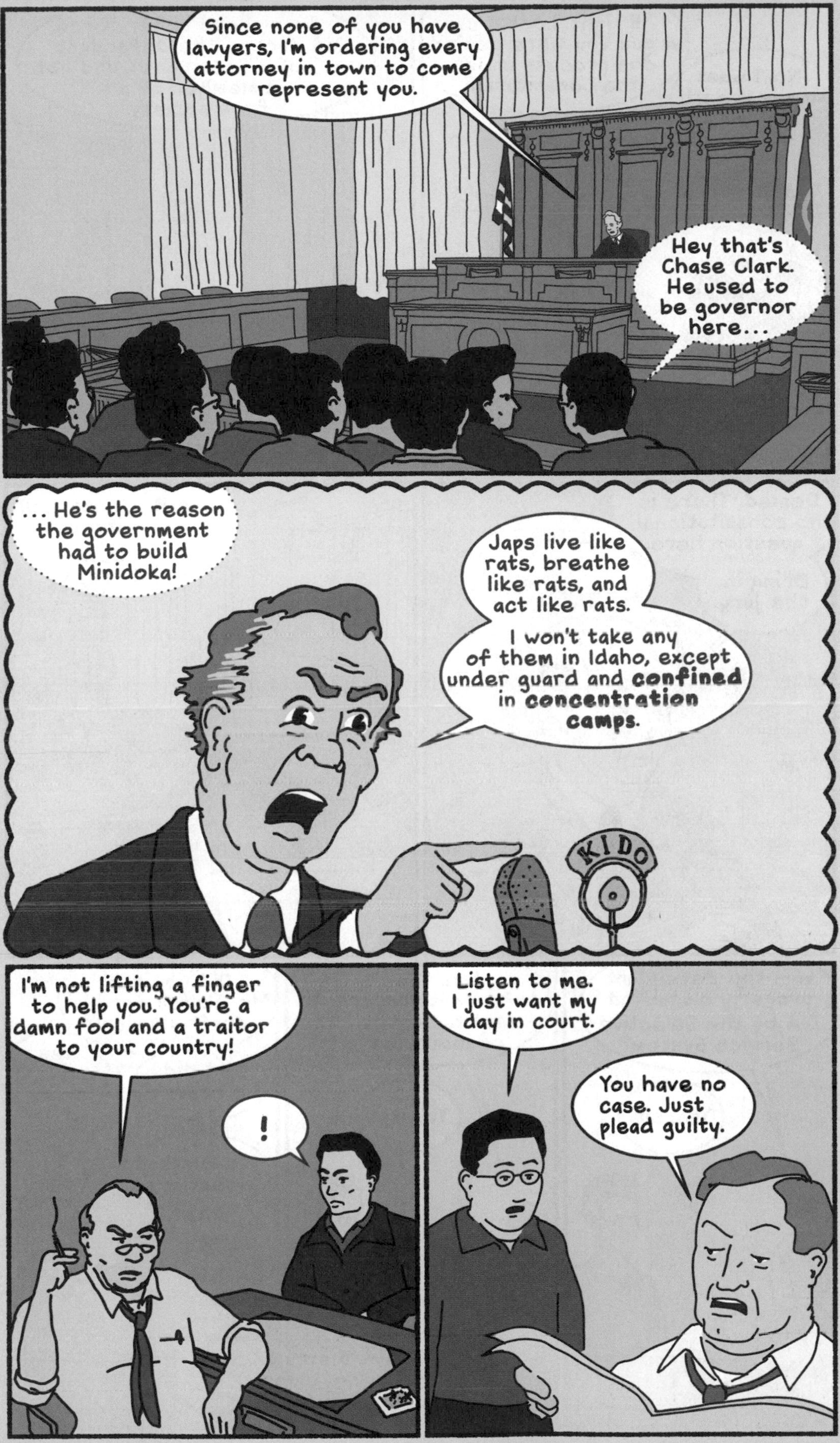
Since none of you have lawyers, I'm ordering every attorney in town to come represent you.
Hey that's Chase Clark. He used to be governor here...
... He's the reason the government had to build Minidoka!
Japs live like rats, breathe like rats, and act like rats.
I won't take any of them in Idaho, except under guard and **confined** in **concentration camps**.
KIDO
I'm not lifting a finger to help you. You're a damn fool and a traitor to your country!
!
Listen to me. I just want my day in court.
You have no case. Just plead guilty.

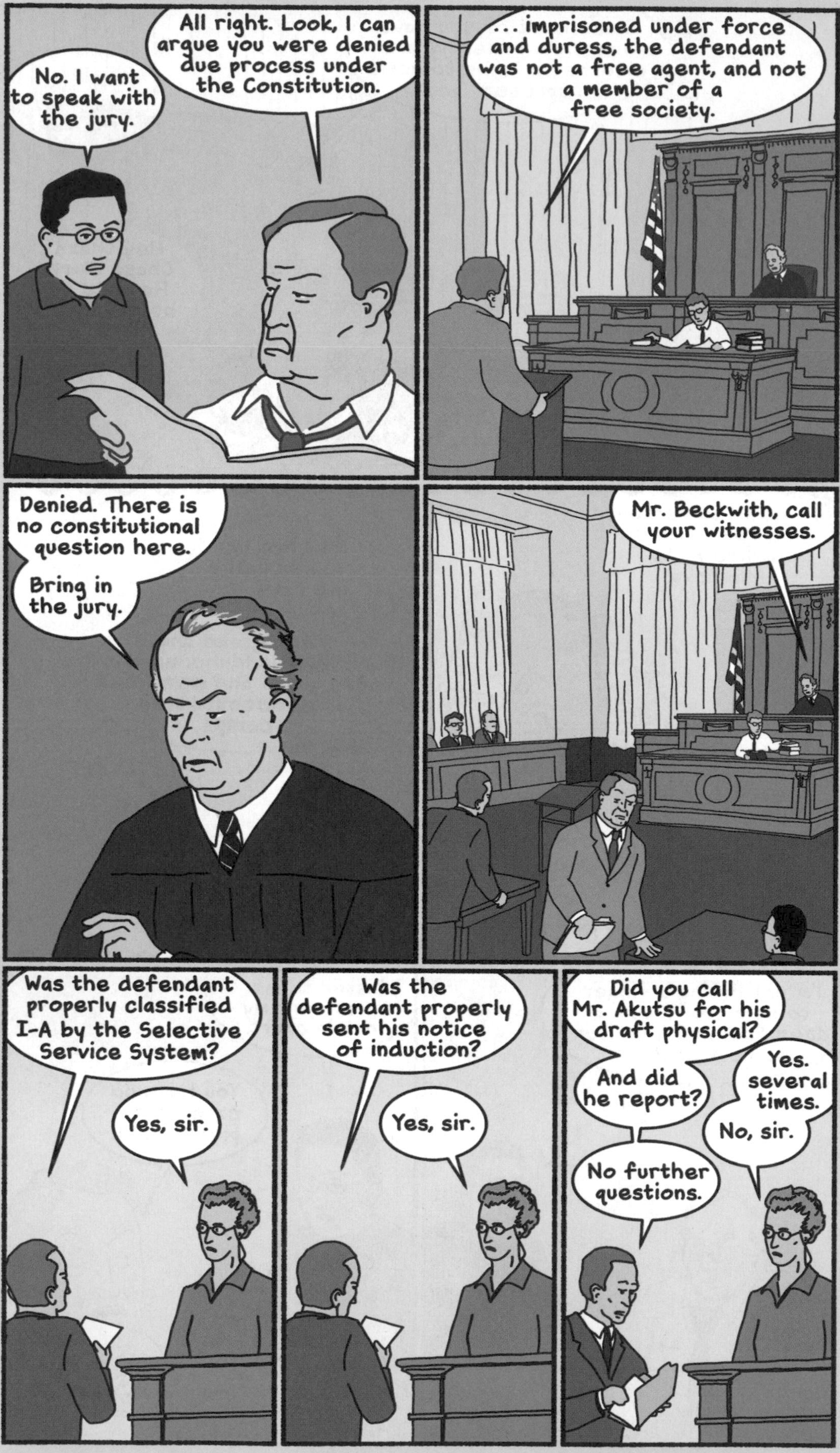
No. I want to speak with the jury.
All right. Look, I can argue you were denied due process under the Constitution.
... imprisoned under force and duress, the defendant was not a free agent, and not a member of a free society.
Denied. There is no constitutional question here.
Bring in the jury.
Mr. Beckwith, call your witnesses.
Was the defendant properly classified I-A by the Selective Service System?
Yes, sir.
Was the defendant properly sent his notice of induction?
Yes, sir.
Did you call Mr. Akutsu for his draft physical?
Yes. several times.
And did he report?
No, sir.
No further questions.

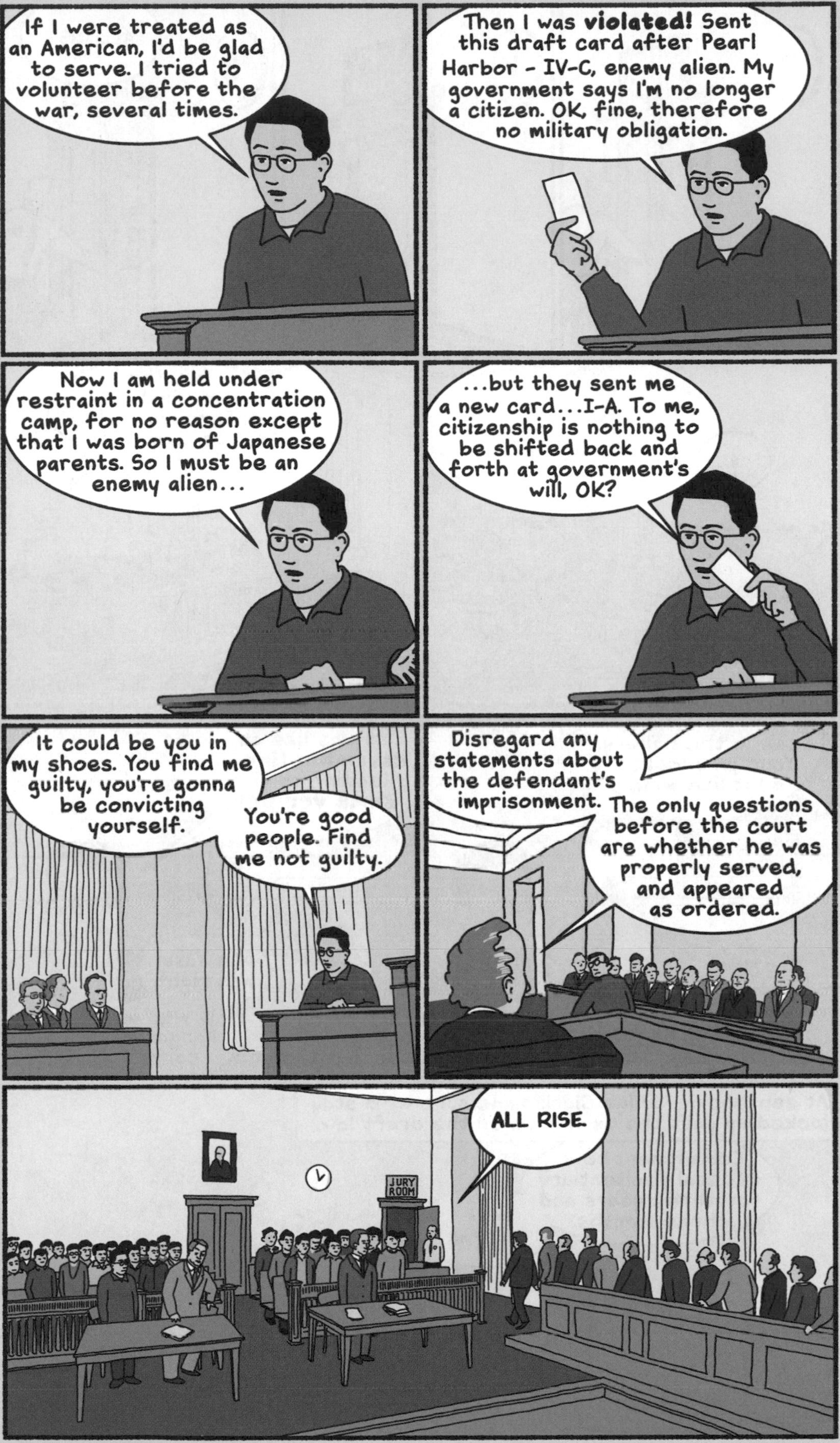
If I were treated as an American, I'd be glad to serve. I tried to volunteer before the war, several times.
Then I was **violated!** Sent this draft card after Pearl Harbor - IV-C, enemy alien. My government says I'm no longer a citizen. OK, fine, therefore no military obligation.
Now I am held under restraint in a concentration camp, for no reason except that I was born of Japanese parents. So I must be an enemy alien...
...but they sent me a new card...I-A. To me, citizenship is nothing to be shifted back and forth at government's will, OK?
It could be you in my shoes. You find me guilty, you're gonna be convicting yourself.
You're good people. Find me not guilty.
Disregard any statements about the defendant's imprisonment.
The only questions before the court are whether he was properly served, and appeared as ordered.
JURY ROOM
ALL RISE.

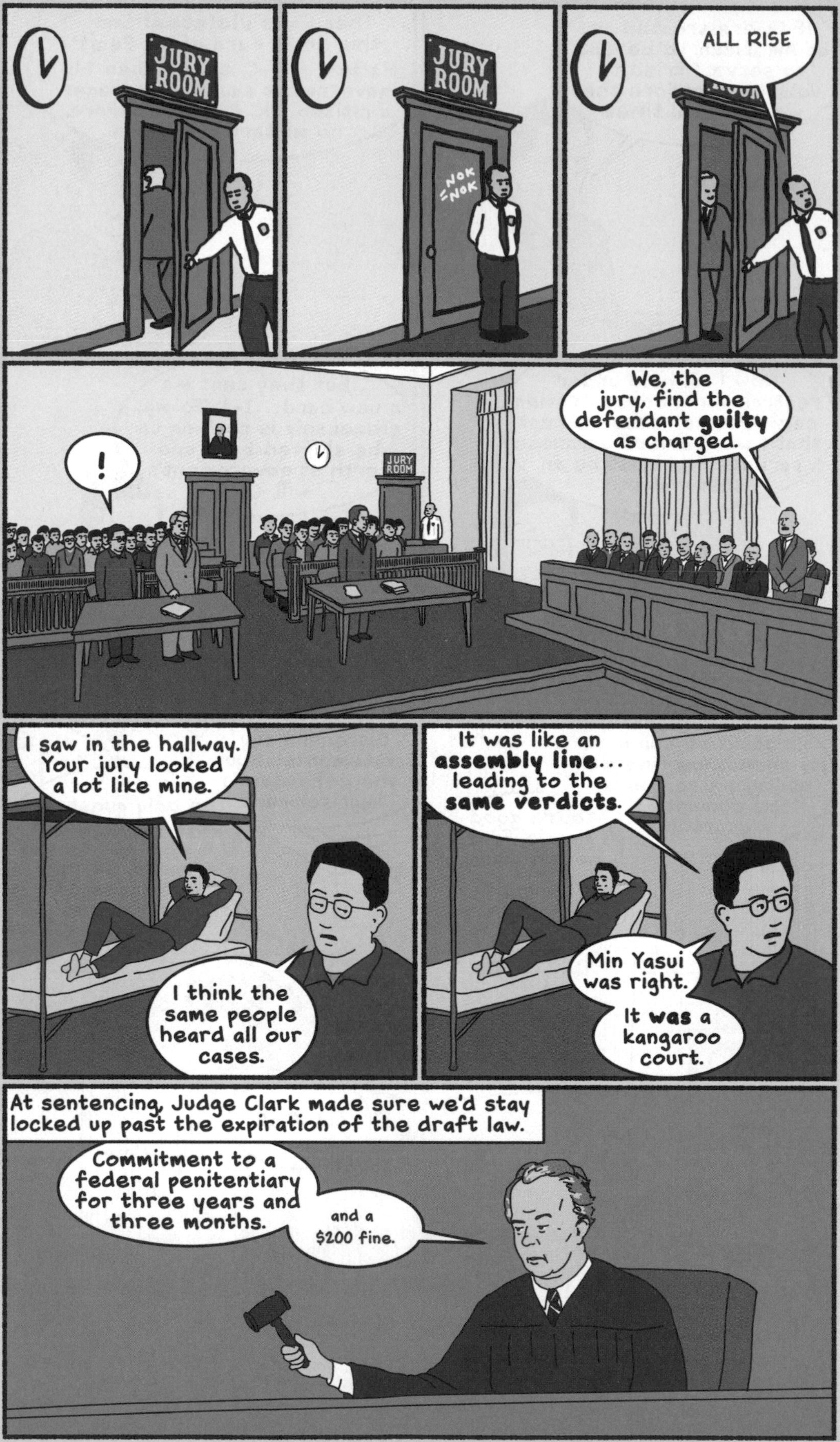
JURY ROOM
JURY ROOM
NOK NOK
ALL RISE
!
JURY ROOM
We, the jury, find the defendant guilty as charged.
I saw in the hallway. Your jury looked a lot like mine.
I think the same people heard all our cases.
It was like an assembly line... leading to the same verdicts.
Min Yasui was right.
It was a kangaroo court.
At sentencing, Judge Clark made sure we'd stay locked up past the expiration of the draft law.
Commitment to a federal penitentiary for three years and three months.
and a $200 fine.

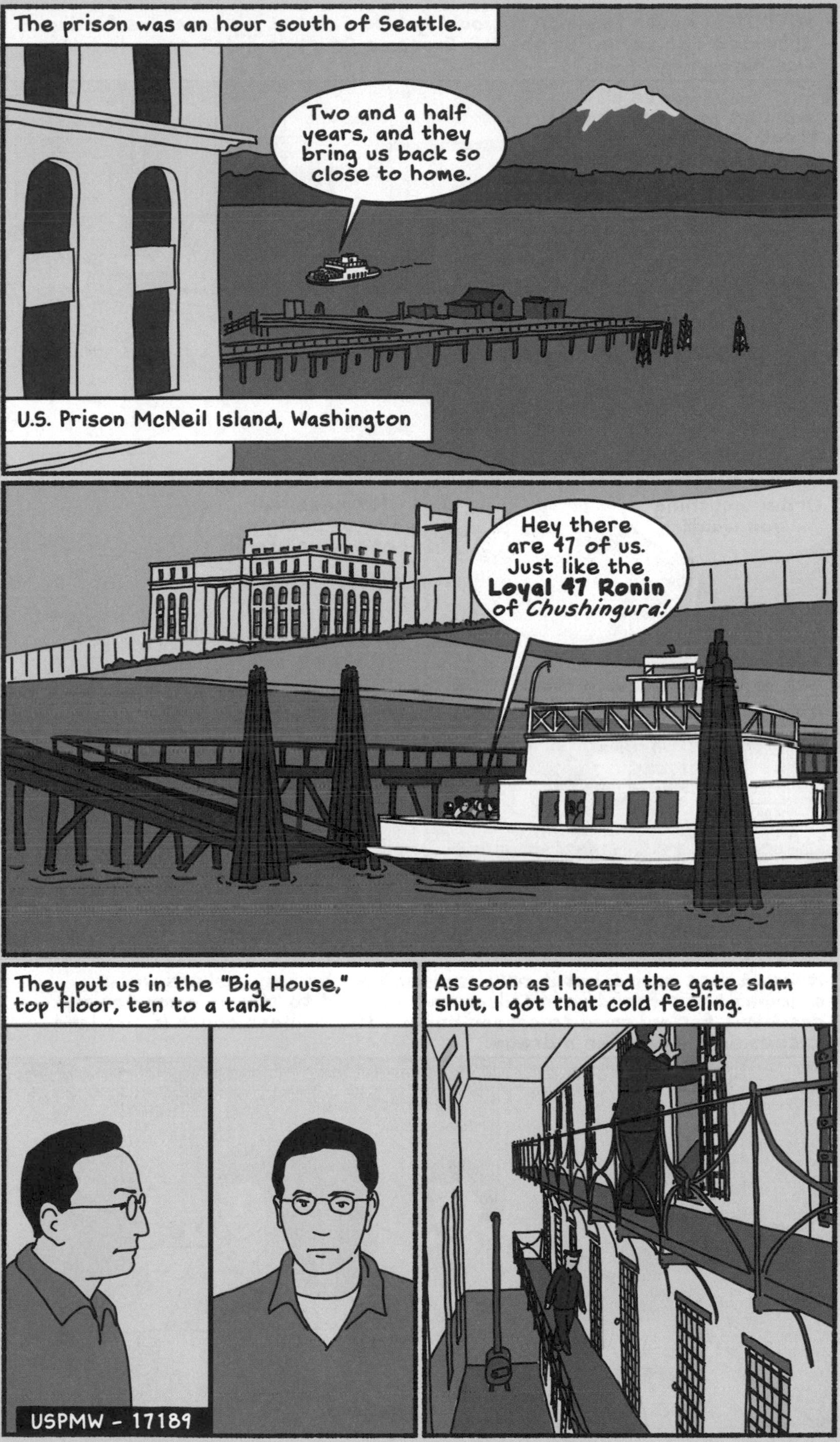

The prison was an hour south of Seattle.
Two and a half years, and they bring us back so close to home.
U.S. Prison McNeil Island, Washington
Hey there are 47 of us. Just like the Loyal 47 Ronin of Chushingura!
They put us in the "Big House," top floor, ten to a tank.
USPMW - 17189
As soon as I heard the gate slam shut, I got that cold feeling.

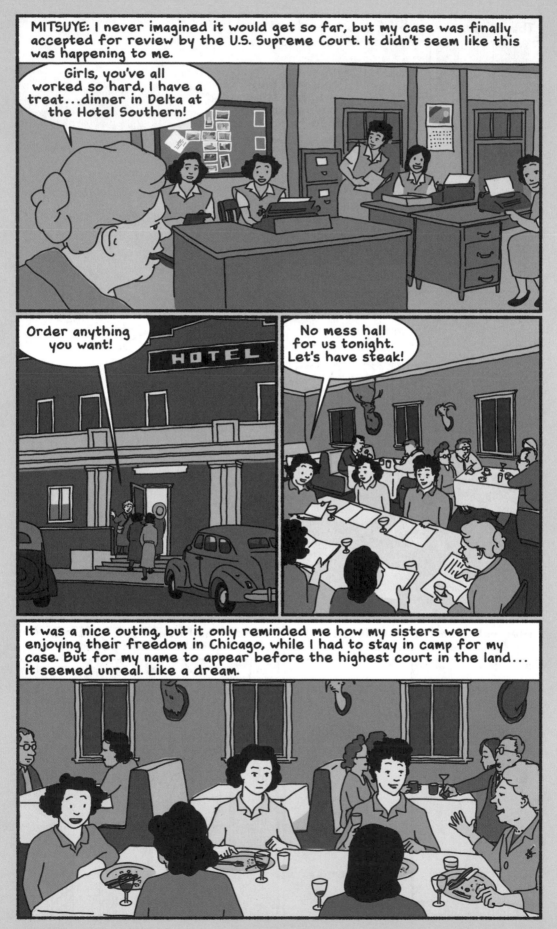

MITSUYE: I never imagined it would get so far, but my case was finally accepted for review by the U.S. Supreme Court. It didn't seem like this was happening to me.

Girls, you've all worked so hard, I have a treat...dinner in Delta at the Hotel Southern!

Order anything you want!

HOTEL

No mess hall for us tonight. Let's have steak!

It was a nice outing, but it only reminded me how my sisters were enjoying their freedom in Chicago, while I had to stay in camp for my case. But for my name to appear before the highest court in the land... it seemed unreal. Like a dream.

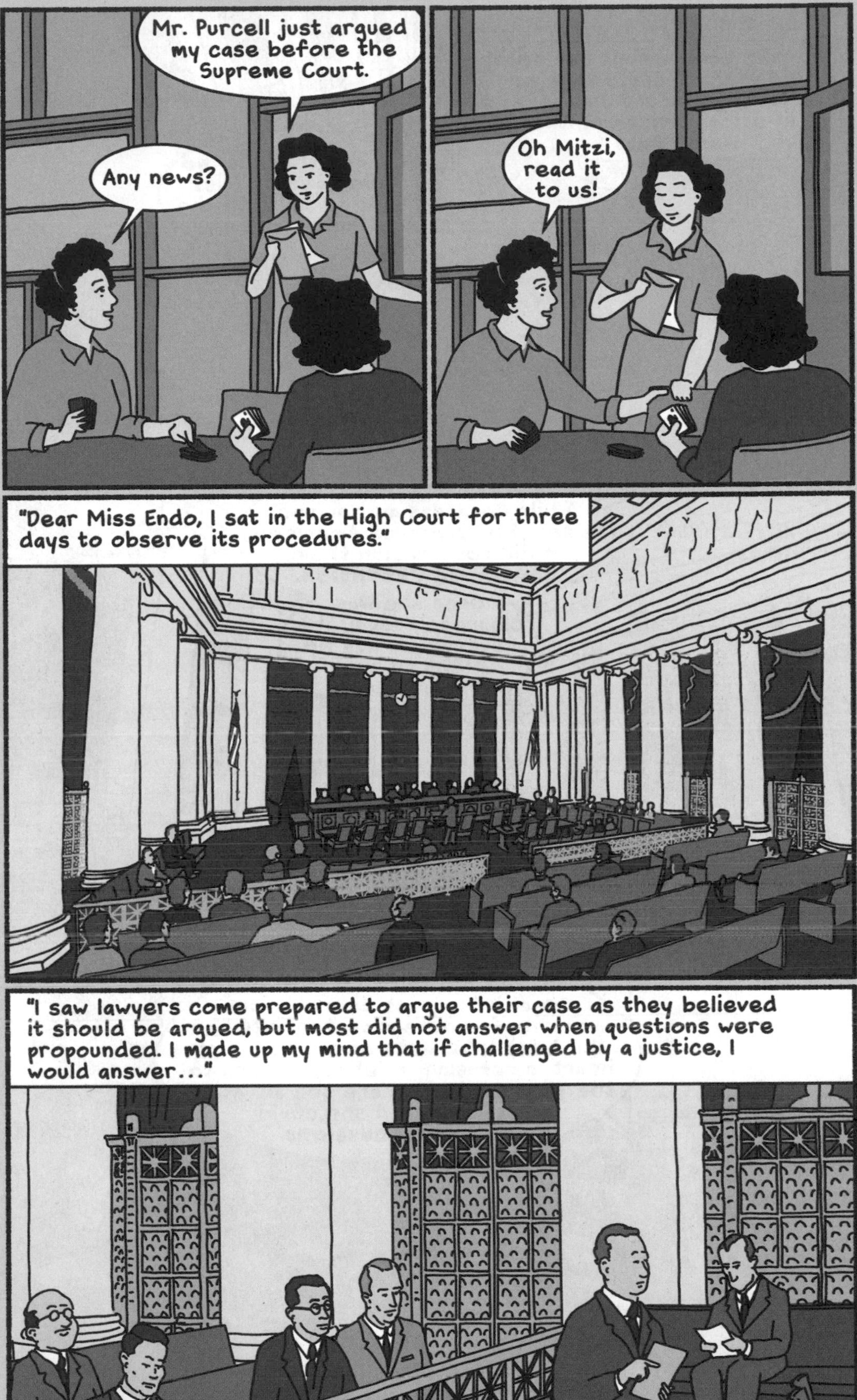
Any news?
Mr. Purcell just argued my case before the Supreme Court.
Oh Mitzi, read it to us!
"Dear Miss Endo, I sat in the High Court for three days to observe its procedures."
"I saw lawyers come prepared to argue their case as they believed it should be argued, but most did not answer when questions were propounded. I made up my mind that if challenged by a justice, I would answer..."

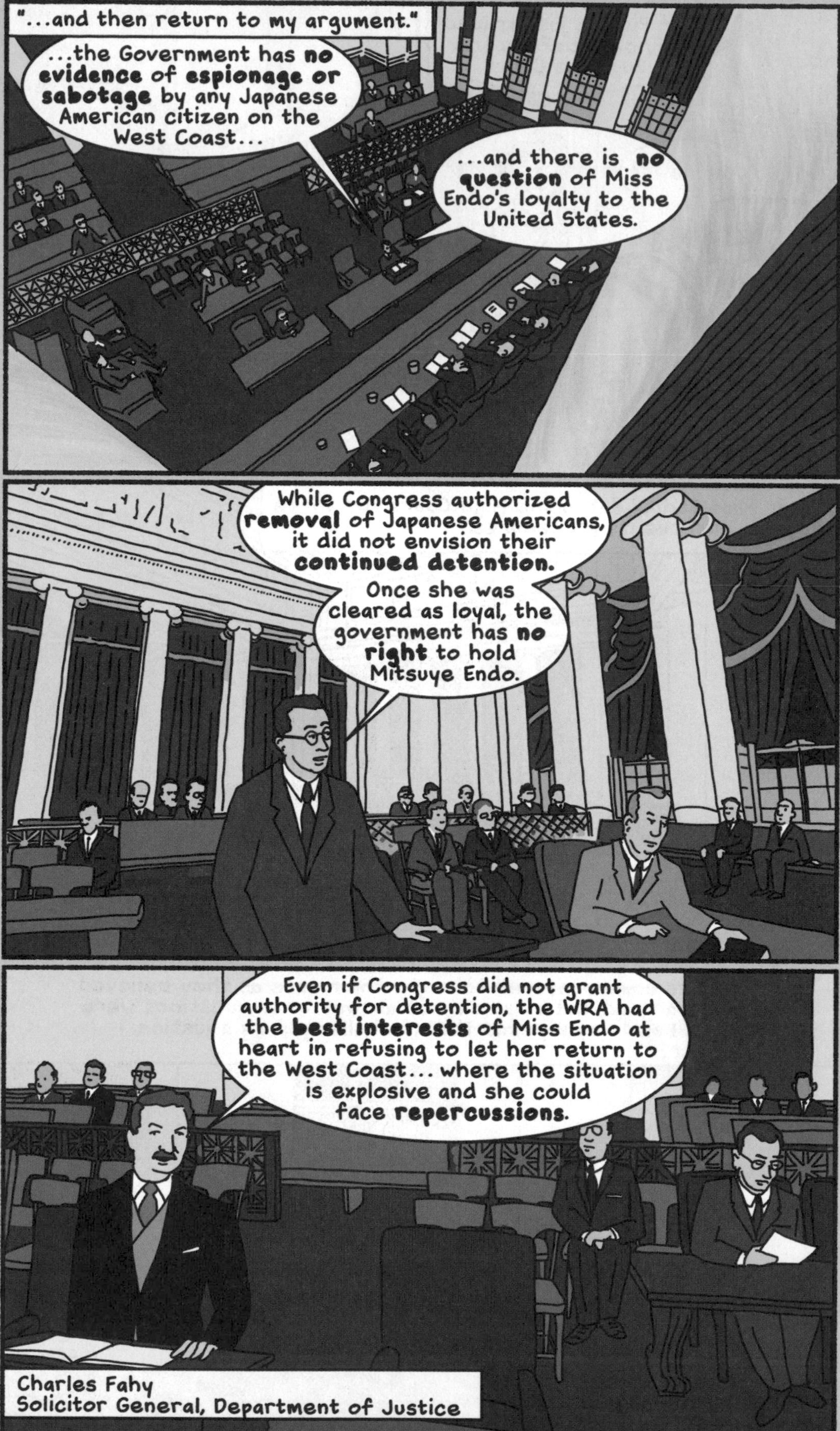
"...and then return to my argument."
...the Government has no evidence of espionage or sabotage by any Japanese American citizen on the West Coast...
...and there is no question of Miss Endo's loyalty to the United States.
While Congress authorized removal of Japanese Americans, it did not envision their continued detention.
Once she was cleared as loyal, the government has no right to hold Mitsuye Endo.
Even if Congress did not grant authority for detention, the WRA had the best interests of Miss Endo at heart in refusing to let her return to the West Coast... where the situation is explosive and she could face repercussions.
Charles Fahy
Solicitor General, Department of Justice

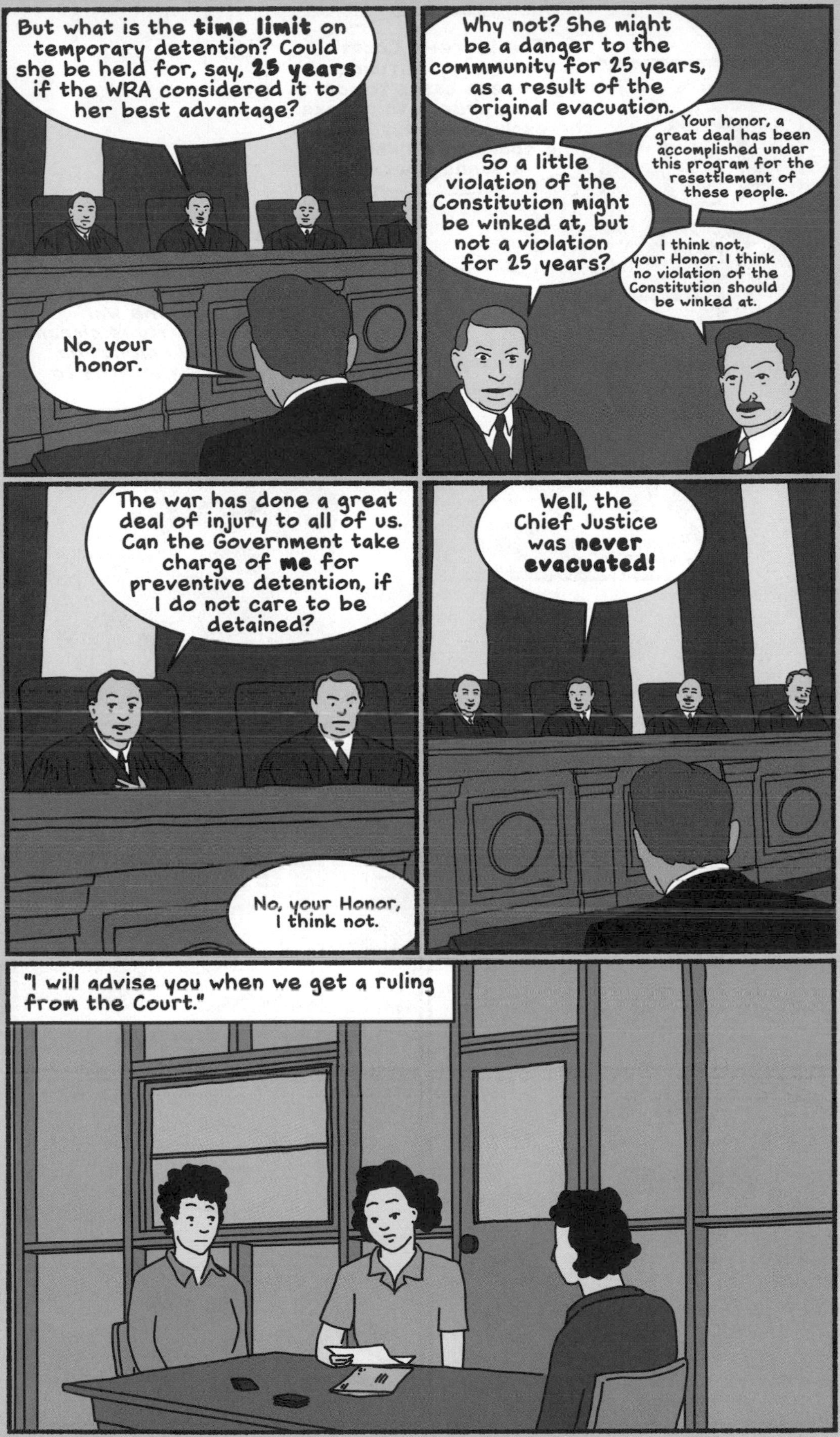
But what is the time limit on temporary detention? Could she be held for, say, 25 years if the WRA considered it to her best advantage?
No, your honor.
Why not? She might be a danger to the commmunity for 25 years, as a result of the original evacuation.
Your honor, a great deal has been accomplished under this program for the resettlement of these people.
So a little violation of the Constitution might be winked at, but not a violation for 25 years?
I think not, your Honor. I think no violation of the Constitution should be winked at.
The war has done a great deal of injury to all of us. Can the Government take charge of me for preventive detention, if I do not care to be detained?
No, your Honor, I think not.
Well, the Chief Justice was never evacuated!
"I will advise you when we get a ruling from the Court."

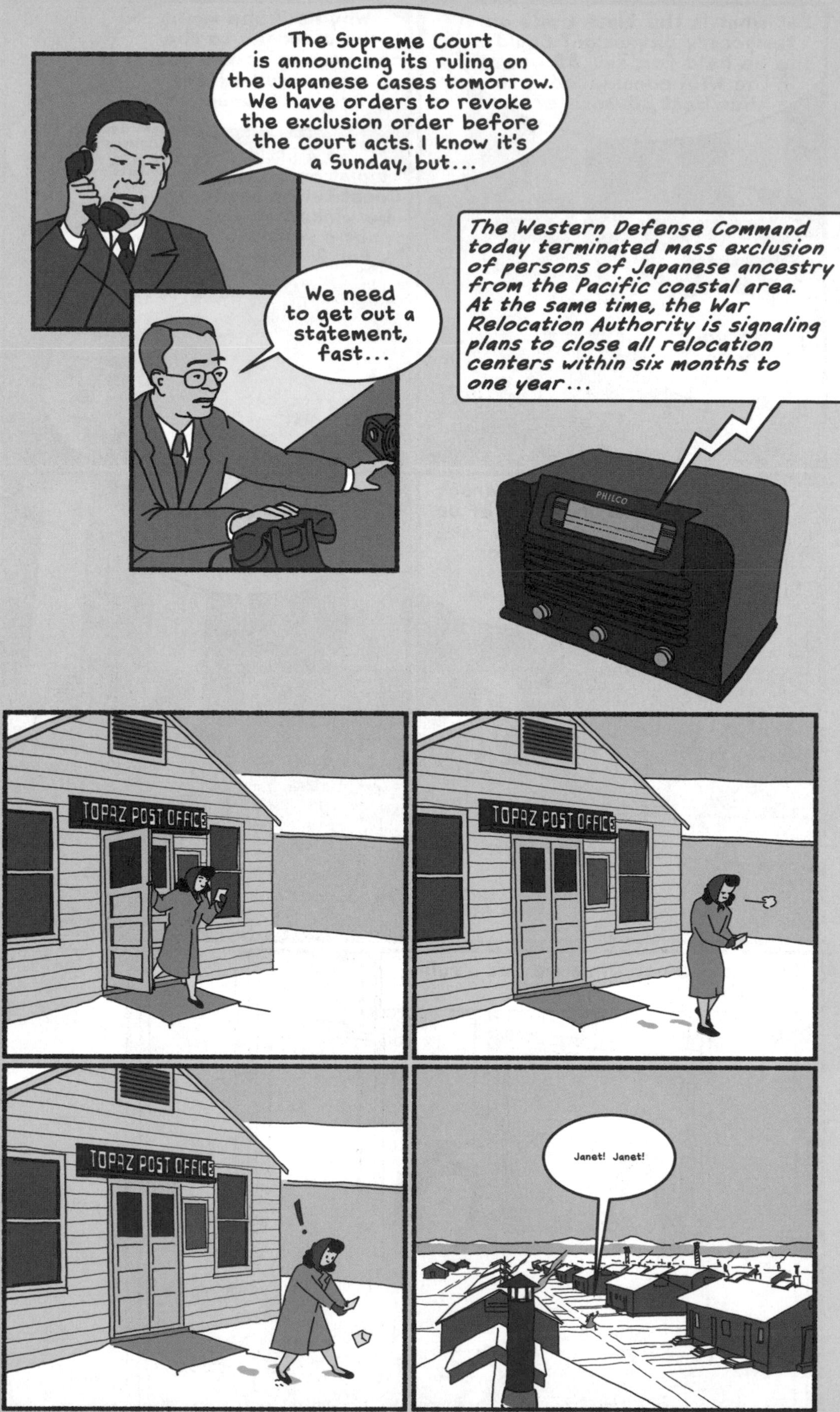
The Supreme Court is announcing its ruling on the Japanese cases tomorrow. We have orders to revoke the exclusion order before the court acts. I know it's a Sunday, but...
We need to get out a statement, fast...
The Western Defense Command today terminated mass exclusion of persons of Japanese ancestry from the Pacific coastal area. At the same time, the War Relocation Authority is signaling plans to close all relocation centers within six months to one year...
PHILCO
TOPAZ POST OFFICE
TOPAZ POST OFFICE
TOPAZ POST OFFICE
!
Janet! Janet!

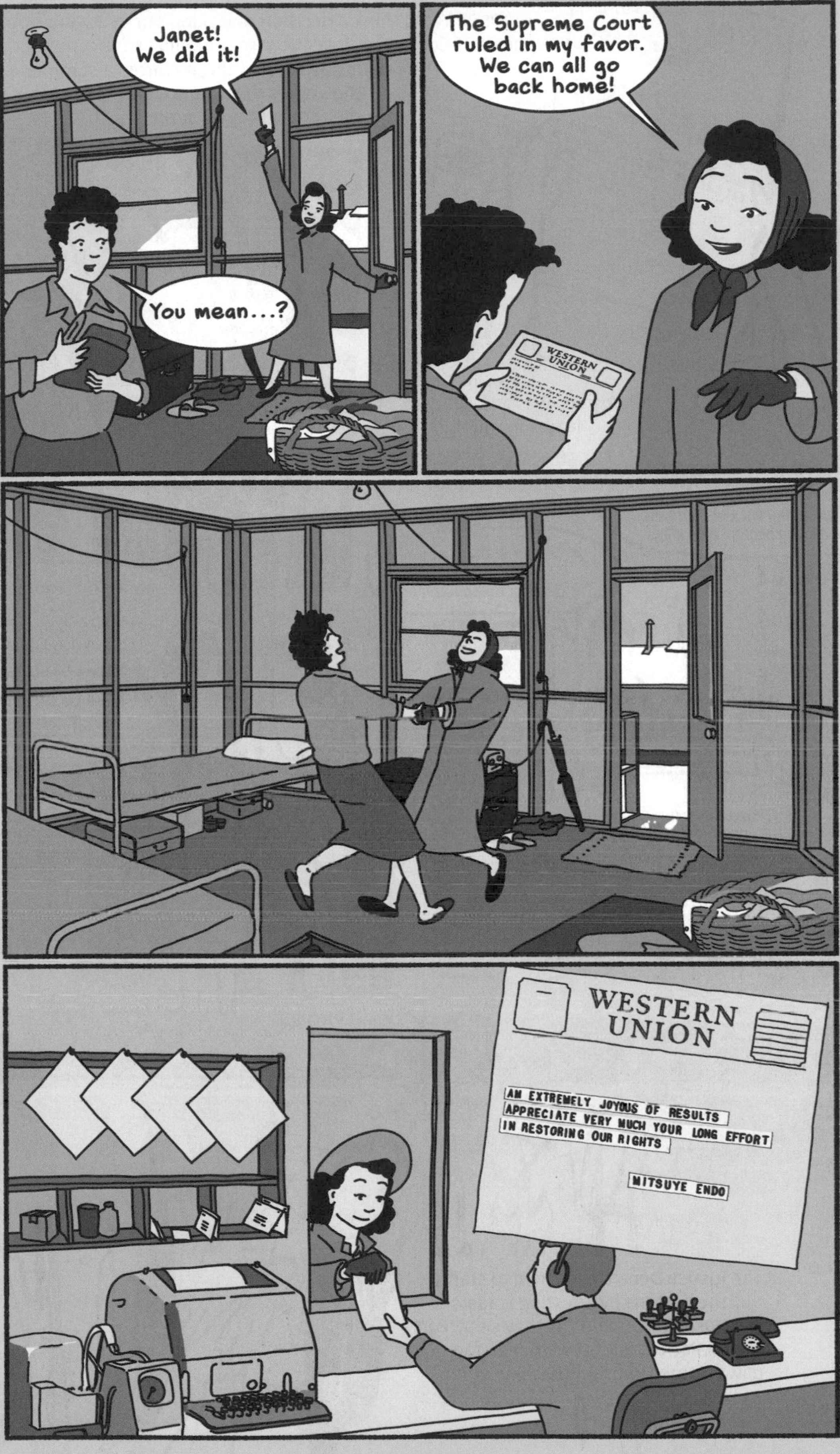
Janet! We did it!
You mean...?
The Supreme Court ruled in my favor. We can all go back home!
WESTERN UNION
WESTERN UNION
AM EXTREMELY JOYOUS OF RESULTS
APPRECIATE VERY MUCH YOUR LONG EFFORT
IN RESTORING OUR RIGHTS
MITSUYE ENDO

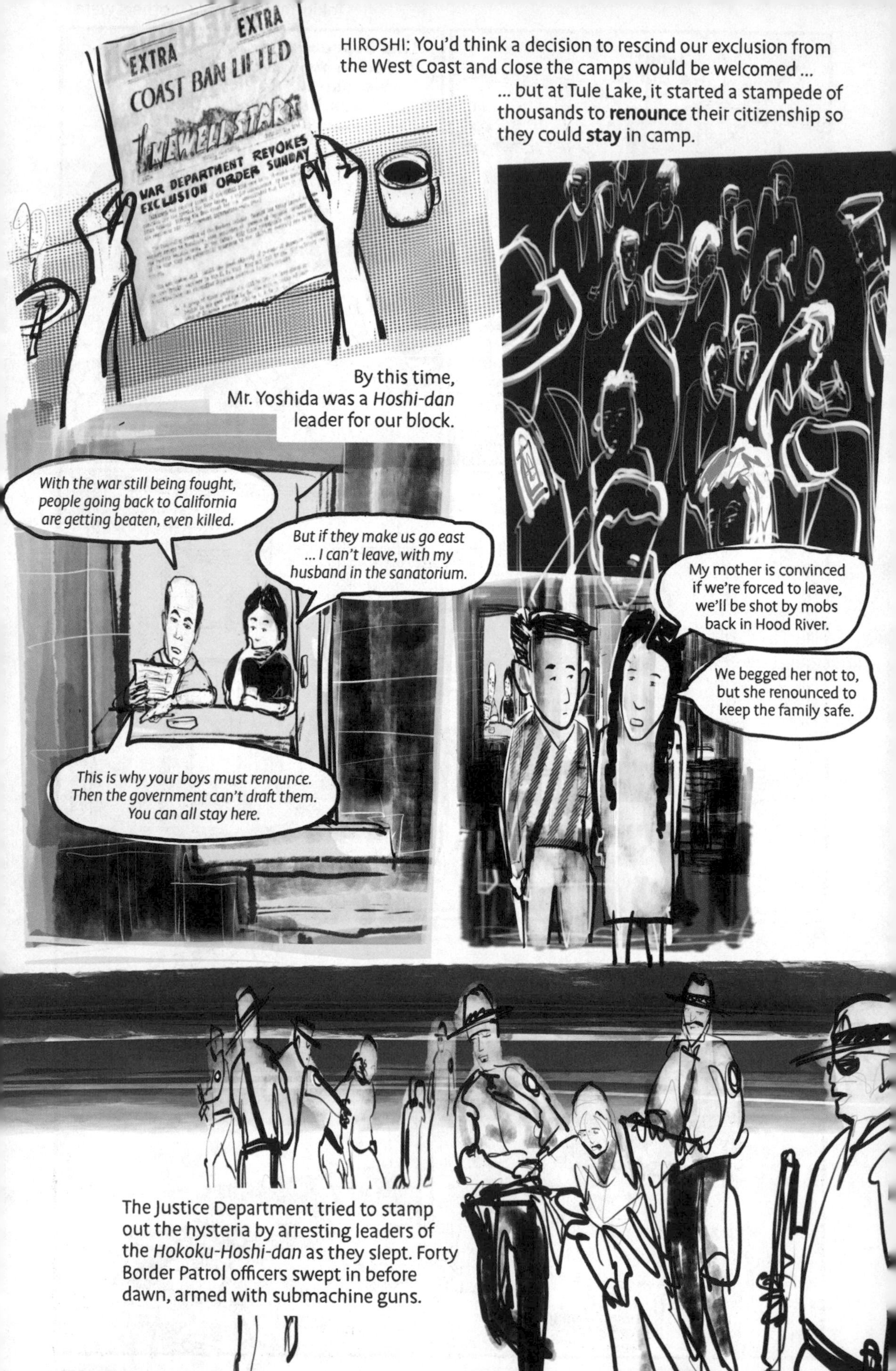
EXTRA
EXTRA
COAST BAN LIFTED
WAR DEPARTMENT REVOKES EXCLUSION ORDER SUNDAY
HIROSHI: You'd think a decision to rescind our exclusion from the West Coast and close the camps would be welcomed ...
... but at Tule Lake, it started a stampede of thousands to **renounce** their citizenship so they could **stay** in camp.
By this time, Mr. Yoshida was a *Hoshi-dan* leader for our block.
With the war still being fought, people going back to California are getting beaten, even killed.
But if they make us go east ... I can't leave, with my husband in the sanatorium.
This is why your boys must renounce. Then the government can't draft them. You can all stay here.
My mother is convinced if we're forced to leave, we'll be shot by mobs back in Hood River.
We begged her not to, but she renounced to keep the family safe.
The Justice Department tried to stamp out the hysteria by arresting leaders of the *Hokoku-Hoshi-dan* as they slept. Forty Border Patrol officers swept in before dawn, armed with submachine guns.

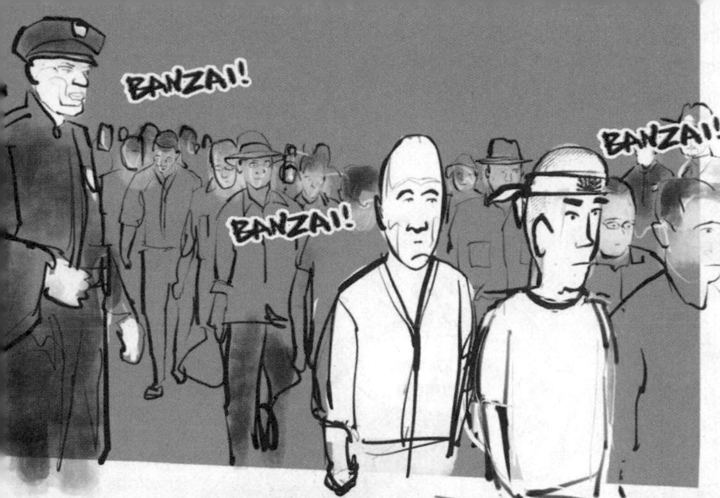
BANZAI!
BANZAI!
BANZAI!

Tokio Yamane and 69 others were celebrated as martyrs as they were put onto trucks bound for a Justice Department camp in Santa Fe, amid cheers, singing, and much bugle-blowing.

Using lists of names seized from the *Hoshi-dan* office, more arrests were ordered. To hold them, Mr. Best built a new concrete jail near the highway and an open field designated "Area 99."

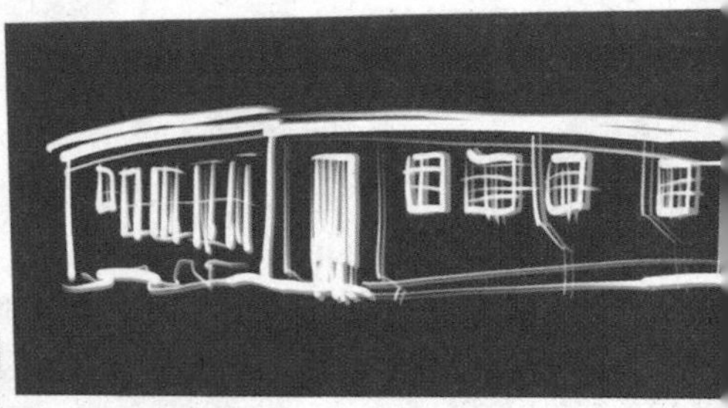

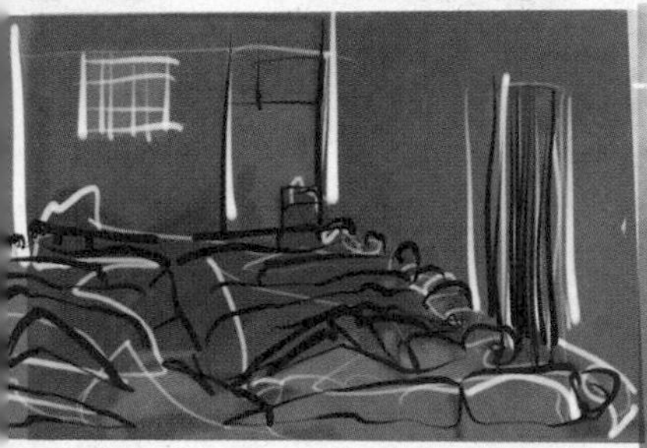

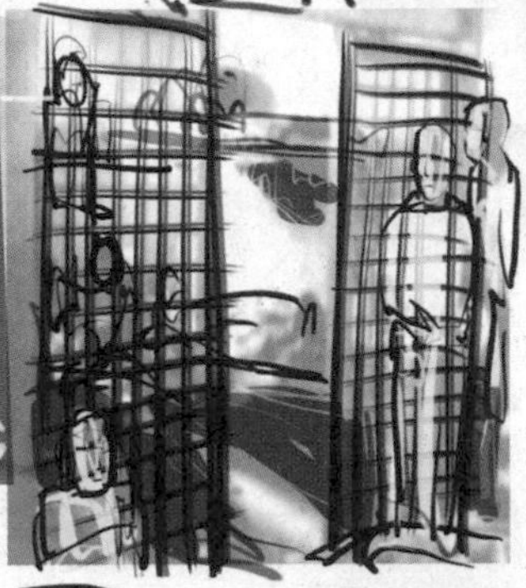

One hundred at a time were packed into space meant for 24, to await transfer to Department of Justice camps in New Mexico and North Dakota.

The leadership purge weakened control of the resegregationists. Bugle-blowing was banned. But diehards still confronted Tuleans about where we stood, as Ryo and Sparky learned while peeling potatoes at the mess hall.

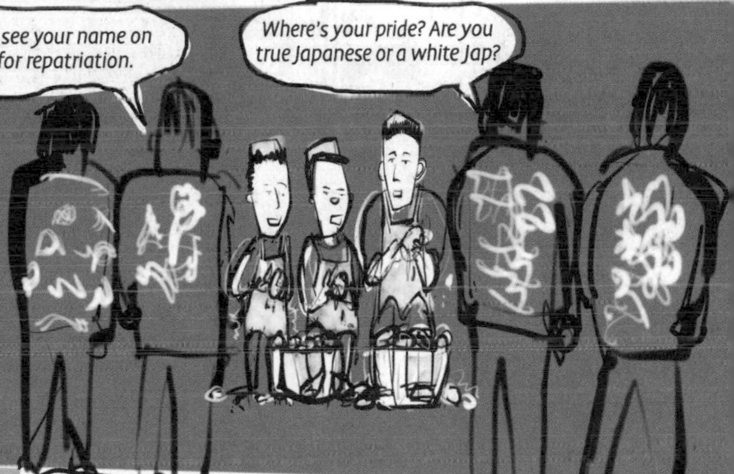
We didn't see your name on the list for repatriation.
Where's your pride? Are you true Japanese or a white Jap?

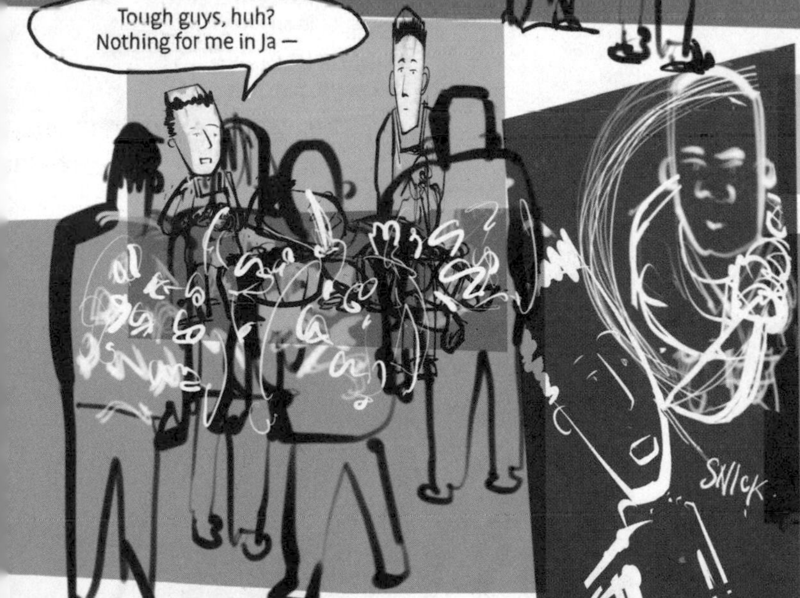
Tough guys, huh? Nothing for me in Ja —
SNICK

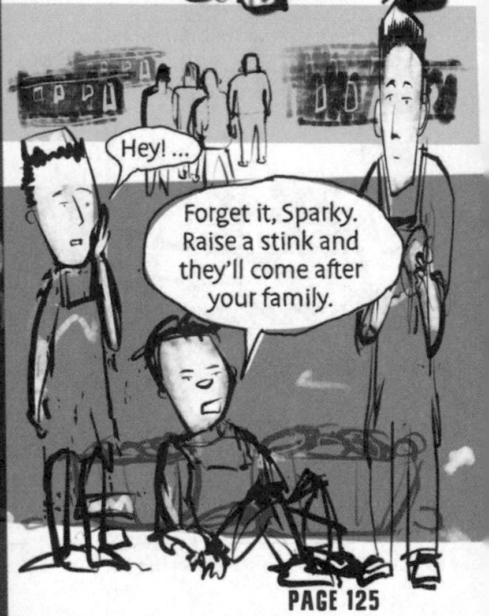
Hey! ...
Forget it, Sparky. Raise a stink and they'll come after your family.

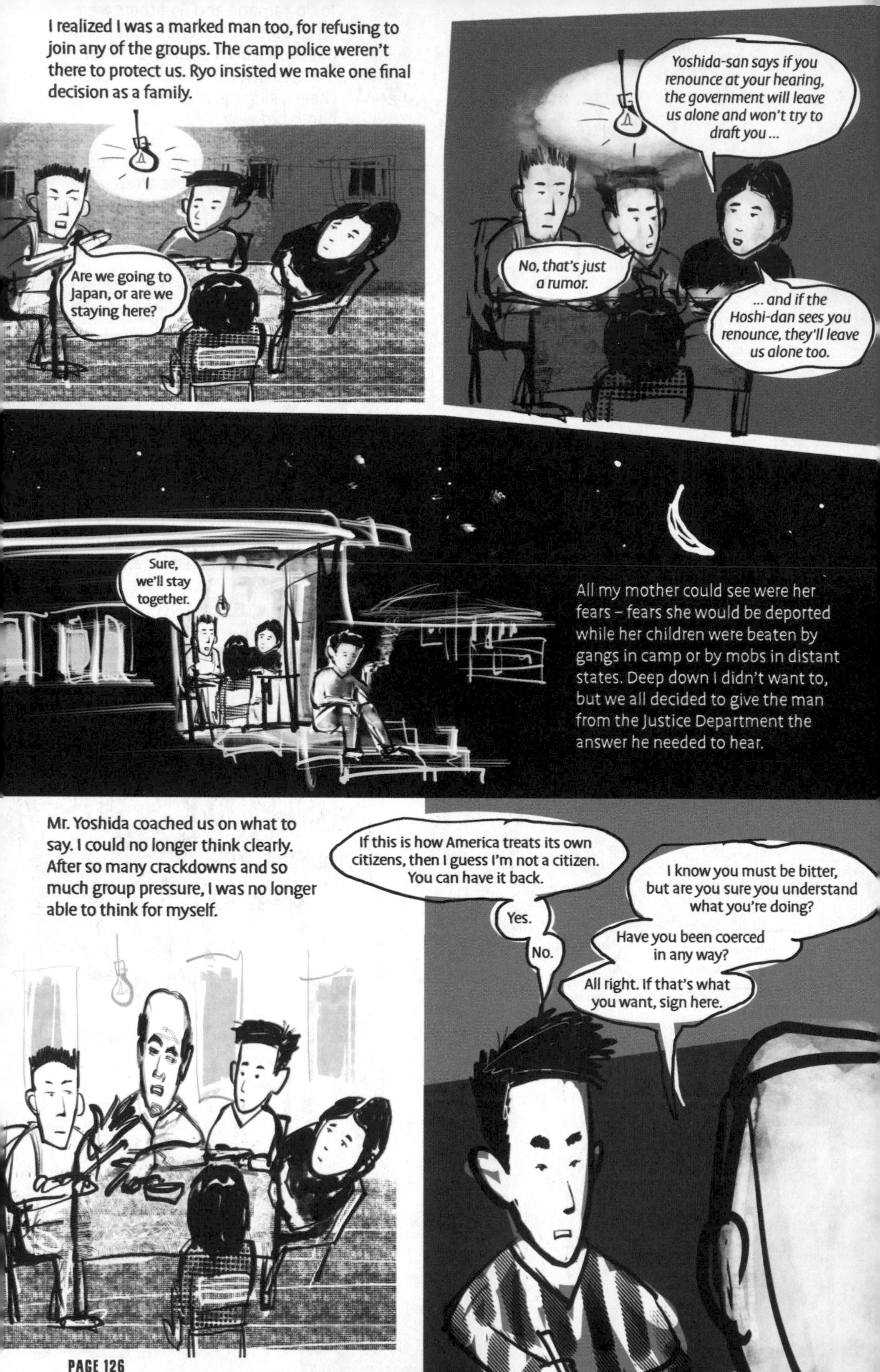
I realized I was a marked man too, for refusing to join any of the groups. The camp police weren't there to protect us. Ryo insisted we make one final decision as a family.
Are we going to Japan, or are we staying here?
Yoshida-san says if you renounce at your hearing, the government will leave us alone and won't try to draft you ...
No, that's just a rumor.
... and if the Hoshi-dan sees you renounce, they'll leave us alone too.
Sure, we'll stay together.
All my mother could see were her fears – fears she would be deported while her children were beaten by gangs in camp or by mobs in distant states. Deep down I didn't want to, but we all decided to give the man from the Justice Department the answer he needed to hear.
Mr. Yoshida coached us on what to say. I could no longer think clearly. After so many crackdowns and so much group pressure, I was no longer able to think for myself.
If this is how America treats its own citizens, then I guess I'm not a citizen. You can have it back.
I know you must be bitter, but are you sure you understand what you're doing?
Yes.
Have you been coerced in any way?
No.
All right. If that's what you want, sign here.

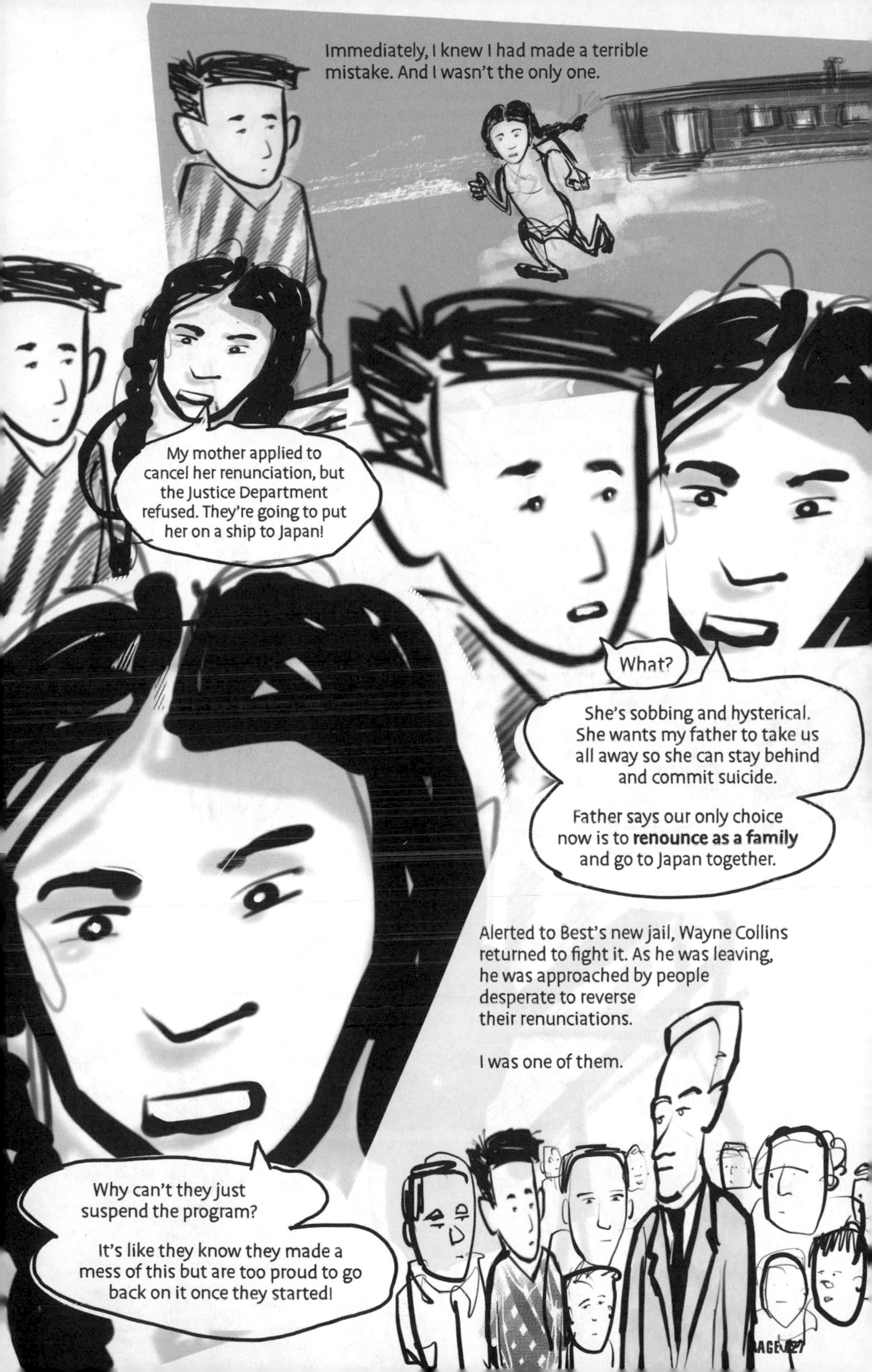

Immediately, I knew I had made a terrible mistake. And I wasn't the only one.
My mother applied to cancel her renunciation, but the Justice Department refused. They're going to put her on a ship to Japan!
What?
She's sobbing and hysterical. She wants my father to take us all away so she can stay behind and commit suicide.
Father says our only choice now is to **renounce as a family** and go to Japan together.
Why can't they just suspend the program?
It's like they know they made a mess of this but are too proud to go back on it once they started!
Alerted to Best's new jail, Wayne Collins returned to fight it. As he was leaving, he was approached by people desperate to reverse their renunciations.
I was one of them.

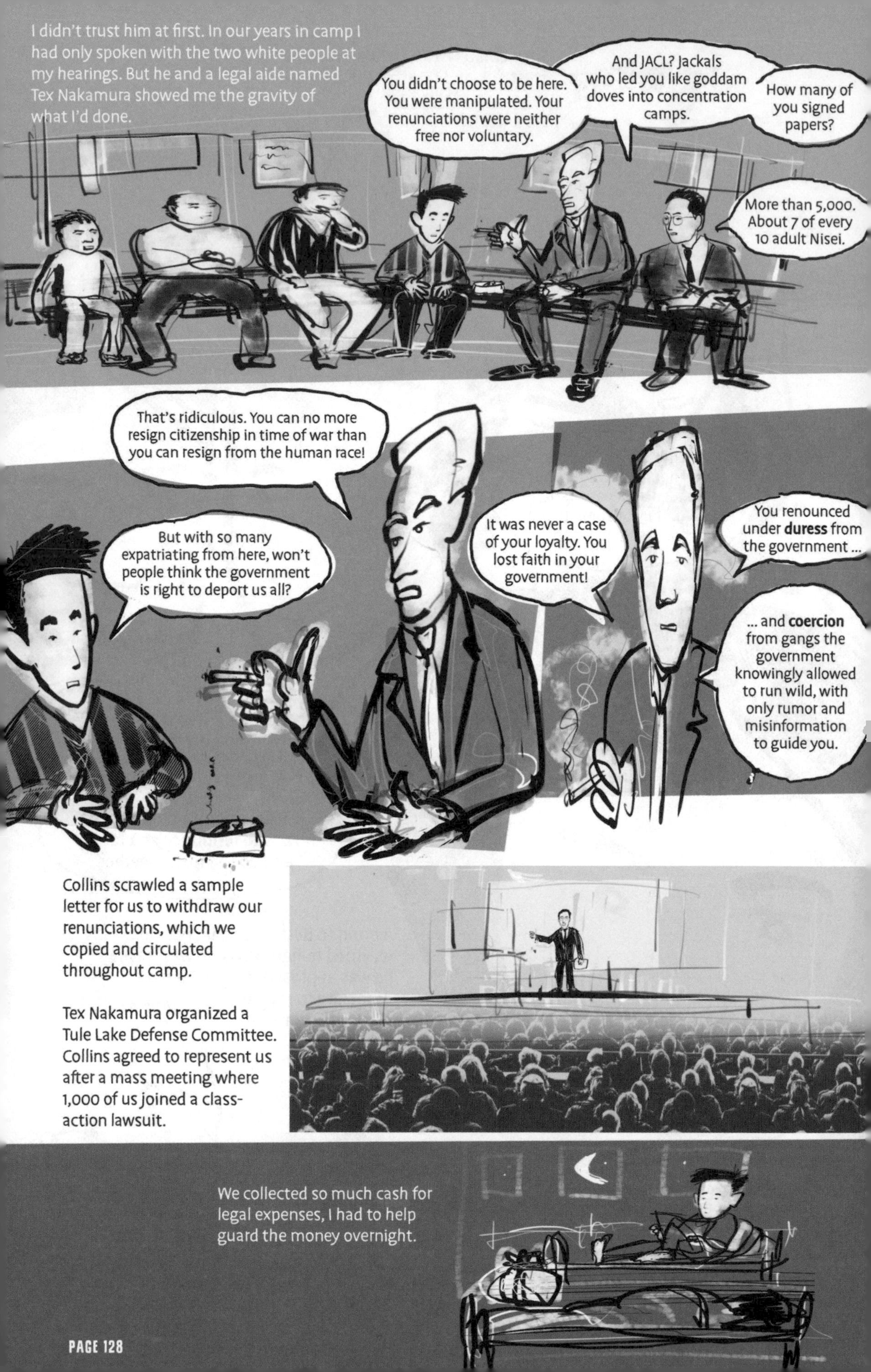
I didn't trust him at first. In our years in camp I had only spoken with the two white people at my hearings. But he and a legal aide named Tex Nakamura showed me the gravity of what I'd done.
You didn't choose to be here. You were manipulated. Your renunciations were neither free nor voluntary.
And JACL? Jackals who led you like goddam doves into concentration camps.
How many of you signed papers?
More than 5,000. About 7 of every 10 adult Nisei.
That's ridiculous. You can no more resign citizenship in time of war than you can resign from the human race!
But with so many expatriating from here, won't people think the government is right to deport us all?
It was never a case of your loyalty. You lost faith in your government!
You renounced under **duress** from the government ...
... and **coercion** from gangs the government knowingly allowed to run wild, with only rumor and misinformation to guide you.
Collins scrawled a sample letter for us to withdraw our renunciations, which we copied and circulated throughout camp.
Tex Nakamura organized a Tule Lake Defense Committee. Collins agreed to represent us after a mass meeting where 1,000 of us joined a class-action lawsuit.
We collected so much cash for legal expenses, I had to help guard the money overnight.

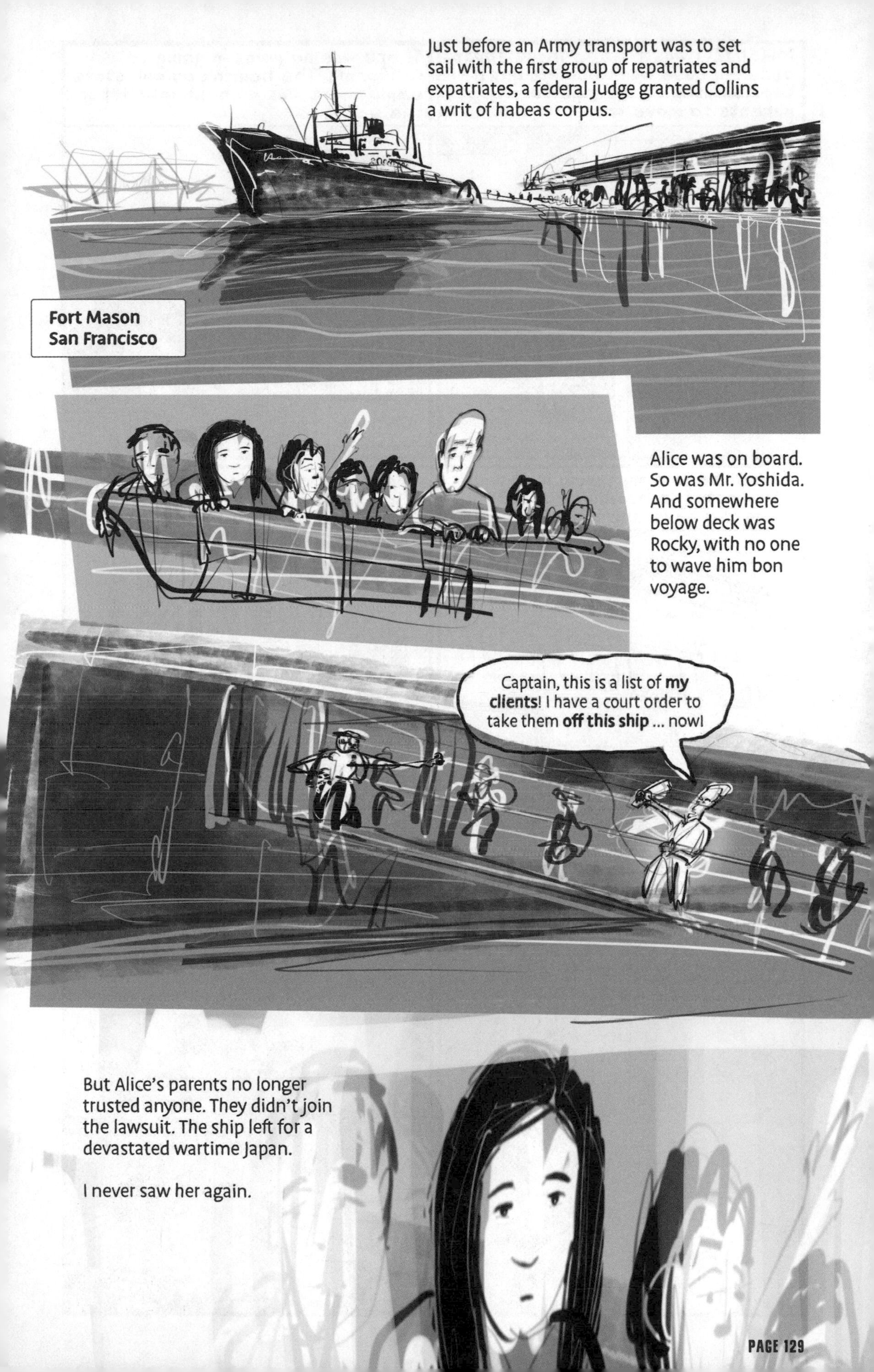
Just before an Army transport was to set sail with the first group of repatriates and expatriates, a federal judge granted Collins a writ of habeas corpus.
Fort Mason San Francisco
Alice was on board. So was Mr. Yoshida. And somewhere below deck was Rocky, with no one to wave him bon voyage.
Captain, this is a list of **my clients**! I have a court order to take them **off this ship** ... now!
But Alice's parents no longer trusted anyone. They didn't join the lawsuit. The ship left for a devastated wartime Japan.
I never saw her again.

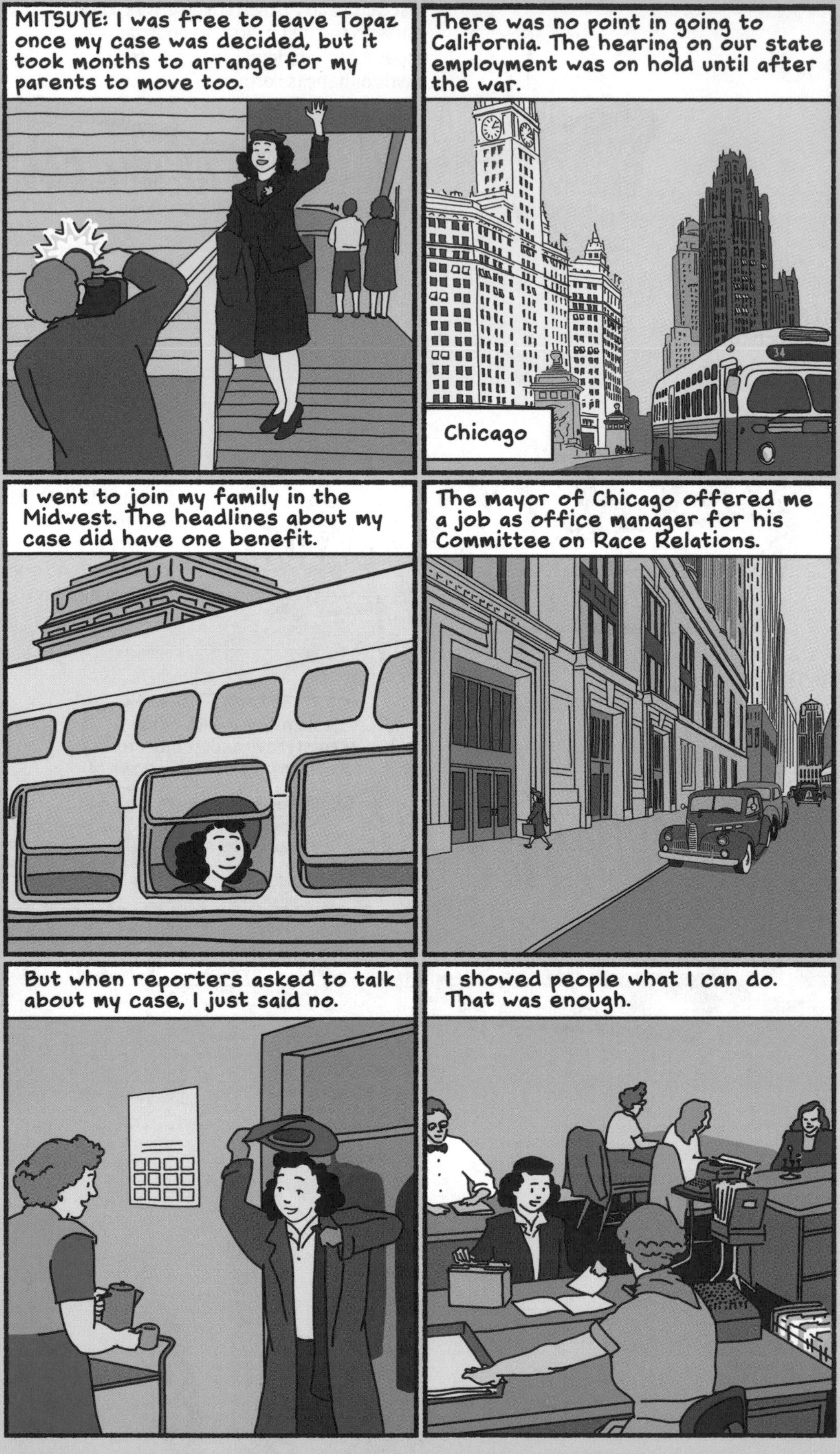
MITSUYE: I was free to leave Topaz once my case was decided, but it took months to arrange for my parents to move too.
There was no point in going to California. The hearing on our state employment was on hold until after the war.
34
Chicago
I went to join my family in the Midwest. The headlines about my case did have one benefit.
The mayor of Chicago offered me a job as office manager for his Committee on Race Relations.
But when reporters asked to talk about my case, I just said no.
I showed people what I can do. That was enough.

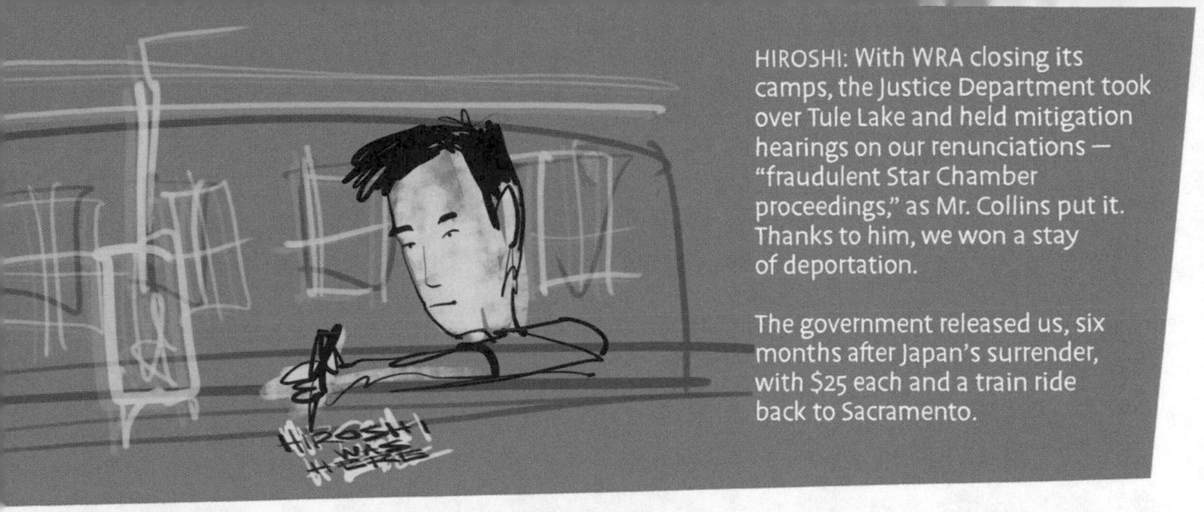
HIROSHI: With WRA closing its camps, the Justice Department took over Tule Lake and held mitigation hearings on our renunciations — "fraudulent Star Chamber proceedings," as Mr. Collins put it. Thanks to him, we won a stay of deportation.
The government released us, six months after Japan's surrender, with $25 each and a train ride back to Sacramento.
HIROSHI WAS HERE

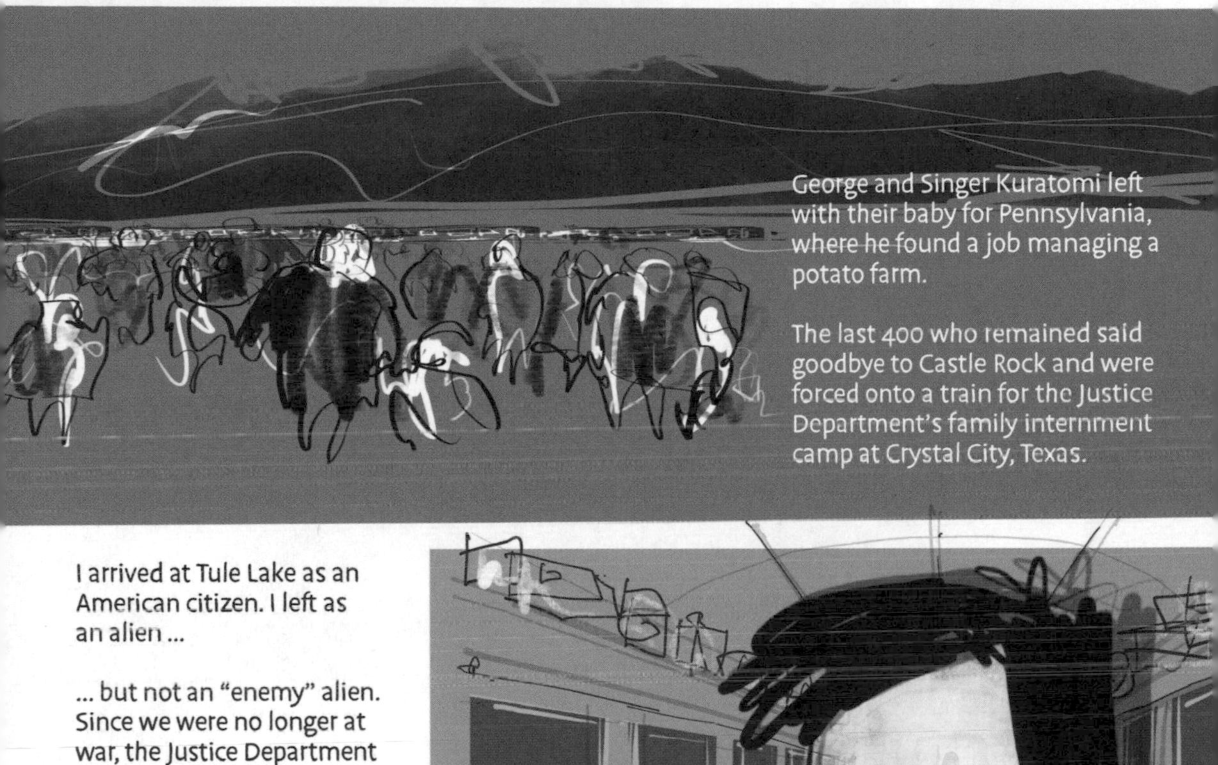
George and Singer Kuratomi left with their baby for Pennsylvania, where he found a job managing a potato farm.
The last 400 who remained said goodbye to Castle Rock and were forced onto a train for the Justice Department's family internment camp at Crystal City, Texas.

I arrived at Tule Lake as an American citizen. I left as an alien ...

... but not an "enemy" alien. Since we were no longer at war, the Justice Department had to invent a new term for us — **"native American alien."**

It meant I was a citizen of no nation, an alien in the country of my birth. And I faced a long struggle to reverse my renunciation and claim back my citizenship.

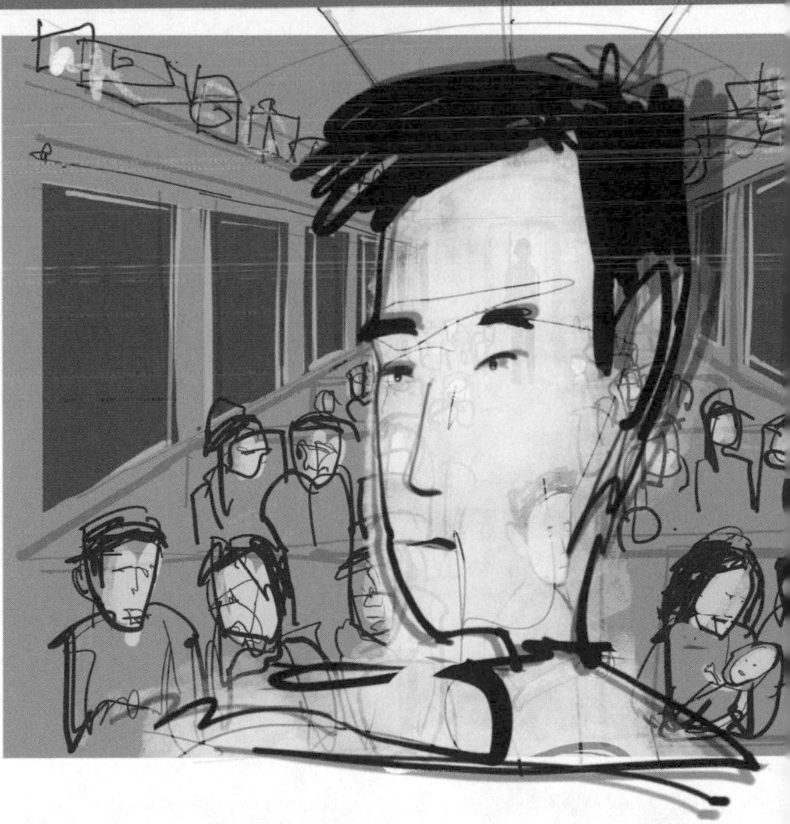

RECORD OF PRISONERS RECEIVED

UNITED STATES PENITENTIARY

McNEIL ISLAND, WASHINGTON

Akutsu, Jim Hajime

Register No. 17189

October 6, 1944

Idaho

Selective Training & Service Act

3 years 3 months

Convicted Boise, Idaho

Convicted October 2, 1944

Arrested Hunt, Idaho

Arrested July 21, 1944

long in Jail From arrest

of Sentence October 2, 1944

ence Begins October 2, 1944

sentence Expires January 1, 1948

d time Expires April 3, 1947

ible for Parole November 1, 1945

upation Farmer

ere Born Seattle, Washington

en Born 1-25-20 Married No

sidence Seattle, Washington

ddress of Relatives Father

Height 5 Ft. 5 in. Weight

Color of Hair Black

Color of Eyes Brown

Complexion Ruddy

Build Slim

When and How Released

U. S. PENITENTIARY
DISCHARGED
APR 30 1946

McNeil's Island, Wash.

— PART FIVE —

NO GOING HOME

1946

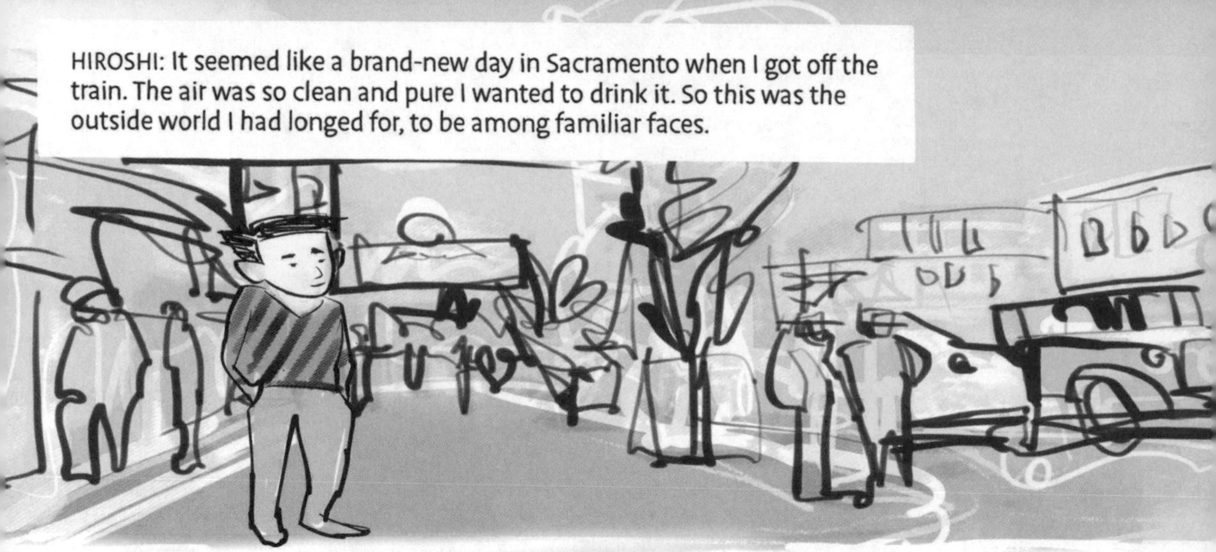
HIROSHI: It seemed like a brand-new day in Sacramento when I got off the train. The air was so clean and pure I wanted to drink it. So this was the outside world I had longed for, to be among familiar faces.

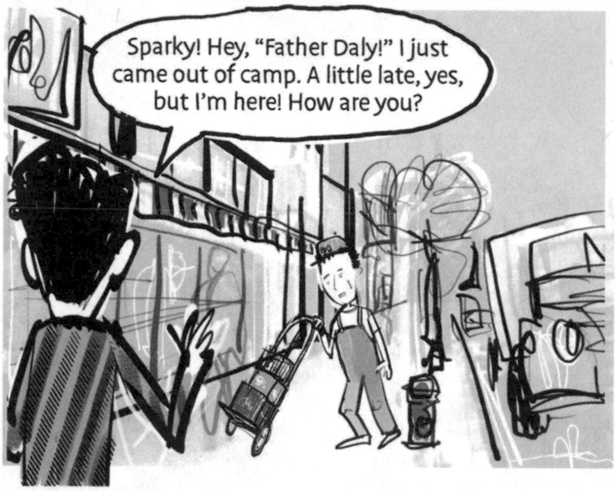
Sparky! Hey, "Father Daly!" I just came out of camp. A little late, yes, but I'm here! How are you?

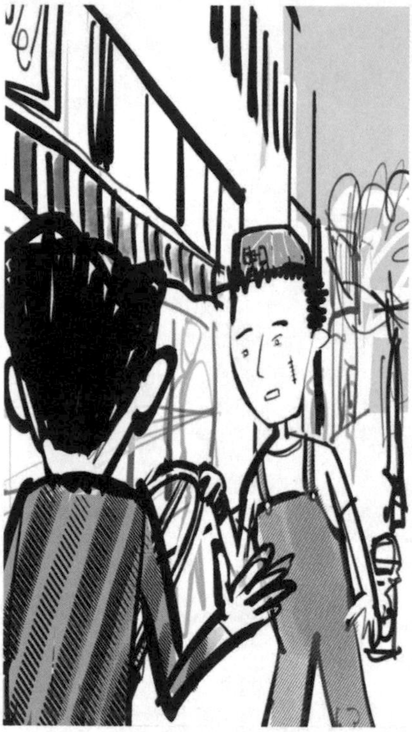

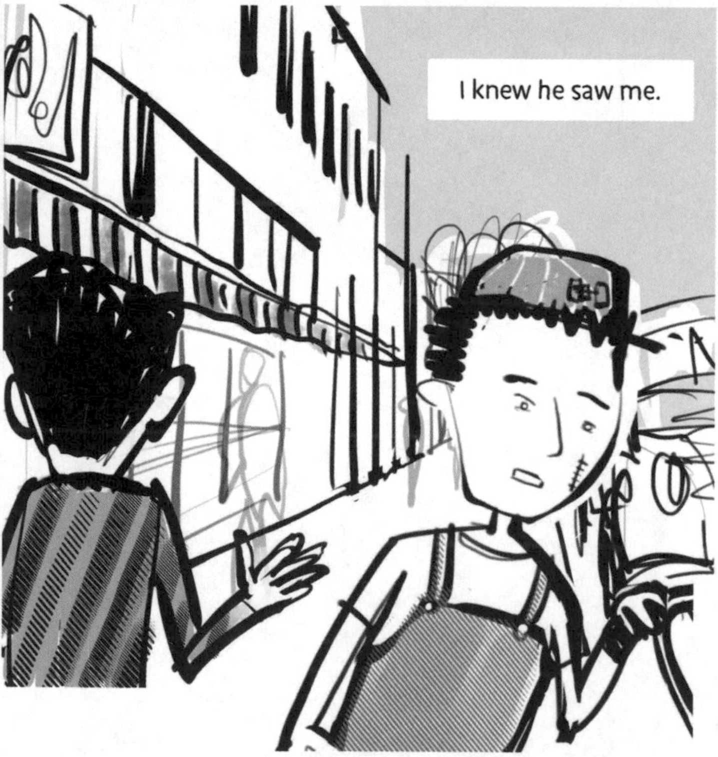
I knew he saw me.

Then I got it. The silent treatment. Camp was camp. Now that we were outside starting over again, you want to put Tule Lake behind you. We were no-no boys. Disloyals, to be avoided. Pariahs ... even to each other.

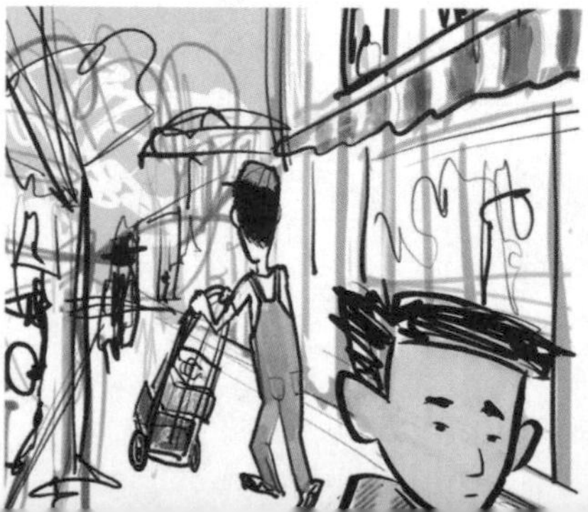

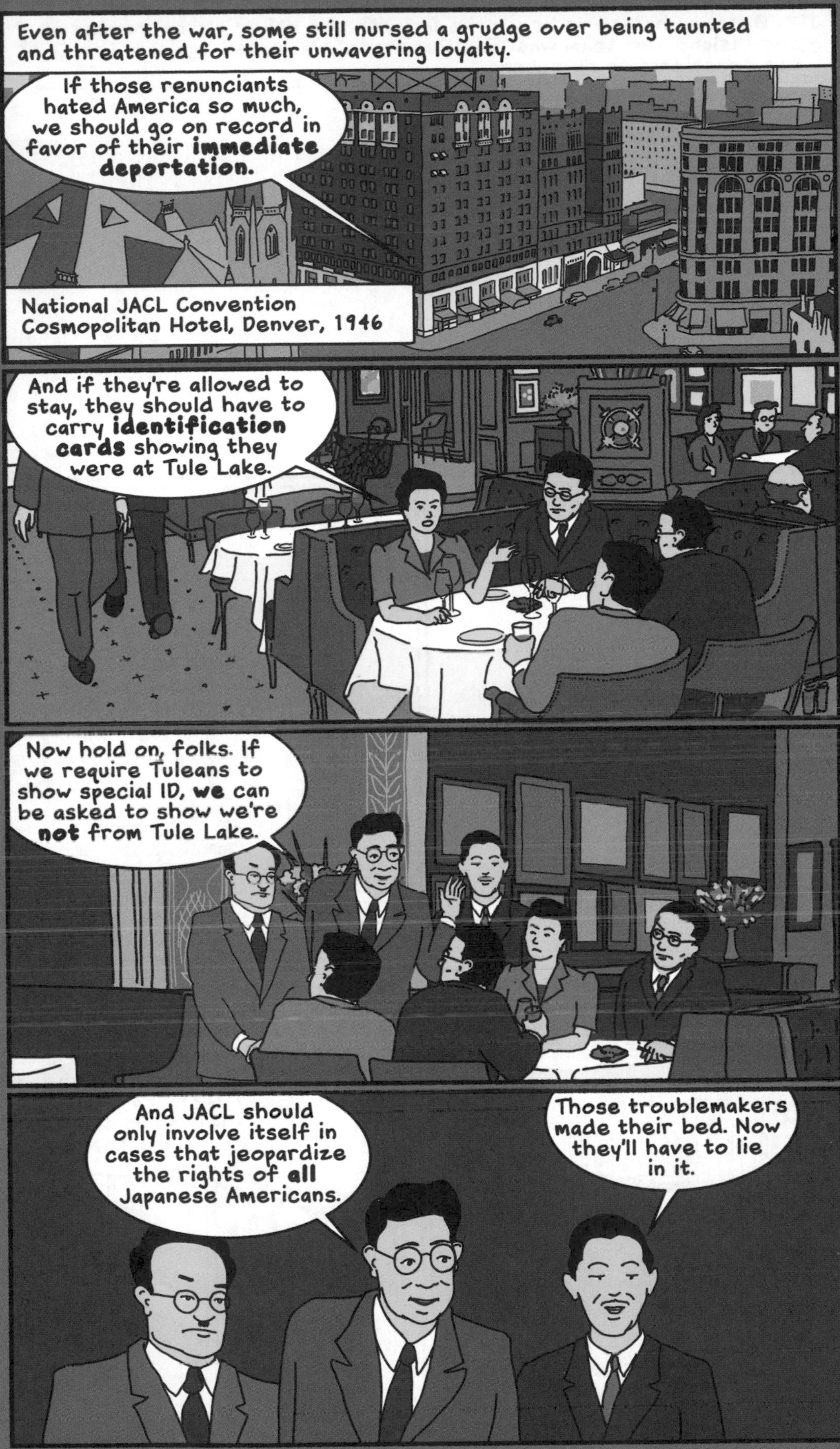
Even after the war, some still nursed a grudge over being taunted and threatened for their unwavering loyalty.
If those renunciants hated America so much, we should go on record in favor of their **immediate deportation.**
National JACL Convention
Cosmopolitan Hotel, Denver, 1946
And if they're allowed to stay, they should have to carry **identification cards** showing they were at Tule Lake.
Now hold on, folks. If we require Tuleans to show special ID, **we** can be asked to show we're **not** from Tule Lake.
And JACL should only involve itself in cases that jeopardize the rights of **all** Japanese Americans.
Those troublemakers made their bed. Now they'll have to lie in it.

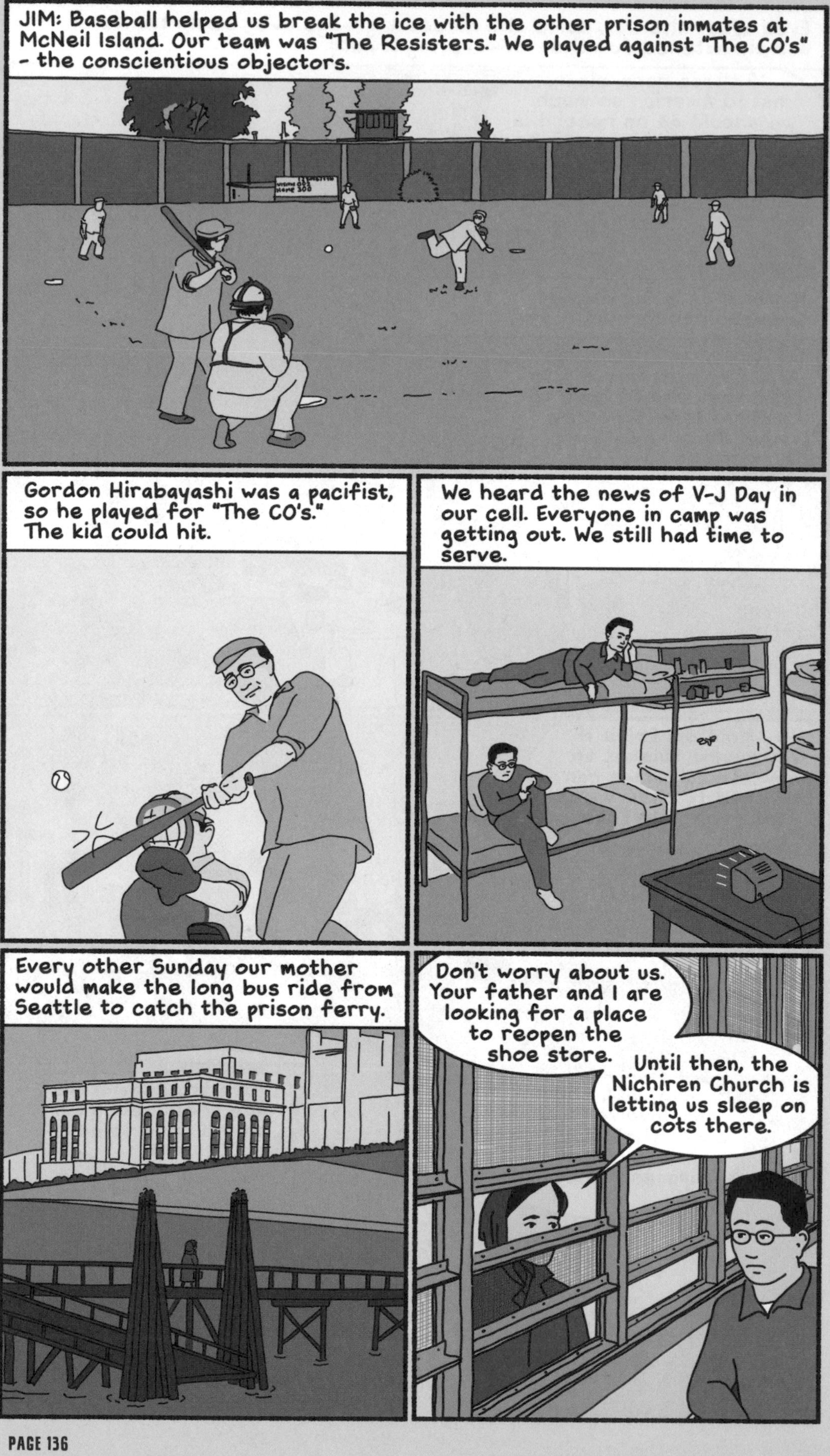
JIM: Baseball helped us break the ice with the other prison inmates at McNeil Island. Our team was "The Resisters." We played against "The CO's" - the conscientious objectors.
Gordon Hirabayashi was a pacifist, so he played for "The CO's." The kid could hit.
We heard the news of V-J Day in our cell. Everyone in camp was getting out. We still had time to serve.
Every other Sunday our mother would make the long bus ride from Seattle to catch the prison ferry.
Don't worry about us. Your father and I are looking for a place to reopen the shoe store.
Until then, the Nichiren Church is letting us sleep on cots there.

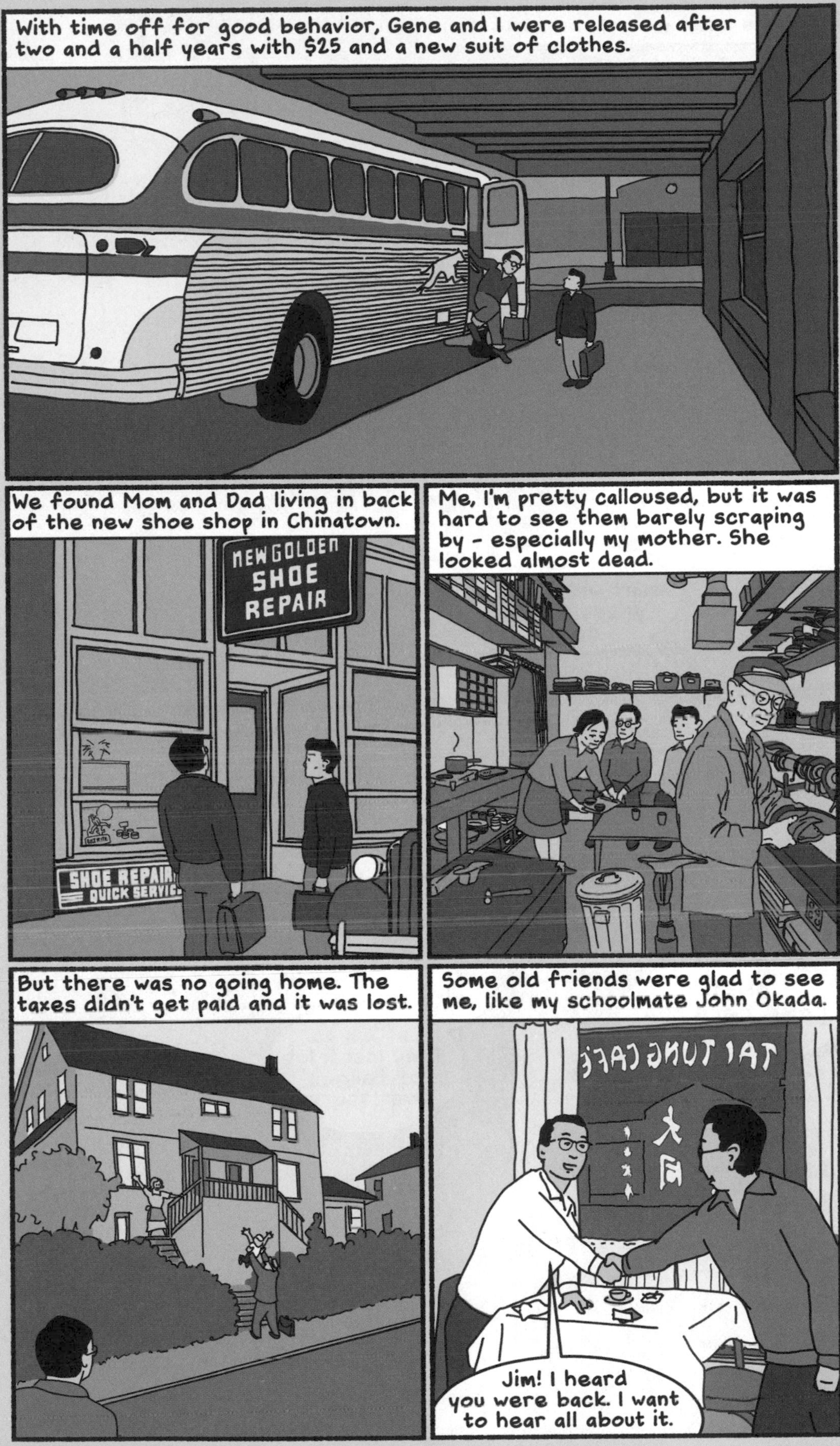
With time off for good behavior, Gene and I were released after two and a half years with $25 and a new suit of clothes.
We found Mom and Dad living in back of the new shoe shop in Chinatown.
NEW GOLDEN SHOE REPAIR
SHOE REPAIR QUICK SERVICE
Me, I'm pretty calloused, but it was hard to see them barely scraping by - especially my mother. She looked almost dead.
But there was no going home. The taxes didn't get paid and it was lost.
Some old friends were glad to see me, like my schoolmate John Okada.
TAI TUNG CAFE
Jim! I heard you were back. I want to hear all about it.

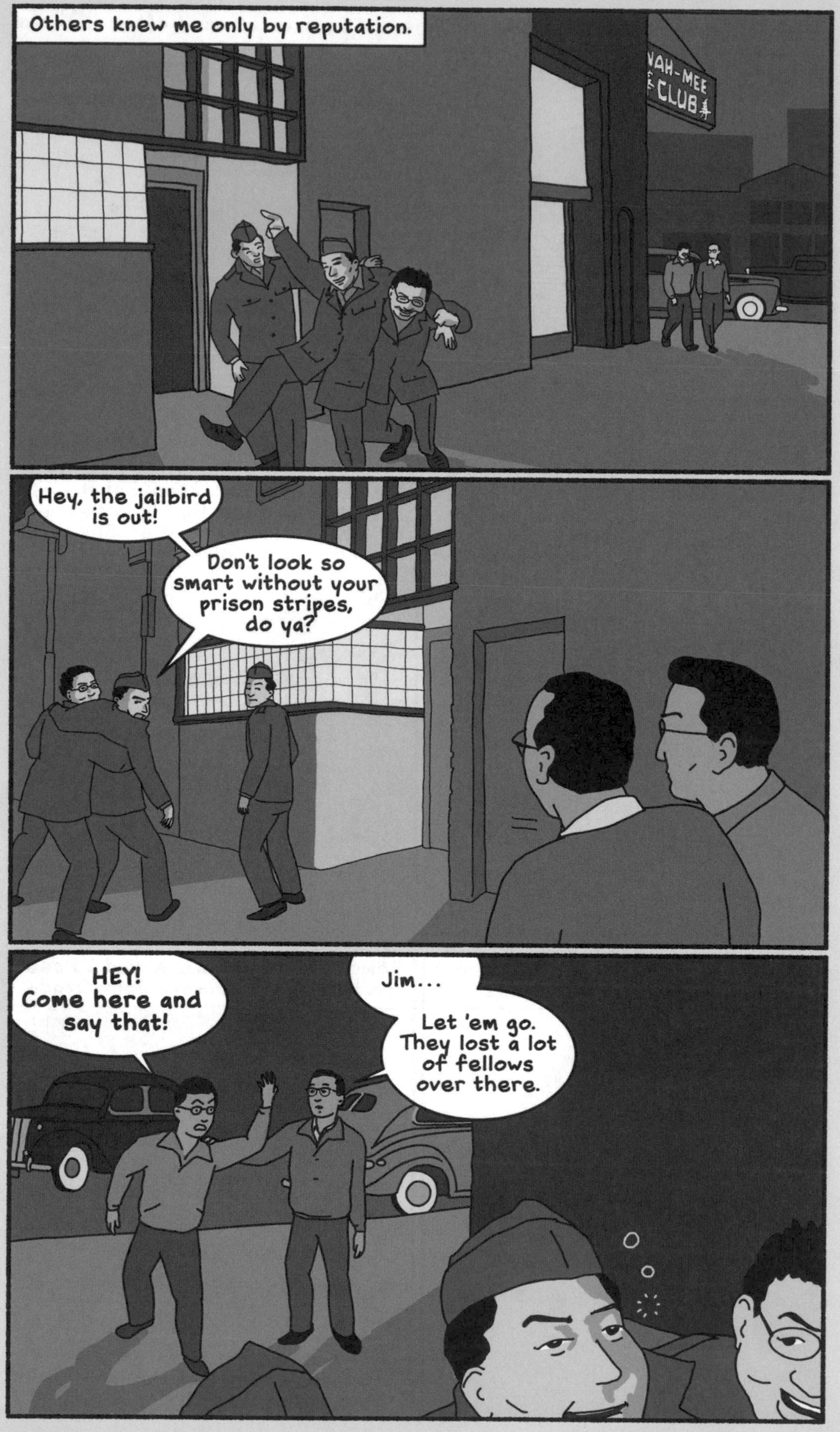

Others knew me only by reputation.
WAH-MEE CLUB
Hey, the jailbird is out!
Don't look so smart without your prison stripes, do ya?
HEY! Come here and say that!
Jim...
Let 'em go. They lost a lot of fellows over there.

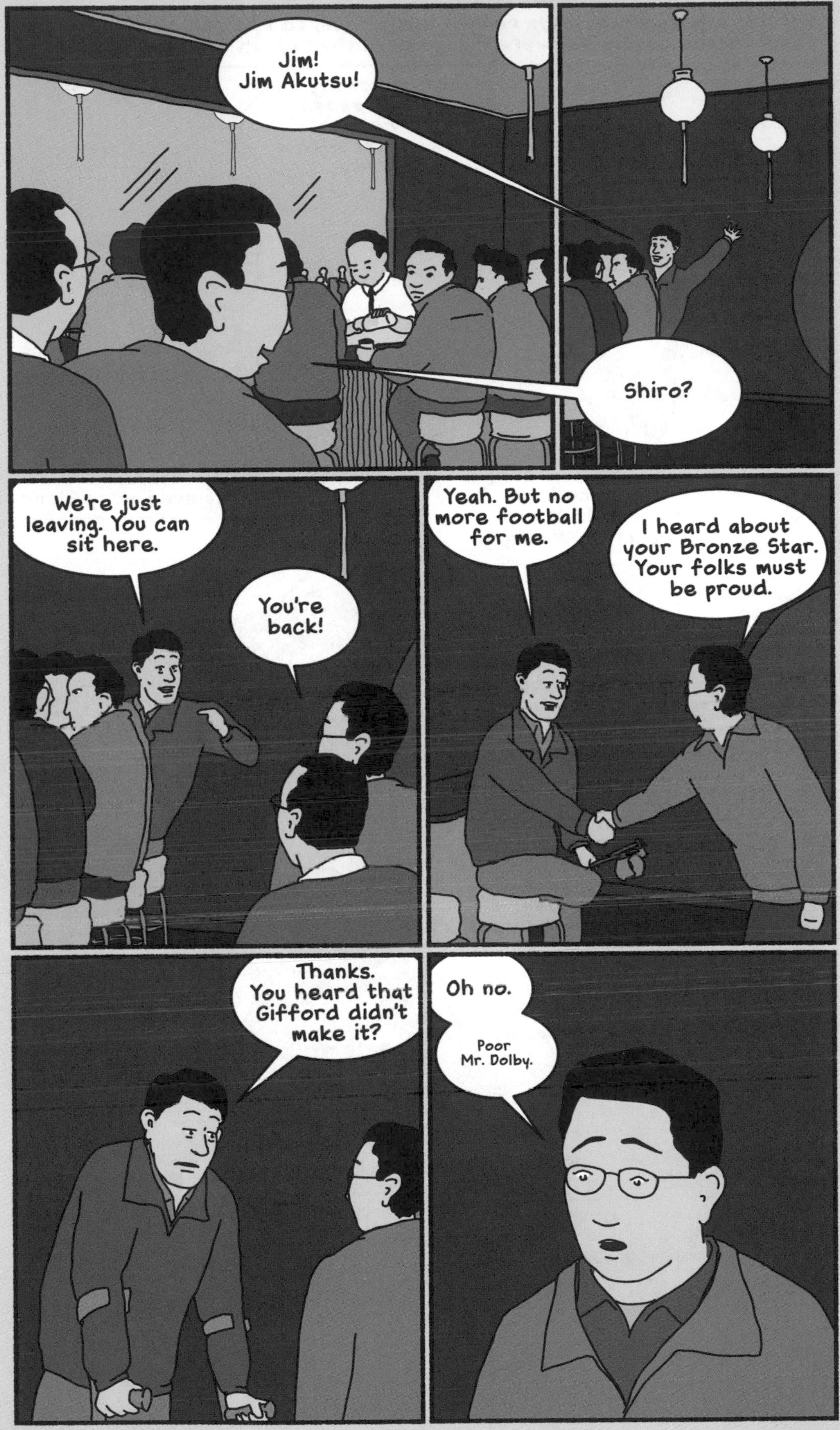
Jim!
Jim Akutsu!
Shiro?
We're just leaving. You can sit here.
You're back!
Yeah. But no more football for me.
I heard about your Bronze Star. Your folks must be proud.
Thanks. You heard that Gifford didn't make it?
Oh no.
Poor Mr. Dolby.

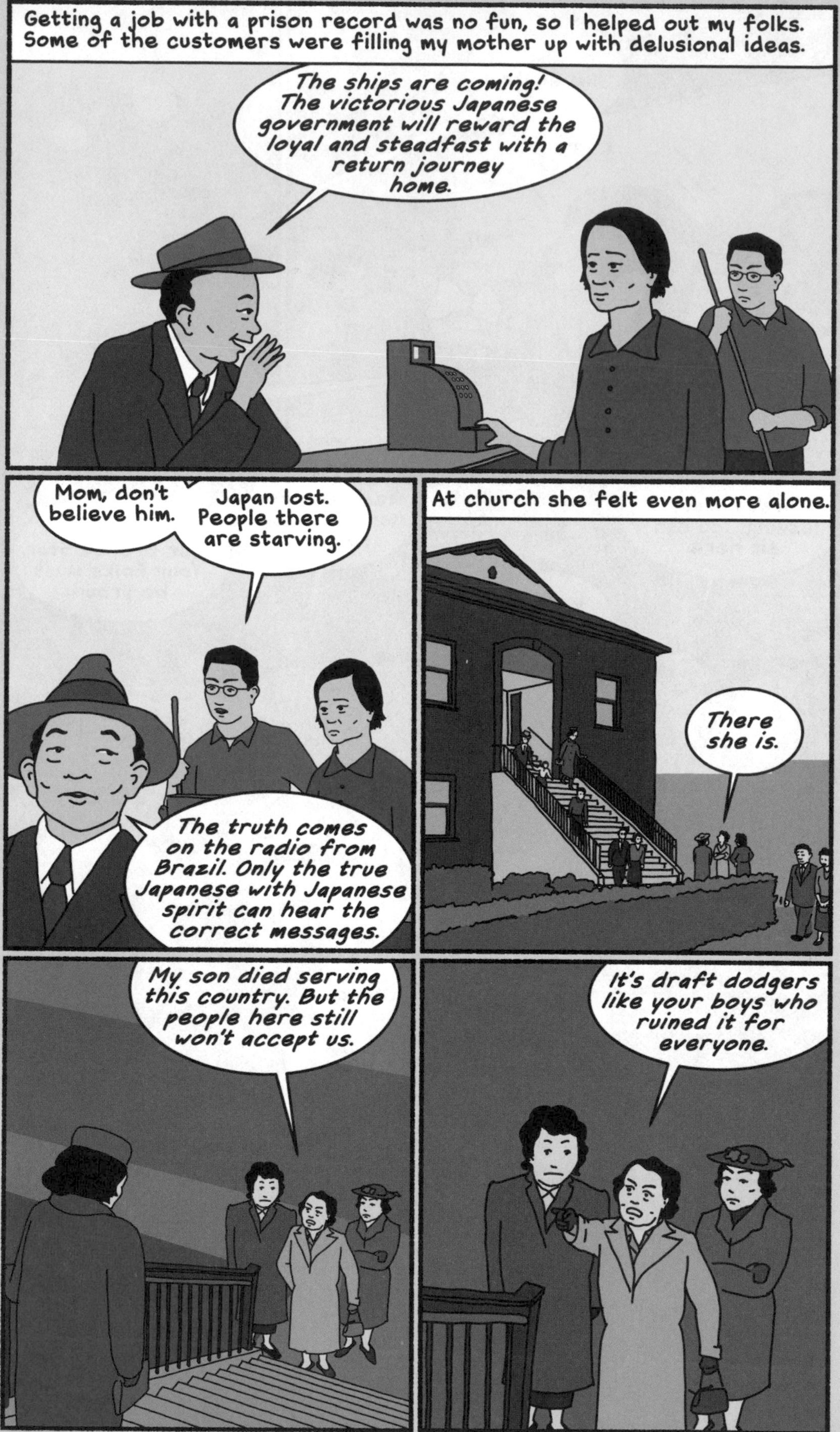
Getting a job with a prison record was no fun, so I helped out my folks. Some of the customers were filling my mother up with delusional ideas.
The ships are coming! The victorious Japanese government will reward the loyal and steadfast with a return journey home.
Mom, don't believe him.
Japan lost. People there are starving.
The truth comes on the radio from Brazil. Only the true Japanese with Japanese spirit can hear the correct messages.
At church she felt even more alone.
There she is.
My son died serving this country. But the people here still won't accept us.
It's draft dodgers like your boys who ruined it for everyone.

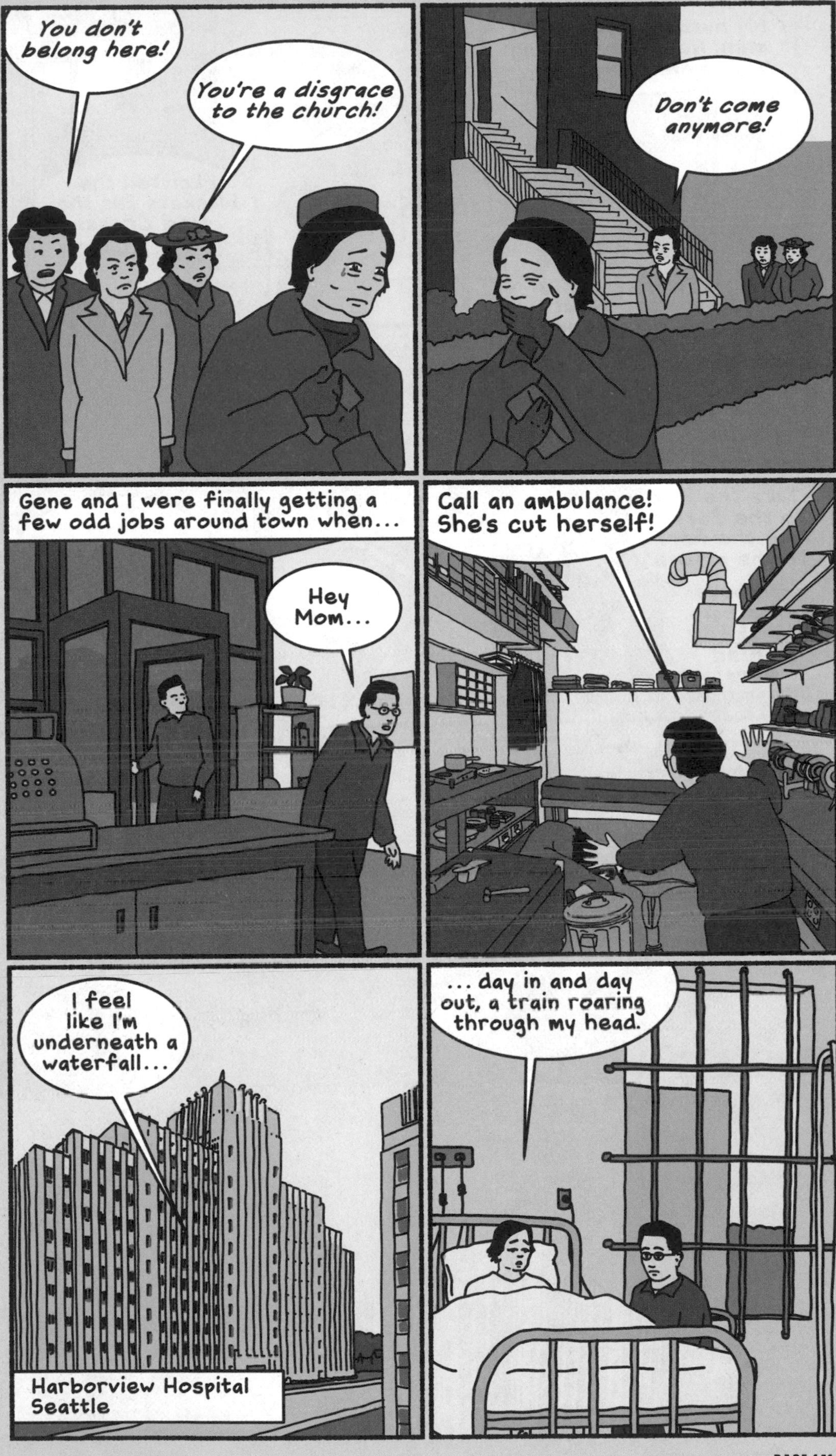
You don't belong here!
You're a disgrace to the church!
Don't come anymore!
Gene and I were finally getting a few odd jobs around town when...
Hey Mom...
Call an ambulance! She's cut herself!
I feel like I'm underneath a waterfall...
Harborview Hospital Seattle
... day in and day out, a train roaring through my head.

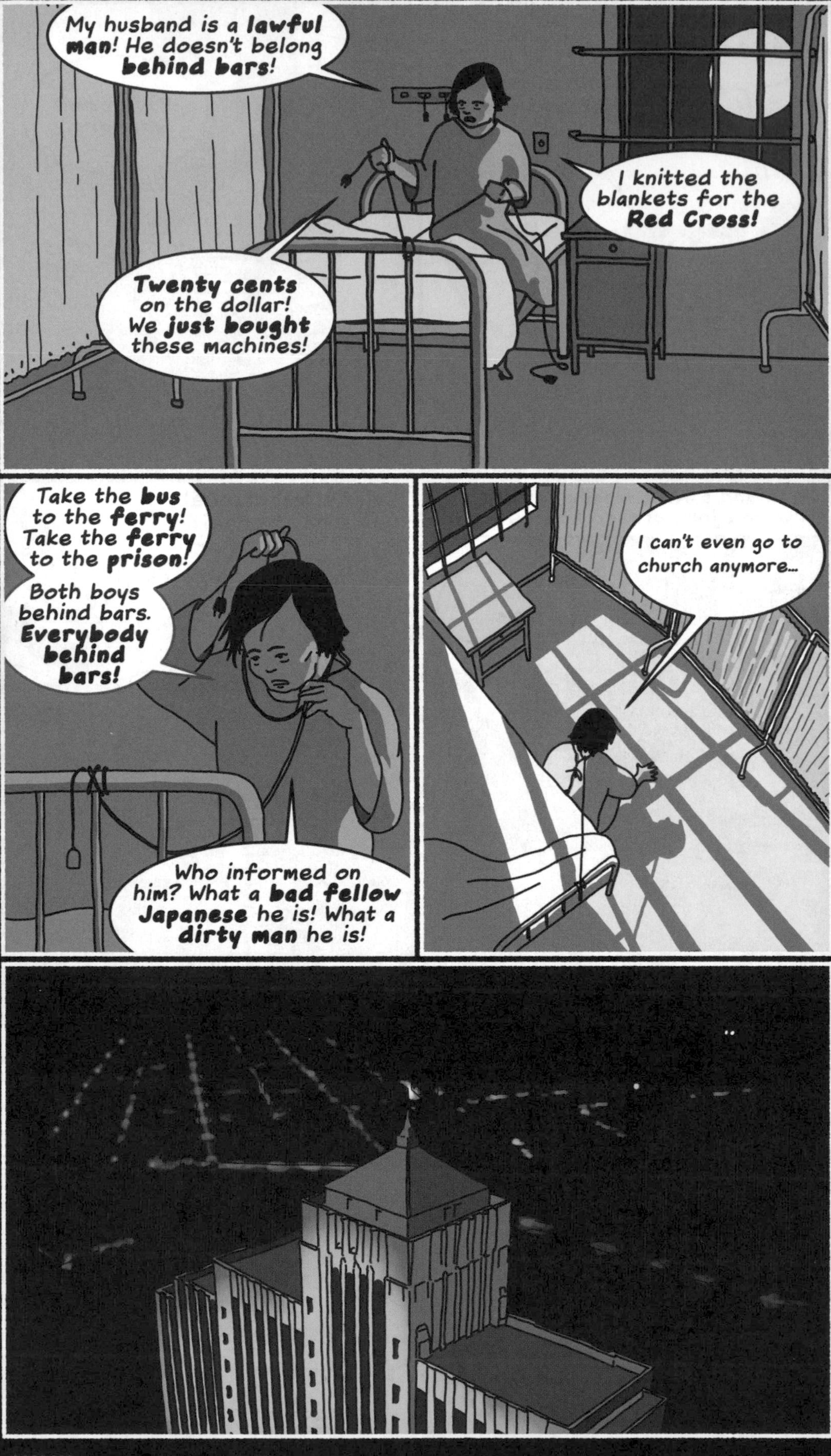

My husband is a **lawful man**! He doesn't belong **behind bars**!
I knitted the blankets for the **Red Cross!**
Twenty cents on the dollar! We **just bought** these machines!
Take the **bus** to the **ferry**! Take the **ferry** to the **prison**!
Both boys behind bars. **Everybody behind bars!**
Who informed on him? What a **bad fellow Japanese** he is! What a **dirty man** he is!
I can't even go to church anymore...

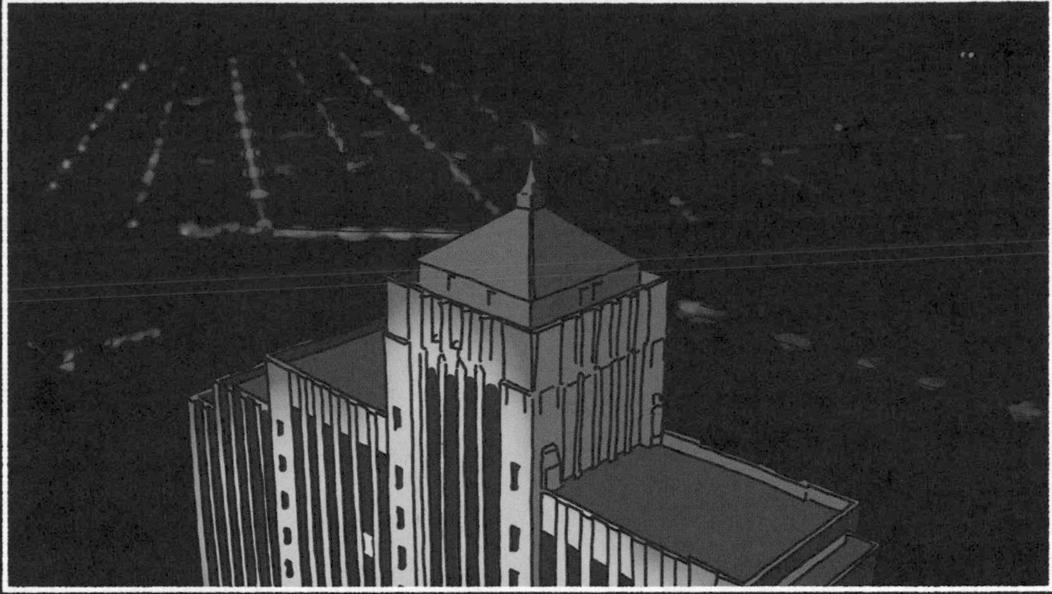

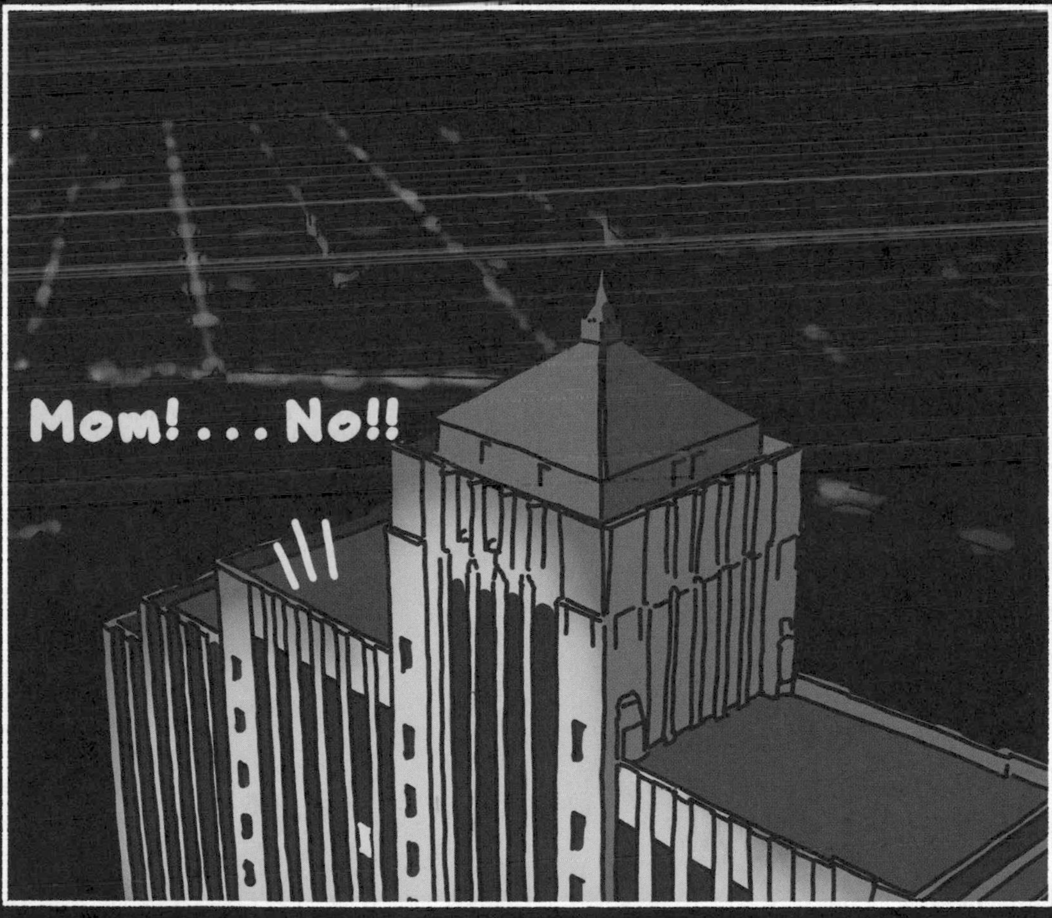
Mom! . . . No!!

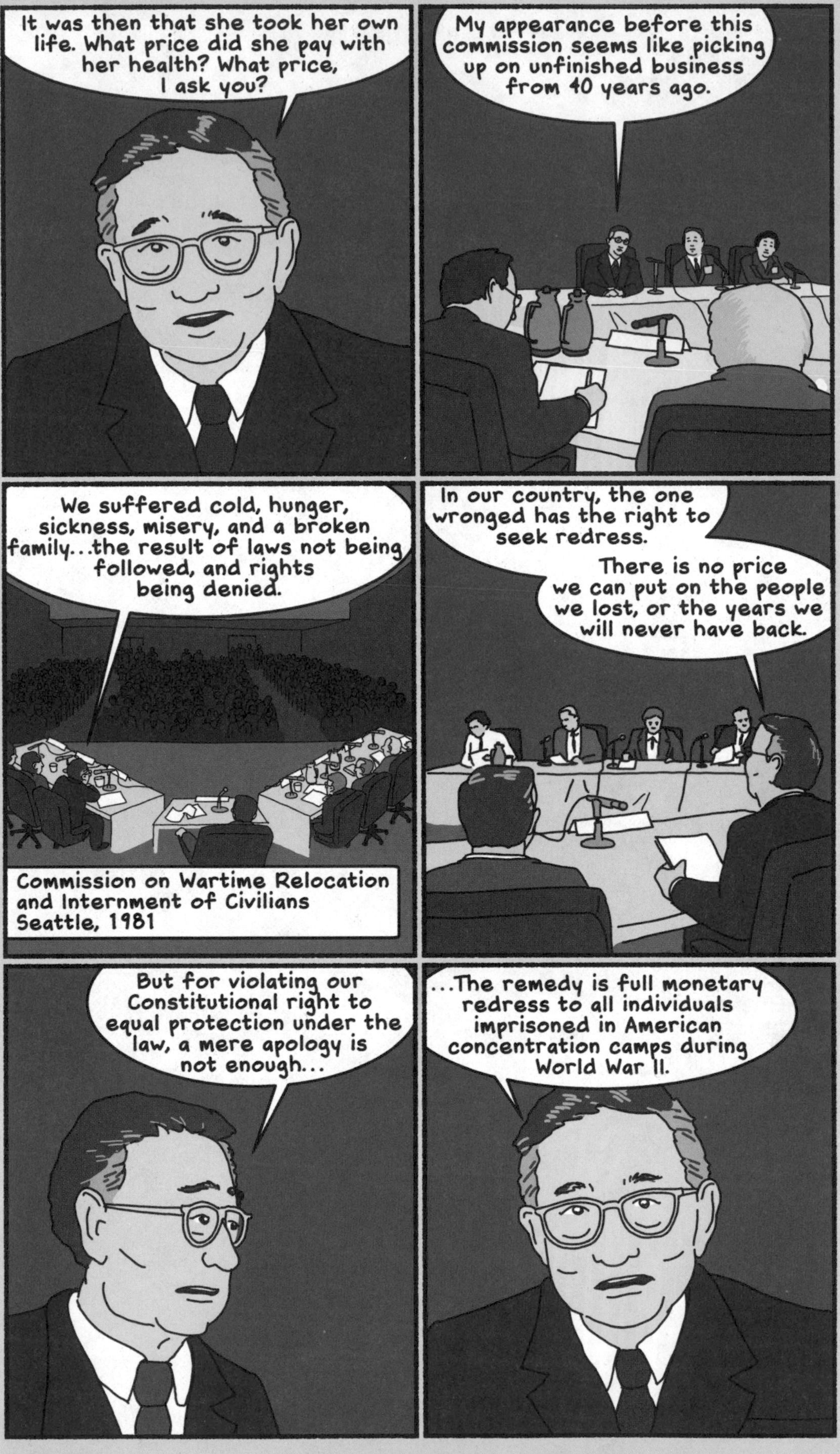
It was then that she took her own life. What price did she pay with her health? What price, I ask you?
My appearance before this commission seems like picking up on unfinished business from 40 years ago.
We suffered cold, hunger, sickness, misery, and a broken family...the result of laws not being followed, and rights being denied.
Commission on Wartime Relocation and Internment of Civilians Seattle, 1981
In our country, the one wronged has the right to seek redress.
There is no price we can put on the people we lost, or the years we will never have back.
But for violating our Constitutional right to equal protection under the law, a mere apology is not enough...
...The remedy is full monetary redress to all individuals imprisoned in American concentration camps during World War II.

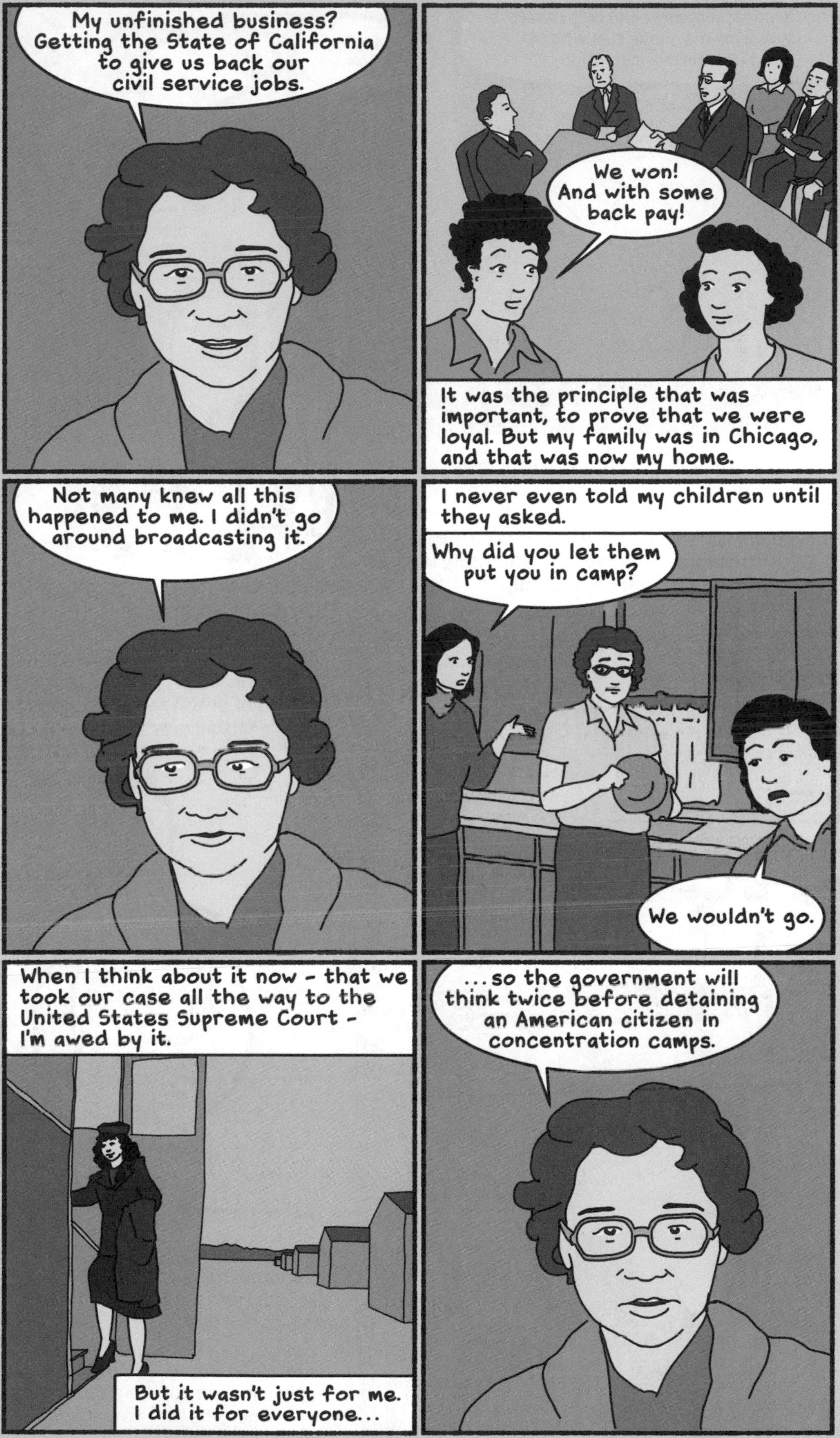
My unfinished business? Getting the State of California to give us back our civil service jobs.
We won! And with some back pay!
It was the principle that was important, to prove that we were loyal. But my family was in Chicago, and that was now my home.
Not many knew all this happened to me. I didn't go around broadcasting it.
I never even told my children until they asked.
Why did you let them put you in camp?
We wouldn't go.
When I think about it now - that we took our case all the way to the United States Supreme Court - I'm awed by it.
But it wasn't just for me. I did it for everyone...
...so the government will think twice before detaining an American citizen in concentration camps.

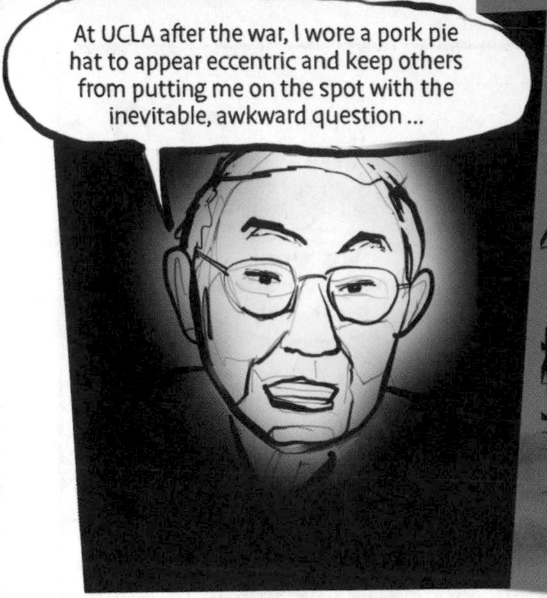
At UCLA after the war, I wore a pork pie hat to appear eccentric and keep others from putting me on the spot with the inevitable, awkward question ...

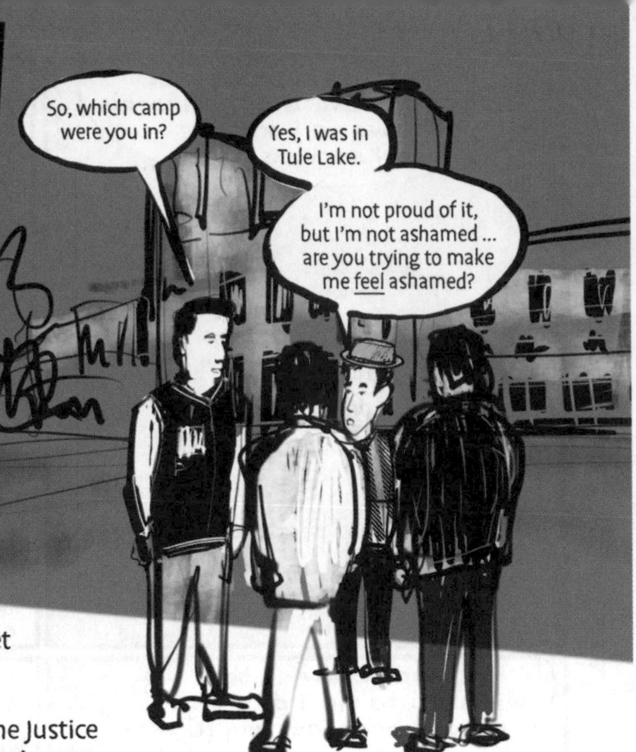
So, which camp were you in?
Yes, I was in Tule Lake.
I'm not proud of it, but I'm not ashamed ... are you trying to make me feel ashamed?

As a citizen of no nation, it was hard to get a job but I was finally hired as a librarian.

Wayne Collins kept filing affidavits until the Justice Department finally restored my citizenship in 1959. All those years, I felt it was my fault.

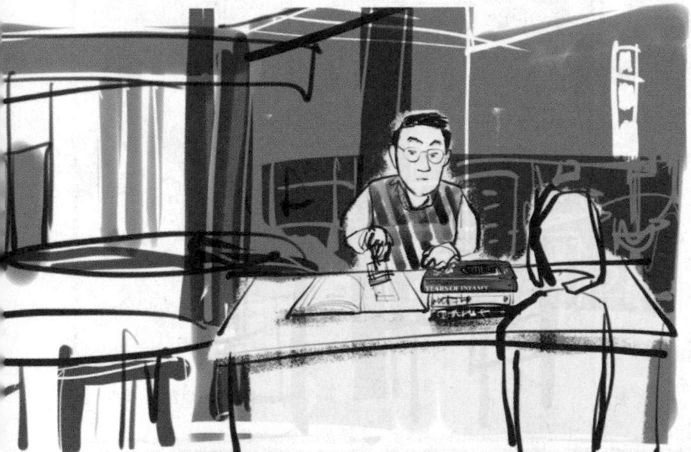

But after 35 years, can you imagine my chagrin, my dismay, when I learned there was no law that required draft-age Nisei to answer that loyalty questionnaire in camp? All those threats of prison and fines ... all lies. I was angry all over again.

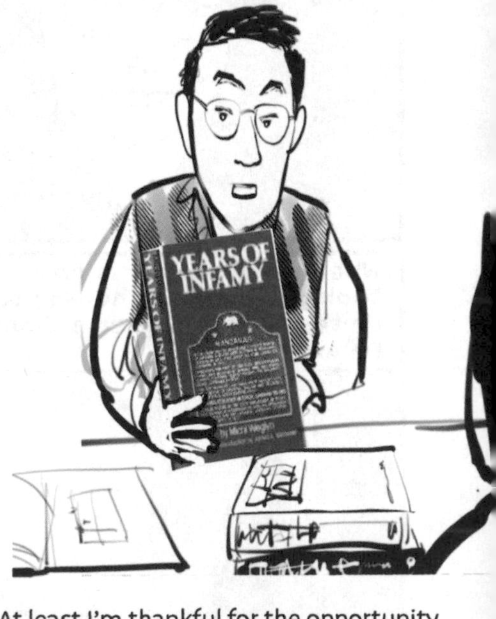
YEARS OF INFAMY

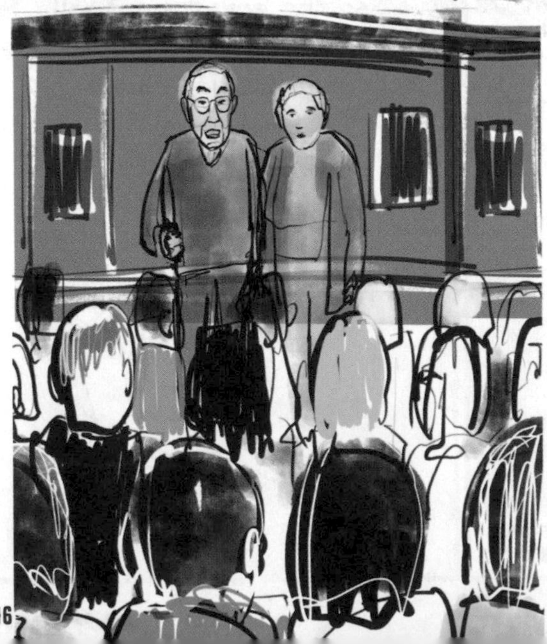

At least I'm thankful for the opportunity to unburden myself with others who were cast out from our own community, even to this day.

To be an American is a privilege I appreciate ... and if there's one thing I've learned, it's that America must unburden itself too.

The government was wrong to single us out for exclusion based solely on our race. It was wrong then, and it would be wrong now.

And whenever we see America turn against a people because of their race, or their religion, or their whatever, we won't just stand by. We won't just go along.

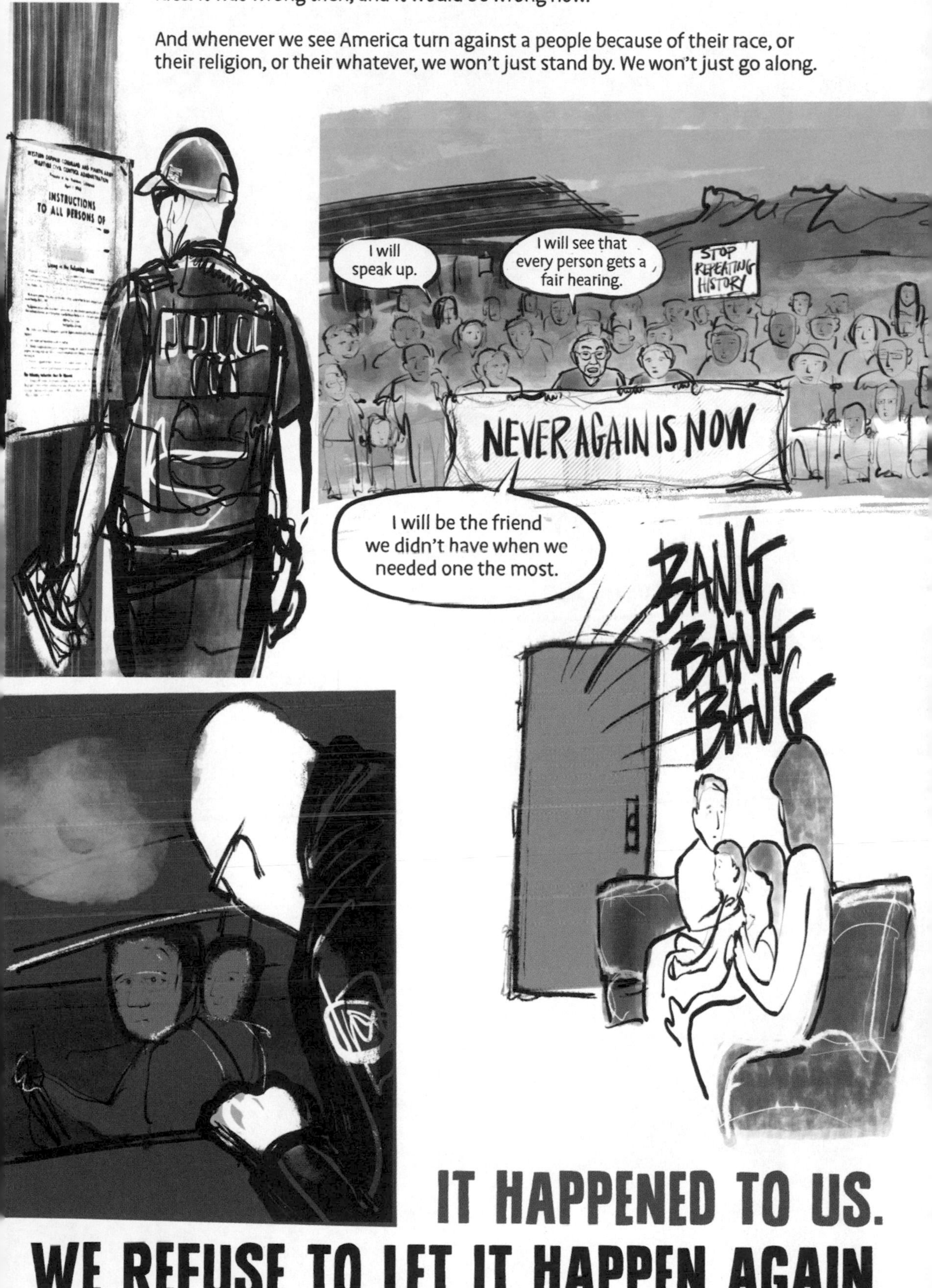

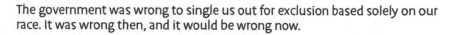

INSTRUCTIONS TO ALL PERSONS OF
I will speak up.
I will see that every person gets a fair hearing.
STOP REPEATING HISTORY
NEVER AGAIN IS NOW
I will be the friend we didn't have when we needed one the most.
BANG BANG BANG
IT HAPPENED TO US.
WE REFUSE TO LET IT HAPPEN AGAIN.

ACKNOWLEDGMENTS

This publication, the full graphic novel and accompanying curriculum guide, produced by the Wing Luke Museum of the Asian Pacific American Experience, is based upon work assisted by a grant from the US Department of the Interior, National Park Service. Any opinions, findings and conclusions or recommendations expressed in this material are those of the authors and do not necessarily reflect the views of the US Department of the Interior.

This material received Federal financial assistance for the preservation and interpretation of US confinement sites where Japanese Americans were detained during World War II. Under Title VI of the Civil Rights Act of 1964, Section 504 of the Rehabilitation Act of 1973, and the Age Discrimination Act of 1975, as amended, the US Department of the Interior prohibits discrimination on the basis of race, color, national origin, disability or age in its federally funded assisted projects. If you believe you have been discriminated against in any program, activity or facility as described above, or if you desire further information, please write to:

Office of Equal Opportunity
National Park Service
1849 C Street, NW
Washington, DC 20240

THE CREATIVE TEAM extends its deepest appreciation to the families of Jim and Gene Akutsu, Mitsuye Endo, and Hiroshi Kashiwagi. Special thanks to Wing Luke Deputy Executive Director Cassie Chinn for conceiving and shepherding this project, and publisher Bruce Rutledge for bringing it to readers.

WING LUKE MUSEUM: Special thanks to community contributors and supporters for this project: Jeffery Akutsu, Marilyn Akutsu, Lorraine Bannai, Bif Brigman, Robert Fisher, Shannon Gee, Toshiko Grace Hasegawa, Meredith Higashi, Debbie Kashino, Leslie Morishita, Gabrielle Kazuko Nomura, Mira Shimabukuro, Paul Tashima-Boyd, Vincent Schleitwiler, and David Yamashita. Thanks also to our project research assistants: Isabella Jaravata, Anatol Steck, and Thien-Kim Vo.

FRANK ABE: For their research and guidance in the writing of this story, I am indebted to Barbara Takei and Hiroshi Shimizu of the Tule Lake Committee; Brian Niiya and the staff at Densho; Jane Beckwith at the Topaz Museum; Barbara Berglund Sokolov of the Presidio Trust; Gwen Whiting of the Washington State Historical Society; and Konrad Aderer, Wayne Collins Jr., Roger Daniels, Takako Day, Art Hansen, Tak Hoshizaki, Peter Irons, Andrew Leong, James McIlwain, Eric Muller, Martha Nakagawa, Melissa Bailey Nihei, Elissa Kikuye Ouchida, Priscilla Ouchida, Yuri Kuratomi Owens, Kathleen Purcell, Greg Robinson, Mira Shimabukuro, Anna Tamura, Shig and Fay Tanagi, Azusa Tanaka, Jim Tanimoto, John Tateishi, Jeffrey Thomson, Jonathan van Harmelen, Hanako

Wakatsuki, Charles Wollenberg, Keith Yamaguchi, and Sharon Yamato, Thanks also to the work of the late Motomu Akashi, Violet Kazue de Cristoforo, Robert Ross, Dorothy Swaine Thomas & Richard Nishimoto, Rosalie Hankey Wax, and Michi Nishiura Weglyn. This one is for Claire and Alice, David and Alden and Seneca. Deepest gratitude to Laureen Mar for being in my life.

TAMIKO NIMURA: I would like to add my thanks to the individuals mentioned above. I am grateful to Sharon Tanagi Aburano, Ben Arikawa, Lorna Fong, and Bif Brigman for additional support. I would also like to thank my partner Josh Parmenter, my daughters Celia and Mira, my mother Helen Nimura, my sister Teruko Nimura, and my extended Nimura family of aunts, uncles, and cousins. I dedicate my work to the memory of my Nisei father (Taku Nimura, 1931–1984) and my uncle Hiroshi Kashiwagi (1922–2019).

ROSS ISHIKAWA: In researching visual sources of the many settings, locations and people in these stories I was struck once again by the efforts of researchers to catalogue, post online and make available for reference such a wealth of information. I wish to specially thank the Densho Digital Repository for their exhaustive and growing collection of images of long gone and otherwise forgotten buildings. Steven J Pickens at the Steilacoom Historical Museum Association tracked down the prison ferry serving McNeil Island in the 1940s. The home movies of Dave Tatsuno from 1943 were an amazing source for locations at Topaz. The evocative artwork by camp artists Eddy Kurushima and Gene Sogioka was invaluable, conveying the chaos and emotion of particularly dark moments at Manzanar and Poston. I want to thank Dylan Enright-Cancino for her help with coloring on some pages. Finally, none of this work would have been possible without the patience, love and support of my wife Edith Szabo and our sons Zoli and Tomo, who withstood years of evenings and weekends without my full attention.

THE WRITERS

Photo: Eugene Tagawa

FRANK ABE wrote and directed the PBS film on the largest organized resistance to incarceration, *Conscience and the Constitution*. He won an American Book Award for *JOHN OKADA: The Life & Rediscovered Work of the Author of* No-No Boy, and is co-editing a new anthology of incarceration literature for Penguin Classics. He blogs at **resisters.com**.

Photo: Josh Parmenter

TAMIKO NIMURA is an Asian American (Sansei/Pinay) writer living in Tacoma, Washington. Her training in literature and American ethnic studies (MA, PhD, University of Washington) prepared her to research, document, and tell the stories of people of color. She can be found at **tamikonimura.net**.

THE ARTISTS

Photo: Brad Kevelin, Adonis Photography

ROSS ISHIKAWA is a cartoonist and animator living in Seattle. In addition to his work on *We Hereby Refuse*, he is working on a graphic novel about his parents and their coming of age during World War II. His work is online at **rossishikawa.com**.

Photo: Courtesy of the Artist

MATT SASAKI is the artist on the previous volume in this series, *Fighting for America: Nisei Soldiers*. He lives with his wife and dog north of Seattle. Samples of his other work are online at **mattsasaki.com**.

Learn more about this story at **curriculum.wingluke.org**.

Based on true events. Some conversations depicted were carried out by correspondence or conducted between staff, but all are drawn from the record.

Library of Congress Control Number: 2020952763

ISBN: 978-1-63405-976-3

Cover art by Ross Ishikawa
Book design by Dan D Shafer
Printed in the United States of America

Published by Chin Music Press. A Wing Luke Museum Book.

CHIN MUSIC PRESS

WING LUKE MUSEUM

CHIN MUSIC PRESS
1501 Pike Place #329
Seattle, WA 98101-1542
www.chinmusicpress.com

WING LUKE MUSEUM
719 S. King Street
Seattle, WA 98104
www.wingluke.org

THIRD PRINTING